W9-ABZ-541

SOUNDINGS IN
MODERN SOUTH ASIAN HISTORY

SOUNDINGS IN MODERN SOUTH ASIAN HISTORY

Edited by
D. A. LOW

★

University of California Press
Berkeley and Los Angeles · 1968

University of California Press
Berkeley and Los Angeles, California
© 1968 by D. A. Low
Library of Congress Catalog Card No.: 68-20442

Printed in Great Britain

TO
Sir Keith Hancock

CONTENTS

★

    TABLE CONFERENCE
        D. A. Low   294

11 SYAMA PRASAD MOOKERJEE AND THE COMMUNALIST
    ALTERNATIVE
        B. D. Graham   330

    Map of India   *between pages* 374 and 375

    Glossary   375

    Index   385

CONTRIBUTORS

★

D. A. Low, M.A., D.Phil. (Oxon.)
Professor of History and Dean of the School of African and Asian
Studies, University of Sussex; formerly Senior Fellow in History,
Research School of Social Sciences, Australian National University.

Ravinder Kumar, M.A. (Panjab), Ph.D. (A.N.U.).
Fellow in History, Research School of Social Sciences, Australian
National University; formerly Research Student and Research
Fellow, Australian National University, and Lecturer in History,
University of the Punjab, Chandigarh.

P. H. M. van den Dungen, B.A. (Western Australia), Ph.D. (A.N.U.).
Lecturer in History, University of Adelaide; formerly Research
Student, Australian National University.

Dietmar Rothermund, M.A., Ph.D. (Pennsylvania).
Associate Professor of History, South Asia Institute, University
of Heidelberg; some time Visiting Fellow, Australian National
University.

H. F. Owen, B.A. (W.A. and Cantab.), Ph.D. (A.N.U.).
Lecturer in History, and Director, Centre for Asian Studies, Uni-
versity of Western Australia; formerly Research Student, Australian
National University.

J. H. Broomfield, M.A. (New Zealand), Ph.D. (A.N.U.).
Assistant Professor of History, University of Michigan; formerly
Research Student, Australian National University.

P. D. Reeves, M.A., Dip.Ed. (Tasmania), Ph.D. (A.N.U.).
Lecturer in History, University of Sussex; formerly Lecturer in
History, University of Western Australia, and Research Student,
Australian National University.

B. D. Graham, M.A. (New Zealand), Ph.D. (A.N.U.).
Reader in Politics, University of Sussex; formerly Research Fellow
in Political Science, Australian National University.

PREFACE

*

This book owes its origin to the work on modern South Asia that has been going on since 1960 in the Departments of History and Political Science of the Institute of Advanced Studies at the Australian National University, Canberra. All of us who have contributed to it were either on the staff or held research studentships there, except Dietmar Rothermund, who came to us for a short time as a visiting fellow. We have now scattered to half a dozen universities in three different continents. But we shall not forget the experience of working together which we enjoyed in Canberra. A genial colleague dubbed us 'the sepoys'. If the ascription may be taken to mean that we are humble foot soldiers – rather than great conquerors who have already won famous victories – we shall be very well satisfied.

We could never have come thus far but for the help of colleagues, archivists, informants, librarians, owners of papers and numerous other people in four different continents. To them we are all most grateful. We are especially grateful to the Australian National University which gave us our unrivalled opportunities and made our field-work visits to the Indian sub-continent financially possible. To those in its Department of History – not least Nan Philips and May Richardson – who helped us on our way, and above all to our *guru*, Professor Sir Keith Hancock we are especially indebted. For their help at the end in Sussex we should like to thank Yvonne Wood and Yvette Ashby.

D. A. Low

Sussex, February 1967

INTRODUCTION

*

D. A. Low

In 1907 the British Labour M.P. Keir Hardie visited India. Wherever he went he met the leaders of the Indian nationalist movement of his day. Almost without exception they belonged to the small westernised élite, to one or other of the high 'twice born' castes, or to one of the traditional small Muslim leadership groups. By following Hardie upon his travels across the continent we can get a remarkably clear picture of the Indian nationalist movement of his day, as seen in terms of the interests and activities of the westernised élite.[1]

I

Wherever he went he met the lawyers and part-time politicians – men who had had a substantial 'English' education in 'English' schools; men who were radical in their liberal political principles; men who felt cheated of their political birthright, and saw themselves locked in a sustained encounter with British imperialism. In many ways they were not men of Hardie's ilk. They were underlings of their British rulers; but they were also successful, rising, 'new', men, who in their own society were rarely more than marginally interested in social and economic reform; they were much more concerned to forge a new élitist society and culture for themselves – one moreover which was well laced with the ideas and ideals of the British aristocracy and the British middle class. The principal figures Hardie saw included such people as Bepin Chandra Pal, Surendranath Banerjea, Harkishen Lal, Bal Gangadhar Tilak, and Srinivasa Sastri. They talked nationalist politics to him whenever they had the opportunity, and took him to meetings in the towns and cities of all the provinces he visited to make speeches on their behalf. It all adds up to a very familiar picture – of the Indian national movement and Indian nationalist leadership at the turn of the century, such as is to be found in all the textbooks on the period.

And yet if one probes a little deeper, some quite new vistas open up, vistas which, for the most part, are not revealed by the standard accounts of the period. Few are more important than the picture one receives of the extraordinary variety in the provincial political situations which Keir Hardie encountered. He visited most parts of British India. In 1907 three areas were politically alight – as one can sense vividly in the reports upon his travels. In Bengal he saw Calcutta and some of the mofussil towns – Dacca, Mymensingh and Barisal among others. Everywhere he travelled in the company of *bhadralok* lawyers from the higher Hindu castes. At every opportunity they vehemently remonstrated with him about the 'pernicious' partition of Bengal which the former Viceroy, Lord Curzon, had carried through two years before. It had clearly been a blow to the heart of all that their Bengal homeland meant to them. Hardie, however, also heard of Hindu–Muslim rioting, and by the time he left Bengal he found himself accused by a leader of Muslim opinion in Bengal of 'seeing things in India through Babu spectacles'. The Partition agitation was engrossing Bengal politics – as the standard accounts correctly affirm – but there was clearly more to Bengali politics than that.

To the north-west, in Delhi and the Panjab (which Hardie visited a little later on) there was scarcely any interest in the troubles of Bengal. But the Panjab, as Hardie found, was scarcely less astir. The main concern of the politicised élite here was not with matters like the Partition of Bengal, but with 'the recent disturbances and high handed dealings in the Panjab'. In recent years discontent in the Panjab had affected two groups, the mainly urban Hindu élite which had been fired by the revivalism of Arya Samaj, and was still smarting under the discriminatory clauses of the Panjab Land Alienation Act of 1900 (by which many of them had been thwarted); and the Panjabi canal colonists who were seething over the regulations governing their tenure of land, and over the further measures concerning these matters which the British plainly had in mind. Two prominent Panjabi leaders, Lala Lajpat Rai and Ajit Singh had recently been deported for their part in the ensuing agitation. Public meetings in Delhi and the Panjab were being vigorously controlled by the Government, and had Hardie decided to address a public gathering the Government would quite certainly have moved in against him. Prominent among his hosts were members of the Arya Samaj. Under their guidance he publicly denounced the Panjab Government's proposed Colonisation Bill and found himself carried along by the local agitation. Its content was quite distinct from that of the one he had encountered in Bengal.

From the Panjab he travelled south to Bombay. There he had once more a warm hearted reception from the local leaders. But in Bombay neither Partition nor colonisation were issues. The nationalist campaign was more diffuse in its concerns; and, by contrast with Bengal and the Panjab, its leaders were divided. In Bombay city Hardie visited the Bombay Presidency Association, the bailiwick of the formidable Pherozeshah Mehta. He visited the Ripon Club, and received a deputation from the Bombay National Union. But Bombay was not the only important centre hereabouts. Hardie had also to go up the railway line to Poona, where Tilak helped him to meet some of the local people. Shortly before he left the town he spoke to separate meetings of its Sarvajanik Sabha and its Deccan Club, referring warmly to Tilak's great rival Gokhale in his address to the former body. He thus touched upon the rifts in the ranks of the nationalist leaders in the Bombay Presidency, rifts of a kind which he had not encountered in the other two provinces which he had found to be politically active. The situation in each of them differed significantly.

It very soon becomes dramatically clear, indeed, that even as between the three provinces in which there were nationalist élites who were politically active at the time of his visit, there were notable differences. From the rest of Hardie's travels it is no less clear that there were other differences of no lesser importance between these three provinces and all the others.

From Bombay Hardie was carried off to Madras by Srinivasa Sastri, not, as elsewhere, to join in a campaign which was already well launched, but to help stir the local élite into some degree of political agitation. The two of them seem to have had some success. To a greater extent than anywhere else in India, Hardie was taken on a tour of small towns, and usually encountered a friendly and eager audience. But there was no local issue preoccupying people's minds hereabouts, and no tradition of nationalist activity. Bengal and the Panjab were a long way off; and when asked by the Government of India to report upon the effects of Hardie's visit the Presidency Government in Madras replied they were not in the least perturbed by what Hardie and his friends had done.

A similar nonchalant reaction had come from the Government of the United Provinces,* where Hardie had been earlier on his travels, in

---

* Abbreviated hereafter to U.P. The British 'United Provinces of Agra and Oudh' became upon independence 'Uttar Pradesh'.

between his visits to Bengal and the Panjab. At Benares he had been met by a few Bengali émigrés who were in the city. In Lucknow he had a friendly but by no means vociferous reception. At Kanpur, however, which is today the great industrial city of U.P., there was no one to meet him on the railway station platform. Admittedly the courts were in vacation. But none of those who practised in them seem to have been the least concerned to come in and play host to this peripatetic British Labour M.P. There was little of the interest in him which was displayed in the neighbouring provinces. So far as nationalist politics was concerned – and there is other evidence in support of this – U.P. at this time, even though it lay between Bengal and the Panjab, stood politically inert. This, surely, is very remarkable, particularly when one remembers the central role played since about 1920 by men from U.P. both in the Indian nationalist movement and in independent India. Apart from Gandhi, few men, man for man, have been more important in modern Indian politics than Motilal Nehru, Jawaharlal Nehru, Govind Ballabh Pant, Purushottamdas Tandon, Lal Bahadur Sastri, and Indira Gandhi; and they have all come from U.P. It is not very difficult to see why it should have played this major role. It is, after all, the largest of the states, the least exclusive, and, for internal Indian purposes, the most centrally placed strategically. It stands, moreover, at the centre of a complex of other states which have many similar characteristics, and which between them comprise not only the Hindu heartland, but the largest single cluster of associated states in modern India. Yet if this be true; if it is really not very difficult to suggest quite a number of reasons why U.P. should have led India in so many ways since about 1920, why was it, so far as nationalist politics were concerned, politically inert in the period preceding?

We may ask here a parallel question. How was it that while Bengalis played such a major part in Indian nationalism up to about the mid-1920s, they have since then played such an ever-decreasing part in the central political leadership of India?

We cannot stay to answer these questions fully here. We may simply note that they arise because of the differing histories of the different Indian regions.

The detail of Keir Hardie's visit to India illustrates the point. It provides us with a political map of India in 1907; and at one level down the contrasts which it presents between different areas of the country are quite remarkable. It is not just, however, that there are contrasts to be noted between different areas at the same time. If we look forwards –

and backwards – there are contrasts within the same area at different times, and different contrasts between different areas at different times as well. This is a consideration which needs stressing. It is only at a rather rarefied level that modern Indian history may be said to comprise a single all-Indian story. At other levels marked variations exist, and if we are to proceed to understanding it further, regional studies, within the orbit of an awareness of the overall story, are now of quite vital importance.

Those of us who have been concerned with this book warmly welcome the increasing emphasis which is now being given to the study of regions and regional variations in the study of modern South Asian history. It is because indeed this seems to us so vital to the current stage of modern South Asian historiography that several of the studies which appear in this book deal in detail with occurrences in a single region. By themselves they will not, of course, be enough. We shall also need to see the whole story of each region in all its complexity over two or more centuries if we are to comprehend the broad history of the Indian peoples in the modern period at all adequately; and this is a much more difficult task. Our hope would be, however, that our essays may do something to help lay the foundations here.

II

As more detailed studies begin to become available one thing will become clear very soon. We shall be involved in mapping out the history of whole societies, and of the seminal changes within them.

No one will underestimate the difficulties and complexities of such a task. We have thought that our conception of it could not, however, be made as clear as we would wish, unless it were illustrated by one specific example. Someone once described a fishing net as a lot of holes tied together with string. This no doubt will prove to be an apt description for the pages which immediately follow. But they are offered as a preliminary exercise in the history of one Indian region; and the example that has come to hand concerns Uttar Pradesh, more particularly in that period prior to 1920 when as we have seen nationalist politics there stood moribund. The key to its life at that time we may suggest lay in its subordination to what we may call a 'husk culture'. An understanding of the genesis, the structure, the persistence, and the residual effects of the phenomenon we have in mind would seem of first importance to an appreciation of the modern history of this key Indian region.

If we cast our eyes across the Indian sub-continent in the late nine-teenth century and consider what were the dominant, locally operative cultural traditions in each of its different regions, a list which might be made in the following way begins to emerge – in Bengal, Bengali bhadralok culture; in Maharashtra, Mahratta revivalism headed by Mahratta Brahmanism, especially of the Chitpavan Brahman type; in Madras, Tamil Brahmanism; in the Panjab, urban Hinduism, especially as associated with the Arya Samaj; and in Bombay (if we may include just one city in the list) Parsi modernism. If there is anything in such characterisations, then it looks as if in U.P. something which was com-pounded of the still extant remnants of traditional 'little' rulership, together with 'big' landlordism, 'urdu' culture, and the aristocratic con-cepts of the Oudh Taluqdars and their associates of the 'Oudh School' of British administrators, stood dominant there.[2] Wherever one looks in U.P. in this period, one soon encounters the pre-eminence of one or other feature of this complex. It is not very difficult, moreover, to see how for all the complexities involved its different elements were related to each other. They had their origins in three separate quarters: in the persistence hereabouts (despite both the Muslim and the British con-quests) of the Hindu 'little kingdoms'; in the immense influence – not least upon such minor matters as 'manners' – of centuries of Muslim imperial courts and Muslim imperial dominance; and, not least, in the British reaction in the post-1857 period in favour of ruling through what they were pleased to call 'the natural leaders of the people' – the Taluq-dars of Oudh, and their compeers, the larger zamindars of Agra Pro-vince. In so far as this élite tradition was characterised by its Indo–Persian cultural traits it can be readily distinguished, because it contrasts so strikingly with what lay submerged beneath it – the most traditionally oriented of all the Hindu cultures to be found anywhere in India.

U.P. is after all the Hindu heartland. Here to the north are the Hima-layas. Here are the Sivalites, the home of Shiva. Here at Ayodhya was Rama's capital; at Mathura Krishna's. Here is the mighty Ganga; at Allahabad its sacred junction with the Jumna and with the mythical Saraswati, and the site of the Kumb Mela. Farther downstream lies Hinduism's Mecca, Benares, with its great centres of sanskritic learning. Centuries of Buddhism, and then of Islam, did not destroy the cohesive-ness of Hindu society in this area. It seems to have been maintained by the manner in which it was structured. There seems to have been much more caste interaction here than was to be found in southern India, and an unusual spatial breadth to marriage connections.[3] At the same time there was a fuller representation of the fourfold *varna* structure of classical Hinduism than could be found anywhere else in India: brahmans, kshatriyas, vaisyas, sudras, were all effectively represented (as they were not, for instance, in South India) and there were, of course, untouchables as well. In Oudh, moreover, there were more brahmans per head of the population than anywhere else in India, occupying places all the way from priests and taluqdars, to merchants, agriculturists and beggars.[4] They were thus unusually well placed to insist upon a long continued adherence to what we may call Brahmanic values. They were strongly placed too to hold their ground against the threats which successive non-Hindu conquerors presented to them.

But while Hindu values remained sacrosanct for the mass of the population in this region, they did not command the allegiance of the élite. This became steeped in a culture that in inspiration was Muslim. Its adherents were, in the first place, the Muslims who came to the area – the Ashraf, as they were called, divided into the four categories of shaikhs, sayyids, moguls and pathans – together with those of the pre-existing hindu élite who became converts to Islam, more particularly the Muslim Rajputs. It also included many other Rajputs, and even Brahmans, and such people as the members of the well-placed writer caste, the Kayasthas, who whilst remaining Hindus adopted much of the Islamised culture. And they were joined by other, smaller groups, of whom perhaps the most famous latterly were the Kashmiri Pandits. There was no intermarriage amongst Hindus and Muslims, and no commensality; but much symbiosis: witness Jawaharlal Nehru's romantic attachment to Urdu culture, or the talk of 'castes' among U.P. Muslims.[5]

So dominant was this Indo-Persian culture, and the élite who held to it, that (as Dr Spear has reminded us)[6] when Englishmen first went in any numbers to India in the eighteenth century, they saw Indian culture as primarily Muslim. In its heyday its reach spread far beyond the borders of present-day U.P., to Bengal in the east, and Hyderabad, Mysore and other southern states in the south. As the Mughal empire collapsed its association with the various petty rulerships which emerged in its aftermath subsisted intact. Together Indo-Persian culture and its associated traditional rulerships might well have been finally swept away by the British, but for the particular events of 1857 when the little rulerships provided the rallying points for those who were in revolt against the British; and the British decided that the best means of recovering their control over the region was to compound with them. In the Canning settlement of 1858, the key figures in U.P., the Taluqdars of Oudh, received sanads guaranteeing them a locally dominant position and this enabled them to survive to become the linchpin of the whole subsequent settlement.[7]

Lucknow was its headquarters.[8] There the Taluqdars had their town houses. There was the centre for their Urdu cultural activities. There they built Canning College in Lord Canning's honour. For over half a century they remained profuse in their loyalty to their British bene-factors. The British reciprocated, and spent their time asserting that the Taluqdars were veritable British gentlemen. Agra province landlords took their cue from their Oudh contemporaries. The Muslims in the province generally, and those who shared their culture, became closely connected both with the British and the Taluqdars; they were used to serving imperial masters in the region, and saw no point in declining to serve the new ones. There was a small western-educated class: but since it too shared much of the dominant Indo-Persian culture, and in any event made its living from rendering services to the British, the Taluq-dars, and the larger Agra zamindars, it too was closely associated with the British and the larger landlords. And the outcome was writ large across the province.

> Where . . . in India [an ecstatic British supporter of the régime asked in 1906] can be found more true happiness and ease under Britsh rule, more solid progress, more unquestioning loyalty? Where such smooth relations between the rulers and the ruled, between the party of order and the party of change? Where a better measure of agrarian peace? Where a more effective combination of old sanctions and young aspiration?[9]

No wonder Keir Hardie found no one to meet him on the railway station at Kanpur.

The élite tradition which all this comprised was to remain dominant for a remarkably long time. It dampened nationalist political activity long after this had become extensive elsewhere. It secured its most dramatic victory as late as the 1920s when the capital of U.P. was trans-ferred from Allahabad to Lucknow, by the then Governor of U.P. Sir Harcourt Butler, who himself was an honorary taluqdar, and the last and, some would think, the greatest of the Oudh School of British administrators; while throughout the dyarchy period of the 1920s and 1930s the most fervent upholders of the élite tradition, the U.P. land-lords, dominated the legislature of the province and for the most of the time the executive as well. This was the only major province in India in which landlords were so pre-eminent for so long.

And yet, for all the dominance of this élite tradition, there was much that was empty about it. The element of traditional rulership within it was not of the pristine kind. With the establishment of British power the 'little kings' had lost their guns, their forts, and their private armies; and the British did not give them thereafter any creative administrative function to perform. In the 1860s some of the Taluqdars became magistrates; but this practice soon seems to have lapsed, and in the period before and after the turn of the century (with which we are mainly concerned here) they fulfilled no administrative or judicial duties for their British rulers. From being traditional rulers they simply became a landed interest. This is nowhere better illustrated than in their concern through the vicissitudes of the first half of the twentieth century to maintain their position as landlords rather than reassert their former position as rulers. For all the insistence moreover of the 'Oudh School' of British administrators in U.P. that the British were working through the 'natural leaders of the people' there was nothing here of 'indirect rule' – that much can be made clear by comparing Harcourt Butler's celebrated pamphlet *Oudh Policy* of 1906 with Sir Frederick Lugard's *Political Memoranda* for northern Nigeria issued in that same year.[10] And this was not all. For all the state which the Taluqdars of Oudh maintained, the Lucknow of the Taluqdars was scarcely the Agra, or the Delhi, or the Lahore, of the Mughals. Once this region had been the home counties of a great empire. Now it was simply the 'north-western provinces' (as the British called it for part of the time). The metropolis had moved elsewhere. What was more, although there might still be Muslim preeminence hereabouts, with the British now in control there was no longer Muslim dominance: and Urdu, although it remained for a time the language of the courts, was a provincial tongue, not the classical language that Persian had been. Sad to relate as well, Urdu poetry, which had once reached a high peak in the eighteenth century, had by the latter part of the nineteenth passed its prime. Urdu culture, moreover, even though it still had its devotees, no longer at the turn of the century served the cultural needs of the bulk of the U.P. élite. Many were looking elsewhere – to theosophy, to arya samaj, to European ideas. The main impression, indeed, which one receives of U.P. at this time is of a great area with little or no cultural, or indeed any other kind of creativity to its credit. The flesh had dried up. The kernel had gone. Only the husk remained.

Yet for a long while there was no challenge to the dominance of the husk culture. There was no pre-existing indigenous ferment which might have been sparked alight by the advent of the British. The heavy pressure, and dispiriting aftermath, of Mughal rule had deadened initiative across the region. After the tremendous upheaval of 1857 the countryside lay inert. There was no indigenous creative minority, like the Maharashtrian Brahmans further south, who proud of their past and still determined to cut a figure in the world, might have turned their minds to the creation of a new future. So many still looked only to the past. In submitting to Muslim rule the Hindu élites in the Ganges valley had in any event long since swallowed their pride: they were not now of a mind to strike out on their own. And the Muslims, while still recovering from the demoralisation which had accompanied the fall of the Mughals, were cowed by the hostility of the British over the part they were alleged to have played in the events of 1857, and their ablest leaders saw their future in terms of assuaging the British, rather than in fashioning a new future on their own. At the same time there were no great numbers of richer peasants in U.P. who might effectively have by-passed the pre-eminence of the existing élite; and little of that combination of landed groups and the new professions which went to the generation of a newly creative élite in Bengal. Above all, perhaps, there was no great metropolis in U.P. to play the engine of change. Unlike Bengal, with its single, great mercantile capital of Calcutta, U.P. was polycentric. There were at least five towns of equal pre-eminence – Agra, Lucknow, Allahabad, Kanpur, Benares. Their character varied; and not one of them could hope to lead the whole province in a new direction. Because for the time being there was no really substantial alternative to the dominant husk-culture, both the innumerable smaller zamindars, particularly of the Agra provinces, and the smaller professional groups in the towns maintained a formal allegiance to it – none more so, until the last decade of his life, than Motilal Nehru, Jawaharlal's father.

This is to paint a picture of one part of South Asia at one period in its modern history with the broadest of brushes. It may well prove to be a very misleading picture. But it suggests that some broader delineation of the history of South Asia in the modern period may well be attempted than is generally indicated by studies of, for example, provincial land revenue systems, the policies of British Viceroys, or, for that matter, of the Indian national movement itself. As, moreover, further investigations on some rather new lines are made, for this and other periods, and of this and other areas, the range of comparisons which will become possible ought to lead to the cutting of all sorts of new historiographical seams – some of them scarcely yet conceived; and from that a great deal might follow.

III

Yet to paint a stationary picture is scarcely to be truly faithful to the historians craft. We must seek to trace out the sea-changes as well; not just the eddies upon the surface, but the deep currents, the undertows, the great shifts of direction. There is no reason why this should not be done. If we take U.P. once again, Dr Irfan Habib has put his finger on one such change when he reports that between the seventeenth and the nineteenth centuries the number of villages in the upper Gangetic valley were halved during a period when the area of land under cultivation was doubled.[11] Why? When? How? With what effect? We do not know the answers, and few suggestions can be offered at present: but it is clear that there is a major historical question here which requires investigation by someone. All we can offer for the moment are some suggestions about another great set of changes – those which have brought about the collapse of that husk culture which we have sought to portray above.

As the twentieth century has worn on there have been marked changes in U.P. One has been indicated already: in 1907 nationalist politics in U.P. were hard to find; by 1921 they were well to the fore – U.P. had a larger number of District Congress Committees (45) than any of the other fifteen Congress provinces.[12] Other changes may be indicated in this way: in the revolt of 1857 against the British the peasants of Oudh flocked to the support of their Taluqdars; by 1920-2 the old nexus was broken and a mounting series of peasant *jacqueries* against the landlords was erupting. Once rajas had competed hereabouts for followers; now peasants were seeking landlords for land. Once this area had been Muslim dominated; today it is Hindu dominated. Once it was Taluqdar dominated; now it is Bhumidar dominated. Once administrators hereabouts had worried about deaths; now they worry about births. Once the official language was Urdu; now it is Hindi. Once the British were in control; now self-governing Indians are in control.[13]

Many of these changes have been linked to one another. As traditional rulers became landlords, so their subordinates moved from being associates and followers to becoming merely tenants. With the growth of population the agrarian balance at first swung sharply in favour of the landlords. There were more tenants seeking land to hold than there was land available for them to occupy. Peasants, moreover, now faced ruling élites of higher castes who had become simply landlords (and seemingly irremovable, and not infrequently rack-renting ones at that); and with the alienation of land to non-agricultural castes, some landlords were now simply rentiers. In Oudh in particular landlords came to hold great power: no less than 78 per cent of the population in the late nineteenth century were tenants-at-will. The old relationships between ruler and follower accordingly became very severely strained. And there was no ready escape. There was not all that much cash-crop development; little opening up of new areas to cultivation as in the Panjab; little industrialisation; and from time to time there were acute and special distresses – famines, price fluctuations, and epidemics. But throughout landlordism reigned supreme. In the end, however, the widespread peasant discontent which was generated erupted in the peasant uprisings of the early 1920s. They might have been very much more effective had not the very size and polycentrism of U.P. made the organisation of an effective *kisan* (peasant) movement there so exceedingly difficult.

These uprisings seem, even so, to have precipitated one of the most important breaches in the old order. One can see the point exemplified in Jawaharlal Nehru's *Autobiography*.[14] He himself states that his encounter with the desperate peasantry of his own Province in the early 1920s constituted a turning-point in his career. His response was typical of his class. The professional middle classes of the towns had formerly battened upon the landlordist husk culture. But in the early 1920s they broke with it. Because it was an empty shell, there was very little about it to attract troubled, thoughtful men once its validity had come to be challenged, and its lack of vitality was becoming plain for all to see. It was particularly objectionable, of course, to urban nationalists because of the close association of its chief adherents with the British. Yet it was not simply a case of the small urban professional groups now striking out on their own. They were soon taking with them large numbers of smaller zamindars (with whom to some extent they overlapped) as well. These men were clearly much discontented with the existing state of affairs. The existing élite tradition was shot through with considerations of status. Status, however, was not linked to achievement: it was tied (in the first place) to sanads and jagirs, or, in general, to the size of one's holding. Amongst the larger landlords there was always great pride of place, and they continually displayed an overweening disdain for all those with lesser possessions. It is clear that smaller zamindars (and there were very large numbers of them) were denied entrance to all the more select quarters, such as the large landlord associations. So that it is scarcely surprising that for all their earlier obsequiousness these smaller landlords should have been ready to look for new openings as soon as these seemed to be available. They found what they were looking for in the further-ance of nationalism and in the championing of (though not, as we shall note, any identification with) peasant discontent. And the outcome can be readily illustrated. The committee of the U.P. Congress which ran the no-rent campaign in the province in 1931 consisted of zamindars – and mostly small zamindars at that – together with professional men from the towns. This alliance exemplified the new forces which were in being in the province by the 1920s; and from this point onwards into the following decades, U.P. Congress leadership consisted almost entirely of *outré* élite-tradition leadership responsive to the mass – A.K. Sherwani and Jawaharlal Nehru being in 1931 its two prime examples.[15]

Before long they and their associates stood in a commanding position. In a situation in which there was no one who could readily undercut them – no non-Brahman movement; no Muslim peasant majority; and no well-organised independent *kisan* movement either – they found themselves in a position of quite unusual political power. The U.P. Congress' dominant role in the All-India scene in the 1920s and in the suc-ceeding decades may be explained to a great extent by its possession of a firm base. Among other things this gave it an unrivalled position from which to destroy its major local opponents, the larger landlords. The U.P. Zamindari Abolition Act of 1951, whatever else it did not achieve, destroyed the position of the Taluqdars and other former big landlords in the province; and great was the fall thereof.

This, however, was not the only means by which the old order was undermined. A crucial development had occurred half a century earlier when the devanagari script had first been allowed in the courts alongside Urdu. Since for every one who used the Persian script in the province three used devanagari, this would seem to have been a reasonable step. However, as a Muslim leader declared at the time, 'It is the coffin of Urdu. Let it be taken out with great éclat.' He was quite correct. Al-though the number of publications in U.P. in Urdu increased in the first half of the twentieth century quite substantially, those in Hindi increased very much faster. By 1921 Hindi publications for the first time began to outnumber Urdu publications, and by 1951 Hindi's triumph was com-plete. It had quite replaced Urdu as the official language, and the number of Urdu publications were now sharply declining.[16] The cultural impli-cations – in the narrower sense – were patently enormous.

There were further developments leading towards the general decline of the existing élite tradition in the province as well. Perhaps the real turning-point came in 1936–7. As Peter Reeves explains later in this volume the landlords National Agriculturist Parties were soundly defeated by the radically minded Congress at the provincial general elections following the Government of India Act of 1935. Shortly afterwards, Congress also won its decisive passage of arms with the British over the issue of whether or not the maintenance of reserve powers in the hands of the Governor meant that they had secured internal self-government or not; while during the same critical few weeks, through its refusal to take a Muslim League member into the U.P. cabinet, Congress not only sounded the death-knell of Muslim pre-eminence in the province (which had lasted by this time for something over six centuries), it gave the *coup de grâce* to the landlord–British–Muslim connection which had been such a prominent feature of the élite tradition in U.P. in the past. It would certainly seem clear that for all Khaliquzzaman's efforts in 1936–7, Congress in U.P. at that time saw in the Muslim League nothing but a wolf in sheep's clothing – the old élite tradition masquerading as the threatened Muslim minority.

The denouement came in 1947. The British pulled down the Union Jack at the Lucknow Residency. With Partition U.P. Muslims like Liaqat Ali Khan and Khaliquzzaman left for Pakistan for ever. The trauma of the old aristocracy can be seen reflected in Attia Hosein's novel, *Sunlight on a Broken Column*, where Aunt Saiva eventually blurts out:

What right have they to steal what is ours? Will they never be content with how much they rob? Is there no justice? Is this a war with custodians for enemy property? . . . If they want to drive out Muslims why not say it like honest men? Sheltering behind the fake slogans of a secular state! Hypocrites! Cowards! . . . The Banias!

Some further aspects of the changes which had occurred were set out by *The Leader* of Allahabad on 5 September 1947 when it wrote:

So it was that saffron robed priests chanted vedic hymns from various corners of the Durbar Hall in UPs Government House as the clock struck 12 on the night of August 14. The boot of history is now on the other leg. We are heading for a new synthesis in the culture of the United Provinces in which Hindu culture will be the dominant partner. It is now the turn of the Muslims to throw up Kayasthas who would attain scholarship in Hindi and Sanskrit.[17]

It is a matter for investigation whether K. M. Panikkar in suggesting in his minority report to the States Reorganisation Committee in 1956 that

U.P. should be divided into two separate states, was trying to salvage something from the wreckage. For he did not suggest that U.P. should be divided down the middle. Rather he suggested that the four western ('Urdu-speaking') divisions should be separated off from the rest into a new state to be called, of all things, 'Agra'![18] What visions that conjures up! But it was not to be.

Yet the fact remains that for all the apparent disappearance of the most striking features of the old order, there was only a very partial social revolution in the state. Although there were serious peasant outbreaks in U.P. in the early 1920s, there were no similar outbreaks ten years later when with a sharp drop in prices as a consequence of the world slump economic conditions became very severe once again. And not only have there been none since: a peaceful, fundamental social revolution has not occurred either. One reason for this is probably that in the early 1930s the Governor at that time, Sir Malcolm Hailey, saw what was coming and took every step he could to avoid it.[19] But another reason is almost certainly to be found in the fact that the U.P. Congress (composed as we have suggested earlier of urban professional men and smaller zamindars) was scarcely less determined than the British to see that no real upheaval occurred, and took steps accordingly. By giving the peasants leadership in an abortive no-rent campaign, while never lending themselves to the notion of a full-scale rural revolution, they checked the development of an autonomous peasant movement (which, as we have suggested, was for various reasons very difficult to manage in U.P. in any event) and none has ever yet developed. Moreover, once the alliance of urban professional men and smaller zamindars had established itself in control in U.P. it seems to have done everything in its power to secure its own interests without overmuch concern for those for whom it had originally agitated. The U.P. land legislation of 1939 was a half-hearted reform. The Zamindari Abolition Act of 1951 got rid, as we have seen, of the larger landlords. But the smaller ones seem mostly to have been reconstituted as Bhumidars, admittedly with official ceilings upon the amount of land they could hold, but with the right to sell and mortgage their land as before, and with most of their previous positions held intact. Certainly provision was made for a larger number of Sirdars – tenants of the state with no rights to mortgage or sell; but, as Daniel Thorner has pointed out, 50 per cent of the land in the U.P. is still held by 10 per cent of the population – an improvement upon the 1·5 per cent who held it previously; a shift, a change, but scarcely a social revolution.[20]

Taluqdars have gone from U.P. Bhumidars, it seems, now reign supreme: and for all the faction fighting to which U.P. has been prone since independence there has been a notable consensus amongst its leaders that it should stay that way. Charan Sing (for so much of the time since independence the U.P. Minister of Agriculture and recently its Chief Minister) has justified the new order in this way:

> By strengthening the principles of private property where it was weakest i.e. at the base of the social pyramid, the reforms have created a huge class of strong opponents of the class war ideology. By multiplying the number of independent land-owning peasants there came into being a middle-of-the-road, stable rural society and a barrier against political extremisms. It is fair to conclude that the agrarian reforms have taken the wind out of the sails of the disrupters of peace and opponents of ordered progress.[21]

Allowing for the changes that have occurred it might have been a supporter of the old élite tradition speaking. It was certainly a small zamindar. Their values are dominant still. As Jawaharlal Nehru grudgingly conceded to a sardonic Bihari audience shortly before his death, his home state Uttar Pradesh had the 'distinction' of still having 'the zamindari mentality'. 'A man with even one bigha of land holds his head high and walks erect like a zamindari', he added amidst loud, appreciative laughter.[22]

One may wonder, however, whether the new Bhumidari régime will be a stable one. Population is growing rapidly in U.P. It has been doing so since the end of the First World War. If the figures are to be believed food production has not kept pace. According to the census the amount of food grains available per head of the population has since 1951 been declining.[23] There is some evidence, moreover, of movements amongst untouchables. Certainly it is notable that (for all the small numbers actually involved) conversions to Buddhism in U.P. – which provides a way out of the caste system – went up by 300 per cent between 1951 and 1961.[24] It may be noted as well that the four lower castes named as being implicated in the peasant upheavals of the early 1920s numbered even then about a third of the population of the province;[25] there is no reason to believe that their number is less today; nor that they could not find numerous allies in related castes. If over forty years ago they could mount a series of peasant risings when conditions became intolerable, it could well be that as conditions become impossible to bear once again, they – or others like them – will make their despair felt in a no less eruptive manner. The situation is certainly a challenge to the politicians.

It must be stressed, however, that what is coming up in U.P. is not just rural discontent. Nothing is more central to twentieth-century U.P. history than the upsurge of the formerly long-subordinated Hindu culture of the mass of the population. After seven centuries of Muslim dominance, as we have seen, Hindu dominance has taken over. The consequences are not all immediately apparent. It can be no coincidence, however, that U.P. should be so aggressively minded in its attachment to Hindi: Urdu has been triumphantly overthrown, and in the circumstances it is hardly surprising that there is little truck with that other alien-based tongue, English. Whether the two great stirrings from below will coalesce or conflict remains to be seen. Both, however, are plainly of singular importance.

IV

This, of course, only constitutes the crudest of sketches, and a good deal of it could well prove to be very misleading. But perhaps it will serve to suggest once again that a broader perspective upon the processes at work in modern South Asian history than has customarily been allowed is conceivable. In tracing it out we must look to the structure of society, to its dominant values, to the interaction between these two; to the prevalent political, economic, social and cultural modes; to the manner in which consensus is secured and conflict contained; and to the way in which a whole society has been the subject of change over time – sometimes almost imperceptibly; sometimes cumulatively, one step here, one occurrence there; sometimes at a key point at a key moment with immense consequences for the whole: each change, moreover, has almost certainly interacted with a whole series of shifts in the related operations of society, and even of the societies round about. If we are to understand what has been afoot our vision will have to be truly kaleidoscopic.

One point is perhaps particularly worth noting. It goes without saying that in the last two hundred years the changes to which India has been subject – to go no further back – have been immense. Many of them cannot be understood without reference to the British. But if we are to understand the processes here, and trace out their course, we have to be quite clear that they were not the consequences of a single encounter between two great monoliths. India upon the British advent was in no sense fixed in a rigid mould. The British 'impact' was in no sense a uniform, once-for-all event. The encounter between Britain and India took an immensely subtle form. As we are at great pains to try and stress

Indian society varied greatly from one region to another and had its own orthogenetic processes. Nowhere was it static, either before or after the British arrival. And the combination of movement with variation meant that most situations were much more different from each other than has sometimes been appreciated. 'The British' for their part differed too. Amongst their number were men with differing interests, conflicting ideals, and varying skills, and those of them who were concerned with India were themselves as much subject to change over time as were the Indian societies with which they were in contact. For all their attempts, moreover, to conceive of what they were doing in all its fulness, their knowledge of the actual and long-term consequences of their actions was plainly very limited. Putting these various considerations together we may be clear that the British impact differed from one area to another quite markedly.

We may remind ourselves as well – as several of the studies in this book will serve to emphasise – that few developments were unilinear here for very long, even in appearance. It will not do, for example, to say that the British 'impact' 'atomised' Indian society; or that it brought about the 'rise' of 'The Indian middle class'. The whole story is much more varied and much more complex.

This brings us up against one of the most serious difficulties in modern Asian historiography – that there seems to be no satisfactory peg upon which to hang our major investigations; no peg of the kind which, for instance, the Meiji Restoration provides in modern Japanese history, the French Revolution in modern French history, or 'the enlargement of scale', we may think, in modern African history. 'British imperialism and the Indian reaction to it in the Indian national movement' (however this may be interpreted) will not suffice. The crucial issues are much more complex, and have still to be fathomed convincingly.

V

It is for these reasons that we are deliberately chary of offering here anything which approximates to an overall view of modern South Asian history. The benchmarks are still exceedingly difficult to discern, and it will probably be some time yet before they become at all clear.

But this is not to say that all-Indian matters are not for us. On the contrary, for all our interest in regions and in regional variations one of our major purposes in this book is to affirm that, alongside these, there are issues of all-Indian significance which can and should be investigated concurrently. There are indeed four such studies of four such issues in this book, and we hope they may help to point the way forward. And we would emphasise that once we have the regional studies which now seem to be more and more in the offing, and once we have extended and deepened the measure of our understanding of all-Indian issues, we should begin fairly soon to relate them experimentally one to the other. No symposium which has been constructed from the work of a group of people who have been investigating a wide range of topics (and which have not been chosen in relation to any one theme) can be expected to touch upon more than a few of the significant issues requiring investigation, particularly when it includes no study, for example, in economic history, or in the history of any part of southern India. This is certainly not the place, therefore, to sketch out a blueprint. Despite the common elements in our thinking all we can offer here is a series of explorations. Nevertheless, taken as they stand, the contributions to this book do combine to make up a story – and this, it may be suggested, runs something like this.

In outlining the social history of Maharashtra in the years after the British conquest in 1818 Kumar begins by showing how British policies in India (particularly in this instance their land revenue policies) generated some quite radical social changes in Maharashtrian society. Van den Dungen follows with a chapter in which he points up by contrast the multifariousness of the changes which occurred in rural society in one other area, the Panjab, and insists that they cannot be explained by reference to British influence alone. The merest outline of a composite picture begins to emerge. In his second contribution Kumar then indicates how changes took place in nineteenth-century India, not only amongst the rural masses, but amongst the sophisticated élite; and in writing about Ranade he opens up the theme which links most of the remaining chapters in this book, viz. the protracted, many-sided debate over what kind of social, political and economic future was to be sought for India as the twentieth century began to overtake it. Close to the centre here stood the debate about what should be the political order which would be most appropriate to India in the twentieth century. Here, Rothermund outlines the opposing views on this issue of the nationalist leader Gokhale and one of the high priests of the Indian Civil Service, Sir Herbert Risley. Risley declared that India was essentially a country of unintegrated communities, and Rothermund shows how in the Morley-Minto reforms of 1909, with which Risley had a great deal to do, this view for the time being prevailed in the constitution of India. But, Owen's chapter then

B

demonstrates how in the period of the First World War the Indian national movement put the lie to this as a conclusive doctrine, mounted a countrywide political campaign against British rule, and set on foot a much more populist, mass-based, nationalist movement than had ever been witnessed in India before.

We have little further to say upon the subsequent central development of the nationalist movement. We have probed instead a number of issues touching upon its development in other respects. Broomfield tells first of how the Muslim majority in Bengal reacted, sharply and positively, to the political developments in the latter part of the First World War period when these threatened to ignore their presence. In a second contribution he shows the other side of this coin by illustrating how as the national movement of the last thirty years before independence gathered momentum one of those groups which had initially made a highly creative response to the new opportunities which the British presence provided found itself fatefully challenged. Reeves then shows how one of the more traditional groups began to face a disastrous future as the growth to power of the Congress grew nearer. Between them they illustrate once again how necessary it is to take account of regional variations, and how very much more elaborate was the story of the movement towards independence than has sometimes been suggested.

In the middle part of the book there are thus several studies of fateful change in twentieth-century South Asian history. The next contribution (by the editor) tells how some Indians held that the right way to contain and direct the developments which had been and were occurring was by the establishment of an Indian version of the liberal British democratic state; and the point is made that in the twenty years that followed independence the aims, albeit the relatively narrow aims, of this relatively very small group of people were remarkably fulfilled – particularly by comparison with what has happened in so many other new states. The book ends, however, with Graham's chapter which demonstrates that this rather particular doctrine was not at all acceptable to those who have a deep attachment to Hindu tradition; and, accordingly, we end upon an inconclusive note – which, as historians, we may think, is as it should be.

Let it be said again that the linkages which have been sketched out here must not be taken as offering a new unilineal theme to modern South Asian history: the uncertainties hanging over mid-twentieth-century India are not confined to those which have been suggested, and a very considerable number of important facets have not been referred to at all. But perhaps this ordering does indicate how specialised – even narrow – studies may be linked to larger themes. It may serve to re-emphasise as well that, for all the importance which is currently attached to regional variations – in our view rightly – there are countrywide connections to be made as well.

Throughout it will be seen that we have been much concerned with such issues as the characteristics of social structure and social change, with the spread of what has been called 'rationality', and with the role of values in society, and particularly of ideology. These are now the stock-in-trade of social scientists. But they are plainly useful concepts to historians as well. We would even suggest that historians may have useful things of their own to say upon them. For example, all that we would wish to say about the importance of social organisation and cultural values, their interrelation and their history, seems to us as true for élites and individuals as it is for whole societies; indeed many of the later contributions to this book explore this problem in some detail.

At the same time we have frequently found ourselves confronting problems of authority in Indian society, and we have sought in each particular instance to see what it was that contributed to it, kept it in being, and/or called it into question. In addition, we have been greatly impressed by the importance of the part played by, the search for, and the firm attachment to, cultural norms – or in other words, by the problem of identity. In our preliminary discussions we assumed that the convergence, or divergence, of political authority and cultural identity would be a recurrent theme in our differing contributions. Occasionally we have been able to glimpse the relationship between them; and whenever we have felt able to say so we have done so. But many of the most difficult problems here clearly remain, and we may perhaps be allowed to leave their further exploration to each of the separate, and larger, studies that each of us hopes to present in the years to come.

One further matter has impressed us – the immeasurable uncertainties which have confronted those who have placed a prominent political role in South Asian history in the last century or so. Lack of knowledge, uncertainty, the need to choose before the manifold implications of the various competing possibilities are at all clear, are part and parcel of a politician's lot, and no study of modern South Asian history that forgot this would, we would now wish to emphasise, tally with our understanding of it. We have no impression of a pre-ordained course of events. On the contrary we have been constantly struck by the uncertainty which seems to have overhung many of the developments with which we have been concerned.

We have one final point to make here. Few things have struck us more than the wealth of material which exists to enable historians to pursue these and other, related, questions a great deal further than they have been hitherto. Sets of private and institutional papers are becoming available all the time. Newspapers of all kinds, stretching back for a hundred years and more, exist in the original in great quantities. Where the originals are no longer extant they can often be followed in précis form in the great series of *Reports on Native Newspapers*. There are, moreover, the tremendous collections of land revenue records. Newspapers contain a great deal more for our use than information about, for example, the history of the Indian National Congress – important though that is: and the land revenue collections contain immense stores beyond those which refer to British land revenue policy alone. Much of the material we have in mind is only to be found in South Asia itself, and it is to the treasures of its various state archives that we would particularly draw attention. Bernard S. Cohn in a series of papers, and Percival Spear in a number of places have shown us the way forward. We shall be happy to be thought to be following in their footsteps.

NOTES

1   I have used the file Home, Political, A, February 1908, Nos 50–63, National Archives of India, Janpath, New Delhi.

2   The chief sources for what follows are [W. C. Benett], *Gazetteer of the Province of Oudh*, Vol. 1, A–G, Lucknow, 1877, Introduction; Percival Spear, *Twilight of the Mughals*, Cambridge 1951, especially Ch. IV; H. C. Irwin, *The Garden of India*, London 1880; S. H. Butler, *Oudh Policy. The Policy of Sympathy*, Allahabad 1906; P. D. Reeves, 'The Landlords Response to Political Change in the United Provinces of Agra and Oudh, India, 1921–1937; Ph.D. Thesis, Australian National University, 1963; Walter C. Neale, *Economic Change in Rural India, Land Tenure and Reform in Uttar Pradesh, 1800–1955*, New Haven and London 1962. I am particularly indebted to Peter Reeves for all his assistance and stimulus, always most generously given.

3   McKim Marriott, *Caste Ranking and Community Structure in Five Regions of India and Pakistan*, Poona 1965, pp. 53–60.

4   Benett, loc. cit., pp. xx–xxi; John C. Nesfield, *Brief View of the Caste System of the North-Western Provinces and Oudh*, Allahabad 1885, pp. 49, 71, 73, 132–3.

5   M. A. Ansari, *Muslim Caste in U.P.*; Jawaharlal Nehru, *Autobiography*, new edition, Bombay 1962, pp. 2, 29, 169.

6   Percival Spear, *The Nabobs*, Oxford paperback edition 1963, 'Historical Introduction'.

7   The most substantial account is in Michael Maclagan '*Clemency*' *Canning*, London 1962.

8   A striking description is in Choudhry Khaliquzzaman, *Pathways to Pakistan*, Lahore 1961, Ch. II.

9   Butler, *Oudh Policy*, p. 28.

10   F. D. Lugard, *Political Memoranda*, London 1906.

11   Irfan Habib, *The Agrarian System of Mughal India, 1556–1707*, Bombay 1963, pp. 12–14.

12   Gopal Krishna, 'The Development of the Indian National Congress as a Mass Organisation, 1918–1923', *Journal of Asian Studies*, XXV, 3, May 1966, p. 417.

13   See note 2 above.

14   *The Pioneer* (Lucknow), 4 February 1921, 29 March, 17 May 1922; Nehru *Autobiography*, Chs VIII–XI.

15 Ibid., p. 297.

16 *Census of India*, 1911, XV, pp. 256, 281, 285; 1951, Uttar Pradesh, Pt 1A, Report, pp. 409, 413.

17 I am greatly indebted to Peter Reeves for this reference.

18 *Report of the States Reorganisation Committee*, 1956, Minority Report by Sardar K. M. Panikkar.

19 This is my initial reading of some of the Hailey Papers for 1931 which I have been permitted to see by the special permission of Lord Hailey.

20 Daniel and Alice Thorner, *Land and Labour in India*, Bombay 1962, p. 7.

21 Charan Singh, *Agrarian Revolution in Uttar Pradesh*, U.P., 1958, p. 41.

22 *National Herald*, 7 March 1963. I owe this reference to the kindness of Dr B.D.Graham.

23 *Census of India*, 1951, II, Uttar Pradesh, Pt 1A, pp. 24, 35, 44, 473.

24 *Census of India*, 1961.

25 See note 14 above.

2

THE RISE OF THE RICH PEASANTS IN WESTERN INDIA

★

Ravinder Kumar

A distinguishing feature of British rule in India was the promotion of social change by the State, as distinct from spontaneous transformations in society, through a rational agrarian policy, through the creation of new institutions of administration, and through the dissemination of new principles of economic organisation. The promotion of social change through deliberate acts of policy was a new departure in the guiding principles of administration in India. For native governments possessed a limited view of their responsibilities towards the community, while the inadequate instruments of social control at their disposal, and their restricted grasp of the principles of economic organisation, prevented them from embarking upon rational programmes of progress. British administrators differed from their native predecessors in their conception of the role of the State in society, and in the sophistication of their insights into social and economic problems. They also recognised the connection between the stability of a régime, particularly one based on conquest, and its ability to satisfy the aspirations of dominant or emerging social groups in the community. British administrators consequently tried to promote progress through fostering social groups whose interests were closely tied to the new régime, and who therefore possessed a vital stake in its survival. In Bengal, for instance, the problems of political control and economic progress were simultaneously resolved through the institution of a landed aristocracy in 1793. Since British administrators in western India looked upon the landed aristocracy as a parasitic group, the tone of their agrarian policy was more democratic. In the provinces of Bombay the British Government sought to encourage the rise of a class of rich peasants who would owe their prosperity to British rule and would therefore be committed to its perpetuation.

I

The effect of agrarian policy on rural society in Western India during the nineteenth century can best be appreciated by looking closely at a small region like the districts around Poona which were taken over by the Government of Bombay from the Peshwa Baji Rao II in 1818. Under the Marathas a typical village in this region consisted of a miniature world, self-sufficient in itself, and geared to a style of life calling for a minimum of contact with the outside world.[1] It would be located on an evenly shaped mound in close proximity to a stream, and would be surrounded by the fields which the villagers cultivated. From a distance it had the appearance of a mass of crumbling grey walls, with a few stunted trees growing out amongst them, and here and there a structure standing out more conspicuously than the rest. All this was enclosed by a mud wall of irregular shape pierced by rude gates of wood at two or more points. The interior of such a village was no more prepossessing than the outside. There was a lack of harmony and an absence of design in its layout. The crumbling walls would turn out to be the homes of the villagers, made of calcareous earth with terraced tops of the same material. These dwellings were constructed without any attempt at regularity, and they were divided by narrow and winding lanes into groups of three or four. While conforming to a basic style, the homes of the prosperous culti-vators were larger in size and more impressive in appearance than the dwellings of the poorer cultivators. The conspicuous structures in the village were the *chowrie*, or the municipal hall, where the public affairs of the village were debated, and the temple, which was built either by a rich and repentant Patel, or by a philanthropic *deshmukh*, in the hope of commuting their earthly sins. Conspicuous, too, were the dwellings of the untouchable castes, whom social taboos prevented from coming into physical contact with the rest of the villagers, and who consequently lived in little hamlets outside the village walls.

The bulk of the villagers comprised cultivators of the *kunbi* caste, who were grouped into *meerasdars*, or hereditary cultivators, and *uprees*, or cultivators who did not have any prescriptive rights in the soil. The *meerasdars* were the descendants of the first settlers of the soil, who had in periods of remote antiquity moved over in *jathas* or family groups to new sites, and had apportioned the available arable land between them-selves, the holdings of each *jatha* receiving the family name to distinguish it from other estates. The proprietary rights vested in the *meerasdars* are brought to light in an account which sets out the circumstances leading to the founding of the village of Muruda in South Konkan. The site of the village originally formed the *rudrabhumi*, or burning ground, of the neighbouring hamlet of Asuda. To Asuda in the sixteenth century came an ubiquitous Brahman called Gangadharbhatta, with two disciples in tow, and after residing in the village for a while he decided to found a new settlement in the neighbourhood. For this purpose Gangadharbhatta applied to Jalandhra, a princeling of the Sekara dynasty who controlled the region from his seat at Jalagama. After securing Jalandhra's permission, Gangadharbhatta persuaded thirteen *jathas* or families to accompany him to the new settlement. He then divided the village lands among these families, the boundaries of their several estates being marked off by *Gadudas*, or huge stones, in the presence of *Kshetrapalas*, or tutelary deities, who provided divine sanction for the allocation of property in land to the founding families.[2]

The original *jatha* estates of a village were jointly held by the family groups, who were responsible as a body for the payment of the land-tax. If the owners of one of the shares in a joint estate let his land fall waste, the family assumed responsibility for his share of the State's dues, and the fields belonging to him were taken over by them for cultivation. Similarly, if the member of a *jatha* died without an heir, his portion of the estate was divided among the surviving relations. He was also free to dispose of his *baproti* or patronymic, but his share was not permitted to pass out of the family if a co-sharer was willing to buy it. Only if no one in the *jatha* wanted to purchase the field did it pass on to an outsider, who now entered the *jatha* on the same terms as the original incumbent, but was referred to as *birader bhaus* or legal brother, instead of *ghar bhaus* or house brother. The *jathas* played an important role in facilitating the collection of the land-tax by the State. A representative of the eldest branch in each *jatha* looked after the interests of the entire family, and collected the land-tax from its members. Similarly, the tax on the village as a whole was collected by the Patel or village headman, who was also the head of the seniormost *jatha* in the village.[3]

When the Government of Bombay assumed control over the Poona territories in 1818, the *jatha* system had lost some of its cohesion, partly through inbuilt tensions, and partly through the attempts of the preceding State to deprive it of the authority which it exercised over its members in questions concerning revenue administration. These attempts were inspired either by a desire to increase the revenue of the State, or to ensure that it received a fair share of the profits of agriculture. It is difficult to say how far the Maratha administration actually succeeded in disrupting the cohesion of the village. For as late as the 1760s, the vitality of the *jathas* is eloquently reflected in the fate of the *kamal* survey which was introduced by the Peshwa Madhava Rao, and which closely resembled the *ryotwari* system later introduced by the Government of Bombay. Despite the care with which the *kamal* survey was conducted, its rates were never applied, because in their place the *jathas* of the village substituted the *rivaj* or the customary rates, which differed significantly from the *kamal* findings. The acquiescence of Madhava Rao's administration in the *rivaj* rates, and in the authority of the *jathas* to determine the distribution of the land-tax within the village, is open to the interpretation that the *kamal* survey only aimed at providing the State with an idea of the productive capacity of the villages under its control. But this hypothesis is difficult to maintain because the *kamal* survey showed the traditional system to be shot through and through with the most glaring inconsistencies. These inconsistencies can be illustrated by a comparison of the *kamal* and *rivaj* surveys of any one village. Taking individual holdings in the village of Oswaree Khuro in Poona district, for instance, we observe that the fields Panduree and Wursola contain one *chowar* of land each, and would therefore be taxed an equal amount on the basis of the *rivaj* survey. Yet these fields were found to possess different productive capacities by the *kamal* survey, which took both the quality and the superficial area of a field into consideration in fixing the land-tax. A comparison of the fields Dhuljote and Amberket shows the *rivaj* rates in an even worse light, with the discrepancy between the actual and assumed productive capacities being greater than in the former case.[4]

Despite the ability of the *jathas* to defy the attempt of Madhav Rao's administration to regulate the internal distribution of the land-tax in the village, only partial memories of the institution remained at the time of the British conquest. These memories found expression in the practice of entrusting the seniormost *jatha* in the village with the responsibility of collecting the land-tax from the villagers, even though joint familial responsibility was no longer rigidly enforced. The members of the *jatha* chosen to represent the village were collectively styled the Patels, and the seniormost among them was called the *mukkadam* Patel. Long after the founding of the village, *meerasdars* descended from the Patel family considered themselves higher in social status than other *meerasdars*, though their pretensions were in no way buttressed by any social or economic privileges. The crucial difference within the cultivators of a village lay between the *meerasdars* and the *uprees*. The former had an indisputable right of cultivating their holdings so long as they paid the land-tax; they could also sell or mortgage their property with the concurrence of other members of the *jatha*. In contrast, the *uprees'* association with the village was tenuous. The Patel leased them the deserted holdings, or the arable waste of the village, either on annual terms, or on a long lease running concurrently for a number of years.

Apart from their tenures, the significant differences between the *uprees* and the *meerasdars* were expressed in social distinctions rather than in economic privileges. They were related to contrasting styles of life rather than to well defined economic differentials. The possession of a *watan*, or a prescriptive right in the land, conferred on the *meerasdar* a status in the village which was denied to the *upree*. Yet the *meerasdar* was not necessarily a richer individual than the *upree*. In the village of Ambola in Poona district, for instance, the holdings of *uprees* like Suntojee Scindiah and Kundojee Scindiah compared very favourably in area and productive capacity with those of a majority of the *meerasdars* of the village.[5] Besides, *meerasdars* like Beerjee Scindiah and Ambajee Scindiah, whose fields possessed the same productive capacity as the holdings of Suntojee and Kundojee, paid a heavier land-tax as their share of the village rental, because the great quantities of cultivable land awaiting exploitation obliged the Patels to offer very favourable terms to the *uprees* to induce them to settle in a village. In contrast to the *uprees*, who moved from one village to another in search for better leases, the *meerasdars* were deeply attached to their fields, and refused to move so long as they could earn enough from their *watan* lands to keep body and soul together. Their attachment to the soil did not stem solely from motives of acquisition; it also flowed from a desire for the social status which they enjoyed in the village, and the prestige which the possession of a *watan* bestowed upon its owner in rural society. The social prerogatives of the *meerasdar* were many and substantial. He was a member of the council which exercised executive authority over the village; he did not pay any house-tax so long as he owned only one house in a village; he was exempted from a tax paid by others in the village on the occasion of marriage, as well as from a dispensation fee paid for marrying a widow or a wife who had been abandoned; and, last but not the least, he and his wife were entitled to precedence over the *upree* on all social occasions in the village.

The absence of well defined economic differentials in the village imparted an air of tranquillity to rural society which exercised a marked effect on the social behaviour of the *kunbis*. The cultivators were a mild and unobtrusive lot and they shrank back quickly from a want of gentleness in others. But while lacking in worldly sophistication, they were not entirely devoid of a natural liveliness and intelligence. The sympathetic observer would have found them minutely informed in matters relating to agriculture, while the concerns of the village would immediately hold their interest. 'On the whole', observed a British Survey Officer who toured the Poona district in 1826, 'they are far better informed than the lower classes of our own population, and actually far surpass them in propriety and orderliness of demeanour'.[6] That this portrayal of rural harmony is not a romantic phantasy is clear from the statistical account we have of the village of Ambola.[7] Of the cultivating families in the village, 60 per cent had fields ranging between 15 to 30 *beegahs*. Holdings of this size provided a reasonable living by the standards of the time, though they did not insure peasants against involvement in debt. The three substantial cultivators in Ambola were the Patel, Baboo Rao Scindiah, and Marojee Scindiah and Bapujee Scindiah, each one of whom had a holding that was not only 60 *beegahs* in extent, but thrice as much as that owned by the average peasant household. At the other end of the social scale stood *kunbis* like Amruta Scindiah and Hykunt Scindiah, who found it virtually impossible to maintain themselves and their families on the profits derived from their holdings. By and large, however, the village comprised a grey mass of peasants, neither ostentatiously affluent nor in the grip of extreme poverty, who held the balance between a few substantial cultivators and a fringe of hopelessly impoverished ryots.

II

Rural society in the districts acquired from Baji Rao Peshwa in 1818 was, therefore, organised into collective institutions like the *jatha* and the village community; and distinctions within the cultivators in this region were expressed in social styles rather than in economic cleavages. The revenue administration of the Marathas flowed from this pattern of social organisation. Since Mountstuart Elphinstone, the Governor of Bombay from 1819 to 1827, was an administrator in the conservative tradition, he was inclined to adopt the Maratha system of revenue administration without any serious modification. But the utter confusion into which the Deccan districts had been thrown during the closing decades of Maratha rule made this impossible, and obliged him to devise an altogether new system of revenue administration.

Elphinstone entrusted the task of devising a new revenue policy to Robert Keith Pringle, a brilliant young Bombay administrator deeply influenced by Utilitarian philosophy and Ricardian economics through Malthus, who occupied the Chair of Political Economy in the East India College at Haileybury. As a doctrinaire Utilitarian, Pringle disagreed with conservative administrators who were concerned primarily with moderation and continuity in the processes of change. His approach to social problems conflicted with the conservative vision of society as a community embracing different groups and interests in a state of over-all equipoise. Instead of looking at social phenomena through collective institutions like the *jatha* or the village, Pringle focused his attention on the behaviour of the individual in the community, and he inferred the attitudes and aspirations of organised groups from the insights he thereby gained into the social process. This approach led Pringle to place a strong emphasis on the discreteness of the individuals who make up a society; it also encouraged him to relegate the social groups and the collective institutions which stood between the individual and the State to a position of secondary importance. To this atomistic view of social phenomena, Pringle added a belief in the effectiveness of rational action. This belief prompted him to assume that social phenomena were governed by laws discernable through the application of human reason; and that once these laws had been discovered, all that remained to be done was to apply them rigorously to the relevant part of the polity.

Since the Maratha revenue system hinged upon collective institutions like the *jatha* and the village community, Pringle looked upon it as a major obstacle in the progress of rural society. He also believed that political economy had discovered the rationale of the rural economy in the Ricardian Law of Rent, and he therefore launched a frontal attack on the traditional system of revenue administration in the Deccan.[8] The settlement of the village rental by the Marathas with the Patel and the village community, he argued, had resulted in gross oppression for the poor cultivators, since in distributing the tax within the village, the Patel and the influential *kunbis* had transferred an inequitable economic burden on them. The *kamal* survey of Peshwa Madhav Rao had attempted to redress this imbalance in taxation through absorbing all the rent, leaving to the cultivator only the wages of labour and profit on the capital invested in the land. But Madhav Rao's attempts to devise a rational basis for the land-tax had provoked the hostility of the dominant cultivators in the village, who had transferred a substantial share of the village rental on to their poorer fellow-villagers through the *rivaj* surveys. The opposition of the dominant cultivators had prevented the Maratha government from levying the *kamal* rates, since it lacked the power and the organisation to undermine their hold over the village.

Pringle proved that cliques of rich peasants dominated the rural communities of Maharashtra by comparing the *kamal* and *rivaj* surveys of the village of Oswaree in Poona district. The unit of measure employed by the *rivaj* survey was the *chower*, which paid a fixed rental irrespective of the quality of the soil. However, the *chower* was a fluctuating unit, and its dimensions varied inversely with the quality of the soil, thus bringing about a measure of equalisation in the assessment. Yet the *kamal* survey of the 1760s, which employed a standard *beegah*, and also took account of the quality of the soil, showed this supposition to be untrue. For instance, the estate of the Mallee *jatha* in Oswaree village amounted to $4 + 4/10$ *chowers*, while that of the Indoree *jatha* comprised 5 *chowers*; their *rivaj* assessments, therefore, were in the proportion 17:20. But the *kamal* survey revealed that the fields of the Mallee family were of a superior quality, and it fixed the assessment of the two *jathas* in the proportion 275:234. Pringle therefore concluded that under the former administration the house of Mallee had exploited its social position in the village of Oswaree to pay a very light land-tax to the State.

To break the dominance of the rich peasants over the villages of the Deccan, Pringle recommended the repudiation of the traditional system of land-revenue, which revolved around the *jatha* and the village community, and which did not employ rational principles in determining the land tax. Since his belief in Utilitarian values predisposed him to look upon individuals rather than organised social groups for creative social action, Pringle was convinced that the principle of joint responsibility for the payment of the land-tax perpetuated the dominance of the influential cultivators over the village and stood as an insurmountable obstacle in the way of progress in rural society. A clean sweep had therefore to be made of the Maratha revenue system, since it was based on irrational premises, and because it sapped the cultivator's will to raise his economic status through hard work. In its place Pringle proposed the institution of a legal and rational relationship between the ryot, as a tenant, and the State, as the supreme landlord in the country. The State's share of the agricultural produce would be the rent payable to the landlord, leaving the wages of labour and profits of capital to the peasant who cultivated the soil. The ryotwari system of land revenue proposed by Pringle sought to undermine the collective quality of life in rural society, and to substitute in its place a competitive and an individualistic social climate. It hinged on the belief that the liberation of the ryots from their obligations to the *jatha* and the village community would create the conditions for the emergence of a prosperous peasantry whose rational values and desire for acquisition would stimulate economic progress and create a stable social order.

III

The taluka of Indapur in Poona district to which Pringle turned in 1826 as the Superintendent of the 'Revenue Survey and Assessment of the Deccan' was typical of rural Maharashtra at the time of the British conquest. The first attempt at regulating its revenue affairs had been made by Malik Amber during Muslim hegemony over the Deccan. The *tankha* settlement introduced by Malik Amber in the 1620s employed a cash rental based on a third share of the gross produce, and it was levied on the villages collectively rather than on the ryots individually. The distribution of the *tankha* on individual holdings in the villages was left to the members of the village community. When Shivaji established his sway over Indapur, its revenue arrangements continued as before, but in 1784–5 the *kamal* survey launched by Peshwa Madhava Rao was extended to the taluka. Unlike the *tankha*, the *kamal* was based on an assessment of individual holdings in the village, and it was undertaken for two reasons: to ascertain the productive capacity of the district, and to effect an increase in the public revenue. While the *kamal* survey was inspired by commendable motives it was unfortunate in its repercussions on Indapur. Though the resources of the *taluka* had increased considerably since the institution of the *tankha*, and a resurvey was therefore called for, the surveyors of Madhava Rao over-estimated its potentiality, and in raising the rental from Rs 1,22,000 to Rs 2,22,000, they imposed a crippling burden on the peasants of Indapur.[9]

Because of the high tax it imposed on the peasants, the *kamal* survey of Indapur remained a fictitious objective. Its failure encouraged the government of the last Peshwa, Baji Rao II, to farm out villages to individuals who were willing to collect the land-tax from the ryots. In delegating responsibility to farmers of revenue who were free of all restraint and who bore no traditional ties with the village communities under their control, the Government of Poona aggravated the economic malaise. For the revenue farmers levied cesses over and above the normal assessment in order to reap quick profits for themselves. Their excesses virtually depopulated Indapur by 1807, when the Government of Poona took alarm and tried to remove the peasants' grievances through a system of leases (*istawa*) providing for a small and annually increasing rent over a period of nine years, when the *kamal* rates were to become operative. However, Baji Rao's revenue farmers had undermined the rural economy so thoroughly that even the reduction of the *kamal* rates failed to induce the ryots to return to their villages, and the Poona administration was desperately turning from one expedient to another when hostilities broke out and the Deccan was annexed by the Government of Bombay.

When the British Government assumed control over Indapur in 1818 the *taluka* had not recovered from the excesses perpetrated by the revenue farmers of Baji Rao. The position was further aggravated by a run of bad harvests in the 1820s, which obliged the new rulers to concede remissions in revenue. However, British problems were partly self-created, since in their ignorance of the productive capacity of the *taluka* British revenue officers assumed that the *kamal* assessment was a reliable guide to the amount of tax which the peasants could pay to the State. The issue was also tied up with the social dominance which the Patel and the principal cultivators exercised over the villages, despite the absence of clear cut economic cleavages in rural society. Misled by the *kamal* survey, British administrators imposed heavy rentals on the villages of Indapur, which it was the responsibility of the Patels to collect for the State. As a result of these high rentals, the Government was compelled to grant annual remissions in revenue. These remissions were particularly large in bad seasons, when a complete or partial failure of the rains reduced the great majority of ryots to a miserable plight. However, the tragedy lay in that the remissions, instead of alleviating the misery of the poor cultivators, were often swallowed up by the Patels and the principal cultivators, to whom the revenue officers were compelled to entrust the detailed distribution of the concessions given by the Government.[10]

The corruption fostered in the villages of Indapur by the annual remissions in tax was brought to the notice of the Government in 1827 by R. K. Arbuthnot, who was in charge of the *taluka*. Arbuthnot pointed out that at the root of the problem lay the 'Present high rates of assessment throughout the country', which led the ryots to believe that the annual remission in the land-tax was a regular feature of the revenue system. By supporting such a system the State played into the hands of the dominant peasants in the villages; it simultaneously undermined the collective sentiment which formed the basis of village society, and encouraged rich and poor peasants to enter into an unholy alliance to defraud the State of its share of the agricultural produce:

> The system of granting large remissions in reference to the quality of crops [Arbuthnot observed] . . . is of so bad an effect, that I feel very averse to putting

it in practice to any great extent: for as soon as it is understood that collections are to be made on this principle, it becomes the object of everyone to deceive the Government. . . . When it is generally understood that all of one family assist each other in their concerns and that if the crops of one should fail, he has recourse to his neighbours to lend him for this year, in expectation, that he will be called upon in his turn in the following year, there appears no injustice, when the assessment is moderate, in insisting on it being paid, nor is it likely to produce injury throughout the country.[11]

The confusion stemming from an inadequate knowledge of the resources of Indapur was heightened by the chaos arising from the changes in the original organisation of the rural communities of Indapur. Villages in the *taluka* were divided into *sthuls* or estates, and these estates were further apportioned into *teekas*, several of which were held by the same cultivator, often in different estates. The cultivable land in the village was also divided into areas of *ghutkool* tenure and *meeras* tenure. *Meeras* land was owned by the *meerasdars*, while the *ghutkool* land belonged to the village collectively, and was administered for it by the Patel. The cultivating community comprised *meerasdars* and *uprees*, of which the former belonged to *jathas* or family groups, each one of which was made up of the *meerasdars* of a particular family, and of those members who were incorporated into it by purchase of land or otherwise. The *sthul* and *jatha* were originally corresponding and coextensive designations, but by the 1820s the same *jatha* often held fields in different *sthuls*, and the same *sthul* was frequently held by different family groups. The complexity of social organisation was heightened by the fact that the *meerasdars* could on occasions occupy *ghutkool* lands, and the *uprees* cultivate the fields of the *meerasdars*, with sometimes each holding a portion of both. All this was hardly designed to simplify the task confronting Pringle as the Superintendent of the Revenue Survey and Assessment of the Deccan.[12]

In order to reduce the confusion in the revenue administration of Indapur to a semblance of order Pringle modified the traditional principles which governed the land-tax. The pitch of this tax, he pointed out, had formerly been based on the exaction of a share of the gross agricultural produce by the State. British administrators like Sir Thomas Munro, who were concerned with the problems of revenue administration, had accepted and acted upon this principle. But despite their acquiescence, the traditional mode of assessment was based on faulty principles, since it made no distinction between rent, which was the landlord's share of agricultural produce and a consequence of the differential fertility of soils, and the profits of capital and the wages of labour, which rightly belonged to the cultivator of the land. The proportion of the gross produce which could be levied without trenching upon the profits of the cultivator varied with the fertility of the land, and decreased progressively from the superior to the inferior soils. It was conceivable that the light assessments of Sir Thomas Munro in the Madras districts, which were based on the gross produce, had left a fraction of the rent to the cultivator even on the inferior soils. But to concede this was no recommendation of the traditional principle of revenue assessment, which took account solely of the gross produce of the soil:

> It is [Pringle observed] obvious that the surplus which remains from the gross produce of the land after deducting all expenses is the fair measure of its power to pay an assessment. But as that surplus varies in its relation to the whole produce in different soils, any tax proportional to the latter only must be unequal. . . . [This] inequality by creating an artificial monopoly in favour of the soils yielding the greatest proportion of net produce . . . will have a tendency to check production. . . . It has always appeared to me, therefore, that, as the net produce is the only accurate standard of exaction, and as in proportion the assessment is regulated by it, it will be distributed in the manner most favourable to the general wealth and prosperity of the community, it might therefore be distinctly recognised as the basis of our operations. . . .[13]

Having defined the bases of a rational revenue policy according to the Ricardian Law of Rent, Pringle applied them to the survey of Indapur. This operation was carried out in three stages: in the first instance, the surveyors measured the holdings of the ryots; next, the assessors classified the fields so measured according to their fertility; and finally, the empirical data collected by the surveyors and assessors was used by Pringle to calculate the net produce of soils of different fertility. The government rental was then fixed as a standard proportion (55 per cent) of the net produce.

In presenting the results of his survey to the Government of Bombay, Pringle emphasised that he had left the natural advantages of different soils unimpaired; and that his rates enabled landlords to levy rents which increased progressively from the worst to the best soils. He also admitted that the survey was fatally dependent upon the accuracy of the data from which the net produce had been calculated. But Pringle found no reason to doubt the honesty of the native officers under his charge, or to question the accuracy of their findings. The crux of the issue was the effect of the survey on the traditional distribution of the land-tax among different social groups in rural society. Pringle was struck by the changes which the survey had produced in the fiscal obligations of individual ryots and of entire villages. But, he argued, these were consequences for which the government ought to have been prepared. If the assessment on individual cultivators had been equal and equitable under the old system, there would have been no need for a new survey. Since it was not so, a scientific survey was bound to change the relative position of different cultivators concerning their obligations to the State.

Although Pringle was convinced that the rates levied under the Indapur Settlement were equitable, he realised that a survey 'is not a mere question of political economy, and that, affecting as it does the rights and interests of a large portion of the community, it must be considered on broader and more general grounds'. He had no fears about cultivators on whom the burden of tax had been reduced by the survey. But the position of cultivators whose rental had been increased required reconsideration on grounds of expediency. For although it was desirable to equalise the land-tax on the poor as well as the 'dominant' cultivators, no re-evaluation could justify the violation of prescriptive rights. It was in this context that alterations in rentals impinged on the status and position of the *meerasdars*, who possessed a property interest in the land. When the idea of a survey had first been broached, it was assumed by administrators who subscribed to conservative views, that a survey based on rational principles would raise the burden of tax on the *meerasdars*, thus assuming for the State a prerogative to which it could not lay any claim. Pringle, however, failed to see anything in the tenure of *meerasdars* which prevented the State from increasing their contribution of rent:

> I am at a loss to discover [he observed] the ground on which this notion of the right of meerasdars to exemption from increased payments on a general revision of the assessment was taken up. I have looked in vain for any confirmation of it in the numerous notices regarding the rights and privileges of this class. . . . I have looked for it in vain in the deeds by which the land is transferred. . . . I have frequently conversed on this subject with intelligent natives, and I have never heard from them but one opinion. . . . Arbitrarily to raise the assessment of an individual meerasdar beyond that of his fellows would be offensive to public feeling. But they have no conception of the existence of any contract to prevent . . . government from causing it to be apportioned on the fields either of meerasdars of uprees in any way which in its wisdom it may think fit.[14]

Luckily for Pringle, the crucial questions concerning the *meerasdars* and their prerogatives were never raised by the Indapur Survey, since it reduced rather than enhanced their burden of land-tax. It was (as we shall soon see) the *uprees* who were adversely affected by the new arrangements, and who had to pay a higher tax under the new rates. But this did not perturb Pringle. He held that since the *uprees* cultivated the land on a tenuous tenure, they had no reason to expect a continuation of the attractive rentals they had formerly enjoyed, and were at liberty to fend for themselves elsewhere. Pringle's attitude towards the *uprees* was not the result of a lack of sympathy for the poor cultivator; and he realised that the surveys would result in a decrease in the area of cultivation. But this did not impair his confidence in the equity of his rates. For he believed that a contraction in the area of cultivation was in some circumstances highly desirable. The idea of attracting *uprees* on low rents was, in his opinion, both ill-conceived and mischievous. It encouraged a ruinous competition against the *meerasdars*, and promoted slovenly and inefficient cultivation on the part of the *uprees*. 'Like the Poor Law in England,' Pringle pointed out, 'it is a system which sets out upon the principle of making the poor rich, by making the rich poor, and ends by making paupers of us all.'[15]

IV

The cogency with which Pringle outlined the principles underlying his survey prompted Sir John Malcolm, the Governor of Bombay, to sanction forthwith its application to Indapur, and the new rates were introduced in the *taluka* in 1830 in a mood of optimism.[16] Yet the survey embraced one feature which would have raised doubts concerning its equity, or its practicability, in the mind of an individual less doctrinaire than Pringle. It is necessary to remember that Pringle believed that the prosperous cultivators in the village had exploited the *rivaj* survey for their selfish ends. Pringle's case for a new survey, and for a *ryotwari* as opposed to a village settlement, rested on the supposition that the dominant cultivators had formerly paid a very low rental to the State. But as the results of his survey poured in, Pringle observed that the burden of tax on the prosperous *meerasdars*, whom he had regarded as the exploiters of rural society, would be decreased instead of being increased under the new rates. In the *talukas* of Pabul and Sewnair in the Poona Collectorate, for instance, the rental of *meerasdars* was reduced from Rs 3,55,827 to Rs 2,17,196, representing a cut of 20 per cent in the total tax.[17] If Pringle had been less confident of the validity of the principles underlying his survey, or of the honesty of the agents employed for its execution, such an alteration in the burden of tax would have shaken his confidence in the Settlement, particularly because he had anticipated an increase and not a decrease in the burden of tax on the *meerasdars*. But his firm belief in Ricardian principles and in the honesty of his native subordinates prevented him from entertaining any doubts about the survey. Executing a neat sleight of hand, he explained away the diminution in tax on the *meerasdars* on the ground that they had formerly paid a heavy tax in order to attract *uprees* to cultivate the *ghut-kool* lands of the villages on low rates.

Because they played an important role in rural society, Pringle found the reduction in the tax on the *meerasdars* a convenient consequence of the Settlement. Ever since the question of a survey had been broached in official circles, conservative administrators had been apprehensive, largely because of Pringle's belief in the existence of dominant cliques of rich peasants in the villages, that an assessment based on rational principles would raise the burden of tax on the *meerasdars*, and would encroach upon their property rights. However, as soon as his survey had been completed, Pringle was able to turn triumphantly on his critics and claim that his settlement had reinforced rather than weakened the position of the *meerasdars*:

There is [he observed] no class of the community which will benefit so much by the survey [as the *meerasdars*]. . . . Indeed, were it otherwise, I should entertain much greater doubts of the advantages of the new rates than I do. I am fully sensible of the importance, with a view to the welfare of society, and every purpose of good government, of maintaining and promoting that independence of spirit, elevation of character, and attachment to the soil, which is the result of proprietary rights. . . . So far from advocating any system which will lead to annihilate them, I should be glad to see them extended to a much wider sphere than they at present occupy.[18]

The real test of a survey, however, was the reaction it evoked among the poor peasants who formed the bulk of the rural communities. So far as the poor cultivators were concerned it soon became obvious that the experiment launched with such hopes was doomed to failure. Early in 1830 reports poured into Poona from the Assistant Collector of Indapur of the difficulty he experienced in persuading the ryots to cultivate their fields under the new rates.[19] Far more disturbing was the desolation of the villages of Indapur through the migration of the peasants to the neighbouring territories of the Nizam in a bid to escape the rigours of the new Settlement. The cultivators had, in effect, voted against Pringle with their feet! The elements, too, joined in a conspiracy against him, since there was a partial failure of the monsoon in 1830. But the state of the government rent-roll made it clear that the vagaries of the weather had been reinforced by an ill-conceived revenue settlement to precipitate a disastrous situation. In 1829 Indapur had been assessed at Rs 58,702 and actually yielded a revenue of Rs 42,299. Pringle had assessed the *taluka* at Rs 91,569. But so many peasants had deserted their villages that even the wildest optimist could not have forecast a collection of more than Rs 16,000 in 1830. The Collector of Poona was reluctant to pronounce on the validity of the survey at so early a date. However, he pressed for the reintroduction of *istawa* leases in order to persuade the ryots of Indapur to return to their villages.

Faced with a virtual collapse of his Settlement through the intransigence of the peasants, Pringle turned to a defence of the principles underlying the Indapur Survey. He touched upon the extensive inquiries into the rights of the ryots, and the nature of their tenures, which had been carried out under his supervision, and referred to the statistical data upon which the calculation of the net produce, and the assessment, were based. To claim infallibility in the prosecution of so complex an operation would be foolhardy. But, Pringle insisted, it was easy to see how a survey seeking to correct inequalities in assessment would provoke the opposition of the peasants whom it affected adversely. The ryots' resistance to the Settlement ought not, therefore, to shake the Government's faith in its accuracy, or its practicability:

> For I am persuaded [Pringle observed] that in the opinion of the majority of the people . . . the magnitude and importance of this work are fully appreciated, and held to be worthy of the government by which it was undertaken. It is certainly looked upon with hope, . . . and will come to be recognised and relied upon with confidence as the charter of their privileges on a point so interesting to our Indian community as the adjustment of the land-tax, and the rights and claims associated with it. . . .[20]

The magnitude of the failure, however, was too calamitous to be dispelled either by pious platitudes or by a reiteration of the principles governing the survey. Conservative administrators like H. D. Robertson, the Collector of Poona, had always been sceptical of Pringle's ability to exploit the Ricardian Law of Rent as the basis of a rational land revenue policy. They now set out to demonstrate how disastrously the survey had altered the distribution of tax in the villages and how seriously it had affected the fortunes of peasants. Through inquiries conducted in the surveyed villages they were able to pinpoint fallacies in the principles of Pringle's revenue policy, as well as in the application of this policy to the survey of Indapur.

When Robertson embarked upon an inquiry into the effects of the Pringle Survey on the peasants of Indapur, what immediately struck his attention was the decrease in the burden of tax on the *meerasdars* through the new rates. This diminution had not escaped Pringle's notice, though he had been hard put to explain a phenomenon which contradicted his thesis of a society dominated by 'rich' peasants. But while Pringle was aware of the diminution in tax on the *meerasdars* in qualitative terms, Robertson's detailed investigations revealed how drastic a change the survey had effected in the economic burden on different groups of cultivators in the villages. In the hamlet of Mouze Kowrey, for instance, the total rent according to the new rates agreed closely with the *kamal* evaluation of Rs 3,304; but rents on fields owned by the *meerasdars*, which were located in the most fertile part of the village, had been lowered from Rs 2,152 to Rs 1,815. Such alterations were brought about through a simple expedient. The fertile rice-fields owned by the *meerasdars*, which were formerly assessed at the maximum rates, had been transferred to an inferior (*jerayet*) category by Pringle's assessors, who had at the same time upgraded the fields held by the *uprees*. The latter now paid Rs 1,489 instead of their *rivaj* evaluation of Rs 1,152. The collection of revenue from Mouze Kowrey before and after the Settlement was an eloquent indictment of the survey operations. In 1829 the village had contributed a sum of Rs 2,690 to the coffers of the State: the anticipated collection in 1930 was Rs 1,819.[21]

The Pringle Survey not only changed the relative burden of tax on the *meerasdars* and the *uprees* to the advantage of the former, but it also altered the proportion in which the *meerasdars* of a particular village distributed the rental amongst themselves.[22] This became obvious to Robertson when he traced the effect of the survey on a *jatha* of six families which held the estate of Kurdela in the village of Kurra (see Table 1). The heads of these families were bound to each other by close ties of kinship, and in the not too remote past their forefathers had divided the estate into six shares according to their several rights of inheritance. By the *rivaj* evaluation the first four families of the *jatha* held equal shares; the fifth a double share; and the last a share and a half. When Pringle's surveyors measured the estate, however, they discovered that the actual area of the different holdings did not correspond with the picture set out by the traditional accounts: Byheroo Kurdela's holdings, for instance, were practically three times those of Pandojee Kurdela, though according to the *rivaj* survey they were only twice the size of the latter's fields. The effect of the survey, therefore, was to introduce radical changes in the traditional distribution of tax among the six Kurdela families, and while the *jatha* had its total rental reduced, the families which it embraced were affected to different degrees. Arjunah and Pandojee Kurdela, for instance, had their rentals halved, while the tax on the rest of the Kurdelas was reduced by only 33 per cent.[22]

TABLE I

EFFECT OF PRINGLE SURVEY ON
KURDELA JATHA

No.	Name of the head of the family	RIVAJ SURVEY		PRINGLE SURVEY	
		Area	Assessment	Area	Assessment
1	Pandojee Kurdela	20 beegahs	24 Rs	21 beegahs	12 Rs
2	Arjoonah Kurdela	20 beegahs	24 Rs	20 beegahs	10 Rs
3	Kassee Kurdela	20 beegahs	24 Rs	24 beegahs	16 Rs
4	Goondji Kurdela	20 beegahs	24 Rs	29 beegahs	17 Rs
5	Byheroo Kurdela	40 beegahs	48 Rs	59 beegahs	34 Rs
6	Andojee Kurdela	30 beegahs	36 Rs	28 beegahs	29 Rs

The members of the Kurdela *jatha* were completely baffled by this inexplicable change in their fortunes. As the two Patels of Kurra, Luxman Gonday and Balloojee Dholay, explained to Robertson, when the Kurdela estate was originally partitioned, the *jatha* had resolved the problem of differential fertility through apportioning shares in *beegahs* of varying superficial extent. The *rivaj beegah*, consequently, took into account both the area and the quality of the field. The measurement of the fields in such a unit simplified the collection of revenue. Thus the former Government had in normal seasons levied a rental of Rs 1·25 on every *rivaj beegah* in the village. If in a particular year it raised the rental on the village, all that was required to divide the enhanced demand among the cultivators was a proportional increase in the rental per *beegah* sufficient to meet the new assessment. By disturbing the traditional distribution of the rental within the Kurdela *jatha*, Pringle had undermined the principles on which the shares of the Kurdelas, and the breakdown of the village demand, were based. To offset the changes effected by the survey, the Patels Gonday and Dholay did not rule out the possibility of the Kurdela *jatha* 'effecting such a redistribution of the land as would bring their shares back to an equality'. Their verdict on the long-range repercussions of the survey, however, was far more ominous: 'All the people do not yet know the effect of the new survey', they pointed out, 'but as soon as they comprehend it, we think that the *meerasdars* will generally quarrel among themselves.'[23]

The confusion into which the survey had thrown the affairs of the Kurdela *jatha* highlights the arbitrary treatment meted out to the *meerasdars* by Pringle. The reasons behind this arbitrary treatment are easy to understand. Notwithstanding the *volte face* he executed once the results of his survey became apparent, Pringle's attitude towards the *meerasdars* was shaped by the suspicion that they had paid very light taxes under the former administration, and that the distribution of tax on them was inequitable and unequal. Such suspicions blinded Pringle to fallacies in the principles of his survey. They also led him to repose complete confidence in the findings of the Survey Department, even when these findings flatly contradicted the traditional *rivaj* accounts. Last, but not the least, came Pringle's belief in the State's discretionary right to raise the rental on the *meerasdars*. This belief led Pringle to commit a grave error, for as his critics pointed out:

that *meerasdars* had their assessment raised or lowered by Government is true; but Government have no right to raise or lower the assessment of only one *meerasdar* of a village. It must raise or lower the assessment of all in equal proportions, for their assessment were originally equalised by their tenures and joint responsibility; and any alteration of these proportions, except in the singular circumstances of fraudulent concealment, is precisely rendering their assessments unequal....[24]

In revealing how the prosperous cultivators of Indapur had emerged with a substantial diminution in rent through the survey, Robertson provided a plausible explanation for the failure of the Pringle Settlement. But it required a detailed investigation by Robert Shortrede extending over fifty villages to establish Robertson's tentative conclusion beyond the shadow of a doubt.[25] The prosecution of the survey had involved two distinct operations, namely, the measurement of the superficial extent of the fields, and their classification on a relative scale according to their fertility. The first operation was carried out by the native officials under Pringle with reasonable accuracy. But the classification of the fields was completely undependable, and throughout the length and breadth of the *taluka*, Shortrede pointed out, 'in two instances only did I find three successive fields correctly assessed';

I have [he observed] called the misclassification general and systematic because had it been otherwise, had the class of each field been determined by lot, then one field in nine should have been correct, and of the remaining eight, four should have been above and four below the proper class. In order to try the classification in this way I made a spinning top in which I made nine marks corresponding to the nine classes, and in several villages I found that the class determined by the spinning top was nearer the truth than that determined by the survey.[26]

Shortrede thus possessed clear evidence that the inaccuracies in classification were deliberate rather than accidental; and that behind them lay the calculated attempt of a section of rural society to defraud the State of its revenues. The significance of the errors in classification is brought out very well in the way in which the surveyors prosecuted their task in the village of Indapur itself. The estate called Brahman *sthul* in Indapur consisted of the best soil available in the Deccan. Yet the portion of Brahman *sthul* belonging to Deputy Patel Massaye Galande, which was of a superior black category, had been classed as inferior red by the surveyors. Similarly, the 750 acres of black soil owned by the Despandya Kulkarnis were grossly under-assessed. In this instance, there were errors both in measurement and in classification: 23 acres of the estate had been classed as first black; 299 as second black; 166 as third black; 140 as red; making in all only 628 acres. The Despandya Kulkarnis thus paid a lower tax than they should have because their fields were wrongly measured and under-assessed.

All this pointed to collusion between the native officials of the Survey Department and the dominant groups in the villages comprising the Patel and the principal cultivators. Shortrede believed this collusion to be the principal reason behind the diminution in the burden of tax on the *meerasdars*. In village after village, he pointed out, the surveyors and assessors sent out by Pringle had been bribed by the prosperous cultivators to under-assess their holdings. The decrease thus effected in the State's rent-roll had been made good by an increase in the burden of tax on the *uprees*, who could least afford to pay anything extra, in order to make up respectable rentals for villages as a whole. 'I am credibly informed,' Robertson pointed out in confirmation of Shortrede's suspicions, 'that in most instances where the aggregate assessment of a village is now less than it formerly was, a contribution was raised from the village officers and the ryots.'[27] Shortrede's verdict on the compact between the dominant cultivators of the village and the native revenue officials under Pringle was equally emphatic:

There can be no doubt [he observed] that the principle of assessing the land according to the net produce is the only one which is necessarily true. . . . I must therefore give my full assent to . . . [Pringle's] general theory of assessment. I must at the same time declare in terms as unqualified my dissent from the general application of that theory to the particular cases I have observed.[28]

Although Robertson and Shortrede had stumbled upon an important reason behind the failure of the Pringle Survey, they failed to grasp the full implications of the *ryotwari* system. The most important feature of the administration of land revenue under the Marathas was the principle of collective responsibility for the payment of the rental by the *meerasdars* of a village. It was the *meerasdars* organised as a community who distributed the collective tax on the village on the basis of the *rivaj* rates, and without reference to any outside authority. Pringle's views on the dominant position of the substantial cultivators were based on sound logic, since it was natural for the Patel and the influential peasants to exercise control over the levers of *social power* in the community. But the further inference, drawn from a comparison between the *rivaj* and *kamal* surveys, that the dominant cultivators were able to transfer a part of their burden of tax to the *uprees*, was incorrect. There was a strict limit to the proportion of the village rental which the *meerasdars* could impose on the *uprees*, since the latter could always express their disapproval of high rentals in a most effective way through the expedient of migrating to a new village. Besides, there was little to be gained by assessing the *uprees* at a rate higher than that they could actually pay, since it was the *meerasdars* alone who stood collectively committed to the State for the payment of the assessment.

All this was no longer true once the traditional relationship between the State and the village community was substituted by a contractual nexus between the ryot and the State through the institution of the *ryotwari* system of land-revenue. Contrary to the situation under Maratha rule, a *meerasdar* now stood to gain positive benefits if he secured a diminution in his share of the village rental, since it was the responsibility of the State to ensure payment of the rental from the villagers severally, instead of the community collectively. In instituting a survey on a *ryotwari* basis Pringle threw open to the *meerasdars* and to the village officers (Patels, etc.) a means for improving their position which had never existed before. The opening up of such an opportunity explains the alliance between the dominant peasants and the native officials of the Survey Department which was responsible for the more

startling features of the Pringle Settlement. Pringle was right in postu-
lating the existence of dominant groups of cultivators in rural society.
But for reasons already explained, the dominance of these groups was
'social' rather than 'economic'; and ironically enough, the means devised
by Pringle to destroy their power strengthened rather than weakened
their hold over rural society.

V

Though the significance and the extent of the *kunbi's* alienation from the
village community, and the destructive impact of the *ryotwari* system
on rural society, were inadequately appreciated by Pringle's critics, the
failure of the Indapur survey scotched all attempts at basing a land-
revenue system exclusively on rational principles. Robert Grant, who
had succeeded Malcolm as the Governor of Bombay, echoed a widely
held view in official circles when he minuted that the only general rule
which could be laid down for the conduct of a survey was that 'there
ought to be a patient, searching and accurate inquiry into the individual
nature and capabilities of every beegah of soil.... No abstract principles
can be applied in such a case.'[29]

But apart from growing scepticism in rational action, the insight into
rural social organisation in the Deccan acquired by British administrators also encouraged them to abandon Pringle's doctrinaire policies.
Some of the confusion in the 1820s concerning revenue policy and
methods of revenue collection stemmed from the fact that a majority of
the Deccan administrators had gained their initial experience under Sir
Thomas Munro in Madras. They were consequently inclined to apply
Munro's methods to Maharashtra without taking local conditions into
consideration. After the Pringle Settlement of Indapur had resulted in a
failure, some conservative administrators in the Deccan re-examined the
Maratha system in the hope of isolating, and emulating, features of the
former administration which had been overlooked in the first instance.
Among these was Thomas Williamson, the Commissioner of the Deccan, who subscribed to Burkean values, and believed in the utter futility
of drastic attempts at reform:

> The result of all my experience [Williamson pontificated in his critique of the
> Pringle Survey] has strongly impressed me with the idea that there is no system
> as good as the established custom of the country, and that when it has apparently
> failed, we have been misled by signs which did not previously belong to that
> system, but were the consequences of confusion, or delay, arising from it being

neglected, or misunderstood... [Of] our own well meant plans for the ameliora-
tion of this country, none have proved so successful as those directed at the
support and restoration of local institutions, and none so unfortunate as those
which have a contrary direction.[30]

In looking for the reasons behind the failure of the Pringle Survey,
Williamson gained a shrewd insight into the former revenue system in
Maharashtra, though he was unable to transform this insight into a practical revenue policy. As opposed to Pringle, Williamson defined a *ryotwari* settlement as a system in which the rights and obligations of individual collectors were first ascertained severally, and then made the basis
of the total village rental. The superiority of such a settlement lay in the
equity with which it determined the ryots' dues, thereby preventing
excessive taxation by the State and arbitrary exactions by the Patels and
dominant cliques of peasants in the villages. Williamson saw a perfect
expression of the *ryotwari* system in the *bhayachara* tenure of the North-
Western Provinces, where a careful inquiry was first instituted into the
productive capacity of a village, and the rental thus evaluated was apportioned into individual shares by the members of the village without
reference to any outside authority. He recognised that the shares so
determined would not necessarily be equal, since some fields would be
better looked after than others. But no additional rent was to be levied on
that account; and this limitation embodied, according to Williamson,
the most striking advantage of the system. For through the economic
incentives it offered to the cultivator without alienating him from the
village community, the *bhayachara* tenure provided a stimulus for effi-
cient agricultural operations. The cultivator no longer drifted from one
village to another in search for holdings with a low rental. Instead, he
was firmly attached to his land, and directed his energy solely to its cultivation and improvement. It would be fatal, Williamson thought, to
weaken this attachment through reassessments which would not only
alter the customary rates, but would also tax improvements effected
under the impression that they would not be subject to any additional
levy.

The conservative principles advocated by Williamson influenced
Richard Mills, the Collector of Dharwar. Mills recognised the basic
weakness of the *ryotwari* system when he observed that the Pringle
Settlement, through alienating the *kunbi* from his fellow-cultivators, had
weakened the cohesion of village society, and had encouraged the dominant cultivators to enter into an alliance with the native officials of the
Revenue Department in order to defraud the State of its revenues and to

impose an oppressive tax on the *uprees*.[31] Yet the alternative proposed by
Mills was open to equally serious objections. In eleven villages in Dharwar Mills had given leases on moderate terms to the Patels for a period of
ten years as an experimental measure. He thereby hoped to preserve the
cohesion of the village community, and to provide its members with
incentives for improving their holdings. Before embarking upon the
venture Mills had been doubtful whether the Patels would be willing to
undertake responsibility for the collection of the village rental. But
what encouraged him to bring the experiment to the notice of the
authorities was the enthusiastic response the idea evoked from the Patels
and the village communities concerned.[32] However, Mills' proposal for
the settlement of villages with the Patels so closely resembled the notori-
ous farming system which had prevailed under Baji Rao, and it could so
easily be exploited by the Patels and the dominant cultivators to their
personal ends, that it did not receive any encouragement from the
Revenue Department.[33]

For it was impossible to revive the former methods of revenue administration. The *rivaj* rates had been ignored for so long that there was little
likelihood of their restoration, not least because they had been 'shock-
ingly mutilated', and in places even 'obliterated', by the arbitrary administration which flourished under Baji Rao.[34] Any practical revenue
policy, therefore, had to be a compromise between traditional methods
of assessment, and the rational principles on which Pringle had based his
Settlement. In his critique of the Indapur Survey, for instance, Shortrede
had advocated an assessment based on a diminishing proportion of the
gross produce from the rich to the poor soils, because of the practical
difficulties involved in calculating rents in a rural society where landlords
did not exist.[35] Shortrede's application of this principle to Indapur shows
to what extent he was willing to abandon rationality when confronted
with practical issues. Setting aside Pringle's ill-conceived attempt to
calculate the net produce of different soils, he proposed that the Government let out land on the basis of the *chower*, in the first instance for a year,
but with a view to an eventual decennial settlement. Williamson threw
himself squarely behind Shortrede's proposal, because he believed that
'from the simplicity of the system, and the moderation of the rent, it
would at once be intelligible and acceptable to the people'.[36] Nor did
Williamson's intuition mislead him. For as soon as Pringle's rates were
abolished, and the light assessments recommended by Shortrede substituted in their place, the situation in Indapur took a turn for the better,
and the peasants returned to their villages. 'An interesting group of

men, women and children who passed my camp the other day,' Williamson noted in his *Journals*, 'said they had left the Nizam's country and were
going to their native villages in Indapur in consequence of the security
now enjoyed there.'[37]

Despite the favourable reaction of the peasants to the virtual revival of
the *rivaj* rates, Shortrede's proposal was too arbitrary, and too unequal in
the burden it imposed on cultivators, to form the basis of a permanent
revenue settlement. It was left to a group of revenue officials led by H. E.
Goldsmid and G. Wingate to devise in the late 1830s a system of revenue
administration which combined the practical features of the Pringle
Survey with the insight of the *rivaj* rates. In devising such a system they
laid down the foundations of land settlement policy in the Deccan.
Goldsmid opposed the idea of rejecting the measurement of holdings
which had been carried out under Pringle's supervision, and of reintro-
ducing the *chower*, which was a fluctuating unit of measure, though it did
not, as it was supposed to, vary inversely in area with the quality of the
soil. Equally ill-conceived, in his opinion, was the attempt to attract the
peasants to the deserted villages of Indapur through the low rates proposed by Shortrede. Such measures, Goldsmid argued, would create an
imbalance in the economy of the surrounding districts by inducing the
peasants residing in these districts to throw up their fields and migrate to
an area where they could rent land on attractive terms.

The most significant feature of the revenue policy advocated by Goldsmid and Wingate was the abandonment of Pringle's doctrinaire use of
the Ricardian Law of Rent, and of his attempt to fix the State demand as
a standard proportion of the net produce. By adopting such a criterion,
Pringle had aimed at rewarding cultivators according to the fertility of
the soil they cultivated, rather than upon the basis of the amount of
capital they invested in the land, or the quality of the effort they put into
their agricultural operations. Such a policy, Pringle had in effect argued,
was neither morally reprehensible nor politically undesirable. As the
Ricardian Law of Rent had demonstrated, it was legitimate that the
profits made by cultivators should be determined by the quality of the
soil they cultivated, decreasing progressively from the best to the worst
soils. The adoption of a revenue policy which contradicted this principle
would interfere disastrously with the rural economy. Politically, there
was everything to be said for the introduction of such an inequality, for
it would enable the substantial peasants to save capital, which could then
be reinvested in the land to secure higher profits. Such an accumulation
of agricultural capital would promote the rise of an affluent class of

peasants whose prosperity would flow from a deliberate and equitable revenue policy, rather than from the exploitation of its dominant position in rural society. Fashioned into the coping stone of rural society under the aegis of the new political order, ran Pringle's argument, this class of prosperous peasants would provide the impetus behind increasing rural prosperity and rising agricultural productivity, and it would serve as a stable social base for British rule in India.

Pringle's attempt to foster the interests of the dominant cultivators, argued Goldsmid and Wingate, was the most serious fallacy in his revenue policy, and the most important reason behind the failure of the Survey. In an inquiry which they conducted in eighty-six villages of Indapur, they discovered, like Robertson and Shortrede before them, that while the measurement of the fields had been carried out with reasonable accuracy, their classification was completely erroneous. Nevertheless, Goldsmid and Wingate did not impute the failure of the Survey solely to errors in classification. True, the ryots had opposed the new scale of rates because it raised the rent on inferior, and lowered it on superior, soils; but this feature of the survey 'cannot be accounted for ... [exclusively] by the numerous cases of error and defect exposed by Lt Shortrede; it is so general and unusual, that we must look for its cause in the system, and not in the execution of the survey'.[38] Goldsmid and Wingate pinpointed in Pringle's application of the net surplus criterion the reason why his survey had dealt so harshly with the poor cultivators. Pringle had defined the net surplus (in Ricardian terms) as the rent which the cultivator was able to pay to the landlord after deducting costs of capital and wages of labour. But, they argued, he had overlooked the fact that the soil of lowest productivity taken into cultivation at any particular moment did not yield any rent to its owner. In taxing soils of the lowest fertility, therefore, Pringle had trenched into the profits of the poor cultivators, and had imposed a scale of assessment which favoured the *meerasdars* as against the *uprees*.

Because his application of the Ricardian law of rent was erroneous, Pringle could not claim that his assessment had left undisturbed the benefits which accrued to the cultivator from the natural fertility of the soil. But having shown where Pringle had erred, Goldsmid and Wingate did not proceed to apply his principles in regulating the land-tax. In subsequent discussions on revenue policy they pointed to the net surplus as the theoretical basis for their assessment, but in practice they employed pragmatic criteria for fixing the rates on different soils. While Pringle's rates were deliberately loaded in favour of the substantial cultivators, and geared to the creation of a rich peasantry which would acquire rational economic behaviour and habits of prudence and thrift under the settled conditions of British rule, Goldsmid and Wingate regarded such a revenue policy as illconceived and injudicious. Wingate, for instance, showed how a ryot having at his disposal a capital outlay of Rs 100 would, according to the Pringle scale of rates, make a profit ranging from Rs 32 as 8 on the best soil, to Rs 12 as 8 on the worst soil[39] (see Table 2). Such an assessment appeared to Wingate to be monstrous in its partiality for the peasant who tilled the superior soils, and contrary to all notions of social equity. What he considered reasonable was a scale of assessment which left the ryot with the same margin of profit, irrespective of the fertility of the soil he cultivated. That a settlement based on Wingate's egalitarian principle would have violated the net surplus criterion is obvious; and a comparison of columns 3 and 6 in Table 2 illustrates how drastic a change in the Pringle evaluation it would have necessitated. Rentals on the best soils like first black, and first red, would have had to be raised by 25 per cent, while those on the worst soils like third red and third burud, would have had to be reduced by 33 per cent of the Pringle evaluation.

TABLE 2

COMPARISON BETWEEN PRINGLE'S SCALE AND
WINGATE'S EGALITARIAN SCALE

Type of soil	Area cultivated by Rs 100	Net Produce per Acre	PRINGLE'S RATES			WINGATE'S RATES		
			Rate per Acre	Total Tax	Ryot's Profit	Rate per Acre	Total Tax	Ryot's Profit
	1	2	3	4	5	6	7	8
1st Black	28-36-0	2-8-0	1-6-0	39-11-9	32-8-3	1-12-1	50-11-1	
2nd Black	29-15-0	1-15-3	1-1-3	31-10-9	25-11-2	1-3-6	35-13-0	
3rd Black	34-33-0	1-7-9	0-13-0	28-4-9	23-6-4	0-13-10	30-2-2	
1st Red	29-13-0	2-0-6	1-1-9	32-8-6	27-0-7	1-4-9	38-0-2	
2nd Red	35-1-0	1-5-3	0-11-9	25-11-6	20-16-9	6-11-5	24-15-4	21-8-11
3rd Red	40-29-0	0-14-4	0-7-9	19-11-3	16-12-5	0-5-10	14-14-9	
1st Burud	40-14-4	1-2-1	0-10-0	25-3-6	20-6-1	0-9-7	24-0-8	
2nd Burud	40-34-0	0-13-2	0-7-3	18-8-2	15-1-7	6-4-9	12-0-10	
3rd Burud	43-33-0	0-10-0	0-5-6	15-1-0	12-5-3	0-2-2	5-13-4	

c

Despite the repudiation of Pringle's attempt to promote the growth of a class of rich peasants, it would be a grave mistake to think that Goldsmid and Wingate shaped their revenue policy on egalitarian principles. The fate of the Pringle Survey showed clearly the dangers of a doctrinaire approach to revenue problems. But Goldsmid and Wingate were even otherwise willing to be guided by experience, and restrained by the *rivaj*, in fixing their scale of assessment. While Pringle had relied solely on the law of rent in devising his scale of rates, and while he had entrusted the practical tasks of the survey to the native officials of the Survey Department, Goldsmid adopted a pragmatic approach and showed a shrewd awareness of the pitfalls it was necessary to avoid in arriving at a workable scale of assessment:

> It is absolutely necessary [he pointed out] that in assessing the land every field should be visited, and its soil and situation carefully assessed by the European Superintendent of the Survey. . . . To conduct such an assessment wholly by myself . . . would be a work requiring years for its completion. Nor is it requisite that I should attempt to do so. For although I can place no confidence in native officials of the class we can afford to employ . . . , still I should entertain 4 natives, unconnected with the districts, whose duty it would be to . . . prepare statements of the quality, quantity and situation of the land, and although not wholly present in the very fields in which the *carcoons* are employed, I should take care to be so near at hand . . . as to prevent the possibility of fraud on the part of the native subordinates. . . .[40]

Goldsmid and Wingate accepted, with minor alterations, the measurement of holdings carried out by the Survey Department under their predecessor. Pringle's classification, however, they found to be completely undependable, and decided to conduct anew, the holdings of the ryots being graded into nine categories of soils according to a diminishing scale of fertility. Further, instead of calculating the net surplus of each grade of soil, and then fixing its assessment at 55 per cent of this figure (as Pringle had done), they derived their rates of assessment 'from local inquiry and the experience of qualified persons, without any very minute investigations into actual produce. . . .'[41] The rates at which they assessed holdings of different fertility are indicated in column 4 of Table 3.

Two features of the rates proposed by Goldsmid and Wingate deserve special mention. Taken as a whole, their rates indicate a considerable diminution in the demand on the land, which was justified on the ground that Pringle had used inflated prices for food-grains in calculating the net produce. More important was the fact that while there was an all-round reduction in rates, the reduction on inferior soils like the *buruds* was significantly greater than that on superior soils like the blacks. As a result, while both the *meerasdars* and the *uprees* had their rentals lowered by the revised settlement, the tax paid by the latter was reduced to a far greater extent than that paid by the former. In this way the imbalance in the burden of tax, which had been the most objectionable feature of the Pringle Settlement, was abolished. Yet how far removed was the new scale of rates from the egalitarian scale devised by Wingate, which would have put all ryots on the same footing, irrespective of the quality of the soil they cultivated, becomes clear through a comparison of columns 3 and 5 in Table 3. To achieve the objective set by Wingate, Goldsmid had not only to reduce the Pringle rates on the poor soils by 33 per cent, but he had also to raise the rates on the black soils by 25 per cent. Goldsmid, however, was guided by practical considerations rather than by abstract notions of social equity. Instead of basing his scale of assessment on theoretical criteria, he relied on 'local inquiry and the experience of qualified persons' in calculating how much rental the different soils could with facility pay to the State.

Though Goldsmid's rates of assessment were less favourable to the

TABLE 3

COMPARISON BETWEEN PRINGLE, GOLDSMID AND WINGATE SCALES

Type of Soil	PRINGLE RATES	WINGATE RATES	*Difference*	GOLDSMID RATES	*Difference*
	I	2	3	4	5
1st Black	1-6-0	1-12-1	$+27\%$	0-12-0	-45%
2nd Black	1-1-9	1- 4-9	$+17\%$	0- 8-0	-53%
3rd Black	1-1-3	1- 3-6	$+12\%$	0- 9-7	-47%
1st Red	0-13-0	0-13-10	$+9\%$	0-6-10	-46%
2nd Red	0-11-9	0-11- 5	$+5\%$	0-5- 2	-57%
3rd Red	0-10-0	0- 9- 7	-7%	0-4- 2	-60%
1st Burud	0-7-9	0-5-10	-25%	0-3-0	-63%
2nd Burud	0-7-3	0-4- 9	-30%	0-2-5	-71%
3rd Burud	0-5-6	0-2- 2	-62%	0-1-0	-67%

'rich' peasants than those of Pringle, they were still instrumental in widening the gulf between the dominant and the ordinary ryots in the villages of the Deccan. This was so because formerly the State demand had pressed very heavily on the village, and had trenched deeply into the profits of the dominant ryots, who were responsible for the total village assessment, and were consequently obliged to make up by large personal contributions the sum which the village had contracted to pay to the State. Under the new revenue system the obligations of the dominant ryots were fixed for the duration of the Settlement, and they could not be called upon by the village community, or by any other authority, to make an additional contribution towards the land-tax. The resulting improvement in their style of life, and the consequential accumulation of capital in their hands, struck the attention of revenue officers forcibly when they revised the tax on land in the districts of the Deccan after an interval of thirty years. The condition of the *taluka* of Indapur in the 1860s, for instance, provides indisputable evidence to the effect that the Goldsmid Settlement had created, at least in a section of the rural community, a degree of prosperity which had been conspicuous by its absence before. The existence of these rich peasants can be inferred from the capital they were spending on agricultural development, and in proclaiming their new status through conspicuous consumption. In 1835-6, when the Goldsmid Settlement was introduced, Indapur possessed only 312 wells employed in irrigation; by 1866-7, the number of such wells had shot up to 1,255. Since the excavation of a well involved a capital outlay of Rs 400, only a prosperous peasant could afford to excavate one, and the total value of new wells in the *taluka* added up to the substantial sum of Rs 250,000. However, this new prosperity also found other channels of expression. A *chowrie*, or a 'municipal hall', and a *dharamsala*, or a resting place for travellers, were the boast of any village with pretensions to respectability in Maharashtra, and during the three decades which intervened between the introduction of the Goldsmid rates and their revision, the rich peasants of Indapur constructed as many as 59 *chowries*, and 27 *dharamsalas*, where none had existed earlier, to flaunt their *nouveau riche* status before the world at large.[41]

The emergence of a group of rich peasants is seen with even greater clarity when we look closely into the effect of the Goldsmid Settlement on individual villages. In five villages located in the *taluka* of Bhimthari in Poona District, for instance, the dominant ryots were able to improve their status in a most dramatic fashion over the thirty years which followed the introduction of the Goldsmid rates. Their new wealth was reflected in the extension of the area under irrigation from 51 to 487 acres, which extension was effected through the excavation of fifty new wells during the period. Besides, four of these villages could now boast of *chowries*, where none had existed earlier; while to accommodate an 80 per cent increase in population (from 2,750 to 4,870), the number of houses in these villages had practically doubled, the rise in number of the superior tiled variety being far more significant than the increase in thatched houses.[42]

Yet it would be incorrect to attribute the growth of the rich peasants in western India *exclusively* to the introduction of the *ryotwari* system. For the emergence of this social group was far more complex a social process. Improvements in means of communication; the growth of new markets and the extension of old ones; the existence of social peace and political stability; and finally, the spread of an acquisitive spirit among the peasants, were some of the factors which heightened inequalities in wealth in the villages, and promoted the accumulation of capital in a section of rural society which was best situated to exploit the opportunities thrown open to it under the new order.

The introduction of British rule in western India was therefore responsible for the creation of a new class of rich peasants whose standards of consumption, and whose accumulations of capital, were 'in every way so superior to what the same people were 40 years ago'.[43] But while this was true of a section of the cultivators, the wealth of this social group stood in striking contrast to the poverty of the overwhelming mass of the cultivators, who bore a crippling burden of debt, whose position became increasingly desperate with the passage of time, and who rose against their oppressors in 1875.[44]

The widening gulf between the majority of the peasants, on the one hand, and a small group of rich cultivators, on the other, was one of the most important consequences of British rule, and it exercised, and continues to exercise, a decisive influence upon social and political developments in Western India.

NOTES

1 T. Coats, 'Account of the Present state of the Township of Lony', *Transactions of the Literary Society of Bombay*, III, London 1823, pp. 183–250.

2 See 'Document (dated A.D. 1663) Giving an Account of the Founding of a New Village named Murunda in South Konkon' in *Writings and Speeches of the Late Rao Saheb Vishwanath Narayan Mandlik*, Bombay 1896, pp. 211–34.

3 H.D. Robertson, Collector of Poona, to W. Chaplin, Commissioner of the Deccan dated 17 October 1820, Revenue Department (hereinafter RD), Vol. 26/5 of 1822, Bombay State Archives (hereinafter BA).

4 R.K. Pringle, Assistant Collector of Poona to H.D. Robertson dated 20 November 1823, RD, Vol. 10/94 of 1823, BA.

5 'Tabular View of the distribution of lands in Village Ambala, Poona Collectorate', being an appendix to Major Sykes Report on Poona District dated nil, RD Vol. 154B of 1826, BA.

6 *Vide* Major Sykes Report on Poona District.

7 *Vide* note 5.

8 R.K. Pringle to H.D. Robertson dated 20 November 1823: RD Vol. 10/94 of 1823, BA.

9 Report by Col. J. Francis of Indapur dated 12 February 1867, *Selections From Records of the Bombay Government*, New Series, No. CLI.

10 R.D. Mills, Collector of Poona, to Bombay Government dated 23 September 1827; RD Vol. 6/212 of 1828, BA.

11 R.K. Arbuthnot to H.D. Robertson dated 1 March 1827: RD Vol. 2c/174 of 1827, BA.

12 R.K. Pringle to Bombay Government dated 6 September 1828, RD, Vol. 225 of 1828, BA.

13 Ibid.

14 Ibid.

15 Ibid.

16 Minute by Sir John Malcolm dated 18 November 1828, RD Vol. 225 of 1828, BA.

17 Letter from Collector of Poona to Bombay Government dated 1 April 1830, RD Vol. 7/287 of 1830, BA.

18 R.K. Pringle to Bombay Government dated 6 September 1828, RD Vol. 225 of 1828, BA.

19 Letter from Collector of Poona to Bombay Government dated 1 April 1830, RD, Vol. 7/287 of 1830, BA.

20 R.K.Pringle to Bombay Government dated 28 January 1832, RD Vol. 426/427 of 1832, BA.

21 H.D.Robertson to Thomas Williamson, Commissioner of the Deccan dated 20 January 1834, Home Dept, (Rev.Br) Con.No.4 dated 30 July 1834, National Archives of India, New Delhi (hereinafter NAI).

22 H.D.Robertson to T.Williamson dated 1 November 1832, RD Vol.434 offi1832, BA.

23 Verbatim Report of an interview between H.D.Robertson and the Patels of the Village of Kurra enclosed in letter quoted in note 22.

24 H.D.Robertson to T.Williamson dated 1 November 1831, RD Vol.434 of 1832, BA.

25 Lt Robert Shortrede's 'Report on the Revenue Survey and Assessment of the Deccan' dated 24 October 1835, Revenue Department Proceedings No. 4 dated 23 January 1837, NAI.

26 Ibid.

27 H.D.Robertson to T.Williamson dated 1 November 1831, RD Vol.434 of 1832, BA.

28 *Vide* Lt Shortrede's Report cited in note 25.

29 Minute by Robert Grant, Governor of Bombay, dated 12 October 1836, RD Vol.11/698 of 1836, BA.

30 T.Williamson to Bombay Government dated 30 July 1834, Home Dept (Rev.Br) Con.No.3 dated 30 July 1834, NAI.

31 R.Mills to Bombay Government dated 30 May 1839, Home Dept (Rev.Br) Con.No.10 dated 14 December 1840, NAI.

32 R.Mills to Bombay Government dated 1 June 1839, ibid.

33 Memo.by L.R.Peid, Secretary to Bombay Government and Rivett-Carnac, Governor of Bombay dated 10 August 1839 and 11 January 1840 respectively, ibid.

34 T.Williamson to Bombay Government dated 16 May 1826, Revenue Department Procs, No.3 dated 22 January 1837, NAI.

35 *Vide* Shortrede's Report quoted in note 25.

36 T.Williamson to Bombay Government dated 26 March 1835, RD Vol. 44/660 of 1835, NAI.

37 T.Williamson to Bombay Government dated 30 January 1836, RD Vol. 12/669 of 1836, NAI.

38 Lt A.Nash to Lt G.Wingate dated 23 March 1838, RD Vol.73/933 of 1836, BA.

39 G.Wingate to R.Mills dated 3 September 1838, RD Vol.73/933 of 1838, BA.

40 H.G.Goldsmid to R.Mills dated 27 June 1835, RD Vol.44/660 of 1835, BA.

41 See Report by Col J.Francis on Indapur dated 12 February 1867: *Selections from Records of the Bombay Government*, New Series, No.CLI.

42   Revision settlement of 5 Villages of the Bhmithadi *taluka* of Poona Collectorate, *Bombay Government Selections* (New Series) No. 230.

43   Memorandum by A. Wingate, Collector of Satara dated 3 October 1874, RD Vol. 87 of 1875, Pt II, BA.

44   Ravinder Kumar, 'The Deccan Riots of 1875', *Journal of Asian Studies* XXIV, 4 August 1965, pp. 613–33.

3

CHANGES IN STATUS AND OCCUPATION
IN NINETEENTH-CENTURY PANJAB

*

P.H.M.van den Dungen

Modern Asian history, it has been charged, has been written too often from a European point of view. Some of the approaches which dominated modern Indian historiography certainly stressed British activities and achievements. The rise of British power in India, the administrative achievements of British officials and Viceroys – these were common themes.

Of late the pendulum has to some extent swung the other way. The old political approaches now have their counterpart in the attention which is given to the Indian nationalist movement, especially in India itself. The difficulty here is that the origins of the nationalist movement are often attributed to European influences. In this context attempts to characterise the revolt of 1857 as nationalist clearly reveal the search for an India-centric point of view.

Important enough as themes in Indian political history, it is clear that neither the growth of the British power in India nor the Indian nationalist movement can be taken as the sole key to the last 200 years of Indian history. Hitherto the most promising approach in this respect is that which suggests that the modern historian should study the Western impact on India, and the Indian response to this impact. This approach focuses firmly on India and gives the old partial approaches their due.

It is understandable that modern Indian histories written from this point of view do not deal adequately with social history. The detailed regional studies of social history on which general histories must depend are only beginning to be written. Nevertheless now that social history is receiving increasing attention, it is worth asking whether the conceptual framework of 'Western impact and Indian response' suffices for this new branch of study.

I

The social historian will certainly find this approach useful in elucidating some of the important changes which took place in Indian society after the British conquest. Let us take the agrarian history of the Panjab in the second half of the nineteenth century as an example. The profound consequences of the establishment of an alien state are inescapable. The novel departures of the British in administrative organisation, land-revenue collection, property rights, communications and civil justice are of great social significance. If one is studying, for instance, the transfer of agricultural land, these factors are of primary importance in any explanation of what happened.[1]

If the story is not carried much further, land transfer and social change may appear almost entirely as the result of the British impact. This is perhaps particularly tempting if the region studied comprised a comparatively homogeneous society. The agrarian Panjab, however, was anything but homogeneous. The proprietary communities of the Panjab belonged to innumerable tribes and castes, differing in social status and religion (Hindu, Sikh and Muslim), affected by various agricultural conditions and the peculiarities of local history, and varying in their attachment to agricultural or pastoral pursuits. In such a region the historian is wellnigh driven to examine the influence of such varied factors on the course of agrarian history. He becomes conscious of the very great influence which indigenous conditions exerted even on something as novel as land transfer. In this way the 'response' side of the explanation gains in importance.

It is in assessing the response to the British impact that the problem of continuity in social history manifests itself. There were important changes during British rule certainly, but were there no changes before the advent of the British? While perhaps few would now deny this, the vital question of establishing a relationship between these changes and the later ones remains unresolved. If certain changes occurred during British rule which appear to be similar to those occurring at an earlier period or even originate in that period, the question arises whether the Western impact is necessarily the best or only point of departure for the social history of modern India. Obviously our framework of 'Western impact and Indian response' lends itself more readily to elucidating some of the important social changes during British rule than to solving the problem of continuity. This is more particularly the case if this framework is allowed to approximate to that which, speaking broadly, informs the British land-revenue records. It was natural enough that British officials, however interested they might be in the antiquities and general history of their districts, were impelled by their position and duties to think in terms of sharp contrasts between the British and pre-British period. The modern social historian can only adopt this point of view at the risk of obscuring elements of continuity.

But if the framework of 'Western impact and Indian response' is not the most useful in revealing the connections between change in the British and the immediately preceding period, it may well be misleading if it is conceived as a complete answer to the study of social change during the British period itself. For after all, the whole framework implies that we are interested in Indian social history only in so far as it is a response to the Western impact. Social developments which are not related to, or only partially affected by the Western impact are thus easily ignored.

In short if we write social history from this point of view it must be admitted that, however much our subject-matter may concern Indian society, our approach still takes the Western impact (and therefore the West) and not India as its starting-point.

An alternative approach is not easy to frame. The Panjab, with its manifold religious and social divisions, no doubt presents special difficulties. There is no single uniform way in which society in this region can be described. It must be recognised that society in the Panjab comprised a very large number of distinct groups integrated into a number of status systems.[2]

Elements of the Hindu varna system were discernible in Panjab society; but any attempt to portray even Hindu society along these lines alone is doomed to failure. Brahmins, Kshatriyas, Vaishyas, Sudras and outcastes – all could be identified. But neither in rural nor urban society did the Brahmins enjoy the favoured social position assigned to them by Hindu religious tradition. Instead it was Kshatriya status which was most ardently prized. The Kshatriyas were represented by distinctive land-holding Rajput castes in the east; but also by Hindu trading castes like the Khatris of the centre and the north-west. Rajputs were especially esteemed in rural and Khatris in urban society, but there was no social bond or mutual recognition. Of the important trading castes it was only the Banias of the south-east who fully accepted Vaishya status, using that term in its later meaning. As for the Sudras – numerically significant landholding castes like the Hindu Jats did not think of themselves as Sudras. They hardly recognised more than the social superiority of the Rajputs, while considering clean artisan and menial castes, supposedly

Sudras, as much beneath them. Of course at the bottom of the hierarchy there were the outcastes – the wandering tribes, eating unclean animals, and artisan and menial castes engaged in degrading occupations – who were universally despised in various degrees.

The egalitarian tradition of Islam had some, though no great, influence on Panjab society. The outcastes were not recognised as orthodox Muslims. Once they relinquished their unclean customs and occupation, however, it was easier for them to enter society than for their Hindu counterparts. The feeling against handicrafts in general was not so strong in the Muslim west. Yet this was probably attributable to the Pathans and Biloches of the frontier, alien Muslim tribes untouched by Indian ideas about occupation, whose example affected the adjacent Muslim areas. As for the landholding castes those of the east and much of the western submontane tracts like the Jats, Gujars and Rajputs were not affected in either name or social position by conversion to Islam. In the western plains, in the absence of Hindu caste restrictions on intermarriage, caste was no more than a tradition of origin, and the tribal name marked the primary social division among indigenous landholding Muslims. The distinction between Rajputs and Jats was in consequence frequently blurred; but for that very reason claims to Rajput status were legion in the western plains.

Islam also superimposed its own status concepts on the indigenous Hindu ones. Muslims generally recognised the superior social position of the Ashraf, i.e. the Sayyids, Shaikhs, Moguls and Pathans. These communities shared the distinction of foreign origin, the claim to be 'original Muslims' as opposed to the mass of indigenous converts. All had special claims. The Sayyids claimed descent from the son-in-law of the Prophet; and some of the Shaikhs descent from the tribe of the Prophet. In consequence the Sayyids and Shaikhs usually possessed an aura of religious sanctity. The Moguls and Pathans derived special social consideration from their descent from the conquerors of India. Taken as a whole the Ashraf were socially exclusive. Only in a few places were marriages contracted with other Muslims and then only with Rajput tribes of the most illustrious lineage. Together with the Rajputs the communities constituting the Ashraf (but more especially the Shaikhs) were a focal point for the aspirations of ambitious Muslims of lower status. In the north-west even tribes of good Rajput status sometimes sought Ashraf status.

The egalitarianism of Islam exercised its most profound social influence indirectly, through the role Islam played in the development of Sikhism. Not that in the central Panjab, the homeland of Sikhism, artisan and menial castes were held in much higher esteem. But the adoption of the egalitarian Sikh religion by the Jats of the central plains and their rise to political power obliterated the traditional status claims of the Rajputs in this area. The Sikh Jats became the Kshatriyas of the central plains without claiming that status. And since Sikhism developed as an indigenous tradition there were no foreign status concepts to replace the indigenous ones.

Independent of the religious traditions were certain occupational factors of great importance. In agrarian society castes and tribes which held land, either for pastoral or agricultural purposes, derived status from that consideration alone. Where village communities existed, as in the east and north-west the landholders looked down on all other village residents – whether they were cultivators, shop-keepers and traders, or menials and artisans – irrespective of their caste affiliations.

In Panjab society in general, employment by Government conferred considerable status.

Society in the Panjab thus conformed to no strict hierarchical pattern. Only the lowest levels of society (menials and artisans) were universally recognised as such.

A common factor can be discerned, however, in the special concern with status which pervaded groups at every level of society. The status of any social group depended to some extent on its hereditary and present occupation; and occupation is a fundamental consideration in any society. A study of changes in status and occupation could therefore be expected to touch on some of the most vital areas of Panjab social history. It would assuredly constitute an approach taking Indian society as its point of departure.

In what follows changes in status and occupation are examined among selected groups at various levels of Panjab society. No attempt is made to present a comprehensive account of social change in the Panjab during the nineteenth century. It is only intended to suggest that an India-centric approach may add an extra dimension to social history, i.e. it may lead to greater appreciation of some of the indigenous forces shaping social history.

II

There is ample evidence that in the second half of the nineteenth century changes in status and occupation were taking place among the lowest and most dependent castes in Panjab society.

The manner in which outcastes improved their status by changing their occupations was discussed at some length by Denzil Ibbetson, a contemporary British observer.[3]

Ibbetson noted instances of wandering tribes with degraded customs settling down in villages and performing low menial functions. He showed that sections of the scavenger castes sometimes took to leather-working, that occupation being considered somewhat less degrading than scavenging. Sections of the leather-working castes, in their turn, sometimes became weavers. Weaving was deemed less degrading than leather-working, and more or less respectable from a religious, if not social, point of view.

Often, Ibbetson pointed out, these occupational changes among the lower menials were accompanied by a change in the name of the section of the caste concerned. The social status of the section rose with its change in name and occupation. Changes in religious belief and practise were also involved. The creed of the section which changed its name and occupation might be modelled more closely on that of their Hindu neighbours. Or the section might substitute Islam or Sikhism for its own creed.

These traditional channels of social mobility were confined to the wandering tribes and the lower menials. Ibbetson speculated that there might be a similar series of changes between water-hunting tribes, on the one hand, and the water-carrying castes, the most respectable of menials, on the other. But for other menial castes, such as potters, washermen, carpenters and so on (excepting only those in the hills), Ibbetson could detect nothing similar.

The effect of the acquisition of land on the status of menials was not discussed by Ibbetson. It is suggestive that during British rule there were here and there a fair number of Tarkhans (carpenters) and a few Lohars (blacksmiths) who were not village servants at all, but the hereditary owners of entire villages. There is evidence that at least some of these Tarkhans and Lohars, while engaged in agriculture, did some carpenter's and blacksmith's work as well. It does seem likely therefore that the landowning Tarkhans and Lohars were the descendants of village menials of the same name.[4]

Many of the Tarkhans and Lohars probably owed their position as landowners to the fact that they had taken the Sikh baptism and had played a considerable military role under Sikh rule. There was certainly a close connection between the Tarkhans and Sikhism. Jassa Singh Ram-garhia, one of the great Sikh chiefs of the eighteenth century, had been a Tarkhan. There were landowning Tarkhans in the Gurdaspur district in

British times who claimed to be the descendants of Jassa Singh and his *misl*. They sometimes styled themselves Ramgarhia Sikhs rather than Tarkhans. Their social position was probably primarily derived from their historical role and buttressed by their ownership of land.

If these landowning Tarkhans and Lohars were an instance of social mobility, they were clearly a rather exceptional instance. During Sikh rule the vast majority of artisans and menials had little or no opportunity to acquire land on any considerable scale. Occasionally they had acquired small plots of land in a village. Sometimes the hereditary landholders of the village had allowed them to cultivate small pieces of land. This land they had cultivated as dependants of the landholders. At other times menials and artisans had been introduced as cultivators by the Sikh officials to enhance the revenue-paying capacity of the village. The hereditary landholders had perforce to accept this intrusion and see how the Sikh official gave them no better terms than the low-caste intruder. In extreme cases of official pressure on village resources the landholders had even accepted this situation as inevitable. To this small extent menials and artisans had occasionally encroached on the position of the landholders during Sikh rule.[5]

The British commonly granted proprietary or occupancy rights to the menials or artisans who held these isolated plots of land. But in many instances the low-caste cultivators were unable to retain their land under the altered conditions of British rule.

More important than this was that under British rule enterprising menials and artisans began to purchase land, or to take it on mortgage. This would have been neither profitable nor possible prior to British rule. For the first time the low castes were able to acquire land not as dependants of the officials or hereditary landholders, but in their own right. And this was as true of the lowest menial, the scavenger, as of the highest.

Naturally the acquisitions of menials and artisans were on a small scale. They might acquire a few plots of land in one village, and perhaps nothing in several others. Their acquisitions in one tract or region might be more prominent than in another.

Nevertheless the acquisition of land by artisans and menials reflected the general process by which these castes were becoming less dependent on the village proprietors during British rule. Indirectly they shared to some extent in the general increase in agricultural prosperity which accompanied the limitation of the revenue-demand, the extension of communications, and the rise in the average prices of agricultural produce. Unlike many agricultural castes, who had social scruples about manual labour, menials and artisans were sometimes able to obtain high wages as labourers on public works. Some went as far afield as Africa to make money. As men out to make their way in the world, they had every inducement to thrift. Their savings were invariably invested in land, and most of them made fair cultivators.

To these artisans and menials the acquisition of land was one of the chief means of raising their status in the village as well as of investing their savings. On occasion their social ambitions carried them beyond the village limits and beyond such a gradual attempt to rise in the social scale. Sometimes they claimed to belong to landowning tribes, even to the high-born Rajput tribes. In the north-western Panjab individual menials and artisans sometimes posed in this way to be able to enlist in the Army. Nor was it entirely unknown for men of these castes to take to education, enter a profession or Government service, and engage in trade and money-lending. The Muslims among them were not averse to passing themselves off as Shaikhs.

Thus in the second half of the nineteenth century the direction of social change among artisan and menial castes was determined to some extent by traditional considerations of status. Change in occupation or acquisition of land led (however slowly) to change in social position. The chief social ambition was to approximate to those of higher rank, but there were many levels of aspiration – from becoming a somewhat less degraded menial, to becoming a small landowner, to usurping the names and service occupations of the highest castes and tribes.

The economic consequences of British rule gave much greater scope to some of these changes than had existed under Sikh rule. It must be remembered, however, that for village artisans and menials the economic consequences were much less direct and made far less impact upon them as a whole than upon landholding tribes and castes. As for the political consequences of British rule – the very stability of British rule prevented that sharp rise in status of the few which accompanied political prominence. Against the landholding Tarkhans we must set the odd and scattered menials and artisans who improved their social position by entering Government service or the professions.

III

Further light may be thrown on social change at the lowest levels of Panjab society by a study of the history of three low castes. The occupation and background of these castes were quite distinct. Yet each of them was held in low esteem because of its hereditary occupation, while none of them was in a dependent economic position like the village menials and village artisans discussed above.

The first case-study concerns a market-gardening caste. Among the landholding and cultivating castes market-gardening was held to be an occupation much inferior to ordinary cultivation. Market-gardening castes accordingly ranked well below, say, Jat landholders and cultivators. There is no direct evidence of market-gardening castes trying to raise their status in pre-British times by switching from vegetable growing to general cultivation. But such changes may well have taken place. In the second half of the nineteenth century castes like the Arains were in some parts of the Panjab engaged in market-gardening, in others they combined market-gardening with general cultivation, while elsewhere they confined themselves to general cultivation. In those parts of the country in which they engaged largely in ordinary cultivation their status in agrarian society was somewhat higher than in the areas in which they engaged in market-gardening.[6]

An instance of social change among a particular market-gardening caste in the second half of the nineteenth century partakes of both traditional and novel elements. At the commencement of British rule a market-gardening caste of Hindu Malis was settled in the north of the Umballa district. The holdings of these Malis were small. They were reaching the stage at which even the greatest skill, industry and thrift did not suffice to feed their families. In the ordinary course of events the Malis would have been expropriated like many other landowners. But the Malis responded to this situation in a way which was quite unprecedented. They had been settled on their land by the Sikh conquerors of Umballa, and once uprooted they had not the intense attachment to their land and homes that was so characteristic of Panjab landowners. They sold what remained of their holdings. They migrated to Pipli in southern Umballa, and with the money obtained from the sale of their holdings they bought large areas of waste in Pipli. The first purchases were made in 1869 and 1873; and thereafter there was a steady flow of Malis into Pipli. They bought land from thriftless agricultural castes, and from non-resident owners and money-lenders who had themselves purchased the land but found difficulty in making it pay. The Malis applied all their skill and industry to their new acquisitions and the waste was soon cultivated. By the late 1880s the Malis in some of the more settled estates had tried to mark their success by abandoning the cultivation of vegetables in order that they might rise in the social scale as landowners.[7]

The administrative and economic framework of these events was provided by the British. Only under British rule could the Malis have bought land in Pipli. Yet the driving force behind the Mali migration lay in their previous history. And the response of some of them to success was rooted in traditional values.

The argument may be taken a step further by the second case-study. It shows not only change grounded in tradition; not merely change influenced by events in pre–British times; but the continuation and development of a change which had begun before British rule. And this in spite of the fact that British rule played a significant role in this example of upward mobility, not, as in previous examples, by favourable and indirect economic and administrative influences but through an economic impact which was, on balance, severe and adverse.

In the second half of the nineteenth century the Hindu and Sikh Labanas were found in the greatest numbers in the Lahore district and in the submontane districts from Gujrat to Umballa. Smaller numbers were located in some of the neighbouring plains districts and in Kangra and Muzuffargarh.[8]

In agrarian society the Labanas ranked well below the Jats. It is possible that the Labanas, or some of them, were in origin related to the wandering tribes. The fact that they were accustomed to making baskets and ropes for sale is the strongest pointer in that direction. At the commencement of British rule, however, the Labanas owned large numbers of cattle, they were engaged in the carrying trade, and to some extent in cultivation. Their hereditary occupation was the carrying trade; and the practice of this occupation would have sufficed to degrade them in the eyes of the landholding castes.

The Labanas' connection with the land and cultivation was comparatively recent, perhaps dating back little further than the first half of the nineteenth century. Allowed to settle in a village for purposes of commerce, the Labanas had stood their ground in times of disorder and acquired some of the village lands. In other instances they had been settled on the soil by the Sikh rulers to extend cultivation. Or they had occupied land to pasture their cattle. By the mid-nineteenth century the Labanas owned in some places not only parts of villages, but entire villages and even groups of villages.

The British brought law and order, and the definition and consolidation of existing rights in land. No longer could the Labanas acquire land in the old way. Despite this fact the British accelerated the transformation of the Labanas into an agricultural caste. The railway all but destroyed the carrying trade. The dependence of the Labanas on the land and on agriculture increased. It was only in the Kangra hills, and perhaps in one or two other places, that the Labanas continued to be carriers to any significant extent. The Sikh Labanas of Muzuffargarh, who owned practically no land, led a wandering life and made a living by making ropes for sale. But almost everywhere in the central and submontane districts agriculture had become the main occupation of the Labanas by the beginning of the twentieth century. They cultivated as owners, as occupancy tenants and, where they held little or no land, as tenants-at-will. In their spare time they sometimes still made ropes, traded in cattle and so on.

As landowners the Labanas were both favourably and adversely affected by the economic aspects of British rule. While they were good, industrious cultivators and market-gardeners, the Labanas could not always avoid serious indebtedness and the alienation of much of their land; more especially because their holdings were small. There was, nevertheless, a spirit of enterprise among many of them, in so far as their straitened circumstances and lack of education permitted. A Labana with some capital at his disposal lent his money out on interest or invested it in land.

Among the Sikh Labanas such capital sometimes represented money made in military service. By the early twentieth century the Sikh Labanas, being men of spirit and good physique, were recruited in fairly large numbers for the Army.

From being carriers, with some interests in land, the Labanas had become, in the space of fifty years, an agricultural caste. In the sense that the railway destroyed the carrying trade this consummation was brought about by new forces. That in these circumstances almost all the Labanas took increasingly to cultivation, rather than to, say, menial occupations, reflects the inroads which they had made in the agricultural world before British rule.

There is no direct evidence that the Labanas were driven in an agricultural direction by a desire to raise their status. In the early twentieth century, however, the Sikh Labanas in the Army were sensitive to any challenge to their agricultural character. And the Labanas of one district, questioned about the matter, insisted that they were true landowners.

They were, of course, over-stating their case. In the early twentieth century the social origins of the Labanas had not been obscured. Nevertheless their social position was gradually improving, as may be seen from the fact that in some places Jats were taking wives from Labanas and the offspring were treated as true Jats.

As a final example of social change among low castes the history of the Hindu, Sikh and Muslim Kalals may be considered. In this, as in previous examples, the direction of change was determined by traditional status concepts. More clearly even than among the Labanas was this change a direct continuation of one which had begun in pre-British times. It was an occupational change made in the pursuit of status; and the social aspirations of the Kalals were more pronounced and varied than those of the Labanas. The history of the Kalals also illustrates the slowness of status changes among low castes. British rule contributed to the story by a mixture of adverse and favourable economic and administrative influences. It hastened and diversified, but did not provide the motivation for particular changes.[9]

The very inferior status which originally distinguished the Kalals derived from their hereditary occupation, the distillation and sale of spirituous liquors. With the rise to political power of Jassa Singh Kalal, the most famous Sikh chief of the eighteenth century, the importance of the Kalals had increased and there had been a tendency among them to abandon their degrading hereditary occupation. The British accelerated the process; for by subjecting the manufacture and sale of spirits to Government regulations they added a form of economic compulsion to the original concern for status. By the first decade of the twentieth century there were few Kalals who still practised distillation.

In addition to abandoning their hereditary occupation the Kalals tried to raise their status by changing their caste names and by claiming more respectable social origins. Jassa Singh Kalal had styled himself Ahluwalia from the name of his ancestral village, a title which was still borne by his descendants, the royal family of the Native State of Kapurthala in British times; and one which the Sikh Kalals generally adopted as the name of their caste. By the early twentieth century some of the Ahluwalias had gone further by claiming Khatri or Rajput origin. Long before British rule some of the Muslim Kalals tried to conceal their antecedents by inventing a Pathan origin and calling themselves Kakezais. A further step was sometimes taken in which the Kakezai became a Shaikh. The Kakezai Shaikhs of Hoshiarpur who ruled the Jullunder Doab in the 1840s, were the most prominent example. The transition from Kalal to Kakezai to Shaikh continued under British rule. Some of the Muslim Kalals also claimed Khatri or Rajput origin.

Inclined or compelled to abandon their hereditary calling and seeking a new station in life, the Kalals, whatever their appellations, showed great energy and enterprise in taking up new occupations. Unlike the Labanas their efforts were not confined to one major direction.

Many Kalals turned to trade and shop-keeping, occupations which probably came easily to those accustomed not only to distil but to sell liquor. In British times the Kalals found an opening in trading in boots and shoes, bread, vegetables and the like, which traders of respectable caste refused to touch.

Both before and during British rule many Kalals took to cultivation. They did not own much land, and did not make good agriculturists, but by the beginning of the twentieth century there were many Kalals whose only hereditary calling was agriculture. Under British rule some of the landowning Kalals did not escape serious indebtedness; others engaged in money-lending and increased their landed possessions.

To trade and agriculture the Kalals added Government service. The Ahluwalias had many men serving in the Army as sepoys or officers. All sections of the Kalals – whatever their religion or occupation – took vigorously to education. Many Kalals occupied high posts in the civil and revenue departments of Government or took to the legal profession. In this way British rule enabled them to become part of the educated élite which was gradually assuming leadership in Panjab society as a whole.

The conclusion need not be laboured. Social change among the Malis, Labanas and Kalals would not have been the same without the administrative and economic framework provided by the British. But the impulse to change in a particular direction came from within and not from without.

IV

Changes in status and occupation among the hereditary landholding tribes and castes such as the Jats, Gujars and Rajputs assume a rather different aspect.

By virtue of their hereditary and continuing connection with the land, the landholding tribes and castes were assured of at least respectable status in agrarian society, irrespective of caste. Most of them attached no stigma to pastoral pursuits or to ordinary cultivation, the chief exceptions being high-born groups like the Rajputs and some pastoral tribes, who looked down on cultivation. The landholding tribes wanted to keep rather than change their hereditary occupation. They were concerned not so much to improve, as to maintain their status. Or at any rate such improvement, with few exceptions, was only desired or feasible in the western plains. Here the Jat might seek Rajput, and the Rajput seek Ashraf status, but even then no change in occupation was involved.

In these circumstances many significant changes in occupation and status among the landholding tribes and castes were, from their own point of view, for the worse. They were not so much sought by the landholders themselves, as induced by outside influences and pressures. It will be shown that during British rule some of these influences were not completely unprecedented. More particularly it will be argued that even changes induced by outside and novel influences cannot be understood in their entirety unless account is taken of the desire of the landholders to maintain their hereditary occupation and status.

During the second half of the nineteenth century there was a distinct though gradual tendency among many pastoral, nomadic and highborn tribes to turn increasingly to agriculture and a more settled existence.

This change was of some importance in the south-western Panjab and in a few adjacent areas (parts of the Shahpur, Gujranwala, Ferozepur and Hissar districts). In the mid-nineteenth century, at the beginning of British rule, there were an appreciable number of landholding tribes in this region who were largely nomadic and pastoral and had little or no attachment to the soil. Some of them had been extremely turbulent under Sikh rule. There were also some tribes who, while still concerned with cattle breeding and grazing, cultivated the soil in a rather half-hearted manner.[10]

At the end of the nineteenth century there remained many tracts in this region in which only a nomadic and pastoral life was possible. But there were many examples of nomadic and pastoral tribes – like the Biloches of Dera Ghazi Khan, the Sials of Jhang, the Gondals of Shahpur, some of the Jat and Rajput tribes of Montgomery, the Pachadas of Sirsa – who were taking increasingly to agriculture. There were also examples of tribes who had been partly pastoral and partly agricultural in the mid-nineteenth century, but who had become wholly agricultural by the end of the century.

It need not be imagined that these sort of changes occurred only during British rule. There is some evidence of similar changes in the period immediately preceding that rule. The references are too scanty, however, to give much idea of the extent and speed of the transition in earlier as compared to British times.[11]

Some tentative judgement may be made on this issue by comparing the forces which produced these sort of changes under Sikh rule with those that produced it under British rule.

The climatic factor was of course common to both periods. In the south-western Panjab conditions always had been more conducive to a nomadic and pastoral life than to a settled agricultural life. The distance from the Himalayas being great, the rainfall was too slight to permit rain cultivation. Agriculture was possible only in the neighbourhood of the rivers. Outside the areas affected by the river floods, the investment of capital in wells or inundation canals was a prerequisite. The maintenance of these wells and canals also required capital. Similar conditions prevailed over parts of the adjacent districts of Gujranwala and Shahpur farther to the north.[12]

In regions such as these the growth of settled agricultural society, where at all feasible, was peculiarly dependent on political stability. In times of disorder a nomadic and pastoral life would seem more attractive than an agricultural life which exposed one to the depredations of contending parties. The Sikh rulers were able at times to provide the necessary stability. Much of the Gujranwala district was re-settled under their auspices in the last decades of the eighteenth century and early in the nineteenth century by Jats who were largely nomadic graziers. In the south-western Panjab order was brought only in the 1820s when Sawan Mal became Governor of the Multan Province; much land having been abandoned before this as the result of military campaigns. It need hardly be added that the British provided a greater degree of political stability and for a longer period; and in this respect provided more favourable conditions for the development of agriculture than the Sikhs had done.[13]

The British were also more powerful than their predecessors. The small Cis-Sutlej Sikh States had hardly been able to control the turbulent pastoral tribes within their jurisdiction. The more powerful Lahore State had kept a better check on the turbulent tribes. They had little control over the Montgomery district, however, where population and cultivation had been especially scant, and the turbulent Jat and Rajput tribes had been able to hide, at the approach of Sikh armies, in the jungle which abounded along the river. There was nothing of this under the British. They established their power over the whole countryside. Everywhere they laid the foundation for the disappearance of those lawless habits which inhibited the transition towards a settled agricultural life.[14]

Both under Sikh and British rule attempts were made to maintain and extend facilities for irrigation. In Gujranwala the Sikh officials and assignees of revenue who ruled the district sometimes constructed wells. In Multan Sawan Mal had the old inundation canals repaired and new ones constructed. Numerous cuts or branches were dug. Careful attention was paid to the working of these canals. Each local official was held responsible for their annual clearance. Against this the British introduced perennial canals in parts of Gujranwala and Shahpur, which made agriculture feasible for the nomadic pastoral tribes of these areas.[15]

Both régimes offered further inducements to prospective cultivators. In the south-west Sawan Mal, recognising the limited capacity of the people as agriculturists, ensured that the local officials exercised close supervision over all agricultural matters. New cultivators were also granted favourable terms in the matter of revenue collection. In the south-west Sawan Mal granted light cash leases for long periods to those who sank new wells or repaired old ones. Alternatively here, and in Gujranwala, part of a new well was held revenue-free for a number of years. The British dispensed with all these inducements. Under their rule the increase in the amount and value of the agricultural surplus left to the landowner provided a more automatic and widespread inducement for cultivation. Yet it may be doubted whether this long-range advantage always made cultivation more attractive to pastoral tribes than the more tangible inducements and aid of the Sikh officials.[16]

Finally it should be noted that the British sometimes only completed what the Sikh rulers had begun. The Sials of Jhang, who ruled the district before the Sikh conquest, are an instance in point. The Sikhs deprived the Sials of the large areas over which they had held sway, but which they had not cultivated. British rule completed the process by vesting the ownership of land in the hands of those whom the Sikhs had settled in these areas. It was partly in consequence of these developments that during British rule the Sials were obliged to cultivate their remaining land themselves to gain a living.[17]

On balance it seems likely enough that British pressures and influences compelling or encouraging pastoral and nomadic tribes to turn to agriculture were stronger and more widespread during the second half of the nineteenth century than the equivalent Sikh pressures and influences during the first half of that century.

Nevertheless the rate of change among pastoral and nomadic tribes reflected their attachment to their hereditary occupation and status as much as heightened outside pressures. Some of the turbulent pastoral Jat and Rajput tribes of Montgomery had become a little less lawless by the end of the nineteenth century. But the process was far from complete. Throughout the south-west, and in some adjacent areas, cattle stealing was still endemic. To those accustomed to a nomadic life, to plenty of opportunity for robbery, or only to the occupation of cattle-breeding (which required little strenuous exertion), an agricultural life which demanded industry, patience, regularity and skill was not easily acceptable. To many, if not all pastoral tribes, there was the further difficulty that they considered cultivation a socially inferior occupation to cattle-breeding and grazing. In consequence almost all semi-pastoral tribes, engaged to some extent in agriculture, made poor cultivators, lacking in industry and skill. If improvement in this respect was occasionally evident, it was still remarkably slow.[18]

In addition to tribes with a recent pastoral or nomadic background there were the high-status tribes, without such background, who took increasingly to cultivation during British rule. The Rajputs of the central Panjab were a significant example.[19]

Much of the story sounds familiar. The position of the Rajputs in this region had been seriously weakened during Sikh rule. Nowhere, not even in the Kangra hills, had the Rajputs retained power or independence. At the commencement of British rule those of the western half of the central Panjab were few in number and scattered. In the submontane areas the Rajputs had lost much land to the industrious cultivators favoured by Sikh officials. The British confirmed the rights in land which had grown up during Sikh rule.

The Rajputs of the central Punjab were not pastoral to any notable extent. But their attachment to a superior status involved customs hostile to cultivation. They secluded their women (who were therefore unable to help in the fields), and they themselves had a marked aversion to agricultural labour in general and to ploughing in particular.

The changes in agricultural industry and cultivating skill which occurred among these Rajputs were a product of their reluctance to compromise their status and of various other pressures and influences. The pressures were sometimes intense. In Kangra and the submontane districts the holdings of the Rajputs were very small. Many were obliged to cultivate to avoid starvation. The Rajputs of Kangra began to perform all sorts of field work under British rule, but they often still refused to touch the plough. Some of the Rajputs of the submontane districts were forced to adopt industrious habits. By the 1880s even the aversion to the plough was decreasing in some of the submontane tracts, and the Rajputs here were improving as cultivators. Much also depended on agricultural circumstances. With canal irrigation, which made cultivation easy, the

Muslim Rajputs of Kasur in the Lahore district were as good cultivators as the Hindu Jats surrounding them. Wherever constant toil was necessary to work wells or to cope with difficult soils, the Rajputs made little progress as cultivators.

The role of indigenous social forces was not confined to occupational changes of the sort discussed above. Attachment to hereditary status and occupation shaped developments as novel as voluntary land transfer.

In one respect voluntary transfers of land, on any significant scale, were primarily due to British rule. Under Sikh rule transfers of land for value had occurred only rarely in most of the Panjab. The value which land acquired under British rule, and the facilities afforded for its transfer, provided entirely new conditions in which the steady expropriation of large sections of the landholding tribes could proceed.[20]

Yet if we look at the pattern of land transfer in various parts of the Panjab the influence of indigenous social forces is at once evident. With the exception of those tribes in arid regions whose way of life remained almost entirely pastoral and nomadic, and whose land did not acquire a marketable value, the pastoral and high-status tribes were most seriously affected. They had only begun to adjust themselves to the conditions of settled agricultural life, and were therefore in no position to adjust themselves to the vast increase in credit which accompanied the increase in the value of their land. Their lack of foresight, their thriftlessness and extravagance were only a further reflection of their attachment to the easy-going pastoral life or to claims to high status. These factors not only forced many pastoral or high-status landholders into debt and led them to mortgage or sell their land; but also prevented many of their kinsmen from acquiring this land. In consequence much of the land alienated by these tribes passed into the hands of more thrifty landholders of other tribes and into those of the Hindu trading castes. Even among skilful cultivating tribes, to whom thrift came more easily, bad seasons or wasteful expenditure sometimes led to the alienation of appreciable areas of land. But, other things being equal, the percentage of cultivation transferred among these tribes was often smaller than the percentage transferred among high-status and pastoral tribes. Besides more of it usually passed to other members of the same tribe, and less of it to the Hindu trading castes.[21]

The social consequences of land transfer were also determined by attachment to hereditary status and occupation – among pastoral, high-status and cultivating tribes alike. Those who had mortgaged their land to Hindu traders were often allowed, and almost invariably prepared, to

cultivate their ancestral fields as tenants-at-will. Society offered the expropriated proprietors no real alternative. There were no other means of
livelihood open to them which would give them an equivalent status.
For trade they had neither the ability nor the capital. To turn to handicrafts would be to sink to the lowest levels of society. The old proprietors
were generally intensely attached to their ancestral land, the very em-
bodiment of their status. They clung desperately to what remained of
their old position, agreeing to pay higher cash or produce rents than an
outside tenant would ever pay. To maintain some semblance of their old
status, they often cultivated their ancestral land almost as the slaves of the
landlord.[22]

Ejectment, if and when it came, was the most bitter blow to the old
owners. They were able to make a living as tenants or day-labourers in
or around their village or at a distance. They were perhaps freer men than
the rack-rented mortgagors. But they lost every vestige of their old
status and identity.

The general conclusions are clear. The British made a considerable
impact upon many landholding tribes – much greater than the impact
on ordinary village menials and artisans. British rule presented greater
threats to the status and occupation of many landholding tribes than Sikh
rule. Yet every change which occurred, however novel, was significantly influenced by the desire of the landholders to maintain their traditional status and occupation.

V

It remains to consider occupational changes deliberately sought by castes
of assured status. Such changes occurred during the second half of the
nineteenth century among some of the more skilful and thrifty cultivating and landholding castes and generally among the Hindu trading
castes.

Of these occupational changes there were some in which concern for
status, though not necessarily absent, does not suffice to explain what
happened. Some form of economic motivation seems to be of primary
importance in these changes. This raises a special problem of explanation.
Unless we are prepared to attribute these changes entirely to British
influence, we must consider whether even economic motives were
linked to indigenous considerations.

During the second half of the nineteenth century some of the more
settled, industrious, skilful and thrifty cultivating and landholding castes

took advantage of occupational opportunities made possible by British rule. In the south-eastern, central and north-western Panjab men of the landholding castes not only became soldiers (common enough prior to British rule) but also money-lenders and traders. These were of course strictly supplementary occupations; the landholders who engaged in them were not in any sense cut off from the soil.

Yet it was only among the Sikh Jats of the central Panjab that these changes occurred to a striking degree. It is therefore reasonable to search for special factors which may help to explain the greater economic enterprise of the Sikh Jats.[23]

These factors, it is submitted, may be found in their physical environment, their history and religion.

There was a significant contrast between the agricultural systems of the western and eastern parts of the uplands of the central Panjab. The cultivation of the Jats of the western half of the uplands was dependent on a fairly small rainfall and was less secure and less demanding than the more intensive rain and well cultivation of the submontane districts. Close farming was less rewarding in the western than in the eastern half of the central Panjab. The Jats of the extreme west were not such laborious and skilful cultivators as the Jats of the submontane districts, who were preoccupied with agriculture. Unlike the Jats in the eastern well areas the Jats of the western uplands were not tied to wells from year's end to year's end. Instead in some areas the Jats of the western half of the uplands had time on their hands during certain parts of the year.

This natural division corresponded closely with the religious division. As the less demanding agricultural system of the uplands gave way to the more demanding, the proportion of Sikhs among the Jats quickly dwindled.[24]

It may be deduced that the Jats of the western uplands, their attention less firmly confined to the soil and with more spare time were much more receptive to new influences than the Jats of the submontane areas. This explanation seems particularly feasible when it is remembered that in the mid-eighteenth century Sikhism came less as a religious creed and more as a militant movement, offering opportunities for plunder and personal enrichment. Doubtless Sikhism attracted most strongly those among the Hindu Jats who were ready to leave their homes to make their fortunes elsewhere. If Sikhism attracted the most restless and enterprising elements among the Jats, it also seems likely that participation in Sikh conquests broadened the outlook of the community and reinforced their restlessness and enterprise.

This enterprise could have hardly asserted itself as strongly in the economic sphere during British rule, had it not been for a religious factor. One of the most striking aspects of the history of the Sikh Jats is that their political supremacy did not lead them to assert generally their claims to Kshatriya status. This was due to the egalitarian message of Sikhism. Possibly, in a direct sense by its influence on the Sikh Jats themselves; but certainly in an indirect sense, in that by preventing the adhesion of the Rajputs to the Sikh cause it rendered them an object of hatred to the Sikh Jats. This failure to translate political power into claims to Kshatriya status was of vital importance. The assertion of this claim would have been inimical to husbandry and to the development of thrift. Instead Sikhism enabled the Jats to play a role in the wider world without destroying their character as good, if not the most painstaking husbandmen.

With this background in mind, the readiness with which the Jats of the Sikh areas exploited their economic opportunities to the full during the second half of the nineteenth century, is easily explicable.

Under British rule the Sikh Jats in both rain-dependent and canal-irrigated tracts were industrious and skilful enough to take advantage of the large profits that could be made from cultivation in the western half of the central uplands. In tracts subject to drought they learned to store grain and save money in good times. And at a time of drought they sought temporary work in other parts of the Province. Thrifty in ordinary circumstances, the Sikh Jats were not always proof against extravagant expenditure on marriage ceremonies and the like. But as a rule they stayed out of the hands of the money-lenders of the Hindu trading castes. Land was transferred, but for convenience, or to raise money for investment in trade, as well as for unproductive purposes. Most of the land alienated did not pass outside the community.

The very large number of Sikh Jats in military service during British rule may be directly accounted for by the military tradition which the Sikh Jats had developed during Sikh rule. Much money came into the Sikh Jat villages from this source.

The enterprise of the Sikh Jats asserted itself during British rule in new spheres of economic endeavour. The Sikh Jats of Ferozepur and Ludhiana took to trade, an undertaking facilitated by the fact that their rain cultivation did not require their attention during the whole year. The Hindu trading castes were not well established in the Sikh Jat villages, and they were given little incentive to settle there. Many Sikh Jats stored their surplus produce until such time as prices were most remunerative, and then carried it on their carts to the market town, where competition ensured a fair price. On their return they took anything which might be sold at a profit in the villages. Some took their carts for hire to carry grain. Or they bought up grain where it was cheapest – in or near the village – and sold it at a profit in a distant market-town. In times of scarcity Sikh Jats from Ludhiana and Ferozepur travelled to unaffected submontane districts like Jullunder and Hoshiarpur to buy grain at the lowest possible price. In these ways the Sikh Jats did much to usurp the traditional occupations of the Hindu trading castes.

Almost everywhere in the Sikh tracts of the central Panjab the money-lending business (elsewhere concentrated largely or entirely in the hands of the Hindu trading castes) was taken up by Sikh Jats themselves. These men lent grain or money in return for a usufructuary mortgage of land, redeemable on repayment of principal. There were even some Sikh Jats who lent on the security of bonds and sought by a rapid accumulation of interest to involve their clients in difficulties. There were the profits of cultivation, soldiering and sometimes trade to invest in land. The Sikh Jat with capital made the most of his opportunities, and the harshness of his transactions reflected his passion for the land of his neighbours. Very much attached to the soil, he sought to acquire land in order to cultivate it.

The sort of special factors which help to explain the enterprise of the Sikh Jats in the economic sphere are not required to account for the economic enterprise of Hindu trading castes like the Khatris, Aroras and Banias. By virtue of the acquisitive nature of their hereditary occupations – trade, shop-keeping and so on – the Hindu trading castes were well-fitted to take advantage of the economic opportunities created by British rule.

The Hindu trading castes profited directly from the general stimulation of trade under British rule.

Their position in the grain trade was greatly strengthened. Prior to British rule they had only been able to acquire the grain from the village headmen or from local officials. Now they were able to take the grain directly from the large number of small proprietors, who were obliged to pay a fixed amount of money annually as land-revenue. In much of the Province the trading castes took the grain from the small proprietors at cheap harvest prices and disposed of it at higher market prices. Much of the benefit of the higher average prices of produce which ruled from the 1860s was absorbed in this way by the trading castes.[25]

The scope for grain and money-lending transactions increased enormously under British rule. The Hindu trading castes dominated the business in most of the Panjab. With their thrift, their literacy and acquisitive outlook this occupation came naturally to them, even to those who might have been little more than village shop-keepers before British rule. Some of the smaller men, who started life as petty lenders, as small village shop-keepers selling oil, salt and flour, or as petty traders and carriers, became comparatively wealthy money-lenders or grain merchants. But the business was not confined to the small men. There were traders in the towns, as well as large and small village traders, engaged in lending.

As agrarian indebtedness increased during the second half of the nineteenth century, the Hindu money-lenders began to acquire the produce at little cost. Gradually, and to various degrees in different parts of the Province, they began to acquire the land of their debtors as well.

The enterprise which transformed the economic position of the Hindu trading castes during British rule was inherent in their occupation and outlook. In the south-eastern, central and north-western Panjab that enterprise did not extend itself to the trader's relations with his newly acquired land.

There were many reasons for this situation. Preoccupied with trade and money-lending, having no tradition of, or taste for, husbandry, the Hindu trading castes were content to have their land cultivated by its hereditary owners or by other tenants. As intruders into the agricultural world (who had held little or no land before British rule) the Hindu traders had not that sympathy with agrarian society which derived from an ancestral connection with the soil. In the new situation they applied the old maxims of the trader and usurer, concerned only with making a profit or getting the most out of a debtor. They often made rack-renting landlords – much more so than non-cultivating owners of landholding tribes. Nor were the trading castes inclined to make agricultural improvements. Their means were often too small, the investment of capital in trade and money-lending too easy, and their knowledge of agriculture too limited. There were no classes among the hereditary landholders to set the example. In the case of mortgaged land there was always the possibility that the mortgagor might redeem or re-mortgage. This inhibited any improvement of the soil in the large proportion of cases in which Hindu traders acquired the bulk of their land, at least initially, as mortgagees. It took time before money-lenders acquired appreciable properties by sale, but where they had done so they were sometimes more inclined to build wells, plant trees and so on.[26]

Developments which hardly manifested themselves in most of the

Panjab during the second half of the nineteenth century were common among the Aroras of the south-western Panjab.[27]

In the second half of the nineteenth century the Aroras with land did not, as a rule, go so far as to cultivate their land with their own hands. The self-cultivating Hindu trader was admittedly more common here than elsewhere in the Panjab, but this was usually the result of poverty rather than choice. Aroras who cultivated their own land because this seemed the natural thing to do, were rare, though they did exist. There were many Aroras with fair properties, however, who depended largely on the income from their land. Some of them had given up trade and money-lending entirely. The majority still engaged in these occupations but not to such an extent as to interfere with the management of their land. Men of this stamp made very fair landlords. They managed to get the most out of their tenants without rack-renting them. The energy and enterprise of these Aroras had not disappeared; it had been channelled in a new direction. In a region in which the standards of cultivation were exceptionally low, their land alone was carefully cultivated. They were constantly sinking wells and making improvements to increase their income from the land. In this aspect of the agricultural character they were far superior to the small Muslim proprietors and large Muslim landlords of the region.

How can we explain this development of agricultural enterprise, this transformation in character, among the Aroras of the south-west alone? Four interrelated reasons are discernible; and the most significant of them owe nothing to British influence.

The most important reason relates to the way in which the Aroras initially acquired a hold on the soil. They obtained much land before British rule as a result of Sawan Mal's policy of granting land on favourable terms to all who were prepared to invest capital in land by building or repairing wells. Thus a number of Aroras approached the land at first not as money-lenders trying to get the most out of a debtor, but as capitalists determined to get the most out of their investment in land. This experience seems to have set the tone for later developments.

The nature of the country was also a significant consideration. In Sawan Mal's time grants of land were feasible and desirable because large areas of waste existed on which the occupying tribes had but a slender hold; and because much land and many wells had been deserted during the troubles preceding the Sikh conquest. In British times the large areas of waste which still existed made considerable extension of cultivation possible by means of such agricultural improvements as wells. Most of the rest of the Panjab was more highly cultivated and more densely populated in both Sikh and British times.

Then there was the point, that, having made a start under Sikh rule, the Aroras of the south-west had much larger properties during the second half of the nineteenth century than Hindu traders in other parts of the Province. At annexation (1849) there were many tracts in the south-west in which the Aroras already held a considerable proportion of the cultivated area.

In at least one south-western district (Multan) the agricultural enterprise of many Aroras was firmly established by the beginning of British rule. There is no really conclusive evidence on this point either way for other south-western districts.

British rule enabled the Aroras of the south-west to increase their holdings by lending money and grain to the Muslim proprietors of the region, who were often unable to discharge their debts except by transferring their land. Many Aroras who had held land before British rule added to their estates, while others acquired land for the first time.

In this way British rule certainly affected the development of agricultural enterprise among the Aroras; but the basic motivation was linked to an experience preceding that rule.

Thus the two most striking instances of occupational change motivated by economic considerations – among the Sikh Jats and the Aroras – cannot be explained purely in terms of British influence. The most radical occupational changes during the second half of the nineteenth century depended on indigenous social factors, whether these had expressed themselves in the economic field before that time or not.

VI

On the basis of the evidence presented above it is possible to explore somewhat further the general problems raised at the beginning of the chapter.

It should be borne in mind that the foregoing cannot hope to be a complete or even a balanced account of social change in the agrarian Panjab during the second half of the nineteenth century. Rather it is an attempt to present a side of the story which it is anticipated is in some danger of neglect.

No doubt it is abundantly clear that an India-centric approach is well-suited to eliciting the indigenous motivating forces in Indian social history. Evidence has been given that these forces were of great significance

D

at various levels of agrarian society; and that they help to explain varied and even novel social developments.

From this point of view it is apparent why a 'traditional' backdrop to 'modern' social developments does not suffice. There was significant social continuity in terms of the persistence of indigenous social forces. The values of agrarian society did not change during the second half of the nineteenth century. The character and history of particular social groups remained as relevant as ever.

Historical continuity was least disputable in those instances in which indigenous social factors expressed themselves in changes which had begun before British rule; or which were at any rate similar to changes which had occurred before that time. That these changes were sometimes hastened or diversified under British rule does not detract from a large element of continuity. There was a significant measure of continuity even when social factors affected or produced changes which were in themselves quite novel.

The very fact that we have to deal with novel changes during the second half of the nineteenth century implies the existence of new influences as well as continuity. These new influences were to be found in the administrative, economic and political framework provided by the British. This aspect of the problem has been mentioned above, but not stressed or discussed in the sort of detail warranted in a more comprehensive and balanced account. Nothing in this paper is intended to discount the novel aspects of British rule, or its many novel social consequences. It should be recognised, however, that some aspects of British rule were novel only in degree or at least had their equivalents under Sikh rule.

The studies of social change in this chapter show that one cannot always speak of a uniform British 'impact' on agrarian society as a whole. That 'impact' varied at various economic levels of society. The emphasis that the historian must put on it in studying village artisans is quite different from the emphasis he must put on it in studying land-holders. Indeed, in the social (as distinct from the administrative and economic) sense that 'impact' is not the same even at similar economic levels. The stress that can be placed on it varies with the character and outlook of particular communities. British rule meant something quite different to typical Rajput landholders than it did to typical Sikh Jat landholders. The British 'impact' almost forced change among the first, but only made it possible among the second. If we think in terms of a 'framework' provided by the British, these difficulties are avoided.

Inherent in the above approach is the stress on the history of particular communities. In this way it differs from the approach which is concerned primarily with changes in relationship between occupational groups such as peasants and moneylenders. It would not do to suggest that the latter approach is not meaningful or does not represent part of the story. The study of particular communities does indicate, however, that it is not the whole story and that during the second half of the nineteenth century social change in the Panjab assumed many and varied forms.

To put it briefly, then, the approach delineated above consists of the study of indigenous and varied social forces, deriving from the values, character and experience of particular communities, and expressing themselves in various ways in an administrative, economic and political framework of some novelty.

Perhaps sufficient has been said to show that the social historian of modern India cannot allow himself to be confined completely by the conceptual framework of 'Western impact and Indian response'. It may well be asked, however, whether the additional approach suggested in this chapter is capable of extension in such a way as to throw light on the more familiar themes treated in the general histories of India. Social history, after all, can hardly be isolated from general history.

The matter may be put to the test (admittedly in a tentative way) by considering the social origins of the Indian nationalist movement on the basis of evidence drawn from the Panjab. Here surely we have a movement which (unless one sees its origins in revolts such as that of 1857) appears to be due to Western influences. There was nothing remotely resembling it in the period preceding British rule.

Nevertheless the topic may be approached as a further example of changes in status and occupation among particular communities.

The first point – that the nationalist movement owed its impetus to people from certain castes – has been generally recognised. Its significance has been partly obscured by the tendency to speak of these people as a 'middle class'. The analogy is drawn of course from British history and society. But the forces and circumstances which produced the British and the Indian 'middle class' were admittedly quite different. And to designate a group as 'middle class' merely because they included professional people (who are in the West considered 'middle class') is only thoughtless application of Western notions of society to the Indian situation. The use of the term 'class' can be justified in the Indian context only if it is understood in the loosest possible sense. The whole approach completely ignores the fact that Indian society possessed its own well-defined social divisions and hierarchical concepts.

A 'middle class' implies the existence of an 'upper class' of a kind which can hardly be identified in the nineteenth century. In the Panjab at least the class ties of the Indian aristocracy (the miscellaneous remnants of men of various communities who ruled before the British) were even less impressive than those of the 'middle class'. Besides the position of the 'middle' and 'upper' classes derived essentially from the same source – association with Government. The 'middle class' was associated in a subordinate capacity with the British; the 'upper class' had exercised political power in the past and was maintained in a favoured position by the British.

It is here that we have the key to the formation of the 'middle class', or rather to the emergence of a new élite. Government in India was above and beyond the subject. Prestige was attached not only to the exercise of political power but also to the service of Government in a subordinate capacity. Men sought Government service, at least in part, because it was the occupation which conferred the greatest prestige. The most popular profession in the nineteenth-century Panjab (the legal profession) was indirectly connected with Government institutions.[28]

As far as Government service was concerned, this was not a new phenomenon. Nevertheless, British rule influenced the emergence of a new élite in a number of special ways.

Initially British rule in the Panjab ensured that most of those engaged in the professions and civil administration came from groups of similar background. The British civil administration and the professions required literacy and training or English education. In an agricultural country where illiteracy was widespread, this gave an enormous advantage to the Hindu trading castes (such as the Khatris, Aroras and Banias) who, by virtue of their hereditary occupation, were already literate to a greater or lesser extent. Thus in the second half of the nineteenth century Hindus of the trading castes dominated the professions and almost all branches and levels of the civil administration. They easily outnumbered the Muslims engaged in these occupations. The latter were themselves drawn largely from particular communities; namely from the few Muslim trading communities and from the communities constituting the Ashraf. The vast mass of the illiterate landholding and cultivating castes (Hindu, Muslim and Sikh) stood little chance in this field. While they dominated service in the army and police, the British subordination of the military to the civil power ensured that military prowess could not lead (as it did under Sikh rule) to civil power or position.[29]

The position of those serving the British civil administration (and those engaged in the professions) was more secure and stable than that of those who had served the previous Government. In Sikh times much depended on the arbitrary decisions or family interests of the official immediately above – and the latter's own position was for the same reason none too secure. During the second half of the nineteenth century the lower ranks of the civil administration were appointed by local British officials, who had no personal interests to serve. In this situation cliques were often formed which effectively preserved the monopoly of those families or castes which had dominated these positions from the beginning. Higher positions in the civil administration, and the professions, depended on the ability to pass certain educational tests, so that these occupations could become and remain the hereditary occupations of certain communities. In the long run the monopoly of office high and low, and of the professions, by particular communities might not prove unassailable; but in the second half of the nineteenth century there was much more stability and security for these communities than under Sikh rule.[30]

At the upper levels of the new élite British rule was responsible to some extent for a novel horizontal social link. English education enabled the educated to communicate in the same language and gave them a common outlook in some respects. The advent of railways and the press made the link meaningful on an all-India as well as on a regional basis.

Granted that the British framework explains greater unity of social background, greater social stability and a novel social link, the social patterns which emerged were dependent very largely on indigenous social organisation. The horizontal link was meaningful between educated men drawn from castes of similar background, as, for instance, the various Hindu trading castes. It proved of little significance where there was no indigenous basis for social unity – as between the Hindu and Muslim communities engaged in Government service. Besides the new horizontal link did not displace the vertical caste link. Men with an English education were still tied to uneducated or less educated castefellows. It was these vertical ties which gave from the beginning some social basis to nationalist sentiments imbibed by those among the Hindu trading castes who had acquired an English education.[31]

While the idea of nationalism came from European sources (if admittedly influenced by Hindu religious values), it was taken up largely by men from those communities (in the Panjab the Hindu trading castes) whose status would be directly enhanced by its success. It made much less appeal to the Muslim communities seeking status through Government and professional employment. To them Hindu dominance in the civil administration was a major obstacle. Nor did nationalism make as much sense for them on the all-India level.

The British also brought new conditions in which the nationalist ideas could flourish, i.e. they provided scope for the assertion of status outside the limits sanctioned directly by the State. More distinctly alien than their predecessors, the British nevertheless permitted, within certain limits, criticism and organisation.

In short, while the nationalist movement could not have taken place without the British, its driving force may be seen as the pursuit of status by particular communities.

It need hardly be added that the above sketch of the social origins of the nationalist movement is only intended to bring out certain salient points. It fits into the general approach described above and applied throughout this chapter to less familiar themes. If it does nothing else, it does perhaps make it clear that as we probe deeper into Indian social history from an India-centric point of view, we will not only enrich this branch of Indian history itself, but may well be led to reinterpret some of those familiar themes with which hitherto the general histories have been most concerned.

NOTES

1   The references to the Panjab in this paragraph and the next are based on the writer's 'Land Transfer, Social Change and Political Stability in the Punjab, 1849–1901.' Ph.D. Thesis, Australian National University, 1966.

2   The sketch of Panjab society which follows is based on: *Panjab Castes. Being a report of the chapter on 'The Races, Castes and Tribes of the People' in the Report on the Census of the Panjab published in 1883 by the late Sir Denzil Ibbetson*, Lahore 1916 (hereinafter *Panjab Castes*), supplemented by assessment and settlement reports of the second half of the nineteenth century, and by P. Tandon, *Punjabi Century 1857–1947* (1961).

3   *Panjab Castes*, paras 565–9, 596–9.

4   On landowning Lohars and Tarkhans: *Assessment Report* (hereinafter *AR*) *Jagraon*, 1882, para. 45; *AR Jullunder*, 1883, para. 8; *AR Batala*, 1889, para. 80; *AR Ajnala*, 1892, para. 29; memo. by Tupper, Financial Commissioner (hereinafter FC), 1900, para. 10, West Pakistan Board of Revenue Financial Commissioner's Office Files (hereinafter FF), 441/100 (2); Drummond, Deputy Commissioner (hereinafter DC) Gurdaspur's No. 136E, 21 Dec.1900, paras 10–11, FF, 441/100B; note by Humphreys, 13 Sept. 1904, FF, 441/100(11)A; Kitchin, Settlement Officer (hereinafter SO) Rawalpindi's No.1627, 16 Dec.1904, para. 2, FF, 441/104; note by Tupper, FC, 21 March 1905, para. 8, West Pakistan Board of Revenue, Panjab Civil Secretariat Printed Files, Revenue (hereinafter PF), 190, p. 1323.

5   On artisans and menials: *SR Rohtak*, 1879, para.27; extract from *AR Gurgaon*, 1883, para.11, encl. to Govt's No. 231, 7 Nov.1888, PF, 18; Francis, SO Ferozepur's No.31, 2 Feb.1888, para 5 and memo. by Wilson, DC Shahpur, 28 April 1888, para. 5, National Archives of India, Proceedings of the Government of India (hereinafter IP), Revenue (Famine), Dec.1888, 1–24A; *AR Pipli*, 1888, para. 19; *AR Chenab Assessment Circle in Shahpur District*, 1888, para. 20; remarks by Dane, DC Gurdaspur, Extracts from the Revenue (or Land Revenue) reports of local officers, bound with Annual Panjab Revenue (or Land Revenue) Report (hereinafter ERR), 1888–9; *AR Ajnala*, 1892, para. 40; Thorburn, Commissioner and Superintendent (hereinafter CR) Rawalpindi's No. 795/C.I. – 6, 23 March 1895, para. 2, IP, Revenue (Land Revenue), June 1896, 28A; *Thorburn's Appendices* (appendices to next item) 1896, pp. 25, 130, 545, 553; S.S.Thorburn, *Report on Peasant Indebtedness and Land Alienation to Moneylenders in parts of*

the Rawalpindi Division, 1896 (hereinafter *Thorburn's Report* 1896), para. 74; *AR Chakwal and Tallagang*, 1898, para. 62 and statement 6; *AR Sinanwan*, 1900, para. 74; references by Maclagan, Abbott, Hailey, Hari Kishen Kaul, Crosthwaite, Montgomery, Bunbury and Wilson, in 1900, FF, 441/100B and by Lowis and Kensington in FF, 441/100 KW. Also *Annual Report on the Panjab Alienation of Land Act, XIII of 1900*, Lahore 1902–1909 (hereinafter *LAR*), 1901–02, para. 11; Agnew, DC Rawalpindi's No. 96G, 21 May 1906, FF, 441/100(22)A; *LAR*, 1906–7, para. 3; *LAR*, 1907–8, para. 4.

6 *AR Nakodar*, 1883, para. 10; *Panjab Castes*, paras 485–6; *AR Zira*, 1888, para. 7.

7 On Malis: *AR Pipli*, 1888, paras 20, 34, 105; and by Maynard, DC Umballa: No. 19/92R, 18 Jan. 1900, para. 3, National Archives of India, Legislative Department, *Papers* relating to Act XIII of 1900 (hereinafter *Papers*); No. 1666 R, 1 Dec. 1900, para. 6, IP, Revenue (Land Revenue), July 1901, 57–8A; note of 16 Dec. 1900, para. 3, FF, 441/100 KW.

8 On Labanas: *Settlement Report* (hereinafter *SR*) *Gurdaspur*, 1854, Appendix to Report of Pergunnah Adeenanugur; *SR Gujranwala*, 1856, paras 15, 34, 84; *SR Gujrat*, 1859, paras 50, 72; Appendix H and K to Blyth's Report on Narowal, *SR Amritsar*, 1854; *SR Muzuffargarh*, 1881, pp. 53, 60, 61; *AR Ludhiana*, 1882, paras 17, 49, 53; *AR Jullunder*, 1883, paras 8, 10; *Panjab Castes* (1883), para. 548; *SR Sirsa*, 1884, para. 126; *AR Gurdaspur*, 1890, para. 40 and statement 4; *AR Gujranwala*, 1890, para. 26; *AR Pathankot*, 1890, paras 43–44; *AR Raya*, 1891, paras 79, 85; *AR Sharakpur*, 1892, paras 15, 16, 23; *SR Lahore*, 1893, para. 45; *Thorburn's Appendices*, 1896, pp. 392, 406, 409, 429, 444, 545; *AR Sinanwan*, 1900, paras 73–4; references by Maclagan, Connolly, Le Rossignol, Diwan Narendra Nath, Montgomery, Anderson, Fagan, in 1900, FF, 441/100B; No. 7–1/410A, 7 Oct 1902 from Officer Commanding 48th Bengal Pioneers, FF, 441/100(13)A; 1902–3 corresp. partly in FF, 441/100(2½) A, partly in PF, 190, pp. 1259–64; 1904–5 notes and corresp. in FF, 441/100(13)A; other 1905 notes in PF, 190, pp. 1406–15; *Census of India, Vol. XIV, Punjab, Part I, Report*, Lahore 1912, p. 465; H. A. Rose, *A Glossary of the Tribes and Castes of the Punjab and North-West Frontier Provinces*, Lahore 1911–19, Vol. 3, pp. 1–4.

9 On Kalals: Blyth's Report on Turun Taran, para. 138, and Appendix H to Blyth's Report on Narowal, *SR Amritsar*, 1854; *AR Sialkot*, 1863, Appendix 8; *AR Jullunder*, 1883, para. 8; *AR Nawashahr*, 1883, para. 7; *Panjab Castes*, para. 648; *AR Kharar*, 1887, para. 24; *AR Jagadhri*, 1887, paras 21–3; *AR Batala*, 1889, paras 46, 70, 80; *AR Gurdaspur*, 1890, statement 4; *Census of India 1891, Vol. XIX, The Punjab and its Feudatories, Part I, The Report on the Census*, Calcutta 1892, p. 339; *AR Pasrur*, 1893, para. 90; *Thorburn's Appendices*, pp. 15, 365, 449, 545; opinion of Drummond, DC Gurdaspur, 1900, *Papers*; note by Douie, Offg Chief Sec. to Panjab Govt, 10 Sept.

1900 and Rose, Provincial Superintendent Census Operations' No. 745, 11 Sept. 1900, FF, 441/100(2); references by Kitchin, Lowis, Drummond, Le Rossignol, Montgomery, Anderson, Fagan, Bunbury in 1900–1, FF, 441/100B; petition of Umballa Kalals, 6 Oct. 1901 and references by Maynard, Walker, Anderson, FF, 441/100(2½); 1903 corresp. on Ludhiana Kalals, FF, 441/100(15); petition of Central Kakezai Association, 16 June 1905 and note by Walker, FC, 20 June 1905, FF, 441/100K covers; *Census* (1912), Vol. XIV, pp. 460–1; Rose *Glossary*, Vol. 2, pp. 438–9.

10 The south-western Panjab here refers to the districts of Montgomery, Jhang, Multan, Muzuffargarh, and Dera Ghazi Khan. This and the succeeding paragraph is based on: Sec. to Chief Commissioner's No. 196, 9 March 1854, para. 3, quoted in *SR Dera Ghazi Khan*, 1874; *SR Ferozepur*, 1855, paras 17, 200; *SR Gujranwala*, 1856, para. 23; *SR Multan*, 1859, para. 22, Appendix A, para. 17, Appendix C, para. 13; Cust, Offg FC's No. 634, 13 July 1860, para. 23, *SR Jhang*, 1859; *SR Dera Ghazi Khan*, 1874, para. 193; *SR Jhang*, 1881, para. 136; *Panjab Castes* (1883), para. 449; *SR Sirsa*, 1884, paras 81, 104, 210; *AR Zira*, 1888, para. 7; *AR Gujranwala*, 1890, para. 26; *AR Jhelum and Bar circles of Bhera*, 1890, paras 14, 17; *AR Shahpur*, 1891, para 53; *AR Wazirabad*, 1892, para. 28; *AR Plain Portion of Kushab*, 1892, para. 54; *AR Hafizabad*, 1893, paras 31, 65; *AR Gugera*, 1893, para. 19; *AR Sangarh* 1895, para. 62; *AR Jampur*, 1896, para. 72; *AR Dera Ghazi Khan*, 1896, para. 45; *AR Kabirwala*, 1898, paras 36, 38.

11 *SR Ferozepur*, 1855, para. 200; *SR Gujranwala*, 1856, para. 23.

12 Agricultural conditions are treated in detail in assessment and settlement reports of the second half of the nineteenth century.

13 *SR Gujranwala*, 1856, paras 23, 68; *Thorburn's Appendices*, 1896, p. 6; *AR Kabirwala*, 1898, para. 36; *AR Multan and Shujabad*, 1899, para. 33; *AR Chenab Nahri Circle of Jhang*, 1903, para. 5.

14 *SR Ferozepur*, 1855, paras 17–18; *SR Googaira*, 1858, paras 6–7, 38; *SR Sirsa*, 1884, para. 210.

15 *SR Gujranwala*, 1856, para. 46; *SR Multan*, 1859, Appendix C, para. 32; Appendix F, paras 21–2; *SR Montgomery*, 1874, p. 38; *AR Sinanwan*, 1877, para. 47; *AR Jhelum and Bar Circles of Bhera*, 1890, para. 17; *AR Hafizabad*, 1893, paras 31, 65.

16 *SR Gujranwala*, 1856, paras 67–8, 90, Appendix 4, para. 14; *SR Multan*, 1859, Appendix B, para. 38, Appendix C, paras 27, 32; *SR Jhang*, 1859, para. 9; *SR Montgomery*, 1874, pp. 140–1; Wace's review of *SR Multan*, 1880, quoted in S.S. Thorburn, *Musalmans and Money-lenders in the Punjab* (1886), p. 163.

17 *SR Jhang*, 1881, paras 82, 85–6, 136.

18 *SR Montgomery*, 1874, pp. 45–8; *Panjab Castes* (1883), paras 447, 449; *SR Sirsa*, 1884, para. 222; *AR Zira*, 1888, para. 7; *AR Hansi, Hissar, Barwala, Fatehabad*, 1890, para. 24; *AR Jhelum and Bar circles of Bhera*, 1890, para. 14;

AR Montgomery, 1893, para. 64; *AR Jampur*, 1896, para. 72; *AR Dera Ghazi Khan*, 1896, para. 45; *AR Pakpattan*, 1897, para. 62; *AR Kabirwala*, 1898, para. 36; *AR Lodhran*, 1900, para. 31.

19   The central Panjab refers to the districts of Kangra (the Palampur, Kangra, Nurpur, Dera and Hamirpur *tahsils*), Gurdaspur, Hoshiarpur, Jullunder Ludhiana, Ferozepur, Lahore and Amritsar. On the various Rajput communities of this region see: *SR Hoshiarpur*, 1852, paras 11, 184; *AR Una* 1880, para. 34; *AR Samrala*, 1881, para. 72; *AR Ludhiana*, 1881, para. 17; *AR Jagraon*, 1881, para. 10; *Panjab Castes* (1883), paras 431, 456; memo. by Purser, SO Jullunder, 10 July 1884, W. Pakistan Records Office, Panjab Govt. Proceedings (hereinafter PP), Revenue (R), 13–14 A, KW; *AR Batala*, 1889, para. 69; *AR Shakargarh*, 1890, para. 27; *AR Kasur*, 1891, para. 15; *AR Chunian*, 1892, para. 33; *SR Gurdaspur*, 1892, para. 9.

20   This problem is examined in detail in Chapters 1–3 of the writer's Ph.D. thesis mentioned in note 1, p. 89.

21   Based on Chapters 4 and 5 of the Ph.D. thesis mentioned in note 1, p. 89.

22   For this and next paragraph: *SR Dera Ismail Khan*, 1879, para. 706; *SR Jhelum*, 1881, para. 217b; scheme for redemption of mortgages in Gurgaon, 1882, paras 3–4, PP, Revenue (A), April 1883, 5A; remarks by Bartholomew DC Jhang, ERR, 1882–3; *SR Jullunder*, 1886, p. 72; *AR Pipli*, 1888, Appendix 8, para. 7; *AR Zira*, 1888, para. 24; remarks by Maconachie, DC Gurgaon, ERR, 1887–8; references in 1889 by Dane, O'Brien, Grant, Rivaz, IP, Revenue (R), Dec. 1891, 10–11A; remarks by Sardar Gurdial Singh, DC Muzuffargarh, ERR, 1889–90; *AR Shakargarh*, 1890, para. 30; *AR Mamdot*, 1891, para. 6; *AR Lahore*, 1892, para. 30; *Thorburn's Appendices*, 1896, pp. 10–12, 14–17, 19, 27–8, 32, 34–8, 40, 52, 54–5, 111, 277, 549; *Thorburn's Report*, 1896, para. 51; remarks on ejectment in ERR, 1894–5 to 1899–1900.

23   On Sikh Jats: *SR Ferozepur*, 1855, paras 112, 180; *SR Lahore*, 1870, paras 85–6, 225; remarks by DC Ferozepur, ERR, 1874–5; *AR Samrala*, 1881, para. 31; *AR Ludhiana*, 1881, paras 17, 19, 31; *AR Jagraon*, 1881, paras 10, 46; *Panjab Castes* (1883), paras 434, 437; Walker, Assistant Commissioner Kasauli's No. 53, 14 April 1884, para. 6, *AR Moga*, 1886; *SR Sirsa*, 1884, paras 126, 185; *SR Ludhiana*, 1884, paras 48–50, 58, 82, 194–5; *AR Moga* 1886, paras 7–8; *AR Ferozepur*, 1888, para. 29; *AR Zira*, 1888, para. 7; Grant, SO Amritsar's No. 553, 15 Feb. 1889, para. 1, IP, Revenue (R), Dec. 1891, 10–11A; *AR Tarn Taran*, 1891, paras 27, 29, 38, 40; *AR Kasur*, 1891, para. 15; *AR Amritsar*, 1892, paras 24–5, 34, 36; *SR Gurdaspur*, 1892, para. 10; note by King, SO Fazilka, 12 Jan. 1901, FF, 441/100B; Kensington, Divisional Judge (hereinafter DVJ) Lahore's No. 434, 31 July 1903, paras 4–5, FF, 441/105.

24   This account of the agricultural systems refers to the period preceding the introduction of canal irrigation into some parts of the western uplands.

25 This paragraph and the next two are based on various parts of Chapters 1, 2 and 5 of the Ph.D. thesis mentioned in note 1, p. 89. The evidence is voluminous and scattered; much of it is in the settlement and assessment reports.

26 Perkins, CR Amritsar's No. 2899, 4 Sept. 1878, para. 11, PP, Revenue, June 1879, 6A; remarks by Bulman, DC Gujranwala, ERR, 1878–9; references in 1889 by Wilson, Smyth, Grant, IP, Revenue (R), Dec. 1891, 10–11A; *AR Shahpur,* 1891, para. 109; *AR Chunian,* 1892, paras 64, 72; *AR Sharakpur,* 1892, paras. 8, 11, 29, 70; Wilson, DC Shahpur's No. 248, 11 April 1896, para. 8, IP, Home (Judicial), Nov. 1898, 274–439A; Robertson, Director of Land Records and Agriculture's No. –, 28 April 1896, para. 6, IP, Revenue (LR), Nov. 1898, 3–22 A.

27 On agricultural enterprise of Aroras of south-west: *SR Multan,* 1859, paras 26–8, Appendix B, para. 27, Appendix D, paras 11, 20–2; *SR Jhang,* 1859, para. 37; *SR Montgomery,* 1874, p. 52; *AR Sinanwan,* 1877, para. 46; *AR Chiniot,* 1877, paras 209, 217; *SR Jhang,* 1881, paras 64, 136, 168; Hutchinson, DC Multan's No. 520, 7 July 1885, *Selections from the Records of the Office of the Financial Commissioner, Punjab,* New Series, No. 11, No. 37, No. LXV (Lahore 1887) (hereinafter *Selections*), p. 960; Hutchinson, DC Multan's No. 645, 31 Dec. 1888, IP, Revenue (R), Dec. 1891, 10–11A; *AR Montgomery,* 1893, para. 64; *AR Pakpattan,* 1897, para. 62; *AR Lodhran,* 1900, paras 31, 33; *AR Sinanwan,* 1900, paras 73–4, 81; *AR Chenab Nahri circle of Jhang,* 1903, para. 17; Douie, Settlement Commissioner's No. 3765, 20 Oct. 1904, para. 3, PF, 190, p. 1305. The areas of land acquired and owned by Aroras before and during the second half of the nineteenth century are referred to in many south-western settlement and assessment reports of the second half of the nineteenth century.

28 Memo. by Young, 2nd FC, 1 Oct. 1889, para. 4, IP, Revenue (R) Dec. 1891, 10–11A; *Punjabi Century* (1961), pp. 16, 17.

29 On Hindu trading castes and civil administration and professions: *SR South Umballa,* 1853, para. 398; *SR Ludhiana,* 1853, paras 24, 55; *SR Sialkot,* 1863, para. 95; remarks by Naesmyth, CR Hissar, ERR, 1869–70; *SR Bannu,* 1878, para. 73; *SR Dera Ismail Khan,* 1879, para. 148; note by Thorburn, DC Dera Ismail Khan, 29 June 1884, *Selections* (1887), p. 953, 3rd footnote; *SR Ludhiana,* 1884, para. 45; *SR Jullunder,* 1886, p. 84; *SR Hoshiarpur,* 1886 para. 60; *AR Wazirabad,* 1892, para. 28; *AR Hafizabad,* 1893, paras 139, 141; *Thorburn's Appendices,* 1896, pp. 20–6, 31–5, 41–3, 553; *Thorburn's Report,* 1896, paras 60–1; *AR Lodhran,* 1900, para. 31; extract paras 12–13 of note by Thorburn, late FC, *circa* 1900, IP, Revenue (LR), Oct. 1909, 29–31A. On Muslim communities prominent in civil administration and professions: *Musalmans and Money-lenders* (1886), p. 32; *SR Rawalpindi,* 1887, para. 125; *Thorburn's Appendices,* 1896, p. 553; note by Maynard, DC Umballa, 16 Dec. 1900, para. 7 and by Kensington, DVJ Delhi, 1900, FF, 441/100 KW;

SR Delhi, 1910, para. 16; corresp. in FF, 441/100(22)A. Service of landholding tribes in Army and Police is very generally discussed in assessment and settlement reports.

30 *SR Hoshiarpur*, 1852, para. 69; *SR Googaira*, 1858, paras 28–9; remarks by O'Dwyer, SO Gujranwala, on Patwaris and Kanungos, ERR, 1892–3; extract paras 12–13 of note by Thorburn, late FC, *circa* 1900 and Govt's No. 1316 S, 30 July 1909, para. 5, IP, Revenue (LR), Oct. 1909, 29–31A.

31 For significance of vertical caste ties: remarks by Brandreth, CR Jullunder, ERR, 1875–6; remarks by Perkins, CR Multan, ERR, 1881–2; Nisbet, DC Rawalpindi's No. 1820 G, 8 Aug. 1885, para. 7, *Selections* (1887), p. 959; remarks by O'Dwyer, SO Gujranwala, on Patwaris and Kanungos, ERR, 1892–3; *Thorburn's Appendices*, 1896, pp. 20, 21, 33, 42, 43; *Thorburn's Report*, 1896, para. 60; Maconachie, DC Gurdaspur's No. 508 G, 9 June 1896, paras 9, 21, IP, Revenue (LR), Nov. 1898, 3–22A; *AR Pind Dadan Khan*, 1897, para. 75; Govt's No. 1316 S, 30 July 1909, para. 5, IP, Revenue (LR), Oct. 1909, 29–31A.

4

THE NEW BRAHMANS OF
MAHARASHTRA

★

Ravinder Kumar

The attempt of the British Government to control social change in India through deliberate acts of policy is of absorbing interest to the social historian. For not only are such acts of policy susceptible to rational analysis, but they also offer new insights into the over all transformations which took place in India in the nineteenth century. In the first chapter of this book we have seen how British administrators in western India were inspired by Utilitarian ideas to resolve the problems of social progress and political control through the creation of a class of rich peasants which was meant to provide a stable social base for British rule over the country. But besides promoting the rise of prosperous and conservative social groups in rural society, British administrators also tried to disseminate values in the community which would reconcile it to the new order. To achieve this it was necessary to 'convert' the native élite to western ideas. This chapter will be concerned with the creation in Maharashtra, through a calculated policy, of a native élite which was inspired by Western values; which firmly supported the political tie between India and Great Britain; and which attempted, even though with indifferent success, to mediate between the government and the wider community. This élite may be christened: 'The new Brahmans of Maharashtra'.

What was the complexion of the native élite in Maharashtra before the British conquest of 1818? The answer to this question is simple. Since the Brahmans were the guardians of the high culture of Hinduism, and the intellectual leaders of the community, they occupied an important position in Hindu society throughout the subcontinent. But several factors had combined to heighten their influence over Maharashtra during the eighteenth century. In 1742 Balaji Vishwanath, who was a high functionary of the Maratha State, succeeded in seizing power from the hands of the weak descendant of Shivaji. Balaji Vishwanath hailed from the sub-caste of Chitpavan Brahmans, and to strengthen his position he started recruiting his bureaucracy from the Chitpavan community. His successors persisted in this policy. They also granted large estates in land to their caste-fellows in a bid to consolidate their power. As a result, before the British conquest of 1818, the Chitpavans controlled the three most important concentrations of power in Maharashtra, namely, the institutions of religion, the bureaucracy and the ownership of land.

The close connection between Brahman dominance and the rule of the Peshwas, as the Chitpavan rulers were called, is highlighted in the institution of *dakshina* through which the State supported the Brahmans as the defenders of Hindu religion and the disseminators of its values. By means of the *dakshina* the Peshwas disbursed large sums of money to scholarly but impecunious Brahmans who assembled at Poona at a fixed time of the year, and were examined by a body of *shastris* who inquired into their knowledge of the ritual and philosophy of Hinduism. The Brahmans looked upon the *dakshina* as a most important institution, and in return for the recognition which it gave to their role, they supported the political authority of the Peshwas. In explaining the premises of this alliance, the Brahmans of Maharashtra told the British Government at a later stage: 'A knowledge of the Hindu Shasters is of the utmost importance, and the shasters are indisputably necessary, so that those who study them are entitled to the dakshinnah as a gift which has from remote period continued, and many being thereby excited to the study of Hindu science have ultimately become eminent by their great learning....'[1]

However, the secular role of the Brahmans was just as important as their spiritual role. Urban society in Maharashtra revolved around caste organisations which looked after the secular affairs of their members, and were the instruments through which the individual conducted his relations, with the political authority, and with persons belonging to a superior or inferior caste. Caste organisations were thus responsible for enforcing peace and order in society. Since the Brahmans were the most sophisticated section of the community, their assemblies were the most articulate and the most lively of all caste organisations. The Brahmans of Poona, for instance, met frequently on the initiative of a leading intellectual like Waman Shastri Sathe or Neelkunth Shastri Thute to discuss the welfare of the caste, or to settle disputed points of custom. Brahman assemblies were well attended, and they were often centres of lively debate and controversial discussion:

There were present [states one account of a meeting of the Poona Brahmans in the 1820s] Mulhar Shrotee, the most highly respected Brahmin in the country; Nilcunt Shastree Thuthey and Wittal Oppaddea of Pundharpur, esteemed the most able of men, and the most deeply versed in the whole of the Deccan in the learning of the Shasters, who have instructed and still instruct many young Brahmins; Raghoo Acharya, an eminent scholar, the Principal of the school at Poona; Hurbhut Caseekur, a Beneras Brahmin of Great celebrity; Chintaman Dixit, Ganesh Shastree of Rajapur; and many other eminent shastrees from all quarters. The number of persons assembled was at least five hundred, and the streets leading to the Boodwar Palace was filled with people curious to know the results of discussions regarding suttees, and the right of sonars to perform certain Brahmanical ceremonies, which last was also a question appointed to be determined at the meeting.[2]

Because of the absence of articulate members, caste assemblies drawn from the lower and middle ranks of urban society lacked the democratic quality of the Brahman congregations, and the power to make decisions in such assemblies lay in the hands of a small group of individuals rather than in the ordinary members. Brahman assemblies worked on the basis of consensus. But in the middle castes power rested with an 'elective' head who took account of the views of the leading members of the caste before committing himself to any course of action. Castes located at the bottom of the social scale, however, were subject to the will of an hereditary head who imposed his authority without taking anybody into his confidence, probably because there were few individuals of any substance in such castes. Yet the power of the caste heads was not absolute or arbitrary. For even among the lower castes they consulted the *shastris* on all intricate points of custom, and accepted their advice as reflecting values to which high and low castes subscribed with equal enthusiasm. In this manner caste assemblies, despite being instruments of cleavage, served to impart cohesion to the community as a whole through relating its social behaviour and its ethos to a common corpus of values.[3]

I

Mountstuart Elphinstone, who assumed control of the territories of Bombay after 1818, had served for a decade as Resident at the court of Baji Rao Peshwa. He therefore possessed a deep insight into the social structure and religious values of Maharashtra, and realised the important role played by the Brahmans in the affairs of the community. What is more important, Elphinstone was a conservative who saw the supreme task of statesmanship as lying in the politics of moderation rather than in hasty innovation. Elphinstone detested an institution like caste which legitimised social inequality in so gross a manner; he disapproved of the arbitrary principles of government pursued by the Peshwas; and he was convinced of the ethical superiority of Christianity over Hinduism. But despite these views, Elphinstone's commitment to conservative principles prevented him from embarking upon drastic schemes of reform. Instead of attempting to undermine the social and intellectual predominance of the Brahmans at a single blow, he tried to win them over to Western values through exploiting the traditional institutions of Hindu society, and through promoting a gradual change in the intellectual climate of the country.

Elphinstone's policy of gradualism is best illustrated in his decision to continue the patronage which the Peshwas had formerly extended to the Brahmans through the *dakshina*. This decision was taken out of political calculation rather than from any sentimental concern for the caste. What prompted Elphinstone to persist in the *dakshina* was the influence exercised by the Brahmans over the rest of the community. The retention of the *dakshina*, he argued, could attach a most powerful social group to British rule. The *dakshina* could, moreover, be exploited to weaken the hold of traditional values over the Brahmans, and to lead them to explore the new and exciting intellectual horizons which had suddenly opened up. For once British rule had consolidated itself, so Elphinstone observed, 'the *dakshina* might still be kept up, but most of the prizes, instead of being conferred on proficients in Hindu divinity, might be allotted to those more skilled in more useful branches of learning – law, mathematics, etc., and a certain number of professors might be appointed to teach these sciences'.[4]

Like the institution of *dakshina*, the Hindu College established in Poona in 1821 by Elphinstone was designed to win over the Brahmans to Western values by gradually shifting their interest from a study of Hindu religious philosophy to an examination of the rational disciplines of the West. Established with the object, in the first instance, of imparting a catholic education to 'young men of the caste of Brahmins in the several branches of science and knowledge which usually constitute the subjects of study of the learned Indians',[5] the College incorporated Chairs in *Advaita* (philosophy), the *Shastras* (religion and justice), *Vyakaran* (grammar), *Nayaya* (logic), *Jyotish* (astronomy), *Vydic* (medicine), and *Alankar* (belles lettres), apart from junior professorships for the study of the Vedas. Elphinstone had no illusions about the values which the Hindu College would disseminate in the community:

But we must not forget [he pointed out] that we are forming, or rather keeping up with no modification, a seminary among a most bigoted people whose knowledge has always been in the hands of the priesthood and whose science itself is considered a branch of religion. In such circumstances, and supporting the expenses from a fund devoted to religious purposes, I do not think we could possibly have excluded the usual theological professorships without showing a hostility to the Hindu faith which it was our object to avoid, and irritating those prejudices of the people which it was the professed desire of the institution to soothe or remove.[6]

Despite the tenacity with which the Brahmans clung to their traditional values Elphinstone was anxious to prepare them for the changes which he sought to introduce gradually, and Raghu Acharya Chintamum, the *Mukhya Shastri* (Principal) of the Hindu College, was instructed to 'direct the attention of the College principally to the Shastras as are not only most useful in themselves, but will prepare their (i.e., the scholars') minds for a gradual reception of more useful instruction at a late time'.[7] To ensure this objective, only those scholars were admitted to the Hindu College who knew enough Sanskrit to commence straight away with the study of the *Shastras* or *Vyakaran* or *Alankar*. At the same time, while the study of the Vedas was not actively discouraged, it was held inferior to that of the *Shastras*, and no scholar was permitted to devote his time and attention exclusively to them. A Brahman who chose to study the Vedas had to study the *Shastras* as well, and his proficiency in the latter was held to be his main qualification. A strong emphasis on the practical pervaded the whole system; and with the passage of time Elphinstone had every intention of heightening this emphasis at the cost of the metaphysical disciplines. As he argued, once the Hindu College had won a place in the affections of the Brahman community, it would be easy to modify the courses of instruction it offered, and transform it into an affective instrument for the dissemination of Western values.

A commitment to Elphinstone's views on social change was in no way inconsistent with the periodic review, and the reform, of the institutions created by him as the instruments of his policy. His successors, therefore, kept a close watch on the progress of the Hindu College, and the distribution of the *dakshina*. When in 1834 J. H. Baber, the Principal Collector of Poona, turned his attention to the Hindu College, he discovered that the institution had drifted far from the ideals for whose promotion it had been founded by Elphinstone. Instead of providing a classical education in Sanskrit to young Brahmans of outstanding ability, the College had become a refuge for idlers and drones 'having the appearance of men 25 to 30 years old, to whom ... it was never intended the allowance should be continued'.[8] The apparent failure of the institution raised several questions of fundamental importance. The College had been established by Elphinstone in order to impress upon the Hindu community his concern for the religious traditions and the values to which the community was deeply attached. Elphinstone had also hoped that the college would train young men from respectable Brahman families and encourage them to enter into the service of the British Government. But neither of these expectations was realised. The College had provided only one candidate for the public service; and the courses of instruction it offered were so unattractive that not a single Brahman family of repute had deigned to send any member to it. In view of these circumstances, Baber raised the question whether the College was serving any useful purpose, and whether it deserved any support from the Government.

Baber had presented so dismal a picture of the Hindu College that a Commission appointed in 1835 to investigate the institution, and having as its President a conservative like Thomas Williamson, the Commissioner of the Deccan, recommended the outright abolition of the College.[9] However, Robert Grant, the Governor of Bombay, refused to take so precipitate a step, even when it concerned an institution which, as he put it, 'preserves and cherishes the old Brahmanical interest, which is anti-British in all its tendencies'.[10] To abolish the Hindu College, Grant argued, just when the Government of Bombay had established a school in Poona for imparting education in English would be highly offensive to the Brahman community, even though the students of the English school did not receive any financial assistance from the State, unlike the drones who led a parasitic existence at the Hindu College. Since political considerations ruled out its abolition, the only solution open to the Government was to modify the courses of instruction offered in the Hindu College, keeping in view its long-term objectives.

However political expediency was not the only reason which pointed to the need for continued State assistance for the Hindu College. It was left to the Reverend J. Stevenson, a Poona missionary who was also a distinguished Sanskritist, to impress upon the Government the proper role of a Sanskrit College, and the importance of some, if not all, of the disciplines which formed part of a classical education.[11] The existence of parasitic students, Stevenson argued, could be ascribed to the incompetence of Narayan Shastri, who had succeeded Raghu Acharya Chintamum as the *Mukhya Shastri* (Principal) of the Hindu College in the late 1820s, rather than to any inherent defect in the institution. Sanskrit, he continued, was the root of all the languages of India, and its study was therefore essential for the development of the regional languages, and their transformation into media adequate for the transmission of modern ideas to the common people. As Stevenson put it, while 'English is necessary to furnish ideas to the native mind, the SANSKRIT is equally necessary to enable the learned in European science to diffuse their knowledge among the masses of the community'. But in putting forth a plea for the retention of Sanskrit, Stevenson proposed drastic alterations in the disciplines taught at the Hindu College. Instead of any encouragement being given to metaphysical speculation on the nature of the universe and the spiritual quality of man, he argued, emphasis ought to be placed entirely on practical fields of study. Among the 'pernicious' disciplines taught at the Hindu College Stevenson listed *Advaita*, *Jyotish*, *Alankar*, *Nyaya* and the *Vedas*, and he recommended the abolition of the Chairs in these fields. Courses of instruction in disciplines like *Mayukh* (jurisprudence), *Vyakaran* (grammar) and the *Dharamshastra* should continue as before, since proficiency in these spheres could equip a young Brahman for a useful career in life.

The reconstitution of the Hindu College along the lines advocated by Stevenson in 1836 reflected the determination of the Government of Bombay to undermine slowly the hold of traditional values on the Brahman intelligentsia, and to expose it to the influence of modern ideas. A similar objective inspired the changes effected in the 1830s in the distribution of the *dakshina*, an institution to which Elphinstone had extended his support for precisely the same reasons which had prompted him to establish the Hindu College. Of course, for the Hindu community in general, and the Brahmans in particular, the *dakshina* was far more important than the Hindu College, since it not only supported a large number of impecunious Brahmans, but it also identified the State with the values and traditions to which the community was attached.

Whatever be its significance, when Baber looked into the distribution of the *dakshina* in 1834, he discovered that the institution was being thoroughly exploited by the Brahman community.[12] In recommending candidates for the award of the *dakshina*, the Committee of *Shastris* appointed for this purpose by the Government of Bombay was guided by 'caprice' rather than by the merits of the applicants. But apart from the corruption which apparently influenced its distribution, the *dakshina*, Baber argued, hardly promoted any of the objectives which had encouraged Elphinstone to support it. Instead of training the minds of the rising generation of Brahmans 'in habits of respect and attachment to the British Government', it confirmed them in their allegiance to traditional values, and was instrumental in widening the gulf between the rulers and the ruled. Baber's appraisal led the Government of Bombay to appoint a Special Commission to investigate the distribution of the *dakshina*, and to suggest ways and means for its reform. On the advice of this Commission the old Committee of *Shastris* which had thoroughly discredited itself through its corrupt practices was dismissed, and the rules for admission to the *dakshina* were made much more rigorous than before. Again on the advice of the Commission, the Bombay Government decided not to entertain any requests for admission to the *dakshina* after 1836.[13]

The reaction of the Brahman community to a decision which affected its interests so adversely was sharp and instantaneous. For besides providing the means of subsistence to impecunious but scholarly Brahmans, the *dakshina* symbolised the predominance of Brahmanical values over the community, and the acquiescence by the State in this predominance. The Brahmans therefore interpreted the decision to discontinue the *dakshina* as a challenge to their position in Hindu society, and a bid to undermine the traditions of which they regarded themselves as the custodians. After debating the issue in their caste assemblies, in November 1836 the Brahmans of Poona presented a petition to the Government of Bombay. This petition was signed by 800 'Shastris, Pandits and Puraniks, etc.' and it stated in forthright language the serious consequences that were likely to flow from the discontinuation of the *dakshina* grants.[14] The study of the *Vedas* and the *Shastras*, the petition pointed out, was necessary to sustain a creative relationship between the Hindu community and the traditions which gave it moral cohesion, and fashioned its secular and spiritual objectives. In keeping with their traditional role, the Brahmans of Maharashtra had taken upon themselves this responsibility, and in return the State had promised to maintain them, and to encourage them in their labour, through the distribution of the *dakshina*. Such an alliance between the political and the intellectual leaders of the community had worked with the happiest of results in the past, and had protected the interests of the Brahmans as well as the secular authority. Elphinstone, the petition argued, had recognised the benefits which accrued to the State, and to the community, from the *dakshina*, and he had therefore refrained from abolishing it. To do this now, the Poona Brahmans stated in conclusion, would be to undermine the moral foundations of Hindu society, and to bring about social anarchy and political disintegration:

We therefore entreat [ran the petition] that the Sircar will take the whole of these circumstances into consideration, and make such arrangements as to cause all such balances as will have remained in hand, after the distribution of the ensuing Dakshina, on account of the absent Brahmans, to be distributed to all new candidates, who may be admitted after passing the usual examination. This will be the means of disseminating the learning and the people will moreover be happy and it will greatly tend to the honour of the Government but should it be otherwise, both science and religion will be lost and ruined, and people will not act uprightly in their dealings, and everyone will suffer extremely.[15]

But the Government of Bombay refused to be browbeaten into surrender by the spectre of anarchy and disintegration which was raised by the Brahman community. Its confidence in its policies stemmed from the belief that the education being given in institutions like the Poona English School (which was founded in 1832) would, in the course of time, give rise to a new generation of Brahmans who would sympathise with its political ideals and its social objectives. The orthodox Brahmans who had petitioned against the decree prohibiting new individuals from presenting themselves as candidates for the *dakshina* were therefore told that the Government was unable to reconsider its decision.[16] It was, however, pointed out to them that the funds released through the interdict would 'continue to be made available to the general purposes of promoting education and rewarding acquisitions of science'. The Government also committed itself to a *de novo* consideration of the problem after the number of Brahmans who received the *dakshina* had fallen sufficiently low.

Since the Government of Bombay had refused to acquiesce in the demands of the Poona Brahmans, the agitation against the discontinuation of the *dakshina* continued with unabated vigour, and even spread in widening circles to embrace the Brahmans of Satara, Wai, Pandharpur, Kurud, etc. Throughout the 1840s the authorities were made to feel the brunt of Brahman disapproval through representations drawn along the lines of the Poona petition of 1836.[17] But the Government did not retreat before this onslaught, since it was confident that the establishment of institutions like the English School was bound to exercise a liberalising influence over the Brahman community. Nor was it disappointed in its expectations. A series of representations received in 1850 from a group of Poona Brahmans, and from some students of the English School, spoke in clear terms of a cleavage in the Brahman caste, and the emergence of a group of liberal Brahmans who had disowned the values and traditions of their forefathers, and who were anxious to exploit the opportunities open to them to advance their prospects.

The liberal Brahmans threw out an open challenge to the old style *shastris* the moment sufficient arrears had accumulated from the annual *dakshina* subvention of Rs 30,000 to oblige the government to consider ways and means to put to some use the funds at its disposal. Their bid for preference took the form of a representation to Viscount Falkland, the Governor of Bombay, which contained suggestions seeking to extend the scope of the *dakshina* beyond the promotion of studies in Sanskrit, and the assistance of old style *shastris* and pandits. The liberal Brahmans proposed the institution of sixteen prizes, of the total value of Rs 1,000, in Sanskrit; and a similar number of awards, amounting to Rs 2,000, in Marathi and English. These prizes were *to be awarded to individuals of any caste* on the submission each year before a competent body 'of an original useful composition in the Prakrit, or translation from some original works in the Sanskrit, English or any other language'.[18]

In stating the reasons which had encouraged them to propose alterations in the distribution of the *dakshina*, the liberal Brahmans defined their vision and their objectives with unmistakable clarity. Under the Peshwas, they pointed out, support of Sanskrit and the pretensions of the Brahman caste could be justified on the basis of the social values of Hindu society, and the concept of political order from which the State drew its sanctions. But for the British Government to desist from introducing changes in the distribution of the *dakshina* would be a pointless surrender to reaction. The ideals to which it subscribed were in no way related to the values of which the old style *shastris* regarded themselves as the custodians; nor did it draw its sanctions from the traditions which the orthodox Brahmans cherished. On the other hand, with a little boldness and a little imagination the State could be instrumental in disseminating ideas that would widen the intellectual horizons of the community, and spread habits of thought and action conducive to progress and prosperity. It was incumbent on the British Government to adopt such policies for altruistic reasons, and on grounds of equity. Its revenues were largely drawn from a tax on the peasant, and a policy which subordinated the peasant's interests to the interests of the superior castes was morally reprehensible and politically inexpedient:

The present system of the distribution of the Dukshunna Fund [the liberal Brahmans of Poona stated in conclusion] has no tendency to promote learning among and extend its benefits to the great mass of the population. It is found [*sic*] on the old illiberal and barbarous prejudice of confining learning to the Brahman caste and locking it up in stores which the great mass of the people can never be able or hope to open. . . . [The] present plan is calculated to civilise the nation in general and lay open for its benefit these stores of learning and wisdom . . . which have hitherto been inaccessible to the nation at large. Another striking characteristic of the old system of the institution of the Dukshunna is the confinement of its benefits to the caste of Brahmans. . . . The cultivator, the gardner [*sic*], the carpenter, the blacksmith, who are the most useful members of the society, and from whom the Dukshunna Fund is wrung, would not under the old system, share in its benefits nor can be civilised by it. . . . What the nation most wants is useful arts, science, and morals and they shall find them not certainly in the dead Sanskrit, but in the animated English literature.

This essential reform must therefore be introduced and it cannot be commenced too soon.[19]

When the petition from the liberal Brahmans calling for a radical view of the *dakshina* was followed by a representation, couched in identical language, from the 'students of Government English School and other English Schools in Poona',[20] J. G. Lumsden, the Secretary to the Government of Bombay, observed that the time had come when the Government could safely embark upon a policy of reform.[21] The support given by Elphinstone to the *dakshina* and to the study of Sanskrit, Lumsden argued, in no way committed the government to prop up the traditional order in Maharashtra. Elphinstone had yielded to no one in his anxiety to introduce liberal ideas among the Brahmans. But with his Burkean concern for continuity in the processes of change, he had visualised the Westernisation of the Brahman intelligentsia as a gradual process. Since there existed a considerable group within the Brahman caste that was clamouring for a liberal education, and a bold attitude towards the *dakshina*, it was clear that a policy of reform could now be adopted without any fear of social disintegration. That reform would have to be undertaken sooner or later, Lumsden argued, was inevitable. For to retain the *dakshina* as it stood under the Peshwas was to deny the ideals and objectives for whose fulfilment British rule had been established over Maharashtra. Brahmanical values, with their emphasis on rank and order and status, conflicted with concepts like equality (in the eyes of the law) and progress and mobility. To submit to Brahmanical ideals would prevent the British Government from embarking upon any scheme of improvement or reform:

Are the recipients of the Duxxina [Lumsden asked] unable to comprehend that the system at work around them is directly at variance with the social system and the entire body of ethics which have formed the subjects of their studies and which they regard with a bigoted reverence? Or is it to be supposed that a single act of concession like the distribution of this Duxxina will conciliate the views of [those?] who receive it or render them less alive to the fact that the Government is pursuing a course which threatens eventually to deprive them of their cherished social supremacy?

If there be justice in the above remarks the course which it is proper to pursue will not require much consideration. Unless Government are deterred by the apprehension of adding to the dissastisfaction of this class who in the present day are rather subjects for compassion than for admiration it should avoid all occasions of extending to them a direct and prominent support which places them in a false position equally in relation to ourselves and to the people.

What encouragement Government can afford should rather be given to those among them who have come out from their camp and who have been educated under the auspices of Government in ideas more consonant with 'the progress of national education'. The time has arrived when without concern for the result, Government can afford to give a direct and unequivocal support to those men whose ideas it has helped to liberalise and whose minds it has endeavoured to advance beyond the prejudices of their nation and in so doing has placed them in the position of opponents to their own caste and to caste interests while they may unquestionably be regarded as more friendly and partial to ourselves.[22]

Since it recognised the contradiction between Brahmanical values and the political objectives of the British Government, and because it focused attention on the liberal forces at work within the Brahman community, the Lumsden memorandum was the signal for sweeping changes in the *dakshina* and in the Hindu College. No new candidates had been admitted to the *dakshina* after 1836, and the amount of money distributed to the *shastris* and pandits by the Government was reduced from Rs 28,000 in 1839, to Rs 12,000 in 1857.[23] In 1859 the *dakshina* fund was entirely taken over by the Education Department, and a number of Fellowships were instituted, which were awarded to candidates of all castes to enable them to receive a secular education in the schools and colleges of Bombay.[24] The Hindu College had in the meanwhile been transformed into an institution for imparting a modern, as opposed to a classical, education. Through reforms initiated in 1850, the College was thrown open to all castes, and its Sanskrit Professorships were substituted by four Chairs: the first in education, the second in English, the third in Marathi and the fourth and last in the sciences.[25] Students seeking admission to the College were expected to possess a sound knowledge of the Vernacular. It was also obligatory for them to study Marathi, though Sanskrit was optional for candidates whose main interest centred on the English language, and *vice versa*. A second set of reforms introduced in 1856 heightened the importance of the Chairs of English and Science in the College, and stipulated that 'Sanskrit students should be made to learn also the other branches of a useful general education taught in the College....'[26] Finally, in 1864 the Hindu College was renamed the Deccan College, and thereafter played a seminal role in the intellectual development of Maharashtra through giving a liberal education to generations of young Brahman and non-Brahman students.

Despite the changes brought about in the intellectual climate of Maharashtra by a deliberate policy of Westernisation, the radical Brahmans whom a liberal education, and the tacit support of the State, had encouraged to challenge the position of their orthodox caste-fellows were still in a minority. The weakness in numbers of the radical Brahmans is underscored by the fact that while the liberal petition seeking changes in the *dakshina* was supported by only twenty-two Brahmans, the orthodox faction could persuade 500 *shastris* and pandits to endorse a counter-petition to the Government of Bombay.[27] However, while the orthodox Brahmans had the strength of numbers on their side, the winds of change that were blowing across Maharashtra had created a climate that was favourable to the aspirations of the 'new Brahmans' for the leadership of the community. The power of the orthodox *shastris*, it should be borne in mind, did not rest exclusively on their religious role. For besides regulating the spiritual life of the individual, the *shastris* led the caste assemblies which mediated between the caste members and the State, and protected the secular interests of the community. Now the *shastris* could play such a role effectively only if the State subscribed to their values and shared their social ideals and political objectives. Since the British Government stood for social ideals and political objectives which were different, and in some respects antagonistic, to the values of the *shastris*, they were unable to perform their political role adequately after the British conquest. The stage was thus set for the emergence of a new élite, and the development of a new style in politics.

The inability of the traditional élite to act to any purpose in the political climate engendered by British rule, and consequent need for a new leadership, is brought into sharp focus by the riots which broke out in Surat in 1844. The Surat riots of 1844 were no doubt connected with the depressed economic conditions which prevailed in that city ever since its displacement by Bombay as the entrepôt for the trade of western India in the opening decades of the nineteenth century.[28] But the immediate cause of the anti-British upsurge in Surat was a decree which raised the duty on salt to off-set the losses sustained by the public treasury through the abolition of transit duties on commercial goods. In raising the salt-tax the Government unwittingly imposed a new and heavy burden on broad sections of the community: on the cultivators, who were already staggering under the weight of an oppressive land-tax; on the local Brahmans, who were living on the wreck of fortunes of better times, and whose main diet consisted of vegetables cured in salt; and on the poor fishing communities of the coast, which employed large quantities of salt in preserving the fish they caught. The increase in the duty on salt was particularly ill-conceived since the social groups it affected did not gain anything from the abolition of transit duties. Dr Gibson, a missionary who was in close touch with native opinion in Surat, pointed out how the measure had confirmed the natives in their suspicion that the British Government would ultimately burden them with taxation just as arbitrary, and oppressive, as that levied by the Peshwas:

> I have often conversed [Gibson observed] with natives who were ready to twit me with the philanthropy of the British Government in giving up transit duties, and in substituting this tax which brought in a huge sum. . . . It seems to me that one could not have hit on a measure better calculated to excite extreme discontent among the various classes who have suffered by our rule, and whose affection we have no opportunity of conciliating otherwise than by letting them alone. The different classes are numerous – they are influential.[29]

As pointed out by Gibson, and subsequently underscored by the riots, the intensity of feeling against the increase in the duty on salt afforded an excellent opportunity to the traditional leaders in Surat to acquaint the authorities with public reaction to the measure. But to such an extent was the traditional élite now alienated from the centres of power, that it was unable to act to any purpose in the crisis precipitated by the British Government. In the absence of any initiative from their traditional leaders, the citizens of Surat expressed their opposition to the increase in tax on salt through 'spontaneous' action. On 30 August 1844, an angry and excited 'mob' of 30,000 people marched to the *adawlut* in Surat, and demanded a cancellation of the duty on salt from the British magistrate, Sir Robert Arbuthnot.[30] The march on the *adawlut* brings into sharp focus the inadequacy of the traditional leaders in a situation which they could have turned to their advantage; on the one hand, by asserting their leadership over the community, and on the other, by demonstrating to the British Government their proper role as links between the State and its subjects. The spontaneity of the Surat demonstration, and the extent to which the bewildered traditional leaders were compelled to adopt an attitude of belligerency under pressure from their followers, is all too clear from an account of the riots by Sheikh Sharif, the foremost Muslim divine in the city:

> In the hope of seeing you hereafter [Sheikh Sharif wrote to Arbuthnot] I beg now to repeat that since this morning, the whole men of this city have united and assembled at my house and urged me to proceed to the Sirdar [i.e., the British representative]. But I have since morning till this time told them to have great patience and make no disturbance or tumult . . . and that those who have anything to say, should petition on the subject, and to agree to whatever a beneficent Government may desire, but in no way will they be satisfied. At length they have agreed to be satisfied in this manner: the Government to order . . . that an answer will be given to the petition in a few days and for the present, until a final order be given, that all the ryots shall remain in their own homes . . .[31]

That the dilemma which confronted the traditional élite was genuine rather than simulated is obvious from Arbuthnot's description of Sheikh Sharif as 'a very respectable and good man . . . whose followers are a discontented set. . . .'[32] But in the absence of any other channel of communication with the 'mob' on the streets, Arbuthnot was obliged to turn to traditional leaders like Sheikh Sharif, and the Mullah of the Borahs, and the Goswamijee Maharaj of the Hindus, for assistance in bringing the situation under control.[33] However, because the traditional leaders were unable to adjust themselves to the changing style of politics in Maharashtra, the future lay with the liberal Brahmans, who were in a position to convey the sentiments of the people to the government, and at the same time shared the values of, and were inspired by the same ideals as, the British Government. Of course, the traditional leaders were fully aware of their growing impotence, and of the changes which were undermining their predominance over the community. All this is clearly reflected in the retort of an embittered *shastri* of the old school to a liberal Brahman who tried to win him over to the cause of reform: 'We Shastris know that the tide is against us and it is no use opposing. You people should not consult us, but go your own way, and do the thing you think right; and we shall not come in your way. But if you ask us and want us to twist the *shastras* to your purpose and go with you, we must speak plainly and we must oppose. . . .'[34]

Who were these 'new Brahmans' who were seeking to rob the traditional élite of their role as the leaders of the community? What was their social vision and what were their political objectives? How wide was the gulf which separated them from the orthodox leaders, and how fundamental were the changes which they sought to bring about in Maharashtra? Were they an alienated group, or did their enthusiasm for reform stop short of a rupture of their ties with the more conservative sections of the community?

These questions are best answered by sketching brief portraits of some representative new Brahmans of Maharashtra.

Gopal Hari Deshmukh, also known as the *Lokhitwadi* (Advocate of the People's Welfare), was born in 1823 in a Deshasth family which had served the Peshwas, and whose estates were confiscated by the British Government for their loyalty to the *ancien regime*. After completing his education in the Poona English School, the *Lokhitwadi* entered the judicial service of the Government of Bombay, where he rose from a humble position to be a judge in the Nasik District Court. He was a pioneer of Marathi journalism, in which capacity he applied himself to social reform, and to the political education of the common people of Maharashtra. The *Satapatren*, or the weekly letters which the *Lokhitwadi* contributed to a contemporary journal, are not the effusions of a sophisticated or an over subtle mind; nor do they reveal any deep insight into current problems and predicaments. But despite his limited vision, and notwithstanding his superficial acquaintance with Western thought, the *Lokhitwadi* was able to arrive at a shrewd assessment of the impact of British rule on Maharashtra. The British occupation, he pointed out, differed fundamentally from the Muslim conquest of India. While the intellectual impact of Islam had been marginal, British rule had opened the eyes of the intelligentsia to a new and exciting range of social values and political objectives, and it had convinced the educated community of the advantages of representative government and popular democracy. Through promoting a change in the intellectual climate, the British Government had cleared the way for the political emancipation of the country. Once Maharashtrians had exorcised evils like the institution of caste, and reorganised their society on a liberal and democratic basis, they would have no trouble in achieving political emancipation. Social reform rather than political power formed the principal concern of the *Lokhitwadi*, but like many a first generation new Brahman, he did not look upon the political and the social as mutually exclusive, and he believed that liberalisation in the latter automatically assured progress in the former sphere.[35]

Vishwanath Narayan Mandlik was born in 1823 in a distinguished

Chitpavan family which was connected with the Peshwas by ties of kinship, and which had provided the former rulers with many a high officer
of State.[36] Mandlik was endowed with an intellectual stature and with
qualities of leadership which would have assured him an outstanding
political career anywhere. He received his education in Elphinstone
College, Bombay, and after a brief spell of Government service he embarked upon a legal career. But it was through his participation in public
affairs, first in the Bombay Municipality, then in the Provincial Legislative Council and finally in the Imperial Legislative Council, that he
made his mark upon the contemporary scene. A 'Whig' who saw no
contradiction between the British 'connection' and the increasing participation of Indians in affairs of State, Mandlik provided a striking contrast to the traditional leaders of the *jo hukam* (sycophantic) school, from
whose ranks the British Government all too frequently packed the legislatures. Yet his conservative cast of mind, and his regard for traditional
values, alienated him from the more impetuous Brahmans who soon
became impatient of the pace at which power was flowing into their
hands. The image Mandlik has left for posterity is that of an enlightened
conservative who was outpaced by the growth of radical sentiment
among the second generation of new Brahmans; and although he
started public life as a liberal, towards the end of his career he was battling
furiously on behalf of orthodoxy to protect Hindu society from schemes
of reform which, so he believed, would have weakened its fabric by
creating a wide gulf between its leading and its traditional elements.[37]

A new Brahman with a difference, because of his political interests,
was Ganesh Vasudev Joshi, who was born in Satara in 1828, and who
came to Poona in 1848 in search of employment after having completed
his preliminary schooling in the city of his birth. After a brief spell of
service in a Government department, Joshi applied himself to a legal
career, and at the same time started taking an interest in the politics of
Poona. He was a founding member of the *Poona Sarvajanik Sabha*, and
as its first secretary he was responsible (along with M. G. Ranade) for
guiding its agitational activity, and shaping its political style. Like other
Brahmans who subscribed to liberal values, Joshi recognised the wide
gulf which separated the traditional leaders from those who controlled
political power, and in the *Sarvajanik Sabha* he saw 'a mediatory body
which may afford to the people facilities for knowing the real intentions
and objectives of the government .... (and provide them with means)
for securing their rights by presenting timely representations to Government of the circumstances in which they are placed'.[38] His search for a

creative political role for the new Brahmans encouraged Joshi to extend the support of the *Poona Sarvajanik Sabha* to the peasants of the Deccan in their grievances against the Revenue and Survey Department; it also encouraged him to organise protests against the repressive press legislation enacted by the Government of Lord Lytton. None of these agitations, however, was marked by any conspicuous success. But Joshi did not have any illusions about the strength of the entrenched interests against which he battled, within the community, and in the ranks of the administration. Besides, he regarded participation in politics by the new Brahmans not as a short cut to victory, but as an experience which would strengthen their moral fibre and sharpen their intellectual faculties. Joshi's finest hour came in 1877, when he attended the Imperial Durbar as the representative of the *Sarvajanik Sabha*, and invoked a 'parliament' of the princes and feudal chiefs who had assembled there to expound for their benefit the ideals and objectives of liberalism.[39]

The most influential new Brahman of his day was Vishnu Shastri Chiplunkar, who transformed Marathi into a language capable of expressing modern ideas. Besides being a prose stylist of outstanding distinction, Vishnu Shastri was an iconoclast who had an eye for humbug that was pitiless in its appraisals, and a vision that was bold and imaginative in the ideals which it set before the community. Before he died a premature death in 1881, Vishnu Shastri had made a profound impression on the young Brahman intellectuals of his time, and in assessing the loss which Maharashtra had suffered through his demise a contemporary compared him to 'Voltaire (who) made everyone from Stockholm to Rome, and St Petersburg to Lisbon, tremble in his shoes when he took up his pen.... (So) did Shastribua make the Rao Sahebs, the Rao Bahadurs, the Reverends and the Saraswatis squirm and squeak under his literary lash'.[40] While he accepted Western values with more reservations than an intellectual with the limited vision of a *Lokhitwadi*, Vishnu Shastri's basic sympathies lay with the advocates of change rather than with the old style *shastris*, and he looked with hope and optimism to a future in which Maharashtra would play a creative role after having purged itself of its social evils and regenerated itself politically. Such ideals found expression in the New English School, which Vishnu Shastri founded in 1880 together with a group of young Brahmans like Tilak, Agarkar and Apte, who were destined to give intellectual and political leadership to Maharashtra till well into the opening decades of the twentieth century.

II

Despite the deep influence exercised by Vishnu Shastri Chiplunkar on the new Brahmans of his generation, the intellectual impact of the West on Maharashtra found its noblest expression in Mahadev Govind Ranade, who was also the most sophisticated thinker of his time. Born in a poor Chitpavan family in 1842, Ranade received his early schooling in Poona, and in 1859 he proceeded to the Elphinstone College in Bombay, which was then moulding the mind of young Maharashtrians through liberal teachers like Green and Wordsworth. Although his poverty obliged Ranade to enter into the service of the Government of Bombay, he did not permit his official duties to restrict his interests or his activities. Ranade's interests encompassed the entire range of human activity, and once he had entered public life through the *Poona Sarvajanik Sabha* in the 1870s, he continued to play an active role till his death in 1901. But despite the example he set to the new Brahmans of his generation, Ranade compels our attention primarily for the insights which he possessed into the weaknesses of Hindu society, and for the catholicity with which he proposed solutions for their eradication. The intellectual qualities which raised Ranade head and shoulders above his contemporaries restricted him as a man of action, and placed him at a distinct disadvantage in the rough and tumble of politics. A melancholic cast of mind; an inability to compromise on questions of principle; and a lack of the qualities that make the demagogue combined with intellectual sophistication to circumscribe the influence of Ranade's ideas, and to restrict the popularity of his leadership.[41]

Besides being a product of his temperament, Ranade's vision was shaped by his membership of an élite caste which shared its values with the lower and middle castes of Maharashtra, and which retained, even after the lapse of half a century, vivid memories of the dominant position it had enjoyed under the Peshwas. The transfer of power in 1818 had shattered the hegemony of the Chitpavan Brahmans. But because of the strength of their traditions, and the hold they had exercised over the bureaucracy before 1818, they remained even after the transfer of power the most influential group in Maharashtra, flocking in great numbers to the schools and colleges opened by the British Government, and monopolising the junior ranks of the civil service. An examination of Table 4 reveals the extent to which they monopolised education, which, it must be remembered, provided the only means of access to the civil service, and to independent careers in the professions.[42] In the Deccan College in

Poona, for instance, more than 97 per cent of the students were Brahmans, although the caste formed only 4 per cent of the total population of the Deccan. Small wonder then that British civilians viewed the preponderance of the Chitpavans with alarm, and apprehended what their memories of past glory meant for the future of British rule in India:

> Now the Chitpawun tribe [wrote Sir Richard Temple, the Governor of Bombay, to the Viceroy, Lord Lytton, in 1879] still stands in vigour and prosperity. They are inspired with national sentiment and with an ambition bounded only with the limits of India itself. . . . If you were to count heads among our best native employees all over the Deccan and the Concan, and even among our humble village accountants, you would be surprised to find what a *hold* this tribe of Chitpawuns has over the whole administrative machinery of the country. And this position is won over not by favour but by force of merit. For among prizemen and honours holders in the schools and graduates of the University the Chitpawuns are predominant. . . . But nothing that we do now, by way of education, emolument, or advancement in the public service, at all *satisfies* the Chitpawuns. They will never be satisfied till they regain their ascendency in the country, as they had it in the last century.[43]

TABLE 4

CASE BREAKDOWN OF STUDENTS IN THE COLLEGES OF BOMBAY IN 1884

Institution	Kayasth Prabhus	Brahmans	Kshtriyas	Trading Castes
1. Elphinstone College, Bombay	18	59	10	38
2. Deccan College, Poona	3	107	1	1
3. Free General Assembly's Institution, Bombay	—	34	1	6
4. St. Xavier's College, Bombay	7	15	1	5
5. Gujarat College, Ahmedabad	1	3	—	1
6. Rajaram College, Kohlapur	—	23	—	—
Total:	29	241	13	51

The social background of a new Brahman like Ranade deserves special emphasis because of the light it throws on his views, and the significance it bestows upon the ideals he set before the community. It would be futile to deny that Ranade's views were to a considerable extent shaped by a temperament which encouraged him to look upon politics as the art of the possible, and to reject the utopian and the visionary for the concrete and the practical. But it is equally certain that the values to which he subscribed as a member of the 'Chitpawan tribe', and the spiritual outlook which he shared with the *kumbi* (the peasant) through allegiance to a common corpus of religious ideas, inculcated in him a concern for social cohesion, and encouraged him to reject progress achieved at the cost of social alienation.

Ranade's concern for social cohesion as a member of an integrated élite caste was reinforced by the intellectual influences which shaped his views on politics and society. Like other new Brahmans of his generation, he read extensively of the works of Adam Smith, Burke, Bentham and the Mills; and like most of them, he was impressed by Burke's notion of tradition, and Mill's notion of liberty, despite the reservations voiced by the prophet of liberalism about societies which lacked political sophistication and formal education. But it was the social theories of Herbert Spencer, to whom Ranade once referred as 'the greatest living philosopher of the age', [44] that made the most significant impact on his mind, and inculcated in him a belief in evolution, and a vision of progress, which saw social or economic or political activity as organically related rather than as isolated fields of human endeavour. Ranade and the new Brahmans who followed his lead are frequently referred to as liberals. But this label is meaningful only to the extent that it distinguishes them from the old style *shastris* who were committed to traditional values, and from individuals who subscribed to activist theories of political action. For the new Brahmans of Ranade's stamp did not subscribe to the individualism which characterised English liberalism in the nineteenth century, nor did they pin their faith on social action based on the motivations of the individual rather than the group. Indeed, instead of being committed to *laissez-faire* values, Ranade held the economics of liberalism to be responsible for much of the poverty of India under British rule.

Despite the comprehensiveness of his social vision, since the circumstances of India under British rule hinged on a relationship of political superordination and subordination between two societies, Ranade was obliged to place an emphasis on political progress which did some violence to the ideas of Herbert Spencer. The need for such an emphasis became all the more pressing when a group of conservative officials initiated a debate concerning political objectives which (to Ranade) appeared to contradict the manifest principles of political progress, and to violate the basic assumptions which underlay the British presence in India. Admittedly, these officials had been provoked into action by the liberal policies of Lord Ripon, and by the Ilbert Bill in particular. But since Ranade looked upon the devolution of power initiated by Ripon as a process to which the British Government was committed irretrievably, he regarded the conservative reaction to Ripon's policies as an attempt to give a novel and sinister interpretation to the relationship which linked India to England.

The most distinguished exponent of the conservative case was Sir Fitzjames Stephen, a Utilitarian who was influenced by the authoritarian doctrine of Hobbes, and whose experience as the Law Member of the Government of India from 1869 to 1872 reinforced his contempt for popular democracy and representative government, and for the shibboleths of 'Liberty, Equality, and Fraternity'.[45] Stephen regarded Ripon's attempt to promote progressive participation by Indians in affairs of State as a step that would fatally undermine British authority in India; and he subjected the liberal vision of British rule over India to a scathing attack in an article which appeared in the *Nineteenth Century*, and which spelt out his view of 'The Foundations of the Government of India'.[46] At the root of liberal pusillanimity and liberal blunders in India, Stephen stated, lay the feelings of guilt which overwhelmed the heirs of John Stuart Mill when they found themselves upholding two different, and contradictory, political ideals in India and England. The policy to be pursued in a dependency which was also an oriental polity became clear once the principles of Mill were disavowed, and it was recognised that England was a 'belligerent' civilisation in India, and that she could attain her political objectives there only by refusing to share power with any indigenous group. The Government of India, Stephen argued, was

essentially absolute Government, founded not on consent, but on conquest. It does not represent the native principles of Government, nor can it do so unless it represents heathenism and barbarism. It represents a 'belligerent civilisation', and no anomaly can be so startling or so dangerous as its administration by men who, being at the head of a government founded on conquest, implying at every point the superiority of the conquering race, of their ideas, institutions, their opinions, and their principles, and having no justification for its existence except that superiority, shrink from the open, uncompromising, straightforward assertion of it, seek to apologise for their own position, and refuse, for whatever cause, to uphold and support it.[47]

Stephen was convinced that British rule over India was based on principles which were different from, and opposed to, the principles of government in England. These principles hinged on the assertion by the British Government of absolute power. Stephen further argued that absolutism was a legitimate form of government in itself, and not a stage leading to popular democracy, as was assumed by the liberals in India. In justifying British rule over India, the liberals argued that the exercise of absolute power could be justified only as a means to educate the people of India in popular democracy, and in the use of representative institutions. 'I do not think', Stephen pontificated, 'that the *permanent existence* of such a government as ours in India need in itself be a bad thing; that we ought not to desire its permanence even if we can save it; and that the establishment of some kind of parliamentary system instead of it is an object which ought to be distinctly contemplated, and, as soon as it is practicable, carried out'.[48]

For Ranade the authoritarian principles of Stephen were anathema, since they condemned India to permanent servitude and deprived the British Government of a moral basis that could justify its presence in the country. Since Stephen's principles were shared by influential civilians in India, and by powerful politicians in England, their enunciation held implications that Ranade was quick to recognise. To neutralise the insidious influence exercised by Stephen's attack on the liberal position, he outlined his view of 'The True Foundations of British Rule in India'[49] in an article which appeared in an issue of *The Journal of the Poona Sarvajanik Sabha*. This article set forth a cogent expression of the liberal conception of the objectives of British rule, and it set out with remarkable foresight the process by which political power was ultimately transferred into Indian hands.

At the very outset Ranade attacked Stephen's doctrine of absolute power, and the 'practical inferences' Stephen drew from the application of this doctrine to the issues which confronted the British Government in India. It had been argued, Ranade observed, that since the British Government in India was founded on conquest, it should not hesitate to proclaim the superiority of the conquering race, and it ought not to limit its freedom of action by the opinions or the ideals of its Indian subjects. Both the inferences drawn by Stephen, however, were fallacious. If the culture of the ruling caste was superior to the culture of the subject race, then the ruling caste could quite legitimately assert its superiority over the latter, whether it had acquired power through conquest, or through the consent of the governed. But the superiority of the ruling élite did not invest it with the right to completely disregard the sentiments, or even the prejudices, of the subject people. Instead, it imposed on the rulers the responsibility of raising their level of culture. For his own part Ranade was ready to admit the superiority of European civilisation in some branches of human activity, and he proclaimed his willingness 'to receive, from our English rulers, the benefits of the new civilisation'. But the reasons which encouraged him to welcome the liberalising influence of British rule also convinced him that British authority over India could never be absolute or unquestioned:

[We] . . . have no objection [Ranade pointed out] to open and straightforward assertion of the superiority of Englishmen over us, in so far as such assertion is necessary for the spread amongst us of the higher civilisation of which English-men are the representatives. But on the other side, we say such assertion should not be uncompromising as Sir F. Stephen makes it – because it is essential to the spread of that civilisation that at many points it should proceed by way of compromise. . . .[50]

Ranade's opposition to the conservative position stemmed from his disapproval of the authoritarian principles which Stephen applied to the British Government in India, and from his dismay at Stephen's denial of any creative role to the new Brahmans whom he represented. In focusing attention on the dangers of absolute government, Ranade leaned heavily on the classic liberal indictment of authoritarianism. Stephen, he argued, had made a plea for absolute government on grounds of its ability to initiate reform with far greater efficiency than was possible for a government that was subject to the popular will. But was this supposition at all justified? Government, whether absolute or otherwise, was run by individuals who were fallible, and who had therefore to appraise and modify their policies according to the reactions of the enlightened sections of the community. For the British Government in India, so Ranade argued, the new Brahmans constituted the one and only link with the native community. While the great bulk of the population was ignorant and apathetic, a small but significant minority had learnt to appreciate Western values through the education it had received in the new schools and colleges, and as a result of the intellectual climate of the country under British rule. This minority was anxious to see representative institutions work in India, and it sought to apply rational principles to the development of the country. The new Brahmans could be taken into political partnership by the British Government in India with advantage both to the State and the community, and they would in course of time provide a base for the transfer of authority into Indian hands. Only by embarking upon such a policy could British rule in India justify itself, and successfully accomplish its civilising mission:

We dissent almost entirely [Ranade stated in conclusion] from the political principles which Mr Justice Stephen wishes to be prevailing in the government of this country. We consider these principles to be erroneous and of evil tendency. Our general conclusion is, that while the shell and husk .... which belong to the English constitution as it at present rests, may be and ought to be cast aside, the real kernel of it is as suitable in this country, as in the soil where it has had such beneficial growth. We agree, that even this essential portion of that constitution should not be introduced all of a sudden. Let each successive step that is taken be justified by the event before further progress is attempted. But however slowly we may move, however cautiously and circumspectly we may look about us at every step that we take, let our progress be towards the goal which is indicated by the constitution of the great kingdom with which we are now so closely associated as parts of the great empire in which the sun never sets....[51]

The debate in which Ranade participated as an antagonist of Sir Fitzjames Stephen, and the definition he gave to his political views, formed only one facet of his activities as a public figure. With his belief in the organic interdependence between the political, the social, the religious and the economic facets of a society, Ranade was convinced that it would be futile to place an exaggerated emphasis on the achievement of political objectives, to the exclusion of progress in other directions. To be meaningful and enduring, so he believed, progress had to embrace all fields of social activity, and it had to proceed at a uniform pace in all branches of human endeavour.

The insights which Ranade gained through his vision of progress as a comprehensive rather than a fragmented phenomenon, and the importance he attached to the intellectual climate which prevailed in a community, and shaped its values, are seen clearly in an article in which he spelt out 'The Exigencies of Progress in India'.[52] The first prerequisite for progress, he pointed out, was a belief in progress itself. For progress to be achieved, it had first to be desired. The revolution of rising expectations and the growing commitment to social mobility and economic growth were the two most fundamental changes in the climate of opinion in India under British rule. Prior to the British conquest, social values had encouraged the individual to acquiesce in the *status quo* rather than to improve his station in life:

Satisfied with an ancient civilisation [Ranade pointed out], we have never, in recent history endeavoured to fall in line with modern progress; nor, but for our education, it is likely that even now we should cherish any new ideal. Our ruin is attributable to our national apathy, lethargy and torpor, the direct result of past isolation and foreign conquests. The active impediments to progress are the inquisitorial power of religion, and the overpowering influence of custom and tradition, which have associated the highest ideal of happiness in our minds with inactivity and ease. While the western nations have striven to develop human energies and powers and to secure a mastery over physical nature, we have stood before the world with folded hands, a picture of helplessness and despair, but in dutiful veneration of everything pertaining to the past, and yielding ourselves in placid contentment to the guidance of antiquated usages, and to rules of conduct which regulated social life before the dawn of modern civilisation.[53]

If a commitment to values which placed a premium on order and stability had retarded the development of India, how, Ranade raised the question, could the progress of the country be ensured? The most important attribute of a progressive society was a rational approach to economic activity. Reduced to its bare essentials, a modern community was one in which every person was constantly striving to improve his status through rational effort. In this perennial quest for self-improvement there was no place for romanticism; and even where this quality was not wholly eliminated, it was subordinated to the achievement of practical ends. Science and rationality were the foundations of modern society; and as seminal influences they played the same role in modern society as faith and religion had played in the earlier stages of human history.

Since the key to progress lay in rational action, and in the substitution of reason for superstition, Ranade's attempt to effect a religious revival was geared to the promotion of such changes in the intellectual climate of Maharashtra. Alone among the new Brahmans of his generation, he discerned the implications of the rise of protestantism in Europe; alone also of his contemporaries, he recognised the upsurge of creative energy which had reinvigorated the West through the spread of the idea of individual responsibility to God, and through the dissemination of an ethic which promised spiritual fulfilment through dedication to a calling in the secular world. The spread of protestantism in Europe had prepared the ground for progress through creating a social and intellectual climate which undermined the medieval world. The *bhakti* saints of Maharashtra, so Ranade believed, had attempted to stimulate similar changes, and they stood for ideals and objectives identical to those that had inspired the religious reformers of medieval Europe:

There is an curious parallel [Ranade pointed out] between the history of the Reformation movement in Western Europe, and the struggle represented by the lives and teachings and writings of these saints and prophets. . . . The European reformers of the sixteenth century protested strongly against the authority claimed by the priests and clergy with the Roman bishop at their head. . . . The reformation in western India had its counterpart in this respect. Ancient authority and tradition had been petrified there, not in an ambitious Bishop and his clergy, but in the monopoly of the Brahmin caste, and it was against the exclusive spirit of this caste domination that the saints and prophets struggled most manfully to protest. They asserted the dignity of the human soul as residing in it quite independently of the accidents of its birth and social rank.[54]

Ranade's critique of the *bhakti* movement is more convincing as an exposition of the religious values which he sought to propagate in Maharashtra, than as an appraisal of the social objectives which inspired the leaders of the *bhakti* movement. In their attitude towards the religious establishment and towards spiritual privileges which were arbitrary and devoid of any utility, the protestant reformers of Europe resembled the *bhakti* saints of Maharashtra. But the protestant emphasis on the worthiness of the secular life, and on the possibility of salvation through commitment to a calling in the secular world, were conspicuous by their absence in the teachings of the *bhakti* saints. The leaders of the *bhakti* movement were primarily interested in disseminating the values of Hinduism (which had till then remained confined to the Brahman castes) among the lower and middle castes through expressing them in a language, and in an idiom, comprehensible to the common people. They sought to create social cohesion by directing the allegiance of the various castes to a common corpus of religious values. Whether Ranade (like many a reformer before him) deliberately misinterpreted the objectives of the *bhakti* saints is difficult to say. What is unmistakable is that he desired to create in Maharashtra the same intellectual climate which he believed had set European society on the path to progress and prosperity.

Such were the values of the 'Hindu Protestantism'[55] which Ranade preached from the platform of the *Prarthana Samaj*, a religious society which he launched in association with new Brahmans like Dadoba Pandurang and R. G. Bhandarkar, to reconcile Hinduism to the spirit of progress, and to cleanse it of the irrationality that had presumably come to disfigure it over the period of time. While rejecting the philosophy of Sankara as a principle whose arid intellectual quality left the emotional roots of the individual untouched, Ranade acknowledged his debt to *advaita* through attributing the creation of the universe, and the existence of man, to a single and omnipotent God. 'There are not many Gods, nor a hierarchy of Gods, nor deified good and bad powers, nor principles of light and darkness, of matter and spirit, of Prakriti or Maya and Purusha. God is One and without a second and not many persons – not a triad, nor a duality of persons',[56] he asserted in *A Theist's Confession of Faith*. Ranade saw this Being in the compassionate God of the *bhakti* saints, in whose praise Ekanatha and Namdeva and Tukarama had composed their *abhangas*, and who could be reached more readily through devotion than through intellectual inquiry.

Because of the ideas which influenced his approach to social problems, and convinced him of the inevitability of progress, in reinterpreting Hinduism Ranade saw himself rationalising trends within Hindu society, rather than imposing alien values upon it. Nor was such a view unjustified; for all around him he saw changes stemming from the interaction between the traditional society of Maharashtra and the values which the new rulers interjected into its social climate. As early as 1821 the Poona Brahmans had split into conflicting camps over the readmission into the community of a caste-fellow called Gangadhar Dixit Phadke, who had defied custom by residing in Bombay for a short interval. The conservative and liberal factions within the Brahman community had clashed even more violently when Shivprasad Seshadri, a convert to Christianity, had indicated a desire to be readmitted into the Brahman fold. In 1840, barely two decades after the British conquest, a society was launched by a group of Brahmans along masonic principles to propagate the abolition of caste. A more important landmark in the spread of Western and liberal values was the founding in 1848 by young Brahman students of a *Literary and Scientific Society* which served as a forum for the discussion and dissemination of radical ideas. The members of this society were associated with social reform, and they tried to promote the emancipation of women. Encouraged by their initial success in liberalising the institution of caste, and in promoting the education of women, the liberal Brahmans launched in the 1870s an attack on the interdict upon the remarriage of widows. The habits of thought which the liberals encountered in their attempt to promote the remarriage of widows were far too deeply entrenched to be shaken by a single assault. But Vishnu Shastri Pandit, the leader of the radical Brahmans, had the satisfaction of debating the issue publicly with Shri Shankaracharya, the spiritual head of the *Advaitists*; and even though the Hindu pontiff decreed the marriage of widows to be against the letter and the spirit of the *Shastras*, his participation in the debate reflected the deep concern of the orthodox community over the rapidly changing intellectual climate of Maharashtra.[57]

Yet Ranade did not permit his belief in social evolution to blind him to the need for organised action, or to convert him to the view that the ferment at work within Hindu society would spontaneously ensure its development along the right lines. He dismissed the conviction of some new Brahmans in the spontaneity of social change as being compounded in equal parts of 'apathy' and intellectual 'sophistry'; and he argued that change came about only through the active assertion of their will by the liberal sections of the community. It was important for the liberals to promote change actively along desirable channels, and there was no assurance that this would come about spontaneously. Ranade's concept of a liberal élite in the role of a social catalyst was enunciated with great clarity by one of his followers in the field of social reform:

Though a state of transition [stated N.G.Chandavarkar] such as that through which our Hindu society is passing is inevitable under the present conditions . . . we should not declude ourselves with the belief that a period of mere scepticism . . . without any inward impetus or conviction must necessarily and unconditionally give way to a better period in the long run. When a society is being disintegrated . . . no hope of a better integration of it can be held unless there are found even in the midst of the forces that disintegrate it 'organic filaments' or forces which promise to bring the disturbed elements together, and reunite the different and dispersing elements of society on a better and higher principle of life. It is in the formation of those 'organic filaments' that the work and value of the social reformer lies; while the forces around us are slowly loosening our faith in the old . . . , the social reformer has to bring those very forces to his aid and show the way to the formation of a new faith, a new ideal, and a new bond, which shall enable society to enter into a higher and richer form of life, instead of being disorganised.[58]

Equally vital to social progress (as the notion of a leading élite) was Ranade's view of reform as a process which altered values and institutions slowly and gradually.[59] Both his conservative cast of mind, and his commitment to social theories which set a premium on evolution, as opposed to revolution, led him to the view that the advocates of drastic change only harmed the course of progress, and the community which they tried to serve. Ranade was fully conscious of the obstacles in the path of cautious reform. But to assume a contrary course of action, he argued, could well prove disastrous. The reformer had to 'accept the teachings of the evolutionary doctrine . . ., because they teach that growth is structural and organic, and must take slow effect in all parts of the organism...'.[60] The supreme illusion, Ranade pointed out, was the belief that the reformer had to write on a clean slate. Nothing could be further from the truth; for his work was to 'complete the half-written sentence. . . . [and] to produce the ideal out of the actual, and by the help of the actual'. Fortunately, for the reformer in Hindu society the task of maintaining links with tradition presented no serious difficulty. Hinduism had shown remarkable flexibility in the past; and there was no reason to believe that Hindu society had lost this quality in the nineteenth century. It was possible for the liberal Hindu to look upon tradition for guidance; just as it was possible for him to relate the present to the past in a spirit of true catholicity. It was also possible for him to hold in high regard the essence of the *shastras*, though he might on occasion violate their letter. Such was the spirit which inspired Ranade to ally himself with B. M. Malabari in the debate which the Parsi reformer initiated in 1886 through his *Notes on Infant Marriage and Enforced Widowhood*. A similar logic impelled him to seek in the *shastras* and the sacred texts support for the measures of reform proposed by Malabari.[62]

Ranade's desire to create a modern society in Maharashtra without weakening the ties of interest, and the bonds of sentiment, between different castes and social groups provides the key to his social ideals and his political objectives. He fully realised that the *bhakti* movement had mitigated social tensions in Maharashtra to such an extent that 'caste exclusiveness finds no place in the religious sphere of life, and is relegated solely to the social concerns of men, and even there its restrictiveness is much relaxed, as any one can judge who compares [the caste feelings of] the Brahmins of South India . . . with the comparative indifference shown in such matters in the Deccan portion of Maharashtra'.[63] This realisation prompted him to reject the politics of extremism, and to oppose religious movements like the *Brahma Samaj*, whose members alienated themselves from the community because of their radical views on religious and social reform.[64] The loyalties which held together the fabric of society in Maharashtra, and which Ranade was above all things anxious to preserve, impressed themselves forcibly even on a visitor like the Russian traveller I. P. Minayeff, who journeyed extensively in India in the 1880s, and was struck by the intellectual climate of Poona and Bombay. Minayeff noticed how the radical Brahman student of the Deccan College 'admire(d) Spencer and at the same time is devoted to spiritualism'; and how in any discussion on the state of society and the nature of politics with the Brahman intelligentsia, the problems of the *kunbi* occupied a pre-eminence which they rarely did elsewhere.[65]

Both in politics and in social reform Ranade sought to modernise Maharashtra without disrupting the ties of interest and sentiment which linked classes and castes together in a close relationship. Ranade's vision did not reflect any explicit concern for the maintenance of Brahman predominance; nor did it reserve for the Brahman castes a dominant role in society. Notions of caste exclusiveness, and caste superiority and caste monopolisation of social roles had no place in his vision of the future. But because he wanted to usher Maharashtra into the age of rationality and progress without exposing the social fabric to any strain; and because the Brahmans occupied a position of superiority in the community, the changes which Ranade advocated would have left (for some time at any rate) the predominance of the Brahman castes unaffected. Any attempt to undermine this predominance artificially would have struck Ranade as morally reprehensible and incompatible with orderly progress. Thus when in 1884 the Government of Bombay attempted to raise the level of education among the lower and middle castes by reserving scholarships for them in the various schools and colleges, the *Sarvajanik Sabha* launched a bitter campaign under Ranade's aegis against what was characterised as an act of discrimination against the Brahman community.[66]

However, since the notions of progress and rationality propagated by Ranade challenged the traditional values of Hinduism, and the beliefs which sustained the institution of caste, they were bound to undermine the social and intellectual preponderance of the Brahman castes. The implications of Ranade's ideas were clear to the old style *shastris* and pandits, whose grip over positions of power was in any event being undermined by changes in the political scene. The orthodox community therefore opposed Ranade's social ideals and political objectives as subversive of the traditional order, and of Brahman supremacy over society. Its reaction to liberalism and Westernisation was voiced by the deputation of Poona *shastris* headed by Rama Shastri Apte, which apprised Sir James Fergusson, the Governor of Bombay, in 1886 of the strong disapproval with which it would view interference in the social and religious life of the Hindu community along the lines suggested by the advocates of reform. 'According to the Hindu *shastras* marriage was a religious institution regulated by strict rules and injunctions. . .', Rama Shastri told Fergusson, and no 'good government has yet interfered with our religious laws and customs. . . .'[67]

Because of the opposition of the traditional leaders of the Brahman community, and because of the implications of the changes he advocated in Hindu society, Ranade's programme of reform did not commend him to the majority of the Brahmans of Maharashtra. Despite the catholicity of his vision; the insight he possessed into contemporary society; and the incisive rationality of his schemes of social and economic reform, Ranade attracted support from only a small section of the Brahman community whose dominance over Hindu society remained unshaken till the closing decades of the nineteenth century. But the tragedy of the new Brahmans did not lie in their failure to influence the Brahman rank and file. Their tragedy lay in their inability to win over to their side the middle and lower castes of Hindu society. The *Sarvajanik Sabha*, which was created by the new Brahmans to provide an institutional basis for their power, did attempt to lead rural discontent against the Government of Bombay in the 1870s. But this attempt remained an isolated bid on their part to win peasant support for their policies; and apart from the 'no-tax' campaign which preceded the Deccan Riots of 1875, and which was partly inspired by the cadres of the *Sarvajanik Sabha*, the new Brahmans were unable to make any impression on the kunbis whose cause they espoused with such integrity and skill. Their failure to do so robbed them of the role of leadership which they were meant to fulfil by administrators like Mountstuart Elphinstone.

NOTES

1   Petition of 800 Brahmans to the Bombay Government dated 4 November 1836, General Department (hereinafter GD), Vol. 15/305 of 1837, Bombay State Archives (hereinafter BA).

2   H.D.Robertson to W.Chaplin dated 10 December 1823: reproduced in R.D.Choksey, *The Aftermath*, Bombay 1950, pp. 220–5.

3   See A.Steele, *Summary of the Customs and Laws of Hindoo Castes Within the Dekhun Provinces of Bombay*, Bombay 1827. Steele's account is based on information obtained from the *Shastris* of Poona and from the various caste leaders in the city.

4   Minute by Mountstuart Elphinstone in G.W.Forrest, ed., *Selections From the Minutes and other Official Writings of the Honourable Mountstuart Elphinstone*, pp. 334–5.

5   Address by W. Chaplin on the opening of the Poona Hindu College dated 10 April 1821: GD, Vol. 10 of 1821, BA.

6   Minute by Mountstuart Elphinstone dated nil, GD, Vol. 8/63 of 1824, BA.

7   W.Chaplin to Bombay Government dated 24 November 1821, GD, Vol. 10 of 1821, BA.

8   J.H.Baber, Collector of Poona, to Bombay Government dated 31 October 1834, GD, Vol. 8/303 of 1836, BA.

9   Report submitted by the Committee for the Reorganisation of the Hindu College to the Bombay Government dated 29 October 1835, GD, Vol. 17/349 of 1836, BA.

10 Minute by Robert Grant, Governor of Bombay, dated 22 March 1835, GD, Vol. 17/349 of 1836, BA.

11 Report by Reverend J.Stevenson dated 28 November 1836, GD, Vol. 39/409 of 1837; also see Memorandum by W.H.Wathen, Chief Secretary to the Bombay Government, dated December 1836: GD, Vol. 39/409 of 1837, BA.

12 J.H.Baber, Collector of Poona to Bombay Government dated 8 November 1834, GD, Vol. 6/301 of 1835, BA.

13 Report submitted by the Committee for the Reorganisation of the Dakshina dated 20 September 1836: GD, Vol. 17/349 of 1836, BA.

14 Petition by the Brahmans of Poona to the Bombay Government dated 4 November 1836, GD, Vol. 15/385 of 1837, BA.

15 Ibid.

16 Bombay Government to the Collector of Poona dated 19 January 1837, GD, Vol. 15/385 of 1837, BA.

17 See Petition by the Brahmans of Poona, Wai, Satara, etc. dated 19 January 1838, GD, Vol. 9/526 of 1840. Also see Petition by 300 Brahmans of Poona to Bombay Government dated 2 November 1849, GD, Vol. 26 of 1850, BA.

18 Petition by the liberal Brahmans of Poona to the Bombay Government dated September 1849, GD, Vol. 16, of 1849, BA.

19 Ibid.

20 Petition by the Students of the Government English School dated 23 October 1849, GD, Vol. 26 of 1850, BA.

21 Memorandum by J.G.Lumsden, Secretary to the Bombay Government, dated January 1850, GD, Vol. 26 of 1850, BA.

22 Ibid.

23 R.V.Parulekar, *Selections From The Records of The Bombay Government*, Education, Part I, 1819–1852, Bombay 1953, pp. xx to xxv.

24 *Report of the Director of Public Instructions in Bombay for 1857–58.*

25 *Report of the Board of Education of Bombay for 1850–51.*

26 Parulekar, op. cit., p. xlviii.

27 Petition by 500 Brahmans of Poona, Satara, Wai, et., dated 13 December 1849, Judicial Department (hereinafter JD), Vol. 16 of 1849, BA.

28 Petition by 1180 Merchants of Surat to the Bombay Government dated 24 April 1827, JD, Vol. 20/146 of 1827, BA.

29 Memorandum by Dr Gibson enclosed in letter from Sir R.K.Arbuthnot, Collector of Surat, to Bombay Government dated 31 August 1844, Political and Secret Department (hereinafter P & SD), Vol. 92/1625 of 1844, BA.

30 Letters from A.Remington, Judge of Surat, to Bombay Government dated 30 August, 31 August and 2 September 1844, P & SD, Vol. 92/1625 of 1844, BA.

31 Letter from Sheikh Sharif to R.K.Arbuthnot dated 30 August 1844, P & SD, Vol. 92/1625 of 1844, BA.

32 Letter from R.K.Arbuthnot to Bombay Government dated 3 September 1844, P & SD, Vol. 92/1625 of 1844, BA.

33 Letter from R.K. Arbuthnot to Sheikh Sharif dated 30 August 1844, P & SD, Vol. 92/1625 of 1844, BA.

34 Quoted in 'The Mandlik School' by N.G.Chandavarkar: *The Speeches and Writings of Sir Narayen G.Chandavarkar*, Bombay 1911, pp. 32–8.

35 I am indebted to Mrs Indira Rothermund for a biographical note on Gopal Hari Deshmukh, and for translations from the *Satapatren*, on which this paragraph is based. Also see article entitled 'Pioneers of the Reform Movement in Maharashtra' from unpublished source material available with *Bombay State Committee for the History of the Freedom Movement in India* (hereinafter *BSCHFM*).

36 Based on a biographical note on V.N.Mandlik by D.G.Padhya in *Writings And Speeches of Vishwanath Narayan Mandlik*, Bombay 1911, pp. 32–8.

37 *Vide* note 34.

38 *Vide* article entitled 'Note on the Life and Work of G.V.Joshi in unpublished source material available with *BSCHFM*.

39 See *Source Material For A History Of The Freedom Movement In India* (1885–1920), II, Bombay 1958, pp. 1–10.

40 Quoted in D.M.Limaye, *The History of the Deccan Education Society* (Poona 1835), p. 19.

41 J.Kellock, *Mahadev Govind Ranade*, Calcutta 1926, Chapters I and II, *passim*.

42 *Vide Education Commission, Bombay*, Vol. 1, Report of the Bombay Provincial Committee, Calcutta 1884, p. 136.

43 *Vide* the *Hindustan Times* (New Delhi), 8 July 1962.

44 Quoted from a speech given by M.G.Ranade in the Prarthana Samaj; *The Mahratta*, 11 December 1887.

45 See E.Stokes, *The English Utilitarians and India*, Oxford 1959, pp. 273–98. Also see J.F.Stephen, *Liberty, Equality, Fraternity*, London 1874, for Stephen's attack on John Stuart Mill.

46 J.F.Stephen, 'The True Foundations of the Government of India', in *Nineteenth Century*, Vol. XIV, 1883.

47 Ibid.

48 Ibid.

49 M.G.Ranade, 'The True Foundations of the Government of India', *Quarterly Journal of the Poona Sarvajanik Sabha* (hereinafter *JPSS*), April 1894. This article does not appear under Ranade's name, but can be attributed to him on stylistic grounds.

50 Ibid.

51 Ibid.

52 M.G.Ranade, 'The Exigencies of Progress in India', *JPSS*, April 1893. This article again does not appear under Ranade's name, but can be attributed to him on stylistic grounds.

53 Ibid.

54 M.G.Ranade, 'The Saints and Prophets of Maharashtra', in *Rise of the Maratha Power*, Bombay 1901, reprinted in 1961, pp. 66–7.

55 The term 'Hindu Protestantism' is used by N.G Chandavarkar to describe the teachings of the *Prarthana Samaj*.

56 Quoted in Kellock, op. cit., pp. 168–9.

57 N.G.Chandavarkar, 'The Forces at Work (Within) Hindu Society', in *Times of India* (Bombay), 8 December 1887. Also see M.G.Ranade's speech before the *Prarthana Samaj* reprinted in *The Mahratta*, 11 September 1887. For a brief review of social reform movement in Maharashtra see speech by N.G.Chandavarkar before the Bombay Provincial Social Conference in 1901 reproduced in his *Speeches and Writings etc.*, pp. 92–6.

58 From N.G.Chandavarkar's speech on Social Reform delivered on 28 November 1896: *Speeches and Writings etc.*, pp. 62–3.

59 From M.G.Ranade's speech on Social Evolution before the Indian Social Conference 1892, *Miscellaneous Writings of the Justice M.G. Ranade*, Bombay 1895, pp. 114–21.

60 Ibid., p. 118.

61 From M.G.Ranade's speech on 'The Past History of Social Reform' before the Indian Social Conference of 1894, *Writings of Ranade*, etc., pp. 133–42.

62 M.G.Ranade, 'The Sutras and Smriti Dicta on the Age of Hindu Marriage', in *JPSS*, April 1891.

63 M.G.Ranade, 'The Saints and Prophets of Maharashtra', in *Rise of the Maratha Power*, loc. cit.

64 Address by M.G.Ranade to the Indian Social Conference of 1895, *Writings of Ranade etc.*, p. 151.

65 I.P.Minayeff, *Travels in and Diaries of India and Burma* (Trans. by S.Bhattacharya), Calcutta n.d., pp. 49, 52–3.

66 *The Mahratta* dated 20 September 1885; *The Kesari* dated 29 September 1885; *The Bombay Chronicle* dated 27 September 1885; *The Din Bandhu* dated 10 December 1885.

67 *The Mahratta* dated 10 October 1886.

5

EMANCIPATION OR RE-INTEGRATION. THE POLITICS OF GOPAL KRISHNA GOKHALE AND HERBERT HOPE RISLEY*

★

Dietmar Rothermund

National liberty and imperial order were the contending ideas that influenced the minds of men in India at the turn of the nineteenth century. Indian nationalists cherished the vision of India's bright political future; British administrators emphasised the precarious situation of the Indian society which could be saved from chaos only by an orderly reconstruction within the framework of imperial government. These conflicting views were brought into clear focus by the discussion about the representation of the Indian people in the course of the first major constitutional reform in India in 1909. Gopal Krishna Gokhale, the leading spokesman of the Indian nationalists in those crucial years, and Herbert Hope Risley, the Home Secretary to the Government of India, who piloted the constitutional reforms through the various stages of draft proposals, committees and debates, were excellent representatives of these two contending schools of thought. They were not only among the main actors of the contemporary political scene in India, but they were also its best analysts and commentators. In this chapter an attempt is made to outline their ideas as well as to trace their influence on the actual development of the constitutional reforms. The first part of this chapter is devoted to their different assessments of India's social and political situation; these assessments are described within the conceptual

* G. K. Gokhale, 1866-1915, Professor, Fergusson College, Poona. Member of the Legislative Council, Bombay Presidency, and of the Imperial Legislative Council. Secretary and President (1905) of the Indian National Congress.

Sir H. H. Risley 1857-1911, Civil Service career in Bengal. On special duty: survey of the tribes and castes of Bengal (1888). Secretary to the Government of Bengal. Census Commissioner of India (1901). Secretary to Government of India, Home Department. Appointed Permanent Under-Secretary, India Office, London (1911).

framework of alternative directions of social development. The second part contains an analysis of Gokhale's and Risley's role in the preparation of the constitutional reforms of 1909 with special reference to Gokhale's advocacy of territorial representation and Risley's emphasis on a representation of interests. The last part, taking Gokhale's 'Political Testament' as a point of departure, provides a survey of the subsequent constitutional development of India, emphasising the predominant problems of nationality and representation.

I

The standards and values by which men identify their role in a social context and the type of authority which they exercise or acknowledge depend on the general course of social evolution. Sir Henry Maine tried to characterise this course of social evolution by pointing out that the foundations of social relations change from status to contract. But this formula bears the stamp of a legal mind and emphasises the symptoms rather than the causes of social change. The terms integration and emancipation may indicate in a more comprehensive manner the alternatives of social organisation. Integration, as defined in Talcott Parsons'[1] 'pattern variables', stands for a social system which is governed by ascribed and particularistic values, as against the universalist and achievement-orientated value system of an emancipated society. The role of an individual in an integrated system is determined by a code of conduct which provides him with a well-defined identity at every stage and station of life. The Indian system of *varnashramadharma* which regulates the duty (*dharma*) of every man according to his caste (*varna*) and age-grade (*ashrama*) is an ideal example of integration. The emancipated individual, however, is not provided with such a blue-print of the good life. His identity has to be established again and again under varying circumstances and his individuality may be severely strained by the very fact that it is the only common denominator of a random selection of diverse identities. The relationship between authority and identity which moulds the style and consensus of social and political life, is very different in an integrated society from that in an emancipated society. In an integrated system the degree of authority which is wielded or accepted by the individual is directly related to his identity, or, if one may say so, every individual is authorised by his identity and identifiable by the social, religious or political authority vested in him. In an emancipated society, however, the authority exercised by an individual may concern only one of his many identities, e.g. his roles as a father, a citizen, an employee, etc. are distinct and compartmentalised. From this it follows that there will be different codes of conduct for different roles. In the field of public authority this means the rule of law and not of men, which may nevertheless manifest itself in a rule of men who represent the law, i.e. the bureaucrat and the elected representative.

In British India the transition from the indigenous integrated pattern to a new system of public authority in an emancipated society was beset with many problems. In general, social systems develop as a whole, and even in cases of cultural borrowing, assimilation, migration, conquest, and other instances of interference, the impact enters into the system and becomes one of the factors of change or retardation, but does not remain a distinct phenomenon for any length of time. The colonial rule of European powers over Asian and African peoples, however, is a striking example of system-symbiosis, as one may call it, because as in a symbiotic relationship, two different systems maintained a constant but limited contact over a long period of time without losing their distinctive features. The members of an emancipated society came to play a crucial role in the control and development of societies which had still retained most of the elements of integration. As Gokhale once put it when speaking of the British administrators in India:

... man for man they are better men than ourselves, they have a higher standard of duty, higher notions of patriotism, higher notions of loyalty to each other, higher notions of organised work and of discipline, and they know how to make a stand for the privileges of which they are in possession. We have no right to complain that they are what they are.[2]

This generous and realistic appraisal did not prevent Gokhale from deprecating the forces of 'racial ascendancy' and from deploring the 'continuous dwarfing or stunting of our race'[3] that was taking place under British rule. The crux of the matter was that the emancipated men who had entrenched themselves in the positions of power and privilege in India were in no position to emancipate the Indians. The system-symbiosis could only be maintained if everybody remained in his place.

The political control which was exercised by the British–Indian government over a vast territory with a relatively small cadre of officials was embedded in the indigenous pattern of authority. In the traditional social order of India, government was a sectional and a transient matter, limited in its scope by the autonomous structure of communal life. The foreign control of government was not therefore very obtrusive as long as the government did not challenge or undermine the established order. But by being and remaining foreign the government was bound to be both more consistently aggressive and more rigid and inflexible than an indigenous government would have been. Its conduct was informed by alien values, its officers were inspired and united by a sense of integrity that had its point of reference beyond the seas, and its laws and policies effected a cultural change which upset the old pattern of authority. At first this was hardly perceived, because the change was of generational dimensions, and its manifestations, wherever they were noticed, appeared to the contemporary observer as isolated instances of disorder. But at the end of the nineteenth century social and economic forces produced a kind of cumulative effect which could not be ignored. Famines, peasant indebtedness, a growing population, the rise of an indigenous educated class, problems of administrative efficiency and over-centralisation were seen as symptoms of a fundamental change.

The perception of social and cultural change gives rise to different interpretations of its merits. An advance toward social emancipation may be regarded as a step towards disintegration. The most acute observers of social change are often those who would prescribe a therapy of re-integration. The enemies of the open society are usually its best analysts, because it is apprehension rather than appreciation that sharpens the vision. By the end of the nineteenth century the official mind in India was very apprehensive indeed. Many of the officials were prepared to abjure everything for which British rule had stood so far. Freedom of contract, the doctrines of political economy, liberal education, were now considered to be unsuitable to the Indian empire. In the face of mounting population pressure many officials wasted their time on historical disquisitions on customary agrarian relations as a guide to remedial legislation. Custom reigned supreme as the lodestar of bewildered alien 'guardians'. They were even more irritated therefore when they found themselves challenged by an indigenous educated élite that did not fit into the customary cultural background. As this background was no longer static any attempt at putting the upstart educated élite in its place had to be based on some idea of what this place ought to be. Nationalists and 'guardians' would agree that a reconstruction of the Indian body politic was required but they would differ with regard to their recommendations.

This was the setting for the thoughts and actions of Gopal Krishna Gokhale and Herbert Hope Risley. These two men were never actually confronted in a political debate. They rarely met. Their spheres of action were separated by the prevailing code of conduct. Both of them were outstanding men and as such they did not represent the average Indian and British attitudes of their day. But they were perhaps the most perceptive and articulate participants in the interaction of the two social systems at that time. Their opinions and decisions provide a focus for the analysis of this interaction in the realm of imperial policy. Neither Gokhale nor Risley had a complete grasp of the social reality of India at their time. They had to some extent a common background because their thought was based on Western political ideas. John Stuart Mill and the whole spectrum of nineteenth-century British political philosophy were parts of their universe of discourse. Gokhale was the more orthodox British liberal, whereas Risley was deeply affected by the conservatism of the German historical school to which he owed his appreciation of traditional patterns of social and political life. Both Gokhale and Risley therefore did not look at India in terms of indigenous standards. Their vision was determined by conflicting Western theories. Consequently they often appeared to be out of touch with the reality of their environment. Even so they made a major impact on the political development of India at a crucial time.

Gokhale emerged in the first decade of the twentieth century as the main spokesman of the Indian National Congress and the leader of the permanent opposition in the Imperial Legislative Council, while Risley reached at the same time the peak of his civil service career as Home Secretary to the Government of India and trusted advisor to the Viceroy in constitutional affairs. Both men were not true to their type in their respective spheres. Risley was an intellectual in a service in which an overdose of intellectual ability made a man suspect since it was considered to be an impediment to that virile stamina and decisiveness which was the mark of the genuine colonial administrator.[4] As Gokhale attested: 'Risley approached every question from the standpoint of a scholar and a thinker.'[5] His closely reasoned notes are some of the best state papers produced under the British Raj in India, and the weight of his arguments could not easily be resisted. Gokhale was known for a similar thoroughness, and as the first full-time politician of modern India, he set a high standard. He was not an orator and agitator who would rouse his own people but rather an eloquent pleader for the good cause of Indian aspirations, trying to influence British official and public opinion. His case could not rest on political power. He had to rely on whatever impression he could make by marshalling incontrovertible facts and figures and presenting convincing arguments which would captivate the minds of those in power. In this respect the political worlds of Gokhale and Risley were very much alike. They both operated in a restricted sphere; but while the restrictions of bureaucratic policy-making were the natural elements of Risley's career, Gokhale suffered from the stunting effect of the colonial straitjacket.

Gokhale belonged to a dominant minority, the Chitpavan Brahmans of Maharashtra. He came from a poor family, but he inherited the ambitions and the claim to leadership of his community. Yet he himself did not derive the right to leadership from this claim but rather from the hard-earned merit of a long political apprenticeship under his great master Justic Mahadev Govind Ranade. From him he had learnt not to cast his ambitions in a narrow communal mould but to devote his life to a rational and universalist patriotism. Ranade was opposed to all facile forms of revivalism even if they appeared under the respectable guise of Vedanta or Theosophy, because they tended to blunt the feeling for right and consistent action which could only emanate from a burning puritanism.[6] This type of puritanism was the mainspring of Gokhale's political convictions. To him the emancipation of the Indian people was an arduous process of political education. It was not to be achieved by simply breaking the spell of foreign rule and asserting the birthright of national independence, but by a slow progress toward social and economic as well as political maturity. The Western impact was the foundation of this progress, and the British Empire was the framework for the construction of a modern political society in India. The principal political questions were how to co-ordinate the growth of this political society with the evolution of the Empire; how to prevent disparities and how to ward off reactionaries at home and abroad. In this spirit Gokhale founded the Servants of India Society which was designed to provide a band of selfless patriotic workers, disciplined by a long political apprenticeship, which would be able to give coherence and continuity to the public life of India. Gokhale's vision was directed towards the future and not towards the revival of some glorious past. This vision could be challenged by nationalists like Tilak[7] to whom the Indian nation was a living presence, and by those observers of the Indian scene who saw the heterogeneity of India's communities, and therefore rejected the dreams of the educated élite and denied the national unity of India.

Risley was one of the keenest observers of India's infinitely complex social structure. He was the founder of Indian ethnology.[8] While serving the Bengal Government he did the field work for his first major publication on the castes and tribes of Bengal. Later, as Census Commissioner, he was able to collect data on an All-India scale. He also devoted much attention to physical anthropology and tried to arrive at some theory of the racial structure of Indian society. These preoccupations entered into his general assessment of social and political life in India. As early as 1890 he had stated his political views in a terse form in an article on 'The Race Basis of Indian Political Movements'.[9] He stressed the role of caste in Indian history and the imitative transmission of culture, the lower castes always trying to adapt themselves to the rules of the higher ones. He emphasised the relationship of caste and monarchy, the king acting as an arbiter and keeping the claims of different castes in balance; and he feared that under a democratic system the castes might serve as a caucus, and rival castes might compete for power as political machines, imposing discipline by social ostracism. At the same time he diagnosed the growing national sentiment as a preoccupation of the upper castes, and while appreciating the aspirations of the educated class he warned against the creation of a literate oligarchy which would not foster genuine self-government. Having visited Prussia on behalf of the Bengal Government[10] in order to study local self-government[10] Risley praised the Prussian example in the concluding part of his article and reported:

> There a bureaucratic system bearing a surprisingly close resemblance to that prevalent in India has been leavened by the infusion of an elective element. . . . The elective village headmen whose powers had fallen into disuse have been revived with the best effect and a system of communal and provincial councils has been introduced. . . .

Accordingly he recommended a revival of the Indian village councils (*panchayats*),[11] which should have quasi-judicial powers and their own revenue. In this way he hoped the officially discredited *panchayat* would rise once more in dignity and influence. And he added:

> The personal law of a large number of castes is at present administered solely by their councils and much interesting custom has by this means been preserved. Once let the village council be made a reality and the leading men of these caste councils will seek election to it. It will thus assume the representative character which at present is wanting . . . [and] the villagers would cease to be a mere mob of individuals.

This association of existing social institutions at the village level with the advance towards representative government was Risley's main concern. He saw that representative institutions must be granted to India since Britain had decided 'to govern India by British rather than by Asiatic methods', but he felt that the basic problem was the construction of the political society on which such representative institutions could be built. Who should be enfranchised so as to create a truly representative cross-section of Indian political interests? Risley was sceptical about the use of those electorates that existed at that time:

Anyone with a turn for constitution making can construct abundant voting apparatus out of municipal institutions, but a franchise framed on this basis would leave the landed interests practically unrepresented, on the other hand a wider franchise may give undue leverage to caste organisations....

These caste organisations he considered to be dangerous on a larger territorial scale because of the absence of an informed public opinion in India which could keep political bosses and machines in check. At the most this type of public opinion could operate within the narrow confines of the village community. Accordingly Risley stressed the functions of caste organisations at that level but deprecated their activities in a wider sphere. 'Government by social ostracism' seemed to be tolerable in small communities which should be rescued from the fate of being 'mere mobs of individuals'. It would become dangerous only when it transcended these limits and entered the realm of large-scale political strife.

Risley adopted the general attitude of the 'guardian' towards political emancipation which he saw as being accompanied by a disorderly and indecent struggle for power. To him representative government did not mean an arena in which various forces should contend for leadership. He wanted it to be a faithful replica of the complex social structure. In this respect his thought reflected the theories of John Stuart Mill who had conceived of representative government as a microcosm of the society. But as an administrator who was primarily interested in the efficiency of government, Risley had additional reasons for deprecating the struggle for power and looking at the strata of society which ought to be represented from a functional point of view. When he had to deal with new legislation for the Calcutta Municipal Corporation in the early days of Lord Curzon's régime he expressed his disapproval of the narrow oligarchy of the educated class which treated the municipality as a 'Bengali Parliament', and he did not think that 'practical considerations are to be subordinated to the supposed educational influence of local self-government'. He deplored the way in which the European merchants of Calcutta and other commercial groups held aloof from the corporation because it was a close preserve of the educated Bengalis.[12] This strengthened his conviction about the necessity of the representation of 'real interests'. The identification and constitutional reconstruction of these 'interests' was to become his main preoccupation when he was put in charge of the constitutional reforms during the Viceroyalty of Lord Minto.

II

The definition and enfranchisement of 'real interests' in a colonial context was a delicate problem. Because of the lack of an independent and fully differentiated public life, every representative institution was avidly captured by the most active group. As there was more prestige than power attached to these institutions, the 'real interests' often did not care to project themselves into this political arena and preferred to exercise direct pressure on the executive whenever some important issue was at stake. This posed a peculiar problem for the executive. A purely autocratic government might dispense or withhold favours and respond to pressures from various groups *ad hoc* and without concern for the continuity and interdependence of political interests. The very idea of representative government, however, presupposed an institutionalised give-and-take of favours and support, whereby a concession to one group today would constitute a claim on its political support at some other time. This was one very important reason which compelled the colonial executive to aim at a representation of different interests in councils and corporations once the principle of representative government was introduced. The other strong motivation for the representation of 'interests' was provided by the conservative trend towards a re-integration of the Indian society. India was seen as a conglomeration of castes, classes, and tribes. A representation of this kaleidoscopic pattern was theoretically desirable and practically convenient. But the administrators who were responsible for the constitutional evolution of India did not always think of Machiavellian plots. For most of them the quest for the 'natural leaders of the people' and for the 'real interests' was not conceived of as a technical necessity of representative government in a colonial empire. It was meant to lead to a restoration of a sense of order and proportion in Indian society. But whether the motivation was Machiavellian or conservative, representation soon became a piece of 'social engineering'. Previously the colonial government had taken it upon itself to define the interests of 'agricultural' and 'non-agricultural' communities for the purpose of the Punjab Land Alienation Act of 1900. Why should it not delimit the representation of political interests in a similar fashion? In this way the re-integration of Indian society and the construction of the body politic could be co-ordinated. Social and political considerations converged: the educated class was thought to be socially unrepresentative and politically undesirable, and the one because of the other. The British bureaucrats were well prepared to resist any improvement in the constitutional position of the educated class. If they were to lose some ground in a first round of constitution making they were sure to recover it when they had to frame the rules and regulations, the natural weapons of bureaucratic rule.

This was the position in 1906 when the victory of the Liberal Party in Britain opened the way for fundamental constitutional reforms in India. The new Secretary of State, the liberal philosopher, John Morley, was a man revered by the educated classes of India. He was known for his criticism of imperialism. Gokhale had visited Morley several years before and he had conveyed to him this appreciation of India's educated élite. But in his conversation with Morley at that time, he had found him to be rather pessimistic about the political development of India. Morley had told Gokhale that he feared India would have a fate similar to that of Ireland.[13] As Secretary of State for India Morley was not impelled by a reforming zeal when he took office. He actually thought that very little work would be connected with it, and he obviously had no plans of his own.[14] But he was a stern advocate of parliamentary control of imperial affairs and he considered the Viceroy to be his agent just as much as the messengers at his doorstep.[15] He was, therefore, bound to become deeply involved in the duties of his office as time went by. The new parliament had many radical members who professed to be friends of India and could be relied upon to keep a watch on the policy of the cabinet. In India Lord Curzon had been replaced by Lord Minto who was a conservative and owed his appointment to the previous cabinet but was nevertheless inclined to view Indian aspirations in a more liberal way than his predecessor. In general the Minto–Morley constellation seemed to augur well for those Indian politicians who were eager to obtain a generous dose of constitutional reform. But the political atmosphere in India after the partition of Bengal was vitiated by the radicalisation of Indian politics. The moderate nationalists who thought in terms of constitutional reforms were challenged by a growing school of thought which felt that constitutional advance would side-track the main issue of Indian national freedom and corrupt Indian politicians who would glory in a more intimate association with the colonial power and thus forget about the birthright of their nation.

Gokhale reached the peak of his political career at this critical juncture.

In 1905 he was elected president of the Indian National Congress which he had served as a general secretary for several years. He was only thirty-nine years old, but he had already been a member of the Imperial Legislative Council for the past four years, and in this capacity he had impressed Lord Curzon as an extremely well-informed and able leader of the permanent opposition.[16] The Congress at Benares in 1905 was, however, at least as much of a challenge to Gokhale as an encounter with Lord Curzon. A few weeks before the Congress met Gokhale had returned from London where he had interviewed several Liberal politicians. He was hopeful that a definite step toward constitutional reform was imminent. For some time he had even thought of getting himself elected to the House of Commons in order to be able to submit a reforms bill to Parliament from the floor of the house. But the great political boss of the Congress, Sir Pherozeshah Mehta, convinced him that even a sizeable number of Indian members of Parliament would be of no avail and that a private member's bill would do more harm than good because it would not commit the cabinet.[17] He had, therefore, dropped the idea, but he was determined to continue his work for the reforms. In Benares he was faced with an audience excited by the Bengal anti-partition agitation, and in no mood to be carried away by vague promises of impending reforms. He satisfied his audience by condemning Lord Curzon and the partition and he then outlined a reform programme which he hoped could be implemented. He suggested that the number of elected members in the Imperial Legislative Council should be raised so as to form one-half of the total number, and that they should have the power to pass the budget and move amendments; three Indian members should be appointed to the Council of the Secretary of State in London; there should be District Advisory Councils with more comprehensive powers than the existing Local Boards; judicial and executive functions should be separated, and the judicial branch of the Civil Service should be recruited from the members of the legal profession in India; while primary education should be extended on a large scale.[18]

Soon after the Benares Congress Gokhale left again for England in order to promote these reforms. Morley granted him a series of interviews and Gokhale reported home: 'I am pleased that I have come here at a time when Mr Morley's mind is in a fluid condition and his opinions on India are in the process of forming.'[19] Morley was interested in Gokhale's ideas, but what was even more important, he knew that Gokhale acted as political advisor to the Friends of India group of radical parliamentarians, a large but incoherent body which would be rather harmless unless it were roused by some untoward event. Morley, who did not like to be asked too many questions in Parliament was anxious to keep Gokhale on the right side in order to be able through him to influence the radical members of Parliament. He freely described his own difficulties to Gokhale, and Gokhale suggested that Morley should appoint a Royal Commission on Decentralisation in order to seize the initiative and gain time for a thorough preparation of the reforms.[20] Morley accepted this advice, but this initial move did not establish a firm lead for the Secretary of the State in the further development of the reforms. The India Office faded into the background and the Government of India soon dominated the discussions about constitutional reform.

Lord Minto's mind, unlike Morley's, was not 'in a fluid condition' as far as his opinions on India were concerned. Minto wanted first of all a representation of communities and interests.[21] He thought in terms of a synthesis of British and Moghul traditions of government and intended to build a 'constitutional autocracy', which would provide for a better association of the people with the government, but would not enable them to control the executive by means of powerful legislative councils. Risley, who was in charge of the details of the reforms scheme, assisted Minto very ably and knew how to interpret this British-Moghul plan, because it corresponded with his own ideas. Within this frame of reference of the greater association of the Indian people with the government Minto was willing to go very far. In fact, he was eager to demonstrate this principle by a suggestion which he thought would capture the imagination of political India, and he therefore asked for the appointment of an Indian member to his executive council, which had always been a close preserve of the most senior civil servants. This suggestion came as a surprise to Morley who thought it to be a rather bold step and feared that the India Council in London would reject it in the same way as the Viceroy's executive council had rejected it.[22] But in the end this unexpected proposal was the first item of the constitutional reforms that could be put into practice. The appointment of an Indian to the Viceroy's executive council had not even been mentioned in the Congress reforms programme. Gokhale and his friends knew that it would be a dubious boon; they were much more interested in an increasing legislative control of the government than in an association with its executive responsibilities. It was in keeping with this point of view that they had asked for Indian representation on the India Council of the Secretary of State, and for an extension of the powers of the non-official members of the Imperial Legislative Council, but had not demanded a reform of the

Viceroy's executive council. Nevertheless when this reform was granted they welcomed it and persuaded the great Calcutta lawyer Satyendra Sinha to accept the position of Law Member on the Viceroy's council. But it soon became quite obvious that the acceptance of this position meant responsibility without power, and Sinha wanted to resign his office almost within a year of his appointment.[23]

The other items of the reforms programme did not materialise so quickly. Gokhale had a hard time in persuading his friends again and again to withhold their criticism and put their trust in Morley who would see to it that the reforms were not whittled away. But the tide had turned against Gokhale who had been so sanguine about the prospects of an early and comprehensive reform at the time of his visit in 1906. The following year saw a rapid polarisation of political forces in India, and the scene in London changed as well. In 1907 it was not Gokhale but Risley who had a series of interviews with Morley. Risley appeared to Morley somewhat mephistophelian,[24] but he was impressed with his intellectual brilliance and wrote about him to Minto in an enthusiastic vein.[25] Morley had been impatient with the long delay of the reform proposals of the Government of India, but he was now convinced that Risley could handle all reform problems very well. Risley also left a copy of his article on the race basis of Indian political movements with Morley who read it with great interest and noted that it was a remarkable forecast of so much that had happened since.[26] On his return to India Risley drafted a reforms circular which embodied the whole scheme of the representation of communities and interests and relegated territorial representation and the educated class to a marginal position. This greatly discouraged Gokhale and his friends who felt that Indian opinion was in a mood 'to leave these reforms severely alone'. Gokhale complained about Risley who had adopted 'a sneering attitude towards the educated classes', and he hoped that the Government of India would realise the mistake of permitting Risley to draft the circular in this vein.[27] The impending defeat of the reforms by the Government of India could perhaps be forestalled by another intervention in London, and Gokhale thought of going there. In this he found some encouragement in a remark by Lieutenant-Governor Baker, a member of the Viceroy's executive council, who had been outvoted in the council because of his liberal views. Baker agreed that Gokhale should shift the scene of his activities to London once more in order to canvass for support among members of Parliament. Morley was furious when he came to know about this advice and upbraided Baker for this 'hint to Mr Gokhale to set in motion parliamentary opposition to [his] official superior'.[28] But for the time being Morley was not disturbed by the Indian nationalists, because they could not agree among themselves what course they should follow. The political atmosphere became more and more tense towards the end of 1907. Gokhale was afraid that fratricidal struggles of an Irish type would wreck the incipient public life of India, and that fissiparous tendencies would increase the vulnerability of a political society which was anyhow characterised by an excessive indiscipline and had no instinct for united action. Gokhale also predicted that the British officials would not do anything to rally the moderate politicians to their side, but would rather utilise the opportunity that presented itself to put down both sections of Indian politicians at once.[29]

The lack of consensus among the educated class and the dramatic split of the Congress in December 1907 confirmed these fears. Since there could be no agreement about the way towards emancipation, the official doctrine of the re-integration of the Indian society within the framework of a British–Moghul constitution could gain ready acceptance. Risley started a correspondence with Morley in April 1908 because Minto was unable to read all the reforms files and authorised him to keep Morley informed about everything. In his first letter Risley made out a convincing case for not giving up the official majority in the provincial legislative councils. He argued that otherwise subordinate governments such as the Government of Bombay would practically become independent not only of the Government of India but also of the Secretary of State and of Parliament. For instance, an instruction about cotton duties or the restriction of factory labour, which must rest upon a parliamentary mandate, would unite all Bombay non-official members, Indians and Europeans, in one solid body; and if the provincial government sympathised with their views and refused to veto a majority vote the authority of Parliament would be superseded. Risley knew that such concrete examples appealed to Morley.[30] In his next letter to Morley he commented on the recent bomb outrages and blamed the Congress politicians, who had started the practice of drawing students into politics, and who had 'thus demoralised a hysterical and imitative class with no traditions and no backbone'. He also added an outline of the entire reforms scheme, which would contain an Imperial Advisory Council of seven Indian princes, and eight representatives of the different provinces of British India; provincial advisory councils of seven to twelve members representing interests, and provincial legislative councils of thirty-five to forty-five members with separate electorates for landholders and

Mohammedans, and territorial representation, through district boards and municipalities, of the educated class. Risley emphasised that the latter point was an adaptation of Gokhale's proposals 'only changing the scale'. The advisory councils should remain small bodies, their note should be distinction; large bodies of this type would be 'either dummies or Dumas' he added. Provincial advisory councils would be very useful to the governors, because even at present they consulted all kinds of people but they could never say 'I have consulted my advisory council'. These councils would consist of specially selected representatives of important interests, and therefore they fitted well into Risley's scheme. He was more diffident about the usefulness of the Imperial Advisory Council with its native princes and could not cite any cases in which their advice would be useful. But he was convinced that this association of the Government of India with the native rulers would serve at least one good purpose: 'Suppose for example that bomb throwing spreads, British officials will not be the only victims, and if concerted measures are to be taken the Native States must co-operate with us.'[31] The policy of associating natives with the 'constitutional autocracy' was thus designed to extend the front and confound the forces that were attacking it. In general this line was followed very successfully by the Government of India, but the idea of the advisory councils was soon given up, because Minto was afraid that in London 'an attempt may be made to enlarge them on a more representative basis to meet the views of the Indian extremists, who are at home accepted as patriots, and of the present House of Commons'.[32]

Soon after this correspondence had been exchanged between Risley and Morley, Gokhale reached London for another round in the campaign for constitutional reform. The proposals of the Government of India were now before the India Council and in due course Morley would have to issue his reforms despatch which remained the only hope for the moderate nationalists who had been sorely disappointed by the Government of India. Gokhale came to England with fewer illusions than in 1906 when he had had his first series of interviews with Morley, and his days in London were overshadowed by the course of events in India. The political murders, the wave of repression initiated by the government, and particularly the trial in Bombay of the great nationalist leader, Bal Gangadhar Tilak, his old colleague and antagonist, created tensions which affected his negotiations with the Secretary of State and the members of his council. But nevertheless he reported home that he had covered a good deal of ground in these discussions. In

September 1908 he submitted a note on the reforms to Morley and sent a copy of it to Risley for inclusion in the reforms papers of the Government of India.[33] The main issue in these discussions was territorial representation versus separate electorates for different communities and interests. Gokhale tried his best to rescue the principle of territorial representation, because political emancipation and national unity would suffer if this principle had to be given up. The Government of India insisted on the principle of communal representation in separate electorates which was in tune with the idea of the association of diverse interests with an autocratic government. Gokhale was willing to accept separate electorates for certain communities and interests if they were supplementary to territorial electorates so as to give some weightage to groups which otherwise would not have been properly represented. But the Government of India did not conceive of separate electorates as a supplementary device; to them communal representation was the foundation of their constitutional plan and territorial representation was the exception which would be granted only to the educated class which represented nobody but themselves as the government saw it. Morley and his council tried to arrive at a compromise between these two incompatible principles of territorial and communal representation by evolving a scheme of electoral colleges. These colleges would provide a level on which separate and territorial representation could be merged. Each territorial unit would have an electoral college whose members were to be elected by separate electorates of communities and interests. The representatives elected by the college would represent the territorial unit as a whole. This was the main point of Morley's great reforms despatch of 27 November, 1908.[34] Risley, however, was able to undermine the whole scheme by pointing out that it might give adequate representation to minorities of opinion (e.g. Free Traders v. Tariff Reform) but not to minorities of sect (e.g. Hindus v. Mohammedans). In order to prove his contention he cited the following example:[35]

> . . . let us suppose that there are six candidates, four Hindus and two Muhammedans for the five seats on the council. H1 a Hindu pleader, H2 a Hindu journalist, H3 a Hindu barrister having just enough land to qualify as a landholder of the novus homo type, H4 a Hindu landholder of standing, M1 a really representative Muslim, M2 a Congress Muhammedan supported by the Hindus; assume further that the landholders vote solidly for H4 and the Muhammedans for M1, that leaves 60 Hindu votes to be cast (of an electoral college of 100 which includes 20 representatives of landholders and 20 of Muhammedans). How should these (remaining votes) be given so as to carry the Congress ticket?

I suggest that they might be distributed thus: H1–5, H2–5, H3–25, M2–25, M1 and H4 would be defeated by Congressmen with merely nominal qualifications, as the college can elect only one Muhammedan and one landholder the votes cast for M1 and H4 are valueless and the 10 votes still left to the Congress are sufficient to secure the election of a pleader and a journalist, H1 and H2.

The political types which Risley mentioned in this example, which he had copied to a large extent from a Mohammedan newspaper, showed a definite bias. Gokhale, however (who of course did not know about this confidential note) wrote in the same month an optimistic letter to Sir Lawrence Jenkins in which he reported a general change of heart among the leading officials:[36]

> Take Sir Herbert Risley. I know Sir Herbert Risley of Lord Curzon's time, and never wanted to meet him more than I could help. His whole bearing then was . . . a sneer at our aspirations. Well, I saw him the other day at Calcutta and had a long talk with him. He always was brilliant and scholarly . . . but I noticed a new desire in him to be recognised as a friend and I could not help being touched by his evident anxiety to be understood.

Even if this may not have been a case of dissimulation on Sir Herbert Risley's part it was certainly a rather hasty judgement on Gokhale's part. Risley was thinking ahead and he was even scanning the files for issues that might be brought up by the non-official members in the reformed councils.[37] He was preparing himself for new lines of defence, and for the present he was advocating the same political views which he had held consistently over a long period of time, and which he thought were in accordance with the realities in India. His sneer may have disappeared, but his line of reasoning was more effective than ever. Morley was forced to withdraw his suggestions, and when doing so in a speech in the House of Lords, he paraphrased Risley's note and adopted his arguments, substituting Protestants and Catholics for Risley's Hindus and Mohammedans in order to elucidate the matter to his fellow peers. The situation provided an opening for the communal spokesmen of the Mohammedans who could use some of Morley's statements for extracting more concessions than they could have hoped for at any earlier stage. Morley was aware of this fact and he was glad that nobody took the opportunity of raising a question in Parliament which would have greatly embarrassed him.[38]

The only major point which Morley was able to defend against the Government of India was the right of the elected members to take their seats in the reformed councils on the basis of election only, without the prerequisite of a nomination by the government; the government would have preferred the continuation of the existing practice of nomination upon election, so as to be able to discourage the election of undesirable politicians. Morley also objected to the disqualification of all politicians who had been deported in the course of the previous year.[39] But in the end he had to grant to the Government of India a general power of disallowing candidatures in certain cases. For this he was applauded by Risley who wrote to him (while sending him a copy of the Bhagavadgita with some appreciative comments), that he had all along pleaded for this power of disallowing candidatures, instead of having to submit a catalogue of political disqualifications, because he felt that Parliament would be willing to condone such restrictions rather than permit explicit discrimination. Risley added:[40]

> In this as in other matters I have found difficulty in getting people here to realise that Parliament has to be reckoned with. Their tendency is to say: 'this is right, if Parliament choose to upset us, let them do so', – instead of trying to attain their object by means which Parliament are likely to agree to.

After having crossed the hurdles of parliamentary solicitude for India's constitution, the bureaucrats could cut down the reforms to proper size by framing the rules and regulations to the act of 1909. The registration of voters was conducted in such a way as to further reduce the weight of the educated class and strengthened the ranks of those 'who had a stake in the country'. In April 1909 Morley had remarked to his private secretary that he felt the reforms were going a bit too far after all. But at the end of that year his fear proved to be unfounded. 'The triumph of constitutionalism' as the reforms had been called at the Congress of 1908 had turned into a victory of the bureaucracy. In commenting on the regulation for the representation of different communities on the Bengal Legislative Council, Risley stated:[41]

> We did not aim at a numerical balance ... The Hindu professional middle class ought to have a bare majority of elected members by virtue of their numbers and intellectual superiority, but they ought not to have things all their own way.

In keeping with their motto 'association but no control' the officials carefully produced a pattern of representation which would provide them with a system of checks and balances. While pretending to be disinterested umpires they loaded the dice against the educated class and made sure that they would not 'have things all their own way'. At the

Congress of 1909 the Indian politicians could only bewail the innumerable instances of arbitrary disenfranchisement and gerrymandering with which the bureaucracy had secured a representation of those 'interests' that had found official approval and an exclusion of those who were undesirable to those in power.[42] Gokhale who had been so closely associated with the progress of the constitutional reforms received all the brickbats of the nationalist press. Insult was added to injury when the 'Mahratta' surmised that Gokhale was secretly in league with the bureaucrats and had betrayed the national cause.[43]

The final structure of the reformed legislatures under the Morley-Minto reforms showed an overall increase of the elective element, but this element was introduced in such a tortuous and guarded manner, that the executive was thoroughly protected against direct attack by a solid phalanx of elected representatives. Even in the provincial legislatures where the statutory official majorities had been abandoned, the non-official seats were parcelled out in such a way that joint action by the non-official members was rather unlikely. In the central legislature the official majority had been retained so as to safeguard the ultimate control of the Government of India. This combination of provincial concessions with central autocracy became a permanent feature of constitutional reform in India. The central legislature had been enlarged from 16 to a maximum of 60 seats, 33 of these were occupied by nominated members of whom 28 were officials of the Government of India. The elective element was composed of representatives of various electorates, 13 of them had to be elected by the legislative councils of the provinces, whereby the elected members of the councils were the electorate for these seats, 6 were elected by special electorates of landholders, 5 by the separate Muslim electorates of the provinces, one by the Muslim landholders, and 2 by the Chambers of Commerce. The provincial legislatures of the Bombay and Madras Presidencies were composed of the 3 executive council members and the advocate general ex-officio, 21 nominated members of whom only 16 ought to be officials, 2 experts, and 21 elected members. In Bengal the number of elected members was even higher; 28 elected members were confronted with only 21 nominated members. But many of the elected members owed their seats to electorates which could not but produce faithful camp-followers of the official side. The scope of the elected members activity in the new councils was anyhow rather limited. The budget was presented to them and they could ask questions and sponsor resolutions, but in the last resort they could not change the course of government.

When the reformed councils met they were at once faced with an un-pleasant task. The wave of terrorism that had swept India since the split of the Congress had sorely tried and nearly exhausted the traditional means of repression that were at the disposal of the government. The deportation of prominent leaders proved to be abortive. It added to their stature and gave rise to embarrassing questions in Parliament.[44] The executive was therefore eager to place the responsibility for the repression of revolutionary activities squarely on the shoulders of the Indian legislature, and soon after the opening of the reformed legislative council it was Risley's duty as acting Home Member to introduce a Press Bill which was intended to curb the freedom of the radical newspapers; because, as Risley put it, 'sedition has the monopoly of its audience'[45]. His speech contained a good analysis of Indian unrest. Gokhale, how-ever, could only deplore 'the cruel irony of fate that the first important measure that comes before the Reformed Council is a measure to curtail a great and deeply cherished privilege, which the country has enjoyed, with two brief interruptions, for three-quarters of a century'.[46] This was the last time that Gokhale's and Risley's paths crossed. The day before Gokhale gave his speech in the council Risley had been given a farewell dinner by Minto.[47] His term of service in India had come to an end and before he could take up his new position of Permanent Undersecretary in the India Office he died in London in September 1911.

III

Gokhale was to survive Risley only by three and a half years and within that short period he did not witness any progress beyond the established political framework. The beginning of the First World War indicated that further reforms might be due, because India's loyalty would have to be rewarded. Gokhale was therefore asked by Lord Willingdon, Governor of Bombay, to outline a minimum demand that would satisfy Indian aspirations and he finished a draft of this demand a few days before his death in February 1915.[48] Later on this draft was published by the Aga Khan and became known as 'Gokhale's Political Testament'. This desig-nation was somewhat misleading because it tended to obscure the fact that the draft was prepared for a particular purpose, and therefore could not contain any long-range plans for India's constitutional progress. Nevertheless the draft showed Gokhale's realistic appraisal of the poten-tialities of constitutional advance within the peculiar framework fashioned by the Government of India. He suggested a large extension of

provincial autonomy with non-official majorities in the provincial legislatures and Indian members on the executive councils of the governors,
counterbalanced by the retention of an official majority in the central
legislature and special powers for the Viceroy. Later reforms demonstrated that Gokhale had gauged the main trend correctly. But his plan
did not contain any reference to responsible government of the parliamentary type and he stated in his draft:[49]

> The relations between the Executive Government and the Legislative
> Council . . . should be roughly similar to those between the Imperial Govern-
> ment and the Reichstag in Germany . . . the members of the Executive Govern-
> ment shall not depend individually or collectively, on the support of the majority
> of the council for holding their offices.

This combination of an irremovable executive with a Reichstag-type
legislature was in keeping with the spirit of the Morley–Minto Reforms
which did not afford a good point of departure for the introduction of a
parliamentary type of government. The representation of 'communities
and interests' was incompatible with responsible government. It required
an irremovable executive in the same way as the 'functional representation' which was suggested by some constitutional planners in the course
of later discussion before and during the Second World War.[50] The draft
of the nineteen members of the Imperial Legislative Council and the
constitutional proposals embodied in the subsequent pact between the
Congress and the Muslim League in 1916 closely paralleled the suggestions made in Gokhale's 'Testament'.[51] None of these proposals contained any reference to a 'responsible government' which according to
the famous declaration of August 1917 the British war cabinet was prepared to grant to the Indian people. British commentators were quick to
emphasise that the government was prepared to go much beyond the
boldest demands of the Indian nationalists and was willing to grant them
a boon of which they had not even thought as yet. But Indian politicians
had not lost sight of 'responsible government' out of sheer force of habit
or lack of imagination. They had asked for a greater amount of control
of the executive by the legislature, and had consciously refrained from
asking for any share of the executive responsibility of government.
Partial executive responsibility to councils elected along the lines of the
established system of representation of communities and interests would
make confusion worse confounded. Politicians like the Aga Khan and
V. S. Srinivasa Sastri recognised this problem and pointed to the Swiss
and the American federal constitutions as models which would be more

appropriate for India.[52] But nobody would listen to these suggestions and responsible government of a peculiar type was wished upon the Indian people at the next constitutional reform.

The fateful term 'responsible government' was inserted in the declaration of August 1917 by Lord Curzon, after the British war cabinet had repeatedly hesitated to use the more general but emotionally loaded term 'self-government'.[53] But, whereas self-government could have implied even non-parliamentary forms of government, responsible government had a technical meaning which could not be disregarded. This technical meaning was exploited by constitutional experts who had taken a leaf out of Lord Durham's report on Canada and emphasised the inevitable deadlock which would result from the encounter of an irremovable executive with an enlarged legislature of the type which the Indian politicians had demanded.[54] They could demonstrate that the proposals of Gokhale's testament and similar suggestions of other politicians would soon lead to a point of no return whereas responsible government could be established in convenient instalments. The bureaucrats were quick to grasp the potentialities of this new device. Like the control of representation the guarded transfer of responsibility gave a great deal of scope to the skilful manipulator, and the combination of both multiplied the number of checks and balances. The debates on responsible government and on the reconstruction of the Indian polity highlighted once more the problem of the symbiosis of the two social systems. The emancipated system of the imperial power provided the model of political progress, whereas the subject people lived in a half-way house, and their political destiny was to be shaped by whatever new construction the imperial power chose to impose upon them. Responsible government demands an emancipated electorate among which a free party system will operate towards an aggregation of interests. The representation of permanently defined sectional interests is the very antithesis of this system, and yet the imperial government managed to combine these two principles in an utterly confusing synthesis of separate electorates and dyarchic responsibility when the next constitutional reforms were granted. The impact of such constructions on the Indian body politic did not contribute to the development of a united nation. But, of course, the imperial rulers could always argue that this nation was only a dream in the heads of a small minority of Indian nationalists, and that if it did in fact exist it should be able to assert itself in spite of some ephemeral political constructions. When defending the introduction of separate electorates Risley had taken precisely this line:[55]

As for the argument from nationality it is too indefinite to be taken seriously . . . if the growth of nationality can be stopped by what is after all a piece of electoral mechanism, nationality in India is not the force that it pretends to be.

This point of view was very close to that of the extremists in Indian politics who spurned the efforts of the moderate reformers and claimed political freedom as the birthright of the nation. The extremists, like Risley, conceived of nationality as of an innate force which may be submerged, but which would always remain a living reality. The extremists tried to find this living reality in the traditions of Hindu culture and religion and established a solidarity which did not include the Muslims of India. Risley, who was a keen observer of the new traditionalism, knew about this problem, and because of his intimate acquaintance with the intricacies of India's social structure, he was very sceptical about her claim to nationality. But because of the conservative nature of his thought he was basically unable to share the hopes of moderate reformers like Gokhale who trusted that the continuous operation of a progressively emancipated political system would help India to overcome the traditional divisions of its social system and create the conditions for the growth of a nation. Unlike the earlier British Liberals, who had much confidence in the emancipating impact of British rule, and who saw the symbiosis of the two systems in terms of a dynamic transfusion of new blood, Risley, and those who thought like him, knew that the corps of imperial rulers was a small entity encapsuled in a vast and complex body over which it retained a precarious control. The providential rule of the British in India in which the Indian liberals still believed at that time was no longer the cherished ideal of those imperial guardians who had come to look at India with the innate pessimism of the conservative mind. Their attempts at re-integrating rather than emancipating Indian society were motivated by their interest in the traditional forms of authority as well as by their awareness of the foundations and limitations of British power in India. They did not think of any special mandate of British rule but only of its survival, and for this purpose they felt they had to adapt British rule to India rather than work for a progressive adaptation of India to British rule. This is why they had to foist what they themselves called a British-Moghul constitution upon India, thus bitterly disappointing the Indian liberals who had been led to believe by an earlier generation of British guardians that it was the mission of Britain to liberate India from Moghul autocracy, and instruct Indians in the art of democratic self-government. But even though old fashioned Liberalism had died out among the guardians in India, it was still in vogue in the British Parliament, a fact, which gave rise to constant tensions. Parliamentary politics at home and the bureaucrats' struggle for the maintenance of imperial rule in India were ever so often at variance. In all important decisions, Parliament had to trust 'the man on the spot' and that man in turn had to obey the orders of Parliament. The result was a hybrid mixture of parliamentary precedent and bureaucratic practice which left its imprint on India's political life for a long time to come. In this context Indian politicians could only plead for a larger amount of parliamentary precedent and less bureaucratic practice. In doing so they had to demand a closer approximation of the Indian government to the parliamentary model at home. For this they have often been wrongly blamed, because they appeared to advocate a slavish imitation of an alien model while they should have thought of a more adequate constitutional form that would reflect the genius of the Indian people. In fact, several Indian politicians did try their hand at drafting an Indian constitution in the course of later years. C.R.Das, for instance, elaborated a hierarchy of panchayats, with the village panchayats at the base and the national panchayat at the top of the constitutional pyramid, the different levels to be connected by a system of indirect elections.[56] A similar plan was proposed by Jayaprakash Narayan in independent India. Gandhi regarded the constitution of the Indian National Congress as it evolved under his guidance as a suitable model for an Indian constitution.[57] This constitution contained three tiers of committees connected by indirect elections, and a highly centralised executive. The erratic radical, M.N.Roy drafted a very interesting 'Constitution of Free India',[58] in which he provided for provincial government by People's Committees with no division of legislative and executive functions and a federal government consisting of a directly elected Governor-General and a legislative assembly to be elected by electoral colleges composed of the representatives of the People's Committees of towns and villages. He also conceded separate electorates to minorities. However, all these drafts and proposals were of purely academic interest; the official constitutional reforms took no notice of them. Independent India emerged with a constitution which was the product of the interaction of parliamentary tradition and the administrative exigencies of a gradual devolution of power. In this way the Indian constitution was a product of system-symbiosis; it was alien and yet closely related to India's political experience. In spite of frequent setbacks, bureaucratic subterfuges and the many obstacles to the development of territorial representation of the

Indian people, the progress of constitutional reform contributed to the emancipation of India's political society. All constitutional nostrums which were supposed to reflect customary relationships and the traditional structure of Indian society in due course disappeared. The progress of constitutional reform vindicated all those, like Gokhale, who had worked for it, even if many of their efforts were frustrated in their own time. Gokhale was a Moderate who had once adopted the motto 'one step enough for me', but he was also an ardent patriot and a true liberal who hoped that this step would be in the direction of the emancipation of his nation. He knew what this emancipation would mean to the Indian people:[59]

I recognize [he said] no limits to my aspirations for our Motherland . . . I want our men and women without distinction of caste or creed to grow to the full height of their stature.

NOTES

1 See Talcott Parsons and Edward Shils, *Toward a General Theory of Action*, Cambridge (Mass) 1952.

2 Gokhale, *Speeches*, 2nd edn, Madras 1916, p. 1064.

3 Ibid., p. 1080.

4 Risley was not made a governor for these reasons; see comments on Risley by Morley in John Morley, *Recollections*, Vol. II, London 1917, p. 229; also Gokhale Papers, National Archives of India (hereinafter GP), Gokhale to Sir Lawrence Jenkins, 29 January 1909, and Hirtzel Diary, India Office Library, Home Miscellaneous Series 864, 26 August 1907. Sir Frederick Hirtzel was private secretary to Lord Morley from 1906 to 1909.

5 Gokhale, *Speeches*, 2nd edn, p. 678.

6 Ranade to Gokhale, 24 May 1899, GP.

7 For a comparison of the policies of Tilak and Gokhale see Stanley Wolpert, *Tilak and Gokhale—Revolution and Reform in the Making of Modern India*, Berkeley 1962.

8 See the following works of Risley: *The Tribes and Castes of Bengal*, 4 vols, Calcutta 1891; Census Report of India 1901; *The People of India*, London 1908, 2nd edn 1915.

9 Published in the *Contemporary Review*, Vol. 57, May 1890.

10 For Risley's own reference to this visit see National Archives of India, Home Department Proceedings, Political A (hereinafter HDP), October 1908 No. 116–48, Vol. I, p. 556.

11 Risley tried later on to convince Lord Curzon of the usefulness of the panchayats, but Curzon was not inclined to revive institutions which he considered to be dead and gone; see HDP, December 1903, No. 53–8.

12 Government of Bengal, Municipal Department, No. 383 T.M., 17 June 1897; see also John Roy McLane, 'The Development of Nationalist Ideas and Tactics and the Politics of the Government of India, 1897–1905', unpublished Ph.D. thesis, University of London 1961, pp. 270 ff.

13 Gokhale to Morley, 9 May 1897, GP.

14 Hirtzel Diary, January 1906, Hirtzel's summary of his talk with Morley at the time of Morley's accession to his new office.

15 Hirtzel Diary, 4 July 1906 and 26 March 1908.

16 See T. V. Parvate, *Gopal Krishna Gokhale*, Ahmedabad 1959.

17 Gokhale to Krishnaswami Iyer, 10 March 1906, GP.

18 Gokhale, *Speeches*, 2nd edn, pp. 838 f.

19 Gokhale to N.A.Dravid, 25 May 1906, GP.

20 See Hirtzel Diary, 9 May 1906, also Morley, *Recollections*, Vol. II, p. 171; on Royal Commission see Gokhale to N.A.Dravid, 6 July 1906, GP, and Hirtzel Diary, 12 August 1907.

21 See Minto's note HDP, October 1908, No. 116–48, Vol. I, p. 509.

22 Hirtzel Diary, 3 April 1907, also Morley, *Recollections*, Vol. II, p. 209.

23 See Parvate, op. cit., p. 291, about Sinha's intention to resign over the Press Bill.

24 Hirtzel Diary, 16 July 1907.

25 Morley, *Recollections*, Vol. II, p. 229.

26 See Morley's handwritten note appended to the copy of Risley's article preserved in the India Office Library (P/V 323).

27 Copy of a letter of Gokhale to Sir William Wedderburn, 15 November 1907. Morley Papers, India Office Library (hereinafter MP).

28 Morley to Lieutenant-Governor Baker, 6 December 1907, and Baker to Morley, 23 January 1908, MP.

29 Gokhale to Wedderburn, 15 November 1907, MP.

30 Risley to Morley, 30 April 1908, MP.

31 Risley to Morley, 7 May 1908, MP.

32 HDP, October 1908, No. 116–48, Vol. I, p. 509.

33 Gokhale to Vamanrao Patwardhan, 23 July 1908, and 25 September 1908, GP, also Parvate, op. cit., p. 258.

34 See Gokhale, *Speeches*, 2nd edn, pp. 844 ff., see also Files on Indian Councils Reforms, Proposals by Sir William Lee-Warner and T.Morrison, MP.

35 HDP, February 1909, Nos. 205–44, Note of 5 January 1909, the Mohammedan paper referred to was the *Observer*, Lahore, of 23 December 1908.

36 Gokhale to Sir Lawrence Jenkins, 29 January 1909, GP.

37 See Risley's comments on resolutions that would probably be moved in reformed councils in Risley to Morley, 13 May 1909, MP.

38 Hirtzel Diary, 25 April 1909, see also Morley, *Speeches on Indian Affairs*, Madras, n.d., pp. 174–5.

39 HDP, February 1909, No. 205–44, p. 251, Morley's telegram of 12 February 1909; see also Hirtzel Diary, 19 April 1909.

40 Risley to Morley, 13 May 1909, MP.

41 HDP, December 1909, No. 70–162, p. 3.

42 See Report of the 24th Indian National Congress, Lahore 1909.

43 See Reports on Native Newspapers, Bombay, *Kesari*, 21 December 1909.

44 See the notes of Minto and the members of his council in HDP, March 1910. No. 33–44.

45 See HDP, July 1910, No. 5–32.

46 Gokhale, *Speeches*, 2nd edn, p. 400.

47 See the biographical note on Risley in Risley, *People of India*, 2nd edn, p. xv.

48 Lord Willingdon to Gokhale, 26 January 1915, GP; see also Parvate, op. cit., 392 ff.

49 Ibid., p. 394.

50 For a discussion of the irremovable executive and functional representation see K. T. Shah, *Federal Structure*, Bombay 1937, p. 521

51 See V. S. Srinivasa Sastri, *The Congress-League Scheme*, Allahabad, 1917.

52 V. S. Srinivasa Sastri, *Self-Government for India under the British Flag*, Allahabad 1916; also H.H. the Aga Khan, *India in Transition*, London 1918, pp. 162.

53 See S. R. Mehrotra, 'The Politics Behind the Montagu Declaration of August 1917' in C. H. Philips, ed. *Politics and Society in India*, London 1963, pp. 94 ff.

54 See Lionel Curtis, *Dyarchy*, Oxford 1920, pp. 361 ff.

55 HDP, August 1909, No. 182–184, note of 28 March 1909.

56 See C. R. Das, National Convention Memoranda No. 2 of 1923.

57 See Gandhi, *Young India*, 30 March 1921, and 29 June 1921; see also *Indian Annual Register*, 1936, Vol. II, p. 238 (Gandhi's speech in Faizpur).

58 M. N. Roy, *Constitution of Free India – A Draft*, Delhi 1944.

59 Gokhale, *Speeches*, 2nd edn, p. 1104.

6

TOWARDS NATION-WIDE AGITATION AND ORGANISATION: THE HOME RULE LEAGUES, 1915-18

★

H. F. Owen

The First World War was a time of great change in the Indian national movement. During this period it became more aggressive and more truly 'national' than ever before: it grew more critical of the British and more peremptory in its demands upon them, and at the same time it drew new regions into nationalist activity and linked them together under a more genuinely all-India leadership. All these developments foreshadowed and prepared the way for Gandhi's rise to leadership of the national movement in 1919.

These changes did not result inevitably, or even directly, from the war itself, but from the agitation launched by Mrs Annie Besant and Bal Gangadhar Tilak in 1915 and their formation of the Home Rule Leagues in 1916.[1] This paper aims to describe how these two leaders took control of the Indian National Congress and committed it to the agitation which they had initiated on a nation-wide scale; how they drew increasing numbers into it and how, despite their failure to retain the leadership, they helped to mould this movement and set it on the path that it was to follow for the next thirty years.

I

It is easier to gauge the extent of the changes which occurred in this period if one recalls the state of the national movement at the outbreak of war in August 1914. At that time, it was weakened by disagreements over goals and methods, by British repression, by the political inactivity of many regions and by the inadequate co-ordination of those regions which were active. The affairs of the Congress were dominated by the

Moderates: epitomised by such men as Pherozeshah Mehta, Gokhale and Surendranath Banerjea, they wished to promote social reform, and looked forward to India's development into a secular, liberal democracy. They welcomed British rule for having provided India with these goals, and for introducing the public order, the Western style of education and the beginnings of representative government, which alone, they believed, made advance to these goals possible. Their ultimate aim was self-government, but they wanted in the meantime to work with the British to change Indian society sufficiently for self-government to be gradually introduced.[2] They criticised the slowness of advance, but sought to encourage the British to accelerate it by such sober means as public debate and the submission of representations to the government.[3]

The Extremists, on the other hand, were closely associated with the Hindu revival movement, and were pledged to uphold indigenous traditions and values. Their goals were defined in more emotional, and hence vaguer, terms than those of the Moderates, but they clearly contemplated the preservation or restoration of the interests of the traditionally-dominant castes from which most of them came.[4] They argued that Indian nationalists should make their first objective the expulsion of the British from the motherland, and this, they believed, could best be accomplished by the use of sanctions: a few advocated bomb-throwing and other acts of terrorism, and all supported 'passive resistance' – the boycott of British goods and institutions and the refusal to pay taxes.[5]

Tilak was outstanding among those who fostered Extremism in western India in the 1890s, and Lajpat Rai and B.C. Pal fostered it in the Panjab and Bengal and sought to extend it to Madras in 1905–7. In 1907 these scattered leaders linked hands in an effort to capture the Congress, but they were expelled from that organisation by the Moderates during the Surat session at the end of that year. The Extremists had demonstrated little organisational ability up to this time, and now their tentative efforts to build a parallel organisation to the Congress were thwarted by the British, who imprisoned some of the leading Extremists and harried the others and their followers. The rank-and-file Extremists were cowed, and so they remained in 1914.

Certain regions had barely been touched by the nationalist movement in either its Moderate or Extremist guise in 1914. In the United Provinces and Bihar, Provincial Congress Committees had been founded at the time of the 1907 Moderate–Extremist split, but there was little political activity in either of these provinces. This can be explained largely by the fact that the British had won the support of the dominant groups, the landlords or *taluqdars* and *zamindars*, by confirming them in possession of the land. The national movement was hardly more active in the Madras Presidency, which embraced the Tamil-, Telugu- and Malayalam-speaking regions of British India and part of the Kannada-speaking region. Despite sporadic activity in the *mofussil*, politics were mainly confined to Madras city,[6] and with the expulsion of the Extremists from the Congress in 1907, the Moderates were confirmed in control of the Madras Mahajana Sabha (which was practically identical with the Provincial Congress Committee).[7] In western India, Gujarat was politically quiescent. Of the dominant groups in Gujarati society, the peasant proprietors had concentrated their attention upon the acquisition of land while the traders had focused theirs upon building up the cotton-milling industry in Ahmedabad and Bombay, with the result that neither of these groups took much interest in wider political issues. The Gujarati Brahmins, who acquired higher education and who might have organised nationalist activity in the region, tended to be siphoned off to professional posts in Bombay city, where they were absorbed into the political life of the metropolis. Sind, which like Gujarat was a part of the British province of Bombay, was also politically inactive. This may be traced to the fact that a backward Muslim peasantry comprised the bulk of the population.

In fact there were only three regions in the whole of British India which had traditions of nationalist political activity in 1914: Bengal, the Panjab and Maharashtra.

These three regions had, however, failed to co-ordinate their activities and had developed virtually distinct styles of politics. In Bengal, political activity was practically confined to the three upper castes of Hindus, known as the *bhadralok* ('the respectable people'), traditionally professional men and landowners. Many of them, both Moderates and Extremists, participated in the agitation against the Partition of Bengal from 1906 to 1911. The Extremists were scattered by British repression in 1908, and with the ending of the Partition in 1911 agitation in the province as a whole subsided, leaving behind only a network of inactive District Congress Committees.[8] The violent strain in the Bengali *bhadralok* tradition gave rise to the terrorist movement during the anti-Partition agitation: students and young men, who found their qualifications rewarded with inadequate jobs, joined secret societies and pledged themselves to murder Britons and collaborators.

In the Panjab the Hindu money-lending castes had largely succeeded in monopolising educational and professional, as well as business, opportunities under the British. By the turn of the century, they were seeking to woo the Hindu peasants away from their Muslim counterparts and to turn them against the British, by appealing through the Arya Samaj to their sense of Hindu identity and Hindu greatness. Arya Samajists, like Lala Lajpat Rai, fomented the anti-British grievances of the Hindu peasants in the Panjab Canal Colonies as part of the Extremist movement of 1906–7,[9] but the British shattered this opposition by deportations and displays of military strength. The Hindus of the Panjab were thus quiescent in 1914, but the Sikhs had been stirred to take up arms by the *Ghadr* ('Mutiny') movement with its headquarters among Sikhs overseas, while Muslim antipathy towards the British was aroused by the Pan-Islamic movement.[10]

Maharashtra consisted of two areas: the Marathi-speaking areas of the British provinces of Bombay and the Central Provinces and Berar (Maharashtra proper), and the Kannada-speaking areas of Bombay (the Karnatak). In both areas the professional and political élite consisted of Maharashtrian Brahmins and the pattern of nationalist political development was similar, so that for the purpose of this chapter they formed one region. Its nerve centre was Poona, the headquarters of the Chitpavan Brahmins, who had ruled the region before the coming of the British and who continued to dominate its life – in education, in the professions, in the administration, in national politics, and in social status generally. Tilak, a Chitpavan, turned a wide range of Maharashtrians against the British by exploiting their economic grievances and their fears that the British threatened their traditional beliefs. Through the Ganpati and Shivaji Festivals he provided Hindu peasants, workers, business- and professional men with a sense of solidarity even at the expense of causing bad blood between them and the Muslims.[11] The movement which Tilak had fostered in Maharashtra was much more truly popular by 1907 than the one led by the Bengali Extremists, who hesitated to stir up the peasants for fear of being unable to control them. And, while there were instances of bomb-throwing in Maharashtra, terrorism was less thoroughly organised there than in Bengal, and Tilak was much less deeply implicated in encouraging it than was, say, Aurobindo Ghose in Bengal.[12]

Between 1908 and 1914 the Extremists in these three regions had been cowed by the imprisonment of Tilak and the Government's harassment of the other leaders and their lieutenants.[13] In response to the Extremist attempt to take over the Congress in 1907, the Moderates had made plans for stepping up Congress activity, for example through the establishment of a network of District Committees. But the suppression of the Extremists removed the Moderates' rivals and (with them) the immediate incentive to action, and the plans for the District Committees fell through.[14] Outside Bengal, the Moderates allowed the annual Provincial Conferences to lapse, while attendances at the annual Congress sessions fell away.

In 1914, then, the fires of the Indian national movement seemed all but quenched. And yet, beneath the ashes were embers which a determined leader might blow into flame. For one thing, the Extremist agitation of 1904–8 had worked a change in the Indian mentality that could not be reversed. In particular the younger generation which had been at school or at university at that time had been deeply stirred. Its youthful idealism had responded to the Extremists' call for self-sacrifice, and likewise to their defiance of the British, to their proposals for passive resistance and their demands for independence. During the anti-Partition agitation in Bengal, 'national' schools had been established to replace Government institutions, and students had led the picketing of shops selling British goods; indeed, throughout India, the Extremists had aimed their appeal at students.[15] The punishments inflicted by the Government on the Extremist leaders had made them martyrs in the eyes of their young admirers. And, although Tilak, Aurobindo and others were imprisoned or had fled, the eagerness of the young men was maintained by another inspiring example, that of Gandhi who led a series of passive-resistance campaigns in South Africa between 1906 and 1914.[16] This young, Western-educated generation included the majority of those who were to be most active in the national movement by the end of the War: men like Rajagopalachariar in Madras and Jitendralal Bannerjee in Bengal; or Saifuddin Kitchlu, Harkaran Nath Misra and Jawaharlal Nehru, who in 1912 returned from Cambridge to Amritsar, Lucknow and Allahabad respectively. Jawaharlal Nehru spoke for them all when he wrote some years later that

[after my return from England] the idea that we must not tamely submit to existing conditions and that something must be done began to obsess me more and more. . . . I felt that both individual and national honour demanded a more aggressive and fighting attitude to foreign rule.[17]

It was not only the younger men who were disappointed by the inactivity of the Congress. Many, who had identified themselves as Moderates at the time of the Surat split, felt that the choice they had been forced to make between the Moderates and the Extremists was an unreal one. They did not believe that, in avoiding the excesses of passive resistance preached by Tilak and Aurobindo, it was necessary to retreat to the caution and inactivity of Mehta and the Bombay Moderate leaders.[18] The disappointing nature of the Morley–Minto Reforms of 1909 made many of them feel that more vigorous agitation was required to move the British. Indeed, the Bengali Moderate, Bhupendranath Basu, expressed the feelings of many people when he averred in 1914 that Moderates outside Bombay would 'accept any means to lift the Congress out of the present bog'.[19]

Furthermore, in those regions which had hitherto taken little part in the nationalist movement there were groups which, given leadership, might be drawn into it. In the U.P. and Bihar there were professional men, generally Kayasthas, Kashmiri Brahmins and Muslims, who had been traditionally associated with service in the Mughal administration. They had taken up the opportunities for education offered by the British, and had found their way into the service of the landlords or the British administration, and had thus identified themselves with the *status quo*. They had no intrinsic interest in the maintenance of the *status quo*, however, and if they could be imbued with nationalist feeling or brought to see that in an independent India they might wield power, they could be mobilised by the national movement. In the Madras Presidency Congress was inactive but drew a membership of some 400 from the Western-educated, professional and business classes (amongst whom the Tamil Brahmins predominated); many of them felt as restive as did Bhupendranath Basu in Bengal.[20] Again, the younger generation of Gujarati industrialists, commercial and professional men would be able to mobilise their caste-fellows and the dominant peasant groups in Gujarat itself, if once a leader arose who could draw them into the national movement. And in Sind the small Hindu Amil minority, traditionally associated with administration, had taken to English education and to the professions and might be mobilised as a nationalist élite in the area: indeed, early in 1915 some young men from this community were engaged in forming associations for the discussion of political issues.[21]

In 1914 leaders emerged who succeeded in mobilising these groups and reviving and reshaping the Congress, for in that year Tilak was released from gaol and Mrs Annie Besant joined the National Congress.

Six years in gaol, however, had made Tilak more cautious. As the result of the inactivity of his followers during his absence, he had become pessimistic of the practicality of launching a successful passive-resistance campaign,[22] and one of his first acts was to disown this method and to emphasise the common ground between himself and the Moderates.[23] Nevertheless, his followers believed that he still held to his old notions, and his release produced a flurry of meetings among them. He was anxious to enlist Mrs Besant's help in getting back into Congress, both as a shield of respectability against renewed British prosecution and as a source of potential followers, so that as she began to stir up agitation in the south and the Ganges valley he followed her example in Maharashtra, and thus staked out his claim to leadership in that region.

From 1914 to 1917 the pace was set for the Indian national movement by Annie Besant. Already sixty-six in 1914, she was an unusually vigorous woman with a commanding personality and magnetic presence. She had developed her oratorical and journalistic skills in England as a proponent, in turn, of Free Thought, Radicalism, Fabianism and Theosophy. She found much that was persuasive and admirable in Hindu metaphysics, and came to India in 1893 to join the work of the Theosophical Society. Until 1907 her headquarters were in Banaras. Then, having been made World President of the Theosophical Society, she moved to Adyar, a suburb of Madras. Although she spoke no Indian language fluently enough to use it publicly, she contributed substantially to the Hindu revival by lecturing, by writing, by founding schools, and by translating Hindu sacred texts into English.[24] Most of her work was among the Western-educated, especially among groups which had become detached from their traditions or had experienced no religious revival of their own – including the Kayasthas, the Kashmiri Brahmins and Muslims of the United Provinces and Bihar, the Tamil Brahmins of the Madras Presidency, the Gujaratis in Bombay and the Amils of Sind – many of those very groups, in fact, which might become the political élite in hitherto inactive regions.

Of Annie Besant's aims in entering Indian politics, probably the most fundamental was the fostering of Indo-British friendship:[25] she firmly believed that educated Indians were ready to govern their country, but above all she wanted to win a substantial advance toward self-government for India because she believed that this would draw Britain and India together. She wished to woo young Indians away from violence, and from passive resistance which she saw as likely to pass over into violence, since she believed that such methods would embitter relations between the two countries.[26] She had denounced Tilak's earlier advocacy of passive resistance,[27] but she now aimed to bring him and the Extremists back into Congress. It seems she was convinced that Tilak had really undergone a change of heart on the question of passive resistance;[28] more important, however, she hoped by thus turning Congress into a 'united front' of nationalists of all shades of belief, to restrain the Extremists and the young men who had come into politics since 1907, while at the same time instilling new life into the Moderates. There is no doubt that her entry into Congress was also prompted by some awareness of the realities of the Indian national movement, and by personal ambition: as a newcomer to Indian politics, she sought the cachet of authority in the only organisation which might presume to represent educated India, and she hoped ultimately to acquire the leadership of this united Congress and to march at its head to self-government.[29]

These aims could be achieved, she believed, by agitation. Here she had in mind the campaigns waged by British radicals during the nineteenth century – the campaigns for the abolition of slavery, the repeal of the Corn Laws, and for Irish Home Rule, not to mention those she had helped to lead herself in the 1870s and '80s in the company of Bradlaugh and the Fabians.[30] Monster meetings would be held, supplemented by newspaper campaigns and pamphlets; then (as Bradlaugh had taught her) if the Government tried to silence the agitation, more publicity could be sought by appealing to the courts.[31] Local committees would be established to relay these demands to the country at large, and to obtain widespread support for them. Such agitation would move Britain to grant self-government: 'British politicians', she asserted, 'judge the value of claims by the energy of those who put them forward'.[32]

II

Towards the end of 1914 Annie Besant set to work to stir the Moderate leaders of the Congress into activity. The 'younger generation', she declared, 'is growing impatient while the Congress marks time', and she urged the Moderates to establish and (where they already existed) to revive District and Taluq Congress Committees which ought to hold frequent meetings to 'educate public opinion' and 'proclaim the opinion of educated India' to the Government.[33] At the same time she backed Tilak's request that he and his fellow-Extremists should be readmitted to Congress.[34] Mehta and his Moderate colleagues in Bombay city opposed both these suggestions, for not only were they averse to sharing the leadership of Congress with Annie Besant and Tilak, but they were convinced that if Tilak were readmitted he would try to convert Congress to passive resistance against the British, and that this would result in British oppression.

When, during the preparations for the 1914 Congress, it became clear that Mehta had won Gokhale, the Bengal Moderates and others to this view, Mrs Besant and Tilak decided to revive political activity themselves. Mrs Besant was the more aggressive, and from early in 1915 she embarked, through her Madras newspapers, *New India* and *Commonweal*, and at meetings and Conferences, on a campaign of agitation.[35] She had already taken up the question of the reorganisation of the British Empire, and now demanded that at the end of the War India should share the status of the 'white' dominions: to this end she put forward a scheme of self-government for India, based on universal franchise for local *panchayats* and more restricted franchise for the superior legislatures.[36] From April 1915 her tone became even sharper.[37] As President of the United Provinces Provincial Conference in that month, she castigated the House of Lords for its refusal to approve the much-canvassed Executive Council for the United Provinces, and encouraged the members of the Congress and the Muslim League in those provinces to set up the United Provinces Governor-in-Council League to protest.[38] Tilak was probably less optimistic than Mrs Besant that agitation without sanctions would move the British to grant reforms, but he was ready to affirm that 'If you [Indians] carry on such an effort for 5 or 25 years you will never fail to obtain its fruit'.[39]

During 1915 both Tilak and Mrs Besant decided to set up political organisations of their own: generally they do not appear to have co-ordinated their plans closely, but they had probably discussed the advisability of establishing such organisations when they met in December 1914, and they maintained irregular contacts through messengers.[40] As early as February 1915 Tilak threatened to set up a 'separate League' if Mehta and the Bombay Moderates persisted in refusing to readmit him to Congress,[41] and in May he convened a 'Provincial Conference' of his followers at Poona where it was decided to form an agency to 'enlighten the villagers regarding the objects and work of the Congress'.[42] It was not until August and September, however, that local associations were established in a number of Maharashtrian towns, and even then they insisted on the need to reunify Congress rather than to expand agitation.[43] All of this supports the conclusion that, while Tilak wanted to bring pressure to bear upon the more reactionary Moderates to readmit him to Congress by threatening to supplant the Congress with his associations, he hoped nevertheless to convince the bulk of the Moderates of his reasonableness and fitness for readmission.[44] The limited scope of his associations, in terms both of area and activities, also reflected Tilak's lack of any elaborate programme at this stage, particularly by comparison with Annie Besant. Indeed, he was finally prompted to carry out his threat to establish his own 'agency' by the desire to stake out a claim to Maharashtra as his sphere of influence, since she was already planning to establish an organisation of her own on an India-wide basis.

By July Mrs Besant had decided to set up a Home Rule League.[45] To this she expected to attract the 'younger and more vigorous workers' and through them to amplify the agitation she had begun. At the same time, she believed that the formation of the League would persuade the Bombay Moderates not only to readmit Tilak but also to allow her to organise agitation under the aegis of Congress. It was hardly surprising that Mrs Besant was less cautious than Tilak: she was not personally acquainted with the difficulties of political leadership in India, and she had yet to feel the full weight of British repression. In addition, she was more familiar with the British radical movements, the lessons of which she and Tilak were planning to apply, and furthermore she had numerous potential political followers scattered widely throughout India as the result of her Theosophical work.

On 25 September 1915, she announced her decision to start the Home Rule League. This marked a turning-point in the history of the Indian national movement. With regard to the goal of the movement, her announcement envisaged much more rapid progress to self-government than had generally been demanded hitherto: the League's 'only object', she said, would be 'Home Rule for India'.[46] In its simplicity, this provided an excellent rallying cry, although in its comprehensiveness lay the danger that it would arouse expectations among younger and more impetuous Indians such as she would not be able to satisfy. To support the demand for reforms, she proposed to focus attention on India's 'growing poverty', for which she blamed the British,[47] and thus incited Indian animosity still further against them. And she foreshadowed the establishment of a network of branches of the League to carry this agitation throughout the country. Nevertheless, she tried to avoid alienating the Moderates completely. The Home Rule League would only be set up, she said, in consultation with Congressmen and members of the Muslim League, and to this end she arranged to hold a Conference in Bombay at the end of 1915 concurrently with the annual Congress session. Furthermore, she and Tilak agreed that, in order to mollify the Bombay Moderates, he and the Extremists would not attend this

Conference.[48] She felt quite safe in committing the future of the League to a Conference at which Moderates predominated, since she had obtained promises of support from a number of them, including Banerjea in Bengal and Malaviya in the United Provinces.

At the Conference itself, however, she found that the Bombay Moderates had seduced many of these others from their support for her League. Although vexed at being thus out-manœuvred, she abided by her promise to accept the views of the majority of the Moderates, and suspended the formation of the League. In fact, her efforts had not been in vain, for at its concurrent session Congress began to move in the direction she desired: Tilak and the Extremists were grudgingly re-admitted; the All-India Congress Committee (or 'AICC') – the standing executive committee of the Congress – was instructed to draw up by the following September a scheme of reforms demanding popular control over the executive Government (a long step towards the 'only object' of Mrs Besant's Home Rule League); and, to back this up, the session committed Congress to a programme of 'educative propagandist work'.[49] These important changes can be ascribed, in part, to Annie Besant's presence in the Subjects Committee (the guiding body for the Congress sessions), where she provided a rallying point for the younger men and all who disliked the inactivity of the Bombay Moderates, and pressed for these modifications to the Congress programme.[50] In addition, the older Moderates' resistance had been weakened by the deaths of Gokhale and Mehta earlier in the year, and this forced them to give way to some extent before her pressure. At the same time, they hoped to subvert her proposed agitation by appropriating it to the Congress and then allowing it to drop.

Mrs Besant recognised this ulterior motive, and announced that if the Congress failed to take substantial steps to put these resolutions into effect by September 1916 she would launch her League. The logical conclusion to be drawn from the failure of Moderates like Banerjea and Malaviya to remain faithful to their promises of support for her was that she must retain control of the Home Rule agitation herself, and this made her anxious to find some pretext for establishing the League. Most of her young admirers were disappointed with her suspension of it. Some of the young Bombay Congressmen in particular were disappointed, notably Jamnadas Dwarkadas, Shankarlal Banker and Indulal Yajnik. Of Gujarati descent, they had imbibed their nationalism when they had been college students between 1905 and 1914. By 1915 Jamnadas was a staunch Theosophical follower of Mrs Besant, and although only twenty-five had already become a wealthy importer of dyes for the cotton industry. Banker, who was the son of a rich man, was to show remarkable organisational talent, and was anxious to serve his country and its depressed classes. Yajnik, a writer, had committed himself to a life of poverty and social and national service in the Servants of India Society.[51] Mrs Besant needed little prompting from them to sanction the inauguration early in 1916 of Home Rule 'Groups' and of a Bombay paper, *Young India*, to be edited by Jamnadas. She also instituted an All-India Propaganda Fund to publish pamphlets in English and regional Indian languages.[52] The newspaper and the Propaganda Fund were conducted with more vigour than the 'Groups', but all three together constituted in truncated form the Home Rule League she had hoped to set up.

Judging that it was only a matter of time before Mrs Besant launched her League proper, Tilak decided to forestall her in Maharashtra. As he had not attended the Conference in Bombay, he was not bound by her decision to suspend the formation of her League, and he established his Indian Home Rule League on 28 April 1916.[53] This, in turn, provoked Mrs Besant and her Bombay supporters to increased activity. She addressed meetings of 5,000 in Poona at Tilak's invitation, and other meetings and Conferences in south India: and she and her supporters produced pamphlets in Madras, Bombay, the United Provinces and Sind. The failure of Congress to implement its resolution to undertake educative propaganda gave her the desired opportunity to launch her own All-India Home Rule League.[54] In mid-1916 her Theosophical and Socialist colleagues in Britain formed an Auxiliary Home Rule League, and at the same time she appointed her loyal Theosophical follower, George Arundale,[55] as Organising Secretary '*pro tem*' for her League in India. It was formally inaugurated on 3 September 1916 with ten branches and 500 members.[56]

III

Tilak confined the operation of the Indian Home Rule League to Maharashtra and the Karnatak, where he had an assured following. He relied on trusted lieutenants to arrange his speech tours, to undertake similar tours themselves, to hold meetings in the temples and open spaces of their own towns, and to print newspapers and pamphlets. During its first year his League published six Marathi and two English pamphlets (of which 47,000 copies were sold) and one each in Gujarati and Kannada.[57] Much of this work could have been done without formal organisation, but the League served to pre-empt Maharashtra as Tilak's field of operation, leaving the rest of India to Annie Besant – an arrangement in which she concurred.[58]

In its first year the managing committee of Tilak's League was appointed from among themselves by Tilak's lieutenants.[59] At its first Annual Conference in April 1917 a more 'democratic' Constitution was adopted, which provided for the election of office-bearers by the members present at the annual Conference, but, even so, the lieutenants' nominees were returned unopposed. It was agreed that these office-bearers were to form an Executive Committee and were to co-opt a representative from each of the League's six branches, Central Maharashtra, Bombay city, the Karnatak, Berar (where there were two branches) and the Central Provinces.[60] Tilak carefully ensured that each major town and area covered by the League had representatives on both the managing committee and its more formal successor, thus avoiding jealousies.[61] In fact, the day-to-day working of the League was supervised from the Poona office of Tilak's newspapers, the *Kesari* and *Mahratta*, by the League's Executive Assistant (a young Chitpavan Brahmin, named D.V. Gokhale) in consultation with Tilak and his close lieutenant, Kelkar.[62]

Very quickly the Government tried to gag Tilak's Home Rule agitation. In July 1916 bonds of Rs 40,000 were demanded from him on the ground that his speeches were seditious, and local officials took steps to warn people against supporting his movement.[63] Tilak riposted by appealing to the courts, and in November obtained a ruling from the Bombay High Court that the demand for Home Rule was not seditious.[64] Thereupon his League embarked on a recruiting drive. Offices were opened for each of the six branches, his supporters among the professional men in Bombay and other towns turned their rooms into recruiting centres, and his more devoted followers toured the *mofussil*.[65] The League's annual subscription of one rupee per head was retained, but the entry fee of Rs 2 was dropped. From a membership of 1,000 in November 1916 the number rose to 14,000 in April 1917, and 32,000 early in 1918.[66] In addition to recruiting new members, this campaign clearly carried the demand for Home Rule to many who did not actually join the League.

As for Mrs Besant's All-India Home Rule League, this initially had an Executive Council of seven office-bearers elected in September 1916 for three years by the thirty-four 'founding branches'. In practice the names she put forward were returned unopposed: she herself was confirmed as

President and Arundale as Organising Secretary, while C. P. Rama-swami Aiyar, an outstanding thirty-six-year-old lawyer, was installed as one of the General Secretaries and B. P. Wadia, a Parsi Theosophist, as Treasurer.[67] The Council, however, held very few official meetings; in general its business was conducted informally by these four officials from Mrs Besant's headquarters at Adyar.

The constitutional links between the headquarters of this All-India League and its branches were most tenuous. No elaborate organisation was prescribed: any three persons might form a branch.[68] The result was that, unlike the half-dozen branches of Tilak's League each responsible for activities in a relatively wide area, some 200 branches of Mrs Besant's League were set up, each one enjoying virtual autonomy and being con-fined to one town or group of villages. The Organising Secretary simply sanctioned the formation of branches, and these remitted to the Council an entry fee of one rupee from each member. Mrs Besant maintained communication informally through individuals, who were either active in a particular branch or in touch with a number of branches,[69] and her headquarters transmitted instructions through such people, or through *New India*, in which from the beginning of 1916 Arundale edited a page of Home Rule news and advice.

The membership of Mrs Besant's League grew more slowly than Tilak's, until (as we shall see) she was involved in a dramatic clash with the Government in mid-1917. In March of that year it had only 7,000 members but by December 1917 it had grown to 27,000.[70]

In the formation of her League she drew largely on the loyalty of members of the Theosophical Society. Some Theosophists objected to her mixing of politics with Theosophy, but the more ardent believed that by launching the Home Rule League she was carrying out the behests of those who control the affairs of the world.[71] Certainly her League was supported by many non-Theosophists: in December 1917 its membership was five times that of the Indian Section of the Theo-sophical Society,[72] and among those who were prominent in the affairs of the League were such non-Theosophists as Ramaswami Aiyar in Madras, Jawaharlal Nehru in Allahabad, Shankarlal Banker in Bombay, and B. Chakravarti and Jitendralal Bannerjee in Calcutta.[73] Theoso-phists, nevertheless, often provided the initial impetus for the forma-tion of branches of the League, and the strength of the League in each area generally reflected the local strength of the Theosophical Society. In the Madras Presidency, for example, it had more members and a more elaborate network of 'lodges' than anywhere else in India, and by

September 1917 the All-India Home Rule League had 132 branches in that Presidency, which again was more than all those in the rest of India.[74] In Madras Presidency, moreover, the Theosophists who were officers of the League were legion: Manjeri Ramier, for example, was an office-bearer in the Calicut Theosophical Lodge and President of the Malabar branch of the All-India Home Rule League, and there were similar duplications of function at Vijayawada (Bezwada) in Andhra and at Madura and Trichy in Tamilnad.[75]

The number of branches was not an entirely adequate indication of the League's strength. While some of the Madras branches were quite small or relatively inactive, the Bombay city branch had over 2,600 members in September 1917, and, although there were only eight branches in the United Provinces, the four in the main cities were very active in the surrounding *mofussil* as well as in the cities themselves. But in these two areas again, the League reflected the local strength of the Theosophical Society: in Bombay its officers included not only Jamnadas Dwarkadas, but other Theosophists, like P. K. Telang and Ratansi Morarji, and in the United Provinces leading roles were played by Theosophists in Lucknow and the staffs of the Theosophical Colleges in Banaras, Kanpur and Allahabad.[76]

The function of the Home Rule Leagues was to contribute to the rousing of agitation in India. Arundale, the Organising Secretary of the All-India League, first concentrated on what Mrs Besant had called the 'educative' aspect of agitation: through his Home Rule page in *New India*, he advised branches on the sort of activities they should undertake. Their members, he said, should argue the case for Home Rule with their friends and urge them to join the League: they should collect political facts and opinions and discuss them regularly; set up classes to lecture to students on political matters; and establish a library, containing printed speeches by Indian nationalists, newspapers, and works by Seeley, J. S. Mill, and, of course, Mrs Besant herself. They should also print and circulate pamphlets; undertake constructive social work in their local area; participate in local government activities; collect funds, and hold public lectures and meetings.[77]

Most of the branches carried out at least some of these functions. Many opened reading rooms and held regular discussion groups for their members and students, notably in the larger towns and cities like Karachi, Bombay, Madura and Madras. The discussion groups considered such problems as those of Indian Finance or Local Self-Government – or aspects of Tagore's poetry – but the general drift of the discussions was always the desirability of Home Rule.[78] By the time her League was founded in September 1916 Mrs Besant's Propaganda Fund had already sold over 300,000 copies of twenty-six English-language pamphlets, which discussed the machinery of government in India and rehearsed the arguments for self-government, and after the inauguration of the League the branches republished these pamphlets and published new ones in the Indian languages.[79] Most branches held public meetings, too, and they could be relied on to do so whenever Mrs Besant and Tilak wished for a nation-wide protest on a particular issue.

IV

Early in 1916 Mrs Besant had written that, in order to 'lay a solid foundation' for the Home Rule agitation, it was necessary to shake the dependence of both educated Indians and the 'masses' upon the Government and to arouse 'pride in the Motherland'. The Government's shortcomings, she said, must be criticised and Indians must be convinced of India's greatness prior to the arrival of the British.[80] Accordingly, the tone of *New India* became increasingly shrill, and soon reached the point of justifying the Irish rebellion of Easter 1916. As a result in May 1916 the Madras Government demanded that she deposit a security of Rs 2,000 under the terms of the Press Act, and the Bombay Government 'externed' her – that is, barred her from entering the Bombay Presidency.[81] In a wave of public meetings Extremists and Moderates throughout India protested against these actions. Nothing daunted, Mrs Besant continued to denigrate the Government. She accused the Madras Government of favouring the British community and Christian missionaries and of victimising Indian students, whereupon it forfeited the Rs 2,000 and demanded a new security of Rs 10,000.[82] She then appealed to the courts, and thereby parried government action temporarily, while also obtaining much favourable publicity. In November she was externed from the Central Provinces and Berar, and in response to this Arundale urged the branches of her League to hold public meetings and send resolutions of protest to the Viceroy and the Secretary of State. Most branches complied, and similar meetings and similar protests followed Tilak's externment from the Panjab and Delhi in February 1917.[83]

Some Moderates who had wished for greater nationalist activity but who wanted agitation to be controlled by Congress, set out to lend support to the Home Rule campaign. While the Servants of India Society refused to allow its members to join the Home Rule League, it encouraged them to support the demand for Home Rule through speech-making tours and the publication of pamphlets.[84] In preparation for the 1916 Congress to be held at Lucknow (as usual at the end of the year), members of the Servants of India Society and other Moderate Congressmen joined with members of the Home Rule League branches from the main cities of the United Provinces in touring surrounding towns and villages. Usually they went by train, stopping off at each town of any size along the way and addressing the members of the bar library. The library would generally have arranged a public meeting, attended by professional people, students, business people, and by agriculturists if it was a market day. The speakers' arguments (which were usually put in Hindi) were designed to appeal to a wide audience. They outlined European movements for national independence, extolled the glories of India in pre-British times and contrasted these with her current poverty and degradation.[85]

Mrs Besant and Tilak were hoping to win control of Congress, and they set about working through their Leagues to gain this objective at the 1916 Lucknow session. Arundale urged every member of the All-India League to 'get himself elected as a delegate to Lucknow' and ensure that this Congress was 'committed far more definitely to Home Rule than its predecessors',[86] while the officers of Tilak's League organised the first 'Congress Special' trains to take delegates from western India. Home Rulers (as the members of the Leagues were known) were in a decided majority, both in the open session and the Subjects Committee.[87] Nevertheless, the older Moderates controlled the Provincial Congress Committees which enabled them to elect a Moderate President, and in the Subjects Committee they played upon Mrs Besant's and Tilak's desire for unity to prevent the Home Rulers from entirely getting their way. By fostering the demand for sweeping political reform and putting forward her own proposals, Mrs Besant had greatly influenced the Congress/Muslim League Reform Scheme which was adopted by this Congress, particularly its demand for a substantial majority of elected representatives in the Indian legislatures from whom half the Executive Councils should be elected.[88] But when she moved a resolution in the Subjects Committee demanding Home Rule she was constrained to withdraw it in the face of opposition from the Moderates. More important, Tilak proposed that a compact Working Committee be set up for the day-to-day working of Congress and for the direction of agitation. He and Mrs Besant no doubt calculated that the Home Rule majority would elect a majority of Home Rulers to this Committee, and that by being made responsible for agitation it would assimilate the work of the Home Rule Leagues on behalf of Congress.[89] But the Moderate veterans were anxious neither to espouse the increasingly shrill agitation of the Leagues nor to allow Tilak and Mrs Besant to consolidate their leadership. The Moderate President therefore announced that 'the Congress was a mere deliberative body', and ruled Tilak's proposal out of order.[90]

For all that the Home Rule agitation was carried on with renewed vigour after the Lucknow Congress, both Tilak and Mrs Besant making triumphal tours and addressing meetings throughout northern, eastern and central India.[91] Soon afterwards the demand for self-government was further stimulated by events outside India, notably the March Revolution in Russia and President Wilson's message to the United States Congress justifying the entry of the USA into the World War on the ground that it was thereby defending the liberties of small nations.[92] The provincial Governments, seeing that they were being discredited by the agitation, now prevailed upon the Government of India to let them take steps to crush it. The Governments of Bombay, Madras and the Central Provinces banned students from meetings, and in April and May 1917 the Governments of the Panjab, Bombay and Madras publicly deplored the agitation, in terms suggesting they might prohibit it.[93] Mrs Besant's lieutenants responded with denunciations of the Government and with talk of passively resisting any attempts to proscribe agitation. Mrs Besant echoed this in *New India*.[94] Thereupon, in June 1917, the Government of Madras interned her, together with Arundale and Wadia.

This was the signal for a nation-wide outcry: the internments did not crush the agitation as the Governments had hoped – quite the reverse. Prominent men, including Moderates, who had held aloof from her Home Rule League now joined it and its membership doubled,[95] and even Moderates who did not join the League, like Banerjea, Wacha and Sastri, condemned the Government's action.[96] The younger men, especially in Bombay, sought guidance from Tilak and from Gandhi for a campaign of passive resistance, and from her place of internment Mrs Besant expressed her approval of passive resistance and strove 'to think out *methods*, so as to adapt P[assive] R[esistance] to Indian conditions'.[97]

At Gandhi's suggestion, her lieutenants in Bombay, led by Jamnadas Dwarkadas and Shankarlal Banker, collected the signatures of a thousand young men willing to break the internment orders by marching to her place of detention, and also set about collecting the signatures of a million peasants and workers on a Monster Petition for Home Rule. Of more lasting importance, they visited Gujarat repeatedly from this time onwards, addressing meetings in towns and villages and encouraging the formation of branches of the All-India League.[98]

A head-on collision between the national movement and the British was only averted in August by the announcement by Edwin Montagu, Secretary of State for India, that an advance was to be made towards responsible government in India, and that he was to visit India at the end of the year to receive, in company with the Viceroy, Lord Chelmsford, the views of Indians on how this should be done.[99] In September, in a further attempt to lower the political temperature, he had Mrs Besant released.

At the time of her release it seemed that she had the national movement at her feet. The internment had united Moderates and Extremists as never before, and her popularity swept her into the Presidential chair of the Congress session in Calcutta at the end of 1917. By the end of the following year, however, she had isolated herself from the several groups which she had brought together in the Congress, and had lost all claims to leadership of the national movement.

This apparently astonishing change may be ascribed to two things. First, the united front of the Moderates, Extremists and young men in the Congress was basically unstable (and in mid-1917 was becoming increasingly so); and, secondly, following her release Mrs Besant attempted to change her strategy. The united front in the Congress was unstable because a number of the old Bombay Moderates had never accepted her political wisdom, and had never really become reconciled to the readmission of Tilak and the Extremists; even more Moderates in both Bengal and Bombay were jealous of Mrs Besant, whom they considered an upstart newcomer to Congress which they saw as their own preserve. The virulence of the Home Rule agitation had increased the Bombay Moderate leaders' suspicions, and Mrs Besant's espousal of passive resistance reawakened their fears of the Extremist programme.[100] Their adherence to the united front was further undermined by Montagu's announcement of forthcoming reforms, which revived their faith in the possibility of advance to self-government in co-operation with the British. Mrs Besant's nomination as President of the Calcutta Congress so provoked the jealousy of Banerjea and the Bengal Moderates, that in August and September 1917 they opposed her election and quarrelled bitterly with her supporters, led by C.R.Das.[101] The young men and Extremists, however, avoided an open rift with the Moderates at this time by temporarily suspending their demands for passive resistance, and by offering to support Banerjea's nominee for the position of Chairman of the Reception Committee at the Calcutta session. But the spectre of another Congress split had been raised.

It was partly in the hope of laying this unwelcome apparition that Mrs Besant altered her strategy. Following her release, she turned her face against agitation and joined the Congress Moderates in rejecting passive resistance.[102] Her reasons for doing so were probably complex,[103] but among the most important, no doubt, was her awareness of the Moderates' uneasiness and her desire to keep the national movement united. In addition, Montagu's declaration seems to have convinced her that the British were now responsive to Indian demands and that more could be won by consultation in the old Moderate tradition than by agitation. Her nerve, too, may have been shaken: the enforced idleness of internment depressed her and probably made her fearful of her continued ability to control the unrest she had aroused.[104]

Her change of strategy confronted her with the problem of maintaining her influence over the young men and Extremists who had so far followed her so enthusiastically. In her Presidential speech at Calcutta she warned them: 'I cannot promise to please you always', and foreshadowed increasing moderation;[105] but she took no positive steps to restrain or control them. Their blood was up: they were disappointed by her repudiation of passive resistance, and were in no mood to give up agitation, in which they could all participate, in favour of consultations between her and Montagu.[106]

During the later months of 1917 and 1918 she sought to retain the loyalty of these more impetuous Congressmen and, at the same time, the confidence of the Moderates, and this led her to adopt increasingly ambivalent policies. By adopting a peremptory tone toward Montagu after his arrival in India, she tried to avoid alienating those whom she had helped to arouse: toward the end of 1917 she and Tilak announced that the Congress/Muslim League Scheme of 1916 constituted the 'irreducible minimum of political reform which must be immediately granted to India'.[107] In the following February, however, in an effort to placate the Moderates, she agreed to accept considerably less. Tilak's supporters and many young Congressmen found this *volte face* painfully 'surprising'.[108] Again, during April 1918, in response to the Government's call for greater Indian contributions towards the War, she joined Tilak in demanding Home Rule as the price of help,[109] but at a meeting of the AICC in May she swung right round and pushed through a resolution urging Indians to offer unconditional assistance. Tilak only acquiesced in the resolution after much wrangling, and Mrs Besant's popularity with the young rank-and-file suffered a grievous decline.[110] In April, in an effort to maintain her identification with young Congressmen, she had argued in favour of passive resistance if Montagu's proposals for reform should prove inadequate, and when the Montagu/Chelmsford reforms scheme[111] was published in July, she and Tilak denounced it as 'unworthy of Britain to offer'.[112] But, in the hope of retaining the support of the Moderates, she prevailed upon the Special Congress, which met in September 1918 to consider the Reforms, to accept a compromise: the Reforms would not be accepted, but neither would they be rejected! Instead, the resolution demanded that they be amended, providing for complete provincial autonomy in five years, and for the transfer to elected Indian members in the central government of all powers other than those affecting war and internal security. Tilak and the young men would have preferred Montagu's scheme to be 'rejected altogether', but agreed to this compromise resolution on the understanding that it would prevent the Moderates seceding from the Congress.[113]

The Moderates had been estranged, however, by Annie Besant's bellicosity toward the British and by her inconsistency, and they refused to attend either this Special Congress or the annual session in December 1918.

Those who attended the annual Congress – mainly the young men and Extremists – rejected her leadership and demanded immediate provincial autonomy.[114] They were dissatisfied with the compromise resolution which they had accepted at the Special Congress,[115] and the ending of the World War in November imparted a sense of urgency to their demand for responsible government.[116] With the withdrawal of the Moderates, Mrs Besant was no longer able to appeal to the need to preserve the united front in her efforts to restrain the more eager Congressmen. At the December session, moreover, she was unable to call on Tilak's help either, for he had gone to England in September to fight his libel action against Chirol. In doing so, he completely failed to recognise the need for leadership in India itself at this time, and threw away the opportunity for giving a decisive lead to those whose feelings he had helped to foment.

Mrs Besant might have succeeded in carrying the young and impetuous members of the Congress and the Home Rule League with her in her change of strategy, if she had improved the organisation of those bodies and had tightened her control over them. It seems, however, that she over-estimated the powers given to her by her election as President of Congress: in her Presidential address she declared that the Congress President 'is, for his year of service, her [India's] chosen leader', and that the 'duty of a leader is to lead'.[117] As President, she could call the AICC together to formulate policy – the assertion of this right was itself an innovation – but the party still lacked machinery at the local level to put the AICC's decisions into effect. She did impart some vigour to the central organisation of Congress at the end of 1917 by appointing C.P. Ramaswami Aiyar as its principal General Secretary, but she made no attempt to strengthen it at the district level or to integrate the branches of her Home Rule League with it. At the end of 1917 she made a half-hearted move to link the branches and the headquarters of the League more effectively by setting up Provincial Councils, but far from making active use of the League in 1918 she allowed it to decline. She abolished Arundale's position of Organising Secretary, and Ramaswami Aiyar resigned from the General Secretaryship of the League when he transferred to the equivalent position in the Congress.[118] As her position waned in mid-1918 Mrs Besant at last began to realise that she had no organisation for restraining those whom she had excited to agitation, and in June she thought of reviving the League and reappointing Arundale as Organising Secretary.[119]

By then, however, it was too late either to rebuild the League or to adapt it to the purpose of control: the young men of Madras were already starting to revolt against her.[120] In any case, she had no programme of action which would give expression to the feelings of the young Congressmen. By alternatively fostering agitation and then calling it off during the fifteen months preceding the 1918 annual Congress, she simply succeeded in frustrating these feelings. By the beginning of 1919 her leadership had been rejected, and, since Tilak had virtually relinquished his authority, the Congress was leaderless. The stage was set for a new leader who would release the great tensions that these two leaders had managed to set up. In March and April of that year Gandhi emerged to fill this role by leading the Rowlatt Act satyagraha.

V

What then did the Home Rule Leagues achieve? Measured by their initial intention of obtaining Home Rule for India they failed. Nevertheless the British Government's promise of advance towards self-government could be traced very largely to the Home Rule agitation. On his appointment as Viceroy in 1916, Lord Chelmsford had recognised that the Moderates were being drawn into increasingly close alliance with the Home Rulers due to the Government's failure to make any favourable response to the demand for reforms, and at the end of the year, in an effort to reverse this trend, he and his Council had proposed to the home Government that the Indian membership of the legislatures should be increased.[121] Austen Chamberlain, the then Secretary of State, had replied in March 1917 that 'the politicians of India have found out how to agitate', and that if any reforms were to be acceptable to those politicians and to prevent their proposals from receiving 'a large measure of support at home', such reforms would have to involve an increase not only in the Indian membership of the Councils but also in the 'authority and responsibility' of those members.[122] It was Chamberlain who drafted, in outline, the announcement which Montagu made in August 1917.[123]

In the long run, however, the importance of the Home Rule Leagues must be measured by their impact on the national movement; and here their crucial contribution was to deflect it permanently from the courses mapped out for it by the previous Moderate leadership. In 1916 and 1917 agitation had been aroused on a nation-wide scale for the first time. There were still, of course, regional variations in the strength and nature of the response to the Home Rule movement, variations which were in part a reflection of political traditions and legacies from the past and of the local standing of the Home Rulers; these in turn grew out of the different social conditions in each of the regions. Considerable work is now being done upon these questions,[124] and there is only space in a chapter such as this to touch upon them quite briefly. The variations in the Home Rule movement also reflected the relative strength in each province of the young, Western-educated generation, which had been stirred by the political events of the first decade of the century; and they reflected, inversely, the severity of British wartime repression, which differed from province to province.

During this period agitation was almost entirely lacking in the Panjab, and was less intense in Bengal than elsewhere. The situation in the Panjab could be largely traced to the fact that the Government had applied wartime emergency legislation to crush the incipient revolutionary movements among the Sikhs and Muslims, and to stamp out all political activity between 1914 and 1917. In addition, the strength of the Arya

Samaj had inhibited the spread of Theosophy in the province, and Mrs Besant thus had few followers there on whom she could call to found branches of the Home Rule League. In Bengal the Government interned 2,000 young terrorist suspects early in the War, thus depriving the Home Rule movement of many potential members.[125] Here, too, the Theosophical Society was weak. Perhaps more important, Congress politics in Bengal were still dominated by Surendranath Banerjea and the Moderates, and it was only with the emergence of C. R. Das in 1917 that the Extremists and young Congressmen organised to challenge them.

The other regions of British India were effectively involved in nationalist politics by the Home Rule movement. Maharashtra and the Karnatak were deeply stirred, thanks largely to Tilak's network of Chitpavan lieutenants, and to the following he had won during his earlier nationalist campaigns. This indeed was the stronghold of Tilak's League.

The greatest strength of Mrs Besant's League lay in Bombay city, Gujarat, Sind, the United Provinces, Bihar and southern India. Here were the areas where the Theosophical Society was strongest, mainly, it has been assumed, because these areas had not had an indigenous Hindu revival when the Society began its work there. They were also the regions where there was little in the way of well-established political movements, either Extremist or Moderate: the first might have pre-empted the loyalty of the younger generation; the latter might have hampered the Home Rule agitation. The outstanding exception here, of course, was Bombay city, where Mrs Besant's young lieutenants found that, while they could stir up agitation very effectively, they were continually being opposed by the Moderates in their efforts to obtain Congress backing for agitation or for passive resistance.[126] Most active in the Bombay branch of the League were a number of young men, many of them Theosophists, who were members of the Bhatia and other Gujarati trading castes engaged in the cotton industry of the capital of the Presidency. Through their business and social contacts they drew other industrial and professional men into the League, as well as enlisting workers from the cloth mills and markets for their meetings and demonstrations. It was also due to them that the agitation was extended to their native region, for from mid-1917 onward they went out into the towns and the countryside of Gujarat, persuading their fellow caste-men and members of the dominant cultivating castes to form branches of the League.

The Sind branches of the All-India Home Rule League were established by Theosophists, too, most of whom were Amils.[127]

In the United Provinces the initial response of older Congressmen had
been to support the Home Rule demands while holding aloof from the
Home Rule League itself. This was probably because Congressmen like
Malaviya were jealous of Mrs Besant, or because others, like Motilal
Nehru and Sapru, remained loyal to the Bombay Moderates. Here and
in Bihar branches of the League were formed by Theosophists, by
Muslim nationalists and by the younger Congressmen,[128] but after Mrs
Besant's internment, many of the older men joined them.

The Theosophical Society had penetrated most deeply into the four
language-regions of the Madras Presidency, and it was through the
many lodges of the Society here, as we have seen, that Mrs Besant had
the greatest success in setting up branches of the League and mobilising
support for it. The Telugu-speaking Brahmins of the future Andhra had
an additional reason for supporting her League, since they saw in it a
vehicle for their agitation in favour of a separate province, in which they
hoped to replace Tamil Brahmins in the professions and Government
service.[129]

Both in the Madras Presidency, and in Maharashtra and the Karnatak
the Home Rule Leagues were dominated by Brahmins. In both these
regions, however, certain peasant groups and trading castes had been
acquiring wealth and, with it, Western education and an envy of the
Brahmins' superior position.[130] These castes believed that if the British
acceded to the demand for Home Rule they would virtually be handing
the government of India over to the dominant Brahmins, and they therefore organised non-Brahmin movements to oppose the Home Rule
agitation.[131] These organisations were to weaken the national movement in these regions in the 1920s and '30s and to divide Indians in the
post-independence period.

These regional differences carried implications for the later development of the national movement; but the striking thing about the Home
Rule movement is that it drew so many areas which had hitherto been
practically inactive into nationalist activity.

From the point of view of organisation, too, the Home Rule episode
helped to shape the future national movement. For the first time a network of local political committees covered much of British India. In
earlier periods, Congress Committees and Associations had been established in certain parts of India (particularly in Bengal during the Partition
agitation), but most of these had become defunct, and the Moderates had

failed to construct the network of Committees which they had begun in 1908. The Home Rule Leagues also fell into disuse, but in spite of this and in spite of their rudimentary nature they underlined the importance of an all-India organisation at the local level for any leader who would conduct agitation, a lesson of which Gandhi took some heed when he came to reorganise the Congress in 1920.

Although the branches of the Leagues were only loosely linked with their headquarters, the Leagues had created formal and informal channels of communication which were to be important in future political campaigns. Tilak's and Mrs Besant's lieutenants in Bombay city, for example, had co-operated in arranging meetings in the city and in Maharahstra and Gujarat. In Gandhi's Rowlatt Act satyagraha of 1919, Shankarlal Banker of the Bombay Home Rule League used the lists of the Leagues' branch secretaries in Maharashtra, the Karnatak, Gujarat and Sind for the distribution of posters and instructions for the conduct of the campaign.[132] Similarly, many of Gandhi's lieutenants in the United Provinces and Bihar had been active Home Rulers, and used the contacts they had made for arranging tours and meetings in the course of the Rowlatt Act campaign.[133]

Many, moreover, who later became leading figures in the national movement had their first experience of arousing audiences during the Home Rule agitation. Such men as Satyamurti in Madras, and Jawaharlal Nehru, Harkaran Nath Misra and Khaliquzzaman in the United Provinces, who were all still in their twenties, had begun as ushers at the annual Congresses, but now found themselves with responsible work to do in the All-India League.[134] Paradoxically, the looseness of the control exerted by its headquarters, and the Government's restrictions on Mrs Besant's movements, gave them the opportunity to exercise their own initiative.

Mrs Besant and Tilak had sought to win control of Congress by obtaining the readmission to it of Tilak and his Extremist followers, and by inducing members of the Leagues to join it and vote for their policies. When most of the Moderates left the Congress, young men and Extremists comprised the overwhelming majority of Congress members, with the result that, although Mrs Besant and Tilak had begun by establishing the quite separate Home Rule organisations, they were instrumental in the end in reviving the original organisation as the vehicle of Indian nationalism.

With Tilak's help, Annie Besant introduced the agitational style into national politics. This style had been foreshadowed by Tilak in

Maharashtra in the 1890s, and by the Panjab Extremists and the opponents of Partition in Bengal in the first decade of the twentieth century, but it was only in the period 1915–18 that agitation was roused throughout India over a continuous period of years, and was adopted by the major national organisation as a standard technique. It was this style, transmuted by Gandhi, which was to characterise much of Congress political activity during the following thirty years. The Home Rule agitation imparted a sense of impatience to the national movement as a whole, and the effect of this was seen in 1920, when Motilal Nehru and others prevailed upon Gandhi to put forward the demand for Swaraj before they would support his non-cooperation campaign.[135]

The demand for Home Rule and the challenge it offered to British rule were presented not only to Western-educated Indians but also to mass groups. The Leagues never claimed to have more than 60,000 members between them, and so were small compared with what came later under Gandhi. But, as we have seen, the number of members was not an entirely accurate indication of the effectiveness of the Leagues, since their activities reached many who were not members, and they provoked other organisations, notably the Servants of India Society, to similar action. Some of their activities involved only educated groups: establishing study circles for students; holding discussions and debates upon aspects of government; setting up libraries and reading rooms; and delivering speeches to lawyers and other professional men in the course of tours arranged by branches of the League. But on these tours – in the United Provinces, Gujarat or Maharashtra, for example – many speakers addressed crowds in market places or in the open spaces before temples. And meetings to protest against Government restrictions on Home Rule leaders or, say, against the conditions under which Indians were indentured to work overseas, drew much larger audiences than did the discussions and 'educative' lectures. In Bombay, for instance, the Home Rulers commandeered a large open space known as Shantaram's Chawl, near the areas inhabited by millworkers and government employees, for meetings attended by ten to twelve thousand. And on their speech tours Mrs Besant or Tilak drew comparable audiences, even in lesser towns.

The demand for Home Rule was simple and forceful, but it had the great disadvantage of being impossible to satisfy in the short run. By initially demanding the maximum, Annie Besant had limited her room for manœuvre; any attempt to change her strategy in relation to the British exposed her to the charge of apostasy by her followers. By fostering agitation to the point where passive resistance was demanded and then repudiating this programme, she and Tilak finally succeeded in frustrating their followers, and in this way provided much of the head of steam world was to propel Gandhi's satyagraha campaign in 1919.

NOTES

1 R. C. Majumdar in *History of the Freedom Movement in India*, Calcutta 1963, II, pp. 363–76, 382–6, 496, has given the best estimate of the movement's importance, but has only touched on the formation of the Home Rule Leagues [hereinafter HRLs] and their achievement; P. Sitaramayya, in *The History of the Indian National Congress*, Bombay 1935, I, pp. 125, 126, 130–1, 149–50, takes their importance for granted but neither examines the mechanism of agitation and the organisation, nor indicates wherein lay their importance; D. G. Tendulkar, in *Mahatma*, Bombay 1951, I, pp. 262–7, 286, 292, touches on the Home Rule movement and the preparedness of the national movement for Gandhi's emergence but fails to relate the two. Biographies and autobiographies probably convey more convincing (if often fleeting) impressions of the movement's importance: see, e.g., T. V. Parvate, *Bal Gangadhar Tilak*, Ahmedabad 1958, with the fullest account of Tilak's HRL, pp. 334–71; *Toward Freedom: The Autobiography of Jawaharlal Nehru*, New York 1941, p. 42; I. K. Yajnik, *Gandhi As I Know Him*, Delhi 1943, pp. 11–23, 30–5; K. M. Munshi, *I Follow the Mahatma*, Bombay 1940, pp. 3–7; but M. R. Jayakar, *The Story of My Life*, Bombay 1958, I, p. 170 gives a totally misleading account, and the latest in the line of biographies, A. H. Nethercot, *The Last Four Lives of Annie Besant*, London 1963, pp. 213–6, 250–75, is not only inaccurate in important particulars but also fails to convey adequately the importance of his subject's contribution to Indian nationalism.

2 See speech by M. G. Ranade, 1878, in J. Kellock, *Mahadev Govind Ranade, Patriot & Social Servant*, Calcutta 1926, pp. 12–13; G. K. Gokhale to 'Vamanrao', 15 May 1908, Gokhale Papers, National Archives of India.

3 R. N. Mudholkar to D. E. Wacha, 15 July 1906, Mehta Papers, held by Sir H. P. Modi, Bombay; T. V. Parvate, *Gopal Krishna Gokhale, A Narrative . . . Review of His Life . . .*, Ahmedabad 1959, pp. 164, 192, 212, 307; S. Banerjea, *A Nation in Making*, Madras 1925, p. 314. There were distinctions between the Moderates of Bengal and western India which there is not space to examine here.

4 See Tilak, quoted in S. A. Wolpert, *Tilak and Gokhale: Revolution and Reform in the Making of Modern India*, Berkeley & Los Angeles 1962, pp. 138, 150, 268; Aurobindo, quoted in H. & V. Mukherjee, *Sri Aurobindo's Political Thought (1893–1908)*, Calcutta 1958, p. 40; D. F. Pocock, 'Notes on the Interaction of English & Indian Thought in the Nineteenth Century', *Journal of World History*, IV, No. 4, p. 844.

5   See e.g. Tilak, 'Tenets of the New Party', 2 Jan. 1917, in *All About Lok Tilak*, Madras 1922, pp. 492–505; Sri Aurobindo, *The Doctrine of Passive Resistance*, Calcutta 1948, *passim*.

6   See A. Gupta (ed.), *Studies in the Bengal Renaissance*, Jadavpur 1958, p. 565.

7   For organisation of Congress at this time, see M. V. Ramana Rao, *Development of the Congress Constitution*, New Delhi 1958, pp. 1–8.

8   See note by A. C. Majumdar, President, Indian Association, 13 May 1913, in Indian Association Executive Council Minutes; Bengal Police, Abstracts of Intelligence for 1917, e.g. paragraphs 4121, 4220–1, 4223, 4327, 4337, 4466, 4849. [Police abstracts collated by the various provinces are hereafter referrred to by '(name of province) Police (year of report), par(s)'].

9   See Lajpat Rai, 'The Story of My Life' (handwritten memoirs in the keeping of Mr V. C. Joshi, Delhi, written in 1914), pp. 92–3, 137.

10   See Government of India, Home Department Political files [hereinafter 'Home Poll'] A, March 1913, Nos 45–55, and B, Nov. 1913, No. 149. These files include weekly reports from the Criminal Investigation Department, which are referred to by page numbers (where the file is consistently paginated) or by the date of the report ['w.e.', i.e. 'for the week ending']. These files also include fortnightly reports from the provincial governments to the Government of India: these likewise are referred to by page numbers where possible, and otherwise by the province of origin.

11   See Government of Bombay, *Source Material for a History of the Freedom Movement in India (Collected from Bombay Government Records)*, Bombay 1958 [hereinafter cited as '*HFM Bombay*'], II, pp. 204–8. For attempts by Ranade and others to mobilise mass groups in Maharashtra and Gujarat before Tilak's time, see J. S. Masselos, 'Liberal Consciousness, Leadership and Political Organisation in Bombay and Poona, 1867–1895' (unpublished Ph.D. thesis, Bombay University, 1964).

12   See *HFM Bombay*, II, pp. 195–540; India, Sedition Committee 1918, *Report*, Calcutta 1919, pp. 6–7, 14, 22.

13   See, e.g., 'Contribution the Freedom Struggle by S. M. Paranjpye' and Gosavi, D. K., 'Contribution . . . by K. P. Khadilkar' (unpublished papers, Bombay Office, History of the Freedom Movement).

14   See letters of V. S. Srinivasa Sastri to V. Krishnaswami Iyer, 28 Sept. to 17 Oct. 1908, V. K. Iyer Papers, Servants of India Society [hereinafter SIS], Madras; Gokhale to Mrs Besant, 21 Nov. 1914, Adyar Archives.

15   See Gokhale to Wedderburn, 29 April 1910, Gokhale Papers; N. C. Chaudhuri, *The Autobiography of an Unknown Indian*, London 1951, pp. 48, 107; B. Shiva Rao, article in *The Central Hindu College Magazine*, XIII (1913), pp. 215–16.

16   See, e.g., Jamnadas Dwarkadas, 'A Memoire of Gandhiji' (unpublished memoirs held by the author, Bombay), pp. 38, 50, 55, 68–89; *The Central Hindu College Magazine*, VII (1907), pp. 313–14; VIII (1908), pp. 113,

275; IX (1909), p. 109; C.Rajagopalachariar, letter to *Hindu*, 14 Aug. 1916, p. 7.

17   J.Nehru, *Toward Freedom: the Autobiography of Jawaharlal Nehru*, New York 1941, pp. 39, 43.

18   Articles by Congressmen in *New India*, 1914, 17 Oct., p. 6; 7 Nov., p. 6; 9 Nov., p. 13a; 12 Nov., p. 6d; 18 Nov., p. 5; Presidential address, 1911 Congress, in A.Besant, *How India Wrought for Freedom*, Madras 1915, p. 532.

19   B.Basu to Gokhale, 26 Nov. 1914, Gokhale Papers.

20   See *New India*, 22 Oct. 1914, p. 13a–b; 24 Oct. 1914, p. 6c–d; 2 Nov. 1914, p. 13; 7 Nov. 1914, p. 6.

21   Bombay Police 1915, par. 378.

22   See Bombay Police 1915, par. 133; Home Poll B, Aug. 1914, Nos 259–62, p. 9; cf. Home Poll B, Aug. 1917, Nos 195–8, pp. 11–12.

23   *Mahratta*, 23 Aug. 1914, p. 272; 30 Aug. 1914, p. 275; Bombay Police 1914, par. 1446.

24   For the contribution of the Theosophical Society [hereinafter TS] to the Hindu revival, see B.C.Pal, *Memories of My Life and Times*, Calcutta 1932, I, p. 425.

25   'Our Policy', *Commonweal*, 2 Jan. 1914, p. 4: this was the first issue of her weekly newspaper.

26   See *New India*, 4 Jan. 1915, p. 6b; 5 Jan. 1915, p. 6b.

27   See *The Central Hindu College Magazine*, VIII(1908), pp. 113–14, 141, 247.

28   See Gokhale to Mrs Besant 18 Nov. 1914, 9 Jan. 1915, Adyar Archives; A.Besant to Gokhale 23 Jan. 1915, Gokhale Papers.

29   See *Hindu*, 2 July 1910, p. 4; editor of 'Justice' [T.M.Nair], *The Evolution of Mrs Besant, Being the Life and Public Activities of Mrs Annie Besant*, Madras 1918, p. 313; *New India*, 9 Nov. 1914, p. 12a.

30   See G.D.H.Cole, *British Working Class Politics 1832–1914*, London 1946, pp. 77–8, 93–6, 122–4, 130; A.H.Nethercot, *The First Five Lives of Annie Besant*, London 1961, pp. 70–294; A.Besant, *The Birth of New India . . . Writings and Speeches . . .*, Adyar 1917, pp. 70–1. Mrs Besant knew of A.O.Hume's early Congress agitation modelled on the anti-Corn Law movement: see A.Besant, *How India Wrought for Freedom*, pp. 51, 71.

31   A.Besant, *India, Bond or Free? A World Problem*, London 1926, pp. 171–3.

32   *New India*, 19 July 1915, p. 10b.

33   Ibid., 17 Oct. 1915, p. 5b–d.

34   See Gokhale to A. Besant 21 Nov. 1914, 9 Jan. 1915, Adyar Archives; A.Besant to Gokhale 23 Jan. 1915, Gokhale Papers.

35   E.g. *New India*, 7 Jan. 1915, p. 4a–c; 25 Jan. 1915, p. 8c; 22 Feb. 1915, p. 7a; 8 Mar. 1915, p. 5d; 22 Mar. 1915, p. 12b; 2 Apr. 1915, p. 13; 8 Apr. 1915, p. 9b; 4 May 1915, p. 8; 6 May 1915, p. 12.

36   Ibid., 13 Mar. 1915, p. 14; 17 Mar. 1915, p. 8; 20 July 1915, p. 8b; 10 Aug.

1915, p. 8a; A. Besant, *India and the Empire: A Lecture and Various Papers on Indian Grievances*, London 1914, pp. 38, 62 ff. See p. 154, above.

37 See, e.g., *New India*, 1 June 1915, p. 8a; 3 Aug. 1915, p. 8a–b; 9 Aug. 1915, p. 8a; 14 Aug. 1915, p. 10c; 23 Aug. 1915, p. 9b; 26 Aug. 1915, p. 8c.

38 A. Besant, *The Political Outlook* (Presidential Address to the 1915 United Provinces [hereinafter U.P.] Provincial Conference), New India Political Pamphlet No. 2 Adyar, n.d. [1915], pp. 6–13, 26–37; Government of India, Home Dept Public file A, July 1915, Nos 75–90.

39 'Home Rule Speech at Belgaum', 1 May 1916, in *Bal Gangadhar Tilak, His Writings and Speeches*, Madras 1919, pp. 135–6.

40 Interviews of the writer with B. Shiva Rao, 21 Feb. 1963; K. Dwarkadas, 27 May, 1 June 1963.

41 *Mahratta*, 14 Feb. 1915, p. 56; cf. *New India*, 28 Dec. 1915, p. 13a–b.

42 Bombay Police 1915, par. 568(b).

43 Ibid., pars 838, 964, 967, 1083–4, 1260, 1366–7, 1402.

44 He was also seeking to satisfy his more impetuous followers' demands for action: see B. G. Tilak to G. S. Khaparde 7 Dec. 1914, Khaparde Papers; G. K. Gokhale to A. Besant 10 Jan. 1915, Adyar Archives.

45 See *New India*, 10 July 1915, p. 10a–b; 28 July 1915, p. 9 a; *The Theosophist*, LIV, No. 2 (Apr. Sept. 1933), pp. 145–7.

46 *New India*, 25 Sept. 1915, p. 11.

47 See ibid., 14 Sept. 1915, p. 6a; *Mahratta*, 12 Sept. 1915, p. 310.

48 Bombay Police 1915, par. 568(b); 'Report from the Joint Select Committee on the Government of India Bill', Vol. II: Minutes of Evidence, *House of Commons Papers*, 1919, IV, p. 82, Answer to Question 1439; Jamnadas Dwarkadas, op. cit., pp. 133–5.

49 AICC Minutes (held at AICC, Delhi), 30 Dec. 1915; *Report of the . . . Congress held . . . [in] 1915*, Bombay 1916, pp. f, g.

50 Bombay Police 1916, pars 39(i) (j); Home Poll Deposit [hereinafter Dep.], Jan. 1916, No. 36; B, Jan. 1916, Nos 541–4, p. 12.

51 Interviews with Jamnadas Dwarkadas, Bombay, 23 April, 10 June 1963; Kanji Dwarkadas, Bombay, 27 May, 1 June 1963; S. G. Banker, Ahmedabad, 27 June 1963; Jamnadas Dwarkadas, op. cit., *passim*. Others in this group included P. K. Telang, son of the illustrious K. T. Telang and brilliant scholar, who gave up prospects of a legal career to teach at Mrs Besant's Banaras Hindu College until 1916, when she requested him to take up the editorship of *Young India* and HRL work in Bombay; the Muslim, Umar Sobhani, wealthy son of millowner, who followed in his father's footsteps, drawn into the HRL largely through business contacts with Jamnadas; K. M. Munshi, a young Gujarati Brahmin lawyer, and centre of a coterie of Gujarati writers; M. R. Jayakar, a young Maharashtrian lawyer from the non-Brahmin Pathare Prabhu community.

52 *New India*, 4 Jan. 1916, p. 10d; 6. Jan. 1916, p. 10d; 24 May 1916, p. 11a; 4 Sept. 1916, pp. 8c, 11; Bombay Police 1916, pars 255, 529.

53 *Mahratta*, 7 May 1916, p. 223; Bombay Police 1916, pars 122, 609.

54 Initially called the 'Home Rule for India League'.

55 B.A. 1898 and LL.B. (Cantab.) 1899, he arrived in India in 1903 to teach English at the Theosophical Central Hindu College, Banaras; became its Headmaster. Mrs Besant recalled him from England in 1916 to help her run the HRL and edit *New India*. He later became President of the Theosophical Society.

56 *New India*, 4 Sept. 1916, p. 11; see also 24 May 1916, p. 11a; 21 June 1916, p. 3d; Home Poll B, July 1916, Nos 441–5, w.e. 29 July 1916.

57 *Mahratta*, 20 May 1917, p. 241.

58 See references cited in n. 48, p. 190, above.

59 *Mahratta*, 30 Apr. 1916, p. 216; 7 May 1916, p. 223. Those comprising the Committee which set up the IHRL were G. S. Khaparde (from Amraoti, Berar), Tilak, Baptista (Bombay), Dr B. S. Moonje (Nagpur), M. S. Aney (Yeotmal), R. P. Karandikar (Satara), G. B. Phansalkar (Satara), S. K. Altekar (Karad), C. M. Desai LDS (Bombay), D. V. Belvi (Belgaum), and Kelkar; those added to form the Central Committee were Dr Sathaye (Bombay), Dr R. G. Vaze LM &S, C. V. Vaidya (Kalyan), V. R. Patwardhan, N. R. Alekar and V. R. Lele.

60 *Mahratta*, 20 May 1917, p. 239; 27 May 1917, p. 255; complete lists for 1917 in Home Poll A, July 1917, Nos 299–313 and KW; Bombay Police 1917, par. 156(a).

61 *Mahratta*, 4 Feb. 1917, p. 58; 11 Feb. 1917, p. 69.

62 Interview with S. V. Bapat (member of Tilak's HRL office staff), Poona, 21 May 1963. In 1915, D. V. Gokhale, then aged thirty, gave up his legal practice in Bombay to edit a Home Rule journal at Tilak's request.

63 *HFM Bombay*, II, p. 243; *Mahratta*, 5 Nov. 1916, p. 540.

64 *Mahratta*, 12 Nov. 1916, pp. 559–60.

65 See ibid., 3 Dec. 1916, p. 588; Bombay Police 1916, pars 954(b), 1093(d), 1480; ibid., 1917, pars 55(a), 109(l), 182(b) (c).

66 *Mahratta*, 5 Nov. 1916, p. 540; 20 May 1917, pp. 238–40; 10 Mar. 1918, p. 111; Bombay Police 1917, pars 603(h), 949(m).

67 Also P. K. Telang and (later) A. Rasul and Gokaran Nath Misra as General Secretaries for Bombay, Bengal and U.P. respectively: *New India*, 4 Sept. 1916, p. 11; All-India HRL [hereinafter A-I HRL] Council Minutes, 8 Oct. 1916, Adyar Archives.

68 See *New India*, 5 July 1916, p. 8c-d; 25 Sept. 1916, p. 3c-d.

69 See, e.g., letters to A. Besant from Jethmal Parsram Guhajain, Hyderabad, Sind, 6 Dec. 1915; Durgdas Adwani, Karachi, 17 Dec. 1916; Purnendu N. Sinha, Bihar, 19 Dec. 1915, Adyar Archives.

70 *New India*, 31 Mar. 1917, p. 5c; 'Addresses Presented . . . to . . . The Viceroy and the . . . Secretary of State for India', Cd. 9178, p. 17, House of Commons Papers, 1918, XVIII.

71 Interview with R. Shukla (member A-I HRL, Allahabad and Kanpur), Banaras, 8 Aug. 1963; *New India*, 16 Sept. 1916, p. 11c; Home Poll B, Apr. 1917, Nos 700–2, p. 8.

72 TS Indian membership (including Ceylon and Persian Gulf) in 1917: 5649. TS, Indian Section, *Annual Report, 1917*, Banaras 1918.

73 Some of these men had come under strong Theosophical influence, but they were now attracted by Mrs Besant's Indian patriotism rather than her religious ideas.

74 *New India*, 11 Sept. 1917, p. 3. The number of branches in Madras was: 63 in Tamil-, 48 in Telugu-, 12 in Kannada-speaking areas, 9 in Malabar. I estimate the number of other branches as: Sind 6, Gujarat 25, rest of Bombay and Central Provinces 12, U.P. 8, Bihar 8, Panjab 3, Delhi 1, Bengal 1; total 196. Of Indian Theosophists, over 40 per cent were inhabitants of Madras Presidency; 20 per cent of Bombay Presidency; 7 per cent each of U.P. and Bengal. Over 56 per cent of the TS lodges were in Madras. TS *Annual Reports, 1913* and *1914*.

75 See file A 31/2, History of the Freedom Movement Office, Delhi; A.R. Ayar to A. Besant, 18 Dec. 1915, Adyar Archives; Home Poll Dep., Oct. 1916, No. 28, 'Madras'; Dep., Nov. 1916, No. 50, 'Madras'; *New India*, 4 Oct. 1916, p. 6; 8 Nov. 1916, p. 11.

76 Interviews with R. Shukla, 8 Aug. 1963, and Iqbal Narain Gurtu (leading U.P. member of A-I HRL), Banaras, 7 Aug. 1963; U.P. Police 1916, *passim*.

77 *New India*, 7 July 1916, p. 3; 5 Sept. 1916, p. 8; 25 Sept. 1916, p. 3.

78 See ibid., e.g. 10 Oct. 1916, p. 12; 17 Oct. 1916, p. 13; 4 Nov. 1916, p. 3; 9 Nov. 1916, p. 8d; Bombay Police 1917, pars 351(c), 841(g).

79 E.g. in Malayalam, Tamil and Telugu, see *New India*, 28 Aug. 1916, p. 8d; 12 Oct. 1916, p. 12; 11 Nov. 1916, p. 5c; in Sindi, see Home Poll B, July 1917, Nos 426–30, p. 25; in Marathi, Gujarati and Hindi, see Home Rule for India League (Bombay Branch), *First Annual Report . . . 30 June 1917*, Bombay 1917, pp. 1–2.

80 A. Besant, article in *Young India*, reprinted in *New India*, 10 Jan. 1916, p. 3.

81 Section 7(a), file 12/2 (Region VIII), pp. 41–3, History of the Freedom Movement Office, Delhi; *New India*, 27 May 1916, p. 9b; Home Poll Dep., June 1916, No. 25, 'Bombay'; Dep., July 1916, No. 25, 'Bombay'.

82 Home Poll Dep., Sept. 1916, No. 18, 'Madras'; Section 7(b), file 12/2 (Region VIII), pp. 83 ff., History of the Freedom Movement Office, Delhi; *New India*, 29 Aug. 1916, p. 4.

83 *New India*, 10 Nov. 1916, p. 3; and e.g. 16 Nov. 1916, p. 3; 21 Nov. 1916, p. 3; 4 Dec. 1916, p. 3c; 21 Dec. 1916, p. 3b; Home Poll B, Feb. 1917,

Nos 552–5, w.e. 17 Feb. 1917; Dep., Mar. 1917, No. 33, 'Bombay'; Reports on Native Newspapers, Bengal (unpublished, Govt of Bengal), 1917, pp. 64, 302, 339.

84 I.K.Yajnik, op. cit., pp. 14–19; U.P. Police 1916, e.g. pars 1424, 2050, 2445, 2650; H.N.Kunzru to Vaze, 12 Apr. 1917, SIS Papers, Poona; Bombay Police 1915, pars 570, 677(c); 1916, par. 779(c).

85 U.P. Police 1916, pars 2046–7, 2130, 2194, 2273, 2515; interviews with Harkaran Nath Misra (member Lucknow branch, A–I HRL), 5 Aug. 1963; R. Shukla, 8 Aug. 1963; H. N.Kunzru, 27 July 1963.

86 *New India*, 4 Sept. 1916, p. 11; 16 Sept. 1916, p. 3d.

87 Bombay Police 1917, par. 21(b); *New India*, 29 Dec. 1916, p. 5a–b.

88 For the full text of the Congress/Muslim League Scheme, and related documents, see *India's Claim for Home Rule*, Madras 1917, Appendices C, D, and E.

89 See N.C.Kelkar to V.S.Srinivasa Sastri, n.d. [early 1917], SIS Papers, Poona.

90 Bombay Police 1917, par. 21(b).

91 Home Poll A, Mar. 1918, No. 247, p. 34; G.S.Khaparde, Diary (unpublished, extracts held by *Kesari–Mahratta* Trust, Poona), 1 Jan.–9 Feb. 1917.

92 See Austen Chamberlain, Secretary of State for India, to Lord Chelmsford, Viceroy, 19 Mar. 1917, and Sir J.Meston, Lt-Gov. of the U.P., to Chelmsford, 7 July 1917, in Home Poll A, July 1917, Nos 299–313; *The Indian Demands*, Madras n.d., pp. 31–2; Home Poll Dep., Apr. 1917, No. 61, *passim*; Dep., May 1917, No. 70, 'Bombay'.

93 Home Poll A, July 1917, Nos 299–313; A, March 1918, No. 247, p. 35; B, April 1917, Nos 700–2, w.e. 7 Apr. 1917; Dep., May 1917, No. 70, 'Panjab'; B, May 1917, Nos 445–8, w.e. 19 May 1917; Dep., June 1917, No. 68, 'Madras'.

94 4 June 1917, p. 8.

95 Those who joined included Motilal Nehru, Jinnah, H.A.Wadia, Sapru, Chintamani, Jayakar and Horniman: *Hindu*, 20 June 1917, p. 4; 26 June 1917, p. 5.

96 Ibid., 20 June 1917, p. 5; Home Poll Dep., Aug. 1917, No. 3, 'Bihar and Orissa'; Bombay Presidency Association, Council Minutes, 23 June 1917.

97 A.Besant, 'Internment Diary' (unpublished, held at Adyar Archives), 7, 8 and 18 July, and 3 Aug. 1917: emphasis in the original. Apologists for, and critics of, Mrs Besant have generally agreed that she consistently opposed passive resistance: the evidence in her own hand plainly shows this is not true.

98 See Bombay Police 1917, pars 841(f)(g)(h)(j)(o), 859(e)(k), 899(r)(s)(u)(v)(y), 970(f)(j).

99   20 Aug. 1917, *House of Commons Debates*, Vol. 97, cols 1695–6.

100   See D. E. Wacha to C. Vijiaraghavachariar, 11 June, 7 and 8 Aug. 1917, C. Vijiaraghavachariar Papers, Salem [hereinafter Vij. Papers].

101   Bengal Police 1917, pars 4121, 4220–3, 4327, 4337, 4466, 4849; Reports on Native Newspapers, Bengal, 1917, pp. 247, 991, 995, 1031; Home Poll Dep., No. 1917, No. 6; B, Nov. 1917, Nos 43–5.

102   Bombay Police 1917, par. 1109(C).

103   See Reports on Native Newspapers, Bengal, 1917, p. 276; E. S. Montagu, *An Indian Diary*, London 1930, p. 117.

104   A. Besant, 'Internment Diary', July 21 to 30, 1917.

105   *Congress 1917 Report*, p. 59.

106   See P. Kesava Pillai to Vijiaraghavachariar, 23 Oct. 1917, Vij. Papers.

107   Bombay Police 1917, par. 1080(m); N. C. Kelkar, *The Case for Indian Home Rule*, Poona 1917, p. i.

108   G. S. Khaparde, Diary (extracts at Bombay History of the Freedom Movement Office), 25 Feb. 1918; see E. S. Montagu, op. cit., pp. 117–19, 128, 274, 278; V. S. Srinivasa Sastri to 'Ramaswami', 24 Feb. 1918, SIS Papers, Madras.

109   *New India*, 22 Apr. 1918, pp. 3–4; Home Poll B, May 1918, Nos 23–6, p. 12; Dep., May 1918, No. 65, pp. 3–4.

110   AICC Minutes, 3 May 1918; Bombay Police 1918, par. 577; Home Poll Dep., Aug. 1918, No. 28, pp. 6–7.

111   *Report on Indian Constitutional Reforms*, Calcutta 1918.

112   See Reports on Native Newspapers, Bombay, 1918, p. 263; Home Poll Dep., May 1918, No. 65, p. 3; B, May 1918, Nos 581–4, p. 2; Dep., Sept. 1918, No. 19, p. 3; *Mahratta*, 14 July 1918, p. 328.

113   Tilak to Khaparde, 18 July 1918; A. Besant to Khaparde, 25 July 1918, Khaparde Papers; Home Poll Dep., Sept. 1918, No. 41, p. 5; B, Oct. 1918, Nos 191–4, pp. 14–15.

114   Home Poll B, Jan. 1919, Nos 160–3, pp. 11–12; Bombay Police 1919, par. 216(b).

115   For the young men's attitude, see Rajagopalachariar to Vijiaraghavachariar [telegram], 19 Aug. 1918, Vij. Papers.

116   See letters to Vijiaraghavachariar from Malaviya, 14 Nov. 1918, T. V. V. Aiyar, 5 Nov. 1918, J. Nehru, 17 Dec. 1918, Vij. Papers.

117   Presidential Address, 32nd session of Indian National Congress, 1917, in *The Besant Spirit*, Adyar 1939, IV, 19, 147.

118   *New India*, 19 Jan. 1918, p. 3a–b.

119   See A. Besant to Members, A-I HRL Council, 19 June 1918, Adyar Archives.

120   See *New India*, 13 May 1918, pp. 3–4; 3 Aug. 1918, pp. 3–6, 10; Home Poll B, May 1918, Nos 581–4, pp. 20–1; Dep., Aug. 1918, No. 28, pp. 3–4.

121 Government of India to Secretary of State for India, 24 Nov. 1916, pars 1, 10, 30–5, 43, in Home Poll A, Dec. 1916, No. 358.

122 Chamberlain to Chelmsford, 29 Mar. 1917, par. 2; 2 May 1917, par. 11, in Home Poll A, July 1917, Nos 299–313.

123 This is not to deny the enormous contribution of Montagu to the cause of Indian self-government: see, e.g., S.R. Mehrotra, 'The Politics Behind the Montagu Declaration of 1917' in C.H. Philips (ed.), *Politics and Society in India*, London 1963, p. 94.

124 See, e.g., the other chapters in this volume.

125 See Home Poll B, Jan. 1918, Nos 487–90, p. 10.

126 See, e.g., Bombay Police 1917, pars 841(w) (I), 859(n), 949(l).

127 See Home Poll B, May 1917, Nos 445–8, p. 5; Bombay Police 1917, pars 513(a), 815(d), 841(e), 859(a).

128 See U.P. Police 1916, pars 1653, 1933, 2195, 2516; letters to Mrs Besant from P.N. Sinha, Patna, 19 Dec. 1915, N.P. Nigam, Kanpur, 20 Dec. 1915, Adyar Archives.

129 See, e.g., Andhra Provincial Conference Committee (Guntur), 'Reorganization of Indian Provinces, being a Note presented to the . . . Congress, 1916', Adyar Archives.

130 This thesis has been most rigorously elaborated in R. Kumar, 'State and Society in Maharashtra in the 19th Century' (unpublished Ph.D. thesis, Australian National University, 1964), *passim*, especially pp. 484–94, 504–9. Research is required for Madras, but see B.H. Baden-Powell, *The Land Systems of British India*, Oxford 1892, III, pp. 112–17, 156–80; Government of India, *Census of India*, 1911, XII, part i, p. 184; S.S. Harrison, *India: The Most Dangerous Decades*, Princeton 1960, pp. 110, 123.

131 See the writer's 'The Leadership of the Indian National Movement, 1914–20' (unpublished Ph.D. thesis, Australian National University, 1965), chapter 5; E.F. Irschick, 'Politics & Social Conflict in South India: A Study of the Non-Brahmin Movement & Tamil Separatism, 1916–29' (unpublished Ph.D. thesis, University of Chicago, 1964).

132 See Bombay Police 1919, e.g. pars 378(h), 430(a), 476(a), 500(c), 528(j) (k), 542(d), 555(l).

133 Ibid., pars 378(i), 473(d), 474; U.P. Police 1919, pars 279–81, 445, 692–4, 728; Bihar & Orissa Police 1919, pars 569, 600–1, 604, 649.

134 See U.P. Police 1916, pars 2195, 2516; 'Scribbler' [P.C. Sundara Rajan], 'Satyamurti', in *Free India*, 19 Aug. 1962, p. 6.

135 See M.K. Gandhi, *An Autobiography, or the Story of My Experiments with Truth*, Ahmedabad 1940, p. 610; G.I. Patel, *Vithalbhai Patel: Life and Times*, Bombay [1950], I, p. 443.

7

THE FORGOTTEN MAJORITY:
THE BENGAL MUSLIMS AND
SEPTEMBER 1918

*

J. H. Broomfield

Soon after daybreak on 9 September 1918 Muslims were gathering in
the narrow lanes between the stalls and godowns of Burra Bazar in
Central Calcutta. As the crowds grew through that hot, sticky morning
there was angry talk about the Government's prohibition of a rally on
the Maidan the previous day, and when a call came from the Nakhoda
Mosque for a protest march on Government House there was a ready
response. Before midday the men started moving out on to the main
roads leading south, but they had not gone far when they were stopped
by armed constables who forced them back into the side lanes. The mob
milling angrily around the mosque was now swollen to nearly 2,000,
and, fearing damage to their property, some of the local Marwari residents ordered their *durwans* to clear the footpaths in front of their gate-
ways. Blows were exchanged and when a shot was fired from one of the
Marwari houses rioting broke out. The police charged with *lathis* but
were forced back under a hail of bricks. They opened fire, killing and
wounding a number in the crowd. Already looting and arson had begun
in the immediate vicinity, and this spread rapidly to other areas of the
city, with the Marwaris everywhere the chief victims. It took three days
and the bayonets of a regiment of British troops to restore order.

Looking back over a half century disfigured with the scars of communal rioting in Calcutta, the pattern of these events seems too familiar
to excite comment, but there were features of this riot which gave it unusual historical importance. For the first time in modern Bengal – perhaps for the first time in British India – an attempt was made to use mob
violence as a political weapon, and this riot provided a model for many
of the vicious techniques which were later brought to perfection by

Calcutta mobsters. Equally as important as the techniques of violent agitation were the discontents which gave the agitators their chance. The riot of September 1918 was the most extreme expression of a general disquiet in the Bengal Muslim community over the impending reconstruction of the political system of British India, a reconstruction in which it was felt the Muslim leaders would have no effective voice. The outburst signalled a critical loss of confidence in the community's leadership and it can be seen in retrospect to have marked the failure of the two strategies upon which Bengal Muslim politicians had relied since the turn of the century. At the same time it pointed the way to a new course of action which might replace them. The design of Bengal Muslim politics through the twenties was first sketched in these violent days of September 1918.

I

To understand the crisis of that month we must review the Muslims' position in the political system of Bengal in the preceding two decades. Under the Indian Councils Act of 1892 the British had maintained in Bengal a bureaucracy composed entirely of career civil servants responsible through its head, the Lieutenant-Governor, to the Government of India, and assisted in legislation by a consultative council. The majority of the members of this Legislative Council were Government officials, and its powers of discussion and voting were strictly limited to prevent its attempting to control the actions of the executive. Its non-official members were to function as consultants to the Government on legislative and administrative matters, in return for which service they were accorded privileged access to the senior officials and certain incidental patronage. In choosing these non-official councillors the Government had two objectives: first, to secure influential representatives of important interests in the province, and, secondly, to include some members of the local bodies, which were the infra-structure of Bengal's political system and which might in this way be linked to the superior administrative institutions.

The Muslim community was singled out as one of the important interests that should have representation, and to each of the Councils formed under the 1892 Act leading Muslims were invited. Some were eminent jurists and educators, the remainder large *zamindars*, and in all cases their established influence with their co-religionists was enhanced by their new association with the Government. In a community which was politically inexperienced and still subject to traditional controls, their authority was assured, but they had no such assured position in the political system as a whole. Without formal institutional backing among the Muslims they represented and with little influence in the local bodies, which were dominated by Hindu bhadralok, they were dependent upon British nomination, and by the turn of the century this system was under strong attack from the bhadralok nationalists. They demanded that the consultative council be replaced by a quasi-parliament, with an elected membership drawn from the Western-educated and propertied classes, and representing territorial electorates instead of interest groups or communities. The reconstituted council should have some control over the executive.

Whether or not these demands could be realised, the Muslim leaders were ill-inclined to disregard this threat from the Hindu bhadralok, for the political strength of the two communities seemed so unequal. The Muslims in Bengal were superior in number to the Hindus[1] but numbers counted for little in consultative politics, and the Hindu bhadralok commanded the critical resources of wealth and education.[2] Their entrenched position in the system of local self-government and the educational boards, combined with their nationalist organisation, gave them an institutional strength which not even the British could afford to disregard. With growing militancy they asserted the exclusive right of the National Congress to speak for the 'Indian Nation' and increasingly they used Hindu symbols to identify their nationalism. It was a reminder to the Bengal Muslims that, despite their provincial majority, they were part of a subcontinental minority, and a religiously alien minority at that.

II

It was in this situation that the first strategy of Bengal Muslim politics was mapped out. Its architect was Khwaja Salimulla, Nawab Bahadur of Dacca, the most eminent of the Government's Muslim consultants, and the head of Eastern Bengal's oldest and largest Muslim *zamindar* family.[3] His policy assumed that the Muslims, as an educationally and economically depressed community, could not hold their own with the Hindu bhadralok in the rough and tumble of electoral or agitational politics. It also assumed that the British were worried by the growing strength and increasingly aggressive tone of Hindu nationalism, and would welcome the clientage of the Muslim community, whose leaders might serve as a counterpoise to the Congress politicians and whose peasant mass might be kept immune from disturbing nationalist propaganda. The strategy was for the Muslim leaders to proclaim the loyalty of their community to the British raj and offer it in liege to the Imperial Government. In return they would expect to be welcomed as courtiers at Government House – able to advise and receive advice from the Lieutenant-Governor and his officials – and in any constitutional or political resettlement they would expect their community to be given favoured treatment.

The Nawab publicly expounded his policy in 1906 when Congress agitation for constitutional reforms and Hindu bhadralok violence against the partition of Bengal had removed any need for reticence. In a circular letter he proposed the formation of a 'Moslem All-India Confederacy':

> ... to support, whenever possible, all measures emanating from the Govern-ment and to protect the cause and advance the interest of our co-religionists throughout the country, to controvert the growing influence of the so-called Indian National Congress, which has a tendency to misinterpret and subvert British rule in India, or which might lead to that deplorable situation, and to enable our young men of education, who for want of such an association have joined the Congress camp, to find scope, according to their fitness and ability, for public life.[4]

Addressing the conference in Dacca at which the political organisation was formed he said:

> The resolution which I have the honour of moving today has been so framed that the object of our League is frankly the protection and advancement of our political rights and interests but without prejudice to the traditional loyalty of the Mussulmans to the Government and good-will to our Hindu neighbours. Whenever it is necessary to do so, we shall represent our views to the Government and respectfully submit our claims for due consideration. But whenever the intention of any Government is misunderstood by our people, it shall be equally our duty to remove that misconception .... only after a League like the one we propose today comes into existence can the Government find a representative body to which to turn for ascertaining the views of the Mussul-mans of India, and to which the Mussulmans themselves can turn for consistent and firm support, sensible and sincere advice, and a true interpretation of the wishes of the Government.[5]

The British were in need of support, especially in Bengal, and they willingly accepted the arrangement on the Nawab's terms. As a result the Bengal Muslims gained many concessions in the decade up to 1911. In their discussion of the proposals for a partition of Bengal, for example, the members of the Government of India recognised the Dacca Nawab's service in countering nationalist influence in his community, and it was one of their arguments in favour of the final partition scheme that it gave the Muslims a majority in the new province of Eastern Bengal & Assam and made Dacca its capital.[6] Certainly the partition proved an advantage to the Eastern Bengal Muslims. The new provincial Government openly favoured the community, preferring Muslims for appointment to the large number of new posts in the Provincial and Subordinate services which were sanctioned in July 1906,[7] allotting special funds and personnel for Muslim education,[8] preparing plans for a new University and High Court for Dacca, and installing the Nawab as their chief non-official adviser and their main agent for the distribution of patronage.[9]

At the Imperial level the British yielded to nationalist pressure for constitutional reforms, but the Muslims were given the preferential treatment which they had requested. The British rejected the Congress demand for parliamentary institutions, retaining the consultative councils composed of the representatives of interest groups and communities. The right of election was conceded, but the Muslims were provided with separate electorates. The right of Indians to serve on the highest executive councils of the Empire was also conceded, but the Muslims secured *de facto* recognition of their claim that these appointments should be communally apportioned.

For almost a decade the arrangement with the British worked well, but like all systems of patronage this one depended upon the maintenance of a fine balance between the interests of patron and client. In this case the balance would be disturbed if the British considered that it was in their interest to make concessions to communities other than the Muslims, and by 1910 there were officials in Calcutta and London who were convinced that it was no longer politic to disregard Hindu bhadralok anger at British policies in Bengal. In the search for a 'boon' with which King George V might crown his Indian visit in 1911 they hit upon the idea of reuniting the province.

The announcement of this decision at the King's durbar in Delhi in December 1911 appalled the Bengal Muslims. The British, it seemed, had performed a *volte face* to pacify the Hindu extremists, and many of the younger Muslims were convinced that after this betrayal there could be no question of maintaining the old loyalist stance. Others, equally angry, were determined to squeeze every possible concession from the British as indemnity for their treachery,[10] but the Nawab of Dacca cautioned both groups against rash action. He was as perturbed as any of his followers at the loss of their province, but he could see no viable alternative to a policy of dependence on the British. He agreed that the

Muslims should be given reparations for their loss, but he also emphasised that it would be a mistake to offend the Government by pressing too hard. The Muslims had to maintain the right balance between their demands and their expressions of loyalty.[11]

It was essential to the success of this scheme that they should, at all times, have leaders close enough to the Government to sense when the time was right to tip the seesaw one way or the other. Fortunately for his plans the Nawab found the new Governor of Bengal, Lord Carmichael, keen to receive him as a friend and they were soon on intimate terms.[12] The Muslims had two other links with the Government in the persons of Nawab Khan Bahadur Saiyid Nawab Ali Chaudhuri, a large *zamindar* from Mymensingh and an elected member of the Bengal Legislative Council, who had a number of close contacts among the senior officials, and Nawab Syed Shamsul Huda, a High Court lawyer and a member of a great landholding family in Tippera, whom Carmichael appointed to his Executive Council. Both men had formerly been members of the Eastern Bengal & Assam Legislative Council, where they had proved themselves adept exponents of the Dacca Nawab's game of balance.

Once again the courtiers gained favours for their community. When they emphasised Muslim educational backwardness, they were rewarded with the appointment of a separate educational officer for Eastern Bengal and the elaboration of plans for the provision of special facilities for Islamic studies in the proposed Dacca University.[13] Huda urged his fellow Executive Councillors to raise the proportion of Muslims in government service, and at his bidding a circular was issued to subordinate offices instructing that no qualified Muslim candidate should be rejected in favour of a better-qualified Hindu until one-third of all posts in Bengal were held by Muslims.[14]

Despite successes such as these, however, the courtiers no longer had the united backing of their community, for there were now influential Muslim politicians who questioned the premises on which the loyalist strategy rested. After the death of Dacca Nawab in January 1915 the Government felt that there was no Muslim leader on whom it could fully rely for an expression of the community's views, and the old rapport was destroyed.[15] A year later Carmichael and Percy Lyon, the pro-Muslim former Chief Secretary of Eastern Bengal & Assam, left the Bengal Government, and their successors were less willing to show favouritism to the Muslims.[16] Huda's term on the Executive Council expired in June 1917 and his seat was given to the Hindu bhadralok lawyer, S.P.Sinha, the immediate past-president of the Indian National

Congress. The Bengal Muslims had lost their spokesmen at court.

The timing could not have been worse, for in August 1917 Edwin Montagu made his fateful declaration on Indian self-government. The destruction of the consultative system and its replacement with a parliamentary structure, which the old-guard Muslim politicians had always feared, seemed imminent, and at this moment when it was most important for them to be able to influence British decisions they had lost their channels of confidential access to the Government. One of the community's political strategies had failed. So had the other.

III

This second strategy had its origins in Muslim anger at the reunification of Bengal. As we have seen, the Nawab of Dacca had tried to contain this anger, but his cautions were rejected by a number of the younger Muslim professional men in Calcutta. Their retort was that the annulment of the partition showed that the British officials could not be trusted to deal fairly with the community and that the Muslims must adopt a more aggressive stance if they were to improve their lot. The Nawab and his supporters managed for more than a year to prevent any public statement of this dissent, but in a debate in the Bengal Legislative Council on 4 April 1913 Fazlul Huq, a young Muslim representative from Dacca, brushed aside the polite conventions of his aristocratic elders, and in a powerful extempore speech warned the Government that continued failure to heed Muslim demands would lead to trouble. However much the Government might deny it, the Muslims were entitled to compensation for their past ill-treatment, he declared.

> To me it seems that Government has arrived at a parting of the ways, and has got to decide, once for all, its future policy regarding questions affecting the Muhammadan community . . . . in spite of their aversion to agitation, Muhammadans are drifting, owing to sheer force of circumstances, into the arena of political warfare. We feel that we have got to move with the times or else we are doomed. Let not the officials think that the feelings of the entire community can be soothed simply by the bestowal of titles and decorations on our leaders, or by providing for a transitory stay of the officials at Dacca with all the paraphernalia of Government. We require something more than a mere concession to our sentiments, something tangible which can be reasonably set off against our loss by the annulment of the Partition.[17]

Shamsul Huda was quickly on his feet to deny the truth of what he euphemistically described as this 'pessimistic view',[18] but the response which Huq's speech drew from various sections of the Muslim community suggested that there were many who thought as he did. The attention which the speech attracted throughout the province, left no doubt that a new political reputation had been made.

Huq is an important figure for the political historian of this period, for he brought a new style to Muslim politics in Bengal. Born of a family of Barisal *vakils*, he followed the well-worn path to Calcutta for education, finishing on the benches of the élite Presidency College. In 1895 at the age of twenty-two he returned to Barisal with an M.A. and B.L. to teach in the local college and later he assisted his father with his legal practice. After five years Calcutta drew him back and he became an articled clerk to the great High Court lawyer, Asutosh Mookerjee. The discussion over the partition found him keenly supporting the measure and his first opportunity for political work came in 1906 when the Nawab of Dacca used him as a runner in his negotiations with Muslim leaders in other parts of northern India prior to the formation of the Muslim League. The Nawab had at his disposal a number of Government appointments in the new Eastern province and he was thus able to reward Huq with a place in the Provincial Executive Service. By 1908 he had become Assistant Registrar of Rural Co-operative Societies. At the time of reunification, however, he was aggrieved at his non-appointment as Registrar for the whole of Bengal, and he left the service in disgust. Again the Nawab came to his aid, ensuring his unopposed return for the Dacca Muslim seat in the Legislative Council.[19]

Here was a potential Muslim leader of a new kind. Unlike the traditional communal leader, whose influence was locally based on landholding and who was usually a member of one of the great aristocratic families, Huq had made his way by personal ability – for it was his ability which had won him the necessary patronage. His education and his experience in teaching, law, administration and political organisation set him apart from the old leadership, and, what was vital, made him acceptable to the Hindu bhadralok. Here was a Muslim who (to adapt W. S. Gilbert) was the very model of a modern politician. It was important, too, that while retaining his contacts with his Eastern Bengal district he had established himself as a figure in Calcutta, for this enabled him to provide communal leadership on two levels.

To the Government, in search of spokesmen for a dependent Muslim community, Western-educated professional men such as Fazlul Huq were unacceptable, but this was of little concern to them. They had no desire to be courtiers, for unlike the older generation their anger, personal and communal, was directed primarily at the Government. Huq and his fellows scoffed at the credulity of those who would rely on British protestations of good faith, and, at the same time, they insisted that there was no longer any need for the Muslim community to eschew politics, for it now had an educated élite which could hold its own with Hindus or British. They even questioned the wisdom of the old orthodoxy of unremitting Muslim hostility to the National Congress. These new middle-class Muslim politicians shared with the Western-educated of other communities, nationalist aspirations quite foreign to the old leaders, and, while still protesting their primary commitment to their community, they were willing to consider collaboration with Hindu nationalists in campaigns against the British.

Their inclination to collaborate was encouraged by a number of factors. First, the anger in their community at the reunification of Bengal was reinforced in 1914 by concern at Turkey's alliance with Germany in the war against England. Indian Muslims accepted the Sultan of Turkey, the Khalifa, as the leader of all Islam, and the fact that he was now at war with Great Britain imposed a strain on their loyalty to the British raj, especially as Pan-Islamic sentiment was then unusually strong.[20]

The outbreak of war also brought appeals from Congressmen for a Hindu–Muslim alliance. In India, as elsewhere in the British Empire, August 1914 sent a wave of excitement and hope through the educated classes. There was talk of a short and glorious campaign, to be followed by a readjustment of international relations, in the forefront of which would be a new partnership of the nations of the British Empire. A new conception of India caught the imagination of many Indian nationalists: a self-governing India taking its place as an equal beside the other British dominions in an Imperial federation. In preparation for the constitutional discussions which, they thought, could not be long delayed, these nationalists drew up reform proposals and sought endorsement for them from Muslim as well as Hindu politicians. They believed that a united demand from the two communities would command greatest attention.[21] Their hopes for a quick settlement were soon blighted, but the reform initiative was not lost and they found the younger Muslim politicians responsive to their appeals.

In Bengal the death of the Nawab of Dacca in January 1915 opened the way to greater influence for this new group of middle-class professional men, and in the following twelve months they gained control of the Bengal Presidency Muslim League, with Fazlul Huq as secretary.[22] They were now able to implement a new strategy. The political future of the Bengal Muslim community, as they saw it, lay in a nationalist alliance with the Hindu bhadralok against the common enemy, the British. The aim was to wrest power from the British and this power was to be divided according to a prearranged scheme which would give the Muslims their fair share.

It was on this basis that Fazlul Huq and his men entered into a series of negotiations with Congressmen and Muslim Leaguers from other provinces which produced a reform scheme jointly adopted by the Congress and the Muslim League at Lucknow in December 1916. The Lucknow Pact, as this was called, was based on a memorial presented to the Viceroy in October 1916 by nineteen non-official members of the Imperial Legislative Council, calling for Representative Government and Dominion Status for India. To secure Muslim support, clauses were added at Lucknow providing separate electorates for the Muslims and giving Legislative Councillors the right to veto legislation affecting their own community. In addition the proportion of seats which the Muslims should have in each of the provincial Councils was detailed, and in five of the seven provinces they were accorded considerable over-representation on the principle that the minority community should have weightage. On the same principle the Hindus were to be over-represented in the Councils of the two Muslim majority provinces, the Punjab and Bengal.[23]

The Lucknow Pact was a remarkable diplomatic victory for the Muslim League and it was hailed as such by the Muslim press, except in Bengal where the concessions on Hindu representation in the local Legislative Council were denounced as a betrayal of the community's interests. By population the Bengal Muslims were entitled to 52·6 per cent of the Council seats but the Lucknow Pact would give them only 40 per cent.[24] There was great anger at those who had agreed to such disadvantageous terms. The young Muslim Leaguers were accused of selling out their community to the Hindus, and there was a reaction against collaboration. 'Those who apprehend that the Moslems will suffer political death if they do not unite with the Hindus are greatly mistaken,' declaimed a Calcutta Urdu daily, the *Resalat*. 'We have already stood alone 1,300 years. What is wanted is that we should firmly abide by our religious laws and not become faint-hearted.'[25]

It was on this issue that debate among the Bengal Muslim leaders turned in 1917. The supporters of the Congress-League Pact insisted that the first aim of all Indians should be to force the British to yield power, while its opponents maintained that the protection of communal interests was the paramount duty of Muslim leaders. Montagu's declaration in August, bringing as it did the need for action, only added to the acrimony of the dispute.[26]

It was settled quite suddenly, however, by communal rioting in Bihar late in September. When the Muslims of Shahabad District attempted to perform their traditional cow-sacrifice on the *Baqr-Id*, they were attacked by Hindus. The nature and extent of the rioting which followed, more fierce and prolonged than any which previously had occurred in British times, suggested a premeditated attempt on the part of the local Hindus to put an end to cow-sacrifice in the district.[27]

This had serious repercussions on communal relations in neighbouring areas of northern India. In Bengal, where excitement was already running high at the prospect of constitutional reform, the Muslim leaders hurled the accusation of treachery at their Hindu opposites. Here, they declaimed, was an example of the use to which the Hindus would put any power they could wring from the British. This was a foretaste of Hindu raj.[28] All talk of collaboration was drowned in a wave of communal bitterness, and the old religious animosity of the two communities was swept to the surface. 'In the West religion and politics can be separated but in the East never,' declared the *Sadaqat*.[29]

It was in this atmosphere of recrimination that the Bengal Muslims set about drawing up their submissions for Montagu and the Viceroy, Lord Chelmsford, who were shortly to tour India to discuss constitutional reform. Already there had been a number of defections from the ranks of the provincial Muslim League of those who repudiated the Lucknow Pact. The Central National Muhammadan Association, a Calcutta organisation of long standing which had formerly concerned itself primarily with Muslim education, offered these men an alternative body through which to work. They persuaded the Association to form a Constitutional Reforms Sub-Committee, of which they took command.[30] They then prepared an address to Montagu and Chelmsford in its name, attacking the Lucknow Pact and demanding legislative representation for the Bengal Muslims in proportion to their population. The spirit of their submissions was characterised by the concluding sentence of the address: 'For England now to place the Indian Moslems, without proper, definite, and ample safeguards, under the heels of a hostile non-Moslem majority, would, your humble memorialists venture respectfully to submit, be a cruel act of breach of faith and violation of trust.'[31]

In November the same group of League defectors, under the leadership of Golam Husain Cassim Ariff and Dr Abdulla-al-Mamum

Suhrawardy, formed a new and specifically political organisation of their own, the Indian Moslem Association,[32] and drew up another address. Its tone was more extreme. It emphasised its authors' determination to secure communal advantages at any cost, and it characterised the Lucknow agreement as a snare and a delusion for Muslims and British alike. 'Indeed the ink of the compact of fraternity itself has been washed away by the blood of the victims of the Bakri-Id riots at Arrah and the Ram-Lila Moharrum disturbances at Allahabad.'[33]

In the provincial Muslim League the supporters of the Pact were now unchallenged but they were uncomfortably aware of the unpopularity of the Pact's provisions for Bengal and the consequent danger for them of being left out on a political limb. They attempted to save themselves by advocating a modification of the scheme to give the Bengal Muslims 50 per cent of the Council seats,[34] and, at the same time, with the assistance of some United Provinces members of the League, they started a new Urdu daily in Calcutta to support the scheme in this modified form.[35]

Thus when Montagu and Chelmsford came to Calcutta in December 1917, the three Muslim associations were united in their opposition to the representation provisions of the Lucknow Pact and all were demanding more generous treatment for their community. Montagu had little sympathy with this demand. He believed that constitutional protection for minorities, particularly for large minorities like the Muslims, encouraged their separatist tendencies, and at the same time, discouraged them from making the effort to stand on their own feet in politics.[36] He was eager to do away with communal electorates but reluctantly discarded this idea when he realised the strain which such a reversal of British policy would impose on Muslim loyalty.[37] In the joint report which Chelmsford and he presented to Parliament in July 1918, he did make it clear, however, that he disapproved of communal representation in principle, and emphasised that he would not agree to its extension, or even to its maintenance in any province where the Muslims formed a majority of the voters.[38]

The Bengal Muslim leaders were aghast at the implications of this for their community. If the British accepted the provisions of the Lucknow Pact as a fair basis for the distribution of seats in the new legislative councils, as the Montagu–Chelmsford report suggested they might, the Bengal Muslims would not be given a representation proportionate to their overall numerical majority, and yet, if Montagu had his way, that majority would be made the excuse for depriving them of their separate electorates. There were vehement protests from the political associations. 'My Committee have carefully studied the Constitutional Scheme in all its aspects and apprehend that its working in its present shape would be disastrous to Moslem interests, and lead to the political extinction of a great and historic community in India,' the secretary of the Central National Muhammadan Association told the Government of Bengal.[39]

IV

The Bengal Muslims were indeed in a desperate position. At this crisis in Indian constitutional development, with the future of their community hanging in the balance, they were faced with the failure of both courses of action which they had pursued in the preceding decade. The courtiers were out of court and the collaborators had unwittingly bound the community to an agreement which now threatened its political future. Faced with this alarming failure of their efforts the politicians were at a loss for constructive suggestions. Throughout July and August 1918 they talked despairingly of the 'political extinction' of their community. They accused the British and the bhadralok of a desire to cripple its strength, and they accused one another of treachery.[40]

There could have been no worse moment for such a display of weakness, for the Muslim community in Bengal needed the reassurance of firm leadership. Among its educated members, the unwelcome tone of the Montagu-Chelmsford report and the increasingly extreme demands of the Hindu nationalists were the cause of grave anxiety. To the orthodox Muslims, the defeats suffered by Turkey and the widely credited rumours that Britain intended to depose the Khalifa were the cause of deep concern,[41] while the mass of the community was suffering from the effects of a bad harvest, heavy flooding due to an early monsoon and extraordinarily high prices for cotton goods. Added to all this were the ravages of the great influenza epidemic, which had struck Bengal in July 1918.[42]

With this general unrest and a demoralised leadership, the community was an easy prey for extremist agitators and a group of such men were on hand to take advantage of the opportunity. Their leaders were three non-Bengalis – a Punjabi, Habib Shah, a Madrasi, Kalami, and a Bihari, Fazlur Rahman – whose chief influence was among the Urdu-speaking immigrant community of Calcutta: the Muslim traders, manufacturers and lower-class factory labourers.[43]

Throughout 1918 these men had been looking for a chance to stir up trouble and they saw September as their best opportunity, for in that month the Muslim *Bakr-Id* would coincide with the Hindu *Durga Puja*. Such a concurrence of religious festivals always brought the likelihood of communal disorder, and, with bitter memories of the previous year's rioting in Bihar still fresh in Muslim minds, the situation on this occasion promised to be unusually explosive.

The Muslim press was busy whipping up discontent. The Bihar riots were frequently mentioned, with heavy underscoring of the moral: 'The Moslems should be on their guard in time this year.'[44] Hoarders were blamed for the prohibitive price of cotton goods and the finger of accusation was pointed at the Marwaris.

This money-lending Jain community, which came from the Rajputana states, had established itself in force in Calcutta in the preceding decade.[45] In trade its members worked in closely-knit family groups, and, with their flair for a good speculation combined with a large measure of unscrupulous dealing, they had quickly secured an important position in Bengal commerce. Communally exclusive and religiously ultra-orthodox, they kept aloof from both the Muslims and Hindus in Bengal, which did nothing to dispel the jealousy and mistrust which their rapid success had engendered. They offended the Muslims, in particular, by their deep aversion to cow slaughter, and it was an unfortunate accident of geography that threw together large numbers of both communities in the overcrowded lanes around Burra Bazar in central Calcutta. By August 1918 the Marwaris of this area were aware of the hostility surrounding them, and, fearing looting of their warehouses should rioting break out in September, they imported up-country guards. This was noted with disfavour in the Bengali press.[46]

The situation was perfect for the Muslim agitators. All they had to do was to strike the spark which would ignite this tinder. Habib Shah was the incendiary. At the beginning of August in his Urdu paper, the *Naqqash*, he took exception to a paragraph published a few days earlier in the *Indian Daily News*, on the ground that it contained an offensive reference to the prophet Muhammad. This created a furore. The other Muslim papers joined the *Naqqash* in its attack and on 4 August the Bengal Presidency Muslim League called upon the Government to institute proceedings against the editor of the *Indian Daily News*. At a public meeting six days later there was wild talk of a holy war against the infidel, and it was decided to call an all-India gathering of Muslims in Calcutta for 8 and 9 September to consider the religious and political future of the community. 'At this moment, Moslems are being attacked from all sides,' wrote the *Naqqash*. 'They say that their feelings are hurt by everybody. But the mere expression of such a sentiment will not stop the mouths of the enemies of Islam. Practical steps should be taken. They should act on the motto, iron must be hammered by iron.'[47]

Moderate Muslim politicians were becoming alarmed by the trend of events but they were reluctant to denounce the agitators publicly lest this endanger their personal popularity and in some way favour their rivals. They became a little more resolute when they found themselves excluded by the extremists from the reception committee which was formed after the meeting of 10 August to organise the following month's demonstration, but even then they would risk nothing more than a confidential appeal to the Government to prohibit the rally.

The Government of Bengal was slow to recognise the gravity of the situation. It handled the affair of the *Indian Daily News* ineptly and provided much ammunition for the Muslim press before the Government of India intervened to persuade the *Daily News* editor to publish an apology. The Governor, Lord Ronaldshay, was absent from Calcutta and it was not until his return at the end of August that his Government considered the matter of the all-India rally. Twelve Muslim leaders were then called to discuss the question with the Executive Council. The representatives of the reception committee denied any intention of fomenting trouble, but their moderate opponents accused them of deceit and favoured cancelling the gathering. At Ronaldshay's request the reception committee met that evening to reconsider its decision but it used the occasion as an excuse to heap abuse on the heads of the moderates for what it described as their collusion with the Government.

In the meantime there had been much inflammatory writing in the Muslim press and a number of religious leaders had arrived in Calcutta from other parts of northern India. On 4 September the Government banned the gathering, ordered the up-country *ulemas* and *maulanas* to leave Bengal, and stopped the publication of the *Naqqash* and a number of other Muslim papers. The reception committee, in defiance of the order, went ahead with its arrangements.

Most of the moderates were now thoroughly frightened and some went as far as requesting police protection. An exception was Fazlul Huq. For ten days from 26 August he had been absent in Bombay attending the special sessions of the Congress and Muslim League called to consider the Montagu-Chelmsford report, and on his return he had been confined to bed with a fever. As soon as he recovered he made an effort to ensure that the Government's order would be obeyed. Speaking to a meeting of the reception committee on the evening of 7 September, he persuaded all but three of its members to abandon the rally. The three were Habib Shah, Kalami and Fazlur Rahman.

On the following day a crowd of five or six thousand Muslims assembled at the site of the rally but they dispersed when they were told that the Government had granted another interview to the reception committee for the next afternoon. On the morning of the 9th word spread through the city that trouble was brewing in Burra Bazar, and a report on the ugly temper of the crowd around the Nakhoda Mosque brought an order from Government House for the armed police to stand by. Fazlul Huq hurried to the Police Commissioner to ask for permission to talk with the mob, by then advancing towards Government House, but this was refused and instead force was used to stop the march. Within two hours the situation was beyond the control of reasoned appeals or police *lathis*, and Calcutta was exposed to three days of lawlessness.[48]

V

For 1918 this course of events was novel and alarming. Before men of property in general and the Marwaris in particular, it raised an awful vision of the disastrous possibilities of a breakdown of law and order in the face of a malcontent or fanatical rabble. They were uncomfortably aware that in some way the stability of Indian society had been shaken in the war years. The small delegation of businessmen – Marwaris, Bengali Hindus and Muslims – which Byomkes Chakravarti, a prominent Congressman, led to the Writers' Building on 17 September to thank the Government for suppressing the riots,[49] was expressive of a concern for what was to come as much as of relief for what was past.

The political implications of the riots were equally disturbing. For the first time in Calcutta, an attempt had been made to use mob violence as a political weapon. Certainly the political aims of the agitators were not clearly defined, but this did not alter the fact that in its organisation the 1918 rioting differed in kind from previous communal disorders. Habib Shah and his fellows were engaged in a political contest in which they used violence and the threat of violence against their opponents. The organisations through which they worked were political, and they played upon political as well as communal grievances.

Their success showed that there was now latent mass discontent which could be exploited for personal or communal advantage by unscrupulous politicians. This gave new significance to the numerical strength of

H

the Muslim community, and forced the basic fact of its majority on the attention of the British, the bhadralok and the Bengali Muslim politicians – courtiers and collaborators alike – all of whom had been acting as though they had forgotten that majority.

There were other lessons to be learnt from the riot. In the first place it had shown the Muslim politicians that a resort to violence could provide a means of expressing their anger and frustration when other forms of action had failed. Moreover it was apparent that the mere threat of violence could force the British and the Hindu bhadralok to pay more serious attention to Muslim demands. Violence had been proved an effective mode of political action, and the techniques for promoting it had been well noted. Future Muslim agitators appreciated all too well the response which could be evoked with the watchcry: 'Islam in danger', and they valued the agency of the *mullahs* in sounding the alarm. They understood the importance of the mosque as a rallying point, of the migrant groups of the *bustee* areas as a source for rioters, of the Marwaris as an alien and unpopular object of violence, and of the vernacular press as a medium for incitement.

Obviously violence in Calcutta was a sword which the Muslims might use against their communal opponents, but it was a double-edged sword. As this riot had shown, the instigators of an outbreak could never be certain that they would be able to control the disorderly elements which they had set loose, and when the rabble got out of hand no one was free from danger, certainly no one of property. The size of the city; the overcrowding of its older areas, with their jumbled maze of narrow lanes and alley-ways; the mixed racial and religious composition of its population; its drifting and unstable migrant section; its large criminal class; its spectacular inequalities of wealth and opportunity; its influential yellow press – all of these factors contributed to the exceptional difficulty of maintaining order in Calcutta or of arresting disorder once it had begun. And this problem of law and order was a matter of concern for politicians as well as police. After the September 1918 riot no Bengali political leader could ever again disregard the possibility that extreme action on his part might provoke mass violence in Calcutta, with possibly disastrous consequences.

The Government of Bengal was shaken by what had happened. Clearly it had misjudged the situation. Its initial hesitation, and its later reliance upon police and troops to the exclusion of assistance from Muslim leaders, almost certainly cost lives. Its actions were censured by both the Government of India and a non-official commission of inquiry,[50] and the Governor, Lord Ronaldshay, writing his memoirs thirty years later, still felt the need for a lengthy apologia.[51] Some good came of the affair. Apart from a reorganisation of armed police in Calcutta in an attempt to obviate the use of troops, there was a realisation among the officials that new forces were at work in Bengal society and that the politics of the post-war years promised to be very different from those of the past.[52]

VI

The events of August and September left many reputations tarnished. The willingness of most of the Muslim politicians to subordinate public duty to considerations of personal advantage and security, their pre-occupation with petty intrigue and factionalism, had been plain for all to see.

Fazlul Huq had come through the affair better than most, but he was in disfavour with the bulk of his community because of his persistent support of the Lucknow Pact. His election to preside at the December 1918 session of the All-India Muslim League won him few friends in Bengal, and his characterisation, in his presidential address on that occasion, of talk of Hindu raj as a 'gross libel'[53] was particularly unwelcome in the atmosphere of communal acrimony following the Calcutta riot. Huq had tarred himself with the brush of collaboration and it was a long time before he was forgiven. 'He has a strong desire to gain a reputation among all communities,' wrote the *Moslem Hitaishi* contemptuously in October 1919. 'So he keeps himself in the good graces of a certain section of Moslems and is ready, without the least hesitation, to sacrifice Moslem communal interests in order to win fame and position among the Hindus.'[54]

What the Bengal Muslims were looking for late in 1918 was not a leader who would compromise, but one who would put communalism before all else in the battle which was about to be fought over Muslim legislative representation. The man who supplied the need was Nawab Khan Bahadur Saiyid Nawab Ali Chaudhuri, the Eastern Bengal representative in the Imperial Legislative Council.[55] He had much to recommend him. A Bengali and a great landholder, he stood apart from the Urdu-speaking group in Calcutta which had been chiefly responsible for the recent troubles. At that time he had spoken out strongly against the encouragement of violence[56] and yet had retained the appearance, at least, of non-involvement in the various intrigues.

More important, at no stage in his career had he had dealings with the nationalists. He was a communalist first and last. When the non-official members of the Imperial Legislative Council drew up their memorial on reforms in 1916, he had refused to sign on the ground that Muslim interests were not explicitly protected.[57] He had resigned the presidency of the provincial Muslim League in 1917 because of the terms of the Lucknow Pact and in December had argued the case for his community in a personal interview with Montagu and Chelmsford.[58]

His main work lay before him. In August 1918 he was elected president of the Central National Muhammadan Association and immediately set about preparing submissions for the two committees which were to consider schemes for a new franchise, and for the division of functions between the various branches of government. He regarded the address to the Functions Committee as an opportunity for a public protest against the 'serfdom' imposed upon the Muslims by the Bengal Hindus. It would be suicidal for the Muslims to agree to any scheme for the progressive realisation of self-government, the committee was told, for there was 'no common sentiment of nationality between the Moslem and the Bengalee'.[59]

The evidence for the Franchise Committee was of more practical importance, for the distribution of legislative seats was still an open question. The Government of Bengal, preparing its recommendations, had come to the conclusion that no satisfactory franchise qualification could be devised which would give the Bengal Muslims a majority of voters and that, this being so, they were entitled to separate electorates. It accepted the Congress-League scheme as 'a convenient solution' of the problem of apportioning seats between the two communities and recommended a Legislative Council for Bengal of 112 members. Fifty-nine of these should be elected from territorial constituencies, with the Muslims providing 27 and the Hindus 32.[60] The Central National Muhammadan Association strongly opposed this suggestion. The Lucknow Pact was acceptable for the rest of India, it asserted, but for Bengal it was unfair to the Muslims. Their population entitled them to at least 50 per cent of the Council seats.[61]

The Franchise Committee did not agree. It accepted the Government of Bengal's argument for communal electorates and its apportionment of 45 per cent of the territorial seats to the Muslims.[62]

Chaudhuri had not appeared as a witness before either of the committees but he had not been idle. As an old comrade of the Dacca Nawab, he knew the value of personal intercession at the highest level, and he had been active in Delhi talking with members of the Government of India. He had insisted that the Muslim League did not truly represent the Muslim community in Bengal, and that the application of the Congress-League scheme to the province would be regarded by his community as a betrayal similar to that of the annulment of the partition in 1912.

He had spoken persuasively. 'I have been much impressed by the arguments which have since been addressed to the Government of India by Saiyid Nawab Ali Chaudhuri,' wrote Sir William Vincent, the Home Member, in opposing the Franchise Committee's proposals.[63] Vincent spoke for his colleagues. They had all been impressed by Chaudhuri's plea and they insisted that the Bengal Muslims be given 44 seats instead of the 34 recommended by the Franchise committee.[64] The question was referred back to the Government of Bengal, with the request that it prepare a scheme to increase Muslim representation, but it stood by its earlier recommendation that 45 per cent of the territorial seats was sufficient.[65]

Chaudhuri would not give up without a fight. Throughout the remainder of 1919, by personal interviews and letters he kept up his pressure on the members of the provincial and Indian Governments.[66] Through the Central National Muhammadan Association he organised Muslim conferences in various parts of the province, at which resolutions were passed disavowing the right of the Muslim League to speak for Bengal and urging the British to honour their pledges to the Muslim community.[67] Forwarding a final note to the Government of Bengal on 10 January 1920, he warned of the consequences of a failure to satisfy Muslim demands:

> Any decision to adhere to the recommendation of the Southborough [Franchise] Committee would leave the moderate element among the Muhammadans practically without any influence or following in the reformed Council and in the country. Disappointed in securing what they justly regard, and what was also confirmed by the very mature and considerate decision of the Government of India as the proper ratio of representation, the Mussalmans, if they do not maintain a spirit of aloofness, will certainly look with disfavour and rankling discontent on a constitution in which, in spite of their numerical superiority, they shall be in a decided political minority. Should the state of things be left as they are, it does not require much imagination to conceive their eventual capture by the extremists to wreck the constitution.[68]

Chaudhuri's argument here is of great significance. He did not approach the Government as a courtier, with a humble petition for concessions in recognition of his community's loyalty. Nor did he take a stand with the bhadralok nationalists in demanding India's just constitutional deserts. Instead he drew the Government's attention to the fact that the Muslims were in a majority in Bengal, and demanded the constitutional recognition of that majority. As a sanction, he added the comment that a failure to satisfy this demand would endanger political order.

His appeal to the British was unsuccessful – only 45 per cent of the territorial seats in the Bengal legislature were given to the Muslims[69] – but his note was none the less important for that. It recognised the crucial fact that in the new system numbers would count. The small consultative council of the past was about to be replaced by a large quasi-parliament, controlling some departments of government and responsible to a mass electorate. In place of the 28 members of the old Legislative Council elected by 10,000 educated and propertied voters, there were now to be 113 elected members with a total enfranchised population of more than a million, of whom the majority would be peasants.[70] In mass politics numbers could count in two ways. As September 1918 had shown they could be made to count in a crude, negative fashion by provoking mob violence; or they could be made to count more positively through electoral organisation. The vote or violence were the implied alternatives in Chaudhuri's note of 10 January 1920. The vote and violence were to remain for Bengal Muslim politicians the main alternative instruments of power through the next three decades.

Violence was relatively easy to instigate and its advantages were not limited to the occasion of the outbreak, for the British and the Hindu bhadralok élite, fearful of disorder and sensitive to the particular dangers of Calcutta, were susceptible to the mere threat of a recurrence. Violence was always difficult to control, however, and its results could never be accurately predicted. It was a blunt and clumsy weapon.

By contrast the vote could be a keener instrument, but its sophisticated use required organisation, both in the electorate and in the legislature. Under the new constitution the provision of communal electorates was a built-in incentive, where none was needed, to organisation on communal lines, and the politicians' search for means of communication with the new mass electorate also enhanced the value of the traditional structure of communal authority: the institutions and symbols of religion. The *mullah*, the mosque, and the call to defend the Faith were to become as much the stock-in-trade of the Muslim M.L.C. as of the violent agitator. For the Muslim politician it was one of the great advantages of separate electorates that they reduced the demands on his technical initiative which mass politics would otherwise have made.

Another advantage was the assurance which they gave of a fixed minimum of seats in the legislature. While the 1919 constitution lasted, at least 39 of the 140 Legislative Councillors would always be Muslims.[71] This was obviously not enough to give them outright control of the Council, but with its communally segmented constitution it was sufficient to enable them to hold the balance of power, provided all would act together. Here was the rub. It proved rarely possible to secure unity.

For one thing there were attractive opportunities of personal gain for renegades at those critical moments when the balance was held. For another, leadership disputes were chronic, and the rivalry of contending factions was made keener by disagreements over social policy and political tactics. Nationalism still vied with communalism for the allegiance of many, and there were invariably a few Muslim members who could not tolerate the alliance with the British which was necessary to defeat the Hindus in the division lobbies. And how could the backsliders be punished when party organisation outside the legislature remained rudimentary because of the security provided by separate electorates? The voters might reject a wayward member if they were convinced that he was 'not a good Muslim', but it was only at times of acute communal tension that they could be persuaded to scrutinise the company their representative was keeping in the Legislative Council. For this reason there was always the temptation for the Community's leaders to stir up trouble before an important Council vote or at election time.

Under the Montagu–Chelmsford constitution in Bengal it was more often the organisation of the politicians than of the voters which gave the Muslim leaders their headaches, and it was a sign of what was ahead that Ali Chaudhuri should have turned from his discussions with the Government in 1920 to the task of marshalling his co-religionists in opposition to the Congress call for a boycott of the legislatures. His appeal for the Muslims to stand united and apart was to be echoed through the years ahead:

Hitherto the whole history of India since the advent of the Mussalmans in this country is a history of a continued antagonism of the two communities and we need be very cautious in clasping too eagerly the hand of fellowship stretched forward so very gracefully by the other community. ... We want in the Council chamber such men who would by no means allow the Muslim interests to be sacrificed for pleasing either the Government or the other communities.[72]

VII

The most striking fact in this account is the Muslims' assertion, at every point, of their community's right to a separate political existence. The strategies of politics, as we have seen, were not constant; the type of Muslim politician with influence varied; and the political system underwent radical change. But this determination to maintain a distinct political identity was throughout the basic factor in Muslim thinking. The suggestion that the community should take its place simply as one religious and cultural group in a diverse Indian nation was never entertained, and we must ask why.

One immediate reason was the fact that there were ambitious men with social influence who could convert that influence to political power so long as the community had a recognised political existence. Under the old consultative system the influence of these men was underwritten by their nomination as Muslim representatives in the Legislative Council, and when election was introduced in 1909 their position was again guaranteed through communal electorates. By 1919 the distinct political organisation of the Muslim community was a fact which neither the National Congress nor Edwin Montagu could deny, and the massive extension of the franchise under the constitution of that year provided new opportunities for power for the politicians whose communal influence enabled them to sway large numbers of men.

Another spur to separation was a genuine distrust of the Congress by many Muslim politicians. Congress rule would mean Hindu rule, they reasoned, and Hindu rule would be intolerable for the Indian Muslims. If we ask why it would be intolerable we come close to the heart of the problem of Muslim separatist thinking. It would be intolerable, in the first place, because of the history of Islam in India. The memory of Muslim imperial rule was cherished by the community, and if the ambition to rule again was not universal, a determination never to submit to the Hindus was certainly widespread. It would be intolerable, secondly, because of its inconsistency with the character of Islam itself. 'An independent political community as the arena of religious activity is part of the very genius of Islam,' Wilfred Cantwell Smith has observed. 'The existence of such a community is not something peripheral; it lies close to the heart of the faith.'[73]

Another obvious feature of this period was the power of the British to regulate the political relations of the Muslims with other Indian communities, and the consequent attention which the Muslim leaders gave to the British in developing their political strategies. The courtiers depended upon an alliance with the British; the collaborators experimented with an alliance against them; and Ali Chaudhuri's successors in the twenties tried to hold a balance between the Government and the nationalists. Always there was a fundamental difficulty: the British could be influenced but they could not be controlled, and at almost any time they wished they could reshape the entire political system. In these circumstances it is not surprising that the Muslim politicians felt very insecure, their insecurity manifesting itself in an exaggerated emphasis upon 'the special British obligation' to the Muslims, and the British 'duty to honour their promises' to the community. Nor is it surprising that this insecurity should have turned to despair when, as in July 1918, they felt that the British were disregarding their interests.

The cause of the alarm on that particular occasion was the threatened loss of separate communal electorates, and this underlines their significance in Muslim thinking throughout this period. Securing separate electorates was regarded by the newly formed Muslim League as its first task in 1906, and the price which the nationalist Muslims asked of the Congress in return for League support ten years later was endorsement of the principle on which they rested. Before Montagu and Chelmsford, every Muslim spokesman demanded their retention with a vehemence which finally convinced the Secretary of State that they could not be destroyed. Thus, despite repeated British statements that they were incompatible with a parliamentary system, they were written into the 1919 constitution and provided the framework of Muslim political organisation until partition in 1947.

Why did the Muslims value separate electorates so highly? First because they provided the clearest possible recognition of the community's distinct political existence, giving it constitutional sanction. Secondly, because the Muslims thought of themselves as a hopelessly outnumbered minority. On this point one might expect Bengal, with its Muslim majority, to have provided an exception, but there as elsewhere the Muslim leaders usually stood forward as minority spokesmen. The Bengal Muslims were, of course, part of a sub-continental minority, and involved in a political system which encompassed all of British India. As a result they remained vulnerable to pressures from outside the province, even though their numbers gave them power inside. The Lucknow Pact had been an unhappy illustration of this fact.

To the proposition that their minority status entitled them to separate electorates, they always added the rider that they had to be given protection because they were 'educationally backward and economically poor'. There can be no question that, compared with the Hindu bhadralok, the Muslims had a very small share of Bengal's landed property, higher education, appointments in government service and the learned professions, and positions in local self-government. The Muslim intelligentsia were convinced that, because of this inequality, the bhadralok possessed such powers of persuasion and coercion that they would dominate any open system of election. Without separate electorates the Muslims would be shut out of politics or would participate only on Hindu bhadralok sufferance.

The irony of this situation lay in the fact that the Hindu bhadralok politicians approached mass politics with trepidation, for they had no confidence in their ability to persuade or coerce the masses, particularly the peasant masses. By the same token, the Muslim politicians discovered that they had many technical advantages in the new system, and that the sheer size of their community gave them great agitational and electoral strength, which awaited only the perfection of those techniques for its realisation. For years their most eminent men had exerted every effort to preserve the consultative structure, and it was to their surprise that they discovered that they had greater potential power under the parliamentary system that had been forced upon them. That majority, which earlier they had tried so hard to forget and which had seemed in 1918 to provide their opponents with a handle to beat them, was now gladly acknowledged.

NOTES

1 The total population of Bengal proper in 1901 was approximately 42,000,000, of whom 22,000,000 were Muslims and 19,250,000 Hindus. By 1921 the total population had risen to 46,700,000, with 25,210,000 Muslims and 20,210,000 Hindus. (*Census of India*, 1911, Vol. V, pt. i, p. 199; and 1921, Vol. I, Pt ii, pp. 3, 6 & 40–3.)

2 Ibid., 1911, Vol. V, Pt i, pp. 357–8, 450, 551 & 553; and 1921, Vol. V, Pt i, p. 302.

3 For biographical details see C.E.Buckland, *Dictionary of Indian Biography*, London 1906; and *Proceedings of the Bengal Legislative Council*, Vol. XLVII, 19 Jan. 1915, pp. 5–6.

4 Edward E.Lang, 'The All-India Moslem League', *Contemporary Review*, Vol. XCII, July–Dec. 1907, p. 345.

5 Ibid., p. 351.

6 H.H.Risley, minutes 1 Sept. and 6 Dec. 1904, Government of India Home Department Public Branch Proceedings, Feb. 1905, A155–67, National Archives of India, New Delhi (hereinafter NAI).

7 Government of India, ibid., July 1906, A29–31, NAI.

8 Lord Carmichael to Lord Crewe, 21 Aug. 1912, Lady Mary Carmichael, *Lord Carmichael of Skirling. A Memoir*, London 1929, pp. 168–9.

9 The Nawab was jubilant: 'There are many good things in store for us which will no doubt come to us by and by, and the Mahomedans being the largest in number in the New Province, they will have the largest share. . . . This is the golden opportunity which God and His Prophet have offered us, but if we do not now profit ourselves by the opportunity, we may not get another chance. Now or never. Our destiny is in our hands. We must strike while the iron is hot.' (K.Salimolla, 'The New Province – its future possibilities', *Journal of the Moslem Institute*, Vol. I, No. 4, April–June 1906, pp. 410–11.)

10 E.g. see demands of Central National Mahomedan Association's Committee of Management, *Statesman*, 23 Jan. 1912; and Crewe to Carmichael, 15 Jan. 1912, Carmichael, *Lord Carmichael*, pp. 150–2.

11 For an example of his application of this, see his speech in the Legislative Council, 3 April 1914, *Proceedings*, Vol. XLVI, pp. 619–21.

12 Ibid., 19 Jan. 1915, Vol. XLVII, pp. 3–8; and Carmichael to Crewe, 25 Feb. 1915, Carmichael, *Lord Carmichael*, p. 204.

13 *Statesman*, 3 and 4 Feb. 1912.

14   Government of Bengal, Appointment Department Proceedings, Sept. 1917, File 4M-4(1-2), West Bengal Government Record Office, Calcutta (hereinafter W.B. Records).

15   Carmichael to Crewe, 25 Feb. 1915, Carmichael, *Lord Carmichael*, p. 204.

16   Government of Bengal, Appointment Department Proceedings, Sept. 1917, File 4M-4(1-2), A30-31, W.B. Records.

17   *Proceedings*, Vol. XLV, pp. 576–81.

18   Ibid., pp. 595–6.

19   For biographical details see obituary, *The Times*, London, 28 April 1962; and *Indian Year Book and Who's Who, 1939–40*, Calcutta & Bombay 1940.

20   *Report on Native Papers in Bengal*, Sept.–Dec. 1914. (This report is hereinafter referred to as NP. It is the source of all newspaper references in this paper, except where an asterisk indicates that the original was seen.)

21   E.g. see the scheme of reforms and accompanying comments published by Surendranath Banerjea, *Bengalee*, 2 July 1915.

22   Government of Bengal, Political Department Proceedings, 'List of Office-Bearers of Recognized Associations', 1915 and 1916, W.B. Records.

23   *Indian Statutory Commission. Vol. IV, Memoranda Submitted by the Government of India and the India Office*, London 1930, pp. 138–40.

24   How badly the Bengal Muslims had fared compared with their co-religionists in other provinces can be judged from the following figures (ibid., p. 139):

(1)	(2)	(3)	(4)
		% of total	
	Muslim % of	*Legislative seats*	*% (3)*
Province	*Population*	*for Muslims*	*of (2)*
Bengal	52·6	40·0	76
Bihar and Orissa	10·5	25·0	238
Bombay	20·4	33·3	163
C.P.	4·3	15·0	349
Madras	6·5	15·0	231
Punjab	54·8	50·0	91
U.P.	14·0	50·0	214

25   17 April 1917.

26   NP, Jan.–Sept. 1917.

27   *Indian Statutory Commission, Vol. IV*, pp. 97–8.

28   NP, Oct. 1917.

29   22 Nov. 1917.

30   *Central National Mahommedan Association. Calcutta. Octennial Report. 1917–1924*, Calcutta 1925, pp. 5–6.

31   Great Britain, Parliamentary Papers, 1918, Cd 9178, Vol. XVIII, pp. 498–9.

32   *Mohammadi*, 2 Nov. 1917; and *Tirmizee*, 25 Nov. 1917.

33   Great Britain, Parliamentary Papers, 1918, Cd 9178, Vol. XVIII, p. 504.

34   NP, Nov. 1917.

35   *Sadaqat*, 24 Nov. 1917.

36   Edwin S. Montagu, *An Indian Diary*, London, 1930, pp. 100 & 115.

37   Ibid., p. 68.

38   *Report on Indian Constitutional Reforms*, Calcutta 1918, pp. 147–9.

39   Honorary Secretary, Central National Muhammadan Association to Chief Secretary, Government of Bengal, 12 Sept. 1918, Government of India, Home Department Public Branch Reforms Office Proceedings, July 1919, Deposit 15, NAI.

40   NP, July–Aug. 1918.

41   Ibid.

42   *Census of India*, 1921, Vol. V, Pt i, pp. 30–1; and *Proceedings of the Bengal Legislative Council*, Vol. L, *passim*.

43   Lawrence, Marquess of Zetland, *Essayez*, London 1956, pp. 112–13.

44   *Mohammadi*, 6 Sept. 1918.

45   *Census of India*, 1921, Vol. V, Pt i, pp. 132–3; and Vol. VI, Pt. i, p. 32.

46   NP, July–Aug. 1918.

47   *Naqqash*, 15 Aug. 1918.

48   The account of the riot and the events leading up to it, given in the preceding paragraphs and at the beginning of the paper, is based on Zetland: *Essayez*, pp. 108–16; and *Report of the Non-Official Commission on the Calcutta Disturbances*, Calcutta 1919, pp. 4–29.

49   *Bangali* and *Nayak*, 18 Sept. 1918.

50   Zetland, *Essayez*, p. 116; and *Report of the Non-Official Commission*, p. 29.

51   Zetland, *Essayez*, pp. 108–16.

52   Government of Bengal, Police Department Proceedings, Dec. 1918, B15–19, File 2C(4–6), W.B. Records.

53   Typescript collection of Fazlul Huq's speeches compiled by Azizul Huq, Dacca.

54   31 Oct. 1919.

55   For biographical details see *Who Was Who, 1929–1940*, London 1941.

56   Zetland, *Essayez*, p. 111.

57   *Mohammadi*, 20 Oct. 1916.

58   Government of Bengal, Appointment Department Proceedings, Mar 1919, B441–55, File 6R–1(17), W.B. Records.

59   Ibid., A10–19, File 6R–18(1–10), W.B. Records.

60   Ibid., Dec. 1918, A94–152, File 6R–25(1–59), W.B. Records.

61   *Evidence Taken before the Reforms Committee (Franchise)*, Calcutta, 1919, Vol. II, p. 393.

62   *Reports of the Franchise Committee and the Committee on Division of Functions*, Calcutta 1919, pp. 9–10 & 52.

63 *Fifth Despatch on Indian Constitutional Reforms (Franchises)*, Calcutta 1919, p. 388.

64 Ibid., p. 373.

65 Government of Bengal, Appointment Department Proceedings, Aug. 1919, A1–2, File 6R-34(1–2), W.B. Records.

66 Ibid., Feb. 1920, A166–8B, File 6R-8(1–3); and Government of India, Home Department Public Branch Reforms Office, Jan. 1920, B244–5, NAI.

67 *Octennial Report, 1917–1924*, pp. 35–7.

68 Government of Bengal, Appointment Department Proceedings, Feb. 1920, A166–8B, File 6R-8(1–3), W.B. Records.

69 Great Britain, Parliamentary Papers, 1920, Cmd. 812, Vol. XXXV, pp. 295–9.

70 Ibid., 1913, Cd 6714, Vol. XLVII, p. 199; ibid., 1920, Cmd 812, Vol. XXXV, pp. 295–9; Government of Bengal, Appointment Department Proceedings Dec. 1918, A94–152, File 6R-25(1–59); and *Indian Statutory Commission. Vol. VIII, Memorandum submitted by the Government of Bengal*, London 1930, p. 130.

71 Great Britain, Parliamentary Papers, 1920, Cmd 812, Vol. XXXV, pp. 295–9.

72 Syed Nawab Ali Chowdhry, *Views on Present Political Situation in India*, Calcutta 1920, pp. 12 and 34–5.

73 Wilfred Cantwell Smith, *Islam in Modern History*, New York 1959, p. 211.

8

THE NON-COOPERATION DECISION OF 1920: A CRISIS IN BENGAL POLITICS

★

J. H. Broomfield

'. . . through these travail pains a new self-respecting India is being born – an India which will not bow the knee on every occasion, but will stand upright and erect. It is good to be alive in these days, even if one has not the heaven, which Wordsworth speaks of, of being young.'[1] With this letter written from Santiniketan by C. F. Andrews to his colleague Rabindranath Tagore, we can recapture a sense of the enthusiasm and optimism in its political future which gripped India in the last months of 1920 as the Congress prepared to implement Gandhi's programme of non-cooperation. The spirit of this period has been adequately conveyed in general historical writing, very frequently through such metaphors as an upsurge of enthusiasm or a wave of excitement sweeping the country. These figures are not inappropriate, but they have the danger of all metaphors of overgeneralising and oversimplifying, of distracting attention from the details of the historical process and its timing. They have not in this case obscured the fact that there were individuals and groups, inside as well as outside the Congress, who opposed Gandhi in 1920 and who were determined not to be swept off their feet by any tide of passion. There has, however, been no major attempt to measure the extent and significance of this opposition, or to uncover its reasons. The result has been the neglect of one of the crucial disputes in modern Indian political history.

This chapter examines the details of that dispute in one province. Its subject is Bengal politics in the twelve months between the passage of the Government of India Act in December 1919 and the Nagpur session of the Indian National Congress in the last days of 1920. Like the preceding chapter and the three which follow it in this volume, it is concerned with a problem of political strategy: the problem faced by the Bengal nationalist leaders of whether or not to support non-cooperation. It is also concerned with two of the major themes of this volume: identity and order. For the members of the Hindu élite, which led the nationalist movement in Bengal, the events and decisions of 1920 called into question the basic values of their social and political position. In that critical year they were faced with the emergence of a new national leader whose philosophy of politics was diametrically opposed to their own at crucial points, and, simultaneously, with an attack on their social ascendancy from aspiring groups beneath them in Bengal society. As a consequence they were forced, perhaps for the first time, to examine the foundations upon which their separate group identity[2] rested, and to defend their conception of the social order. In 1920 the great issues of this century for Bengal were debated.

I

On 23 December 1919 the royal assent was given to the Government of India Bill. For the Extremist party, in undisputed command of the Congress since the Moderates' withdrawal sixteen months before, this posed a serious problem. Should they persist in their opposition to the Montagu–Chelmsford reforms or should they now accept them as a *fait accompli* and use their power to dominate the new institutions? Certainly their reputation in the preceding two years had been built on their steadfast rejection of all British reform proposals and their condemnation of those Indians who were prepared to co-operate with the British, but they could contend, with some degree of truth, that this had been a stratagem designed to force the British to yield more power. That game was played out (so the argument ran) and the only result of a continued refusal to participate in constitutional politics would be the loss of the field to 'a tribe of timid, little-souled people who will think of themselves first and of their country last or not at all'.[3] Even under the Morley–Minto constitution, the Extremists had had qualms about leaving the legislative councils to the Moderates[4] and the danger seemed greater now that some of the functions of the provincial Governments were to be transferred to Indian ministers.

On the other hand, the Extremists asked, was there any reason to believe that participation in the new councils would be more profitable than it had been in the old? No matter what concessions had been made to Indian demands, the British bureaucracy was still in command, and (the Extremists held) the Amritsar tragedy of April 1919 had shown that it was as reactionary as ever. 'If the fountain remains as it is,' wrote

Motilal Ghose, 'the addition of a few more conduits will not make the water any more drinkable than it was.'[5] What was needed was a change of heart, and this, the Extremists maintained, had not happened. The racial arrogance which had characterised British Indian policy in the past, had been in evidence throughout the reforms discussions. Even the basic assumption upon which the Montagu–Chelmsford scheme rested: that Indians had yet to learn the art of self-government, and its corollary: that they should be given constitutional protection against their ignorance, were considered offensive.[6]

To accept the reforms, even under protest, would be to acquiesce in this judgement of Indian inferiority and this would injure the growth of national self-confidence. Many of the Extremists believed that it was self-confidence, above all else, that India needed. As a subject people, Indians had lost faith in their ability to act independently. For nearly two centuries they had been taught to distrust their own judgement and to accept without demur the decrees of a paternalistic foreign régime. To save their soul they had to repudiate the right of others to think for them. They had to act for themselves. '. . . what makes the difference between the Englishman and you?' Swami Vivekananda had asked his countrymen in 1897.

The difference is here, that the Englishman believes in himself, and you do not. He believes in his being an Englishman, and he can do anything. . . . You have been told and taught that you can do nothing and nonentities you are becoming every day. What we want is strength, so believe in yourselves. . . . What we want is muscles of iron and nerves of steel. We have wept long enough. No more weeping, but stand on your feet and be men.[7]

Vivekananda had a profound influence upon the development of twentieth-century Indian political and social thought, and his gospel of national self-assertion found a particularly rich soil in his native Bengal, where the ground had been prepared by the novels of Bankim Chandra Chatterjee. His teachings were given political application by Aurobindo Ghose, Bepin Chandra Pal and Rabindranath Tagore, who called upon their compatriots to prove their manhood by defying British power. This was the philosophy which had inspired the *swadeshi* and national education movements, and the terrorists at the time of the partition of Bengal, and it was the underlying reason for the Extremists' rejection of the Morley–Minto reforms. They saw that merely to accept institutions provided by the British and work them as the British instructed, would do nothing to advance India's self-reliance. This was just a new form of the old dependence. To prove their independence, to themselves as much as to the British, Indians had to reject what was proffered. They had to have the courage to cut their leading-strings.[8]

The question was, what then? In the Morley–Minto period some individuals in Bengal had avoided this problem by turning away from politics – to religion like Aurobindo Ghose or back to literature like Rabindranath Tagore – and for the Extremist party as a whole no satisfactory answer had been found. The years between 1909 and 1916, the years of negative opposition, had been full of frustration. Again in 1920 they had the chance to reject a British constitution and again they had to ask, what then? This time more depended upon their answer for now they had political power, with all its opportunities and responsibilities. In 1909 they had been outside the Congress but in 1920 they had control of the organisation and commanded a large following. If they did not participate in the new councils, they had to formulate a satisfactory programme of political action of their own.

It was a measure of their uncertainty when faced with this difficult decision, that they vacillated for a year before finally rejecting the Montagu–Chelmsford constitution. The December 1919 Congress at Amritsar resolved to work the reforms, but this decision was reversed by a narrow majority at a special session in Calcutta nine months later, and the plenary meeting at Nagpur in December 1920 voted overwhelmingly for withdrawal of all co-operation with the British.

Between Amritsar and Calcutta, Calcutta and Nagpur, there were some remarkable changes of mind, none more striking than those of the Bengalis. At Amritsar the Bengal contingent, led by Chittaranjan Das, Byomkes Chakravarti and Bepin Chandra Pal, voted against the reforms. At Calcutta they voted for them. At Nagpur they were all for non-cooperation. To understand why they wavered, it is necessary to understand their attitude to the person and policy of M.K.Gandhi. It was Gandhi who commanded the majorities at Amritsar and Calcutta, where the Bengal nationalists voted with the minority, and it was to Gandhi that they capitulated at Nagpur.

II

Gandhi, a Gujerati lawyer who had won a great reputation in South Africa with his work for Indian rights, had emerged in the first rank of nationalist leaders after a spectacular success in leading a protest movement against the indigo planters of Bihar in 1918. It was at his instigation that the *hartals* of April 1919 in protest against the Rowlatt Acts had been organised. The nationwide response to his appeal was testimony to his extraordinary influence, but the violence which resulted, shocked him deeply. He was convinced that without greater self-discipline India could not challenge the British, and for this reason he demanded that the Congress accept the Montagu–Chelmsford constitution. To those, like the Bengalis, who argued that the 1919 Congress session at Amritsar should reiterate the earlier uncompromising resolutions on the reforms, he replied that this would be irresponsible if the Congress had nothing constructive to offer in their place.[9]

Two incidents in January 1920 forced him to think again: the hero's welcome accorded on his arrival in Britain to General Reginald Dyer, the officer responsible for the Amritsar tragedy, and the rejection by the British Government of Indian Muslim protests over the Turkish peace terms. Gandhi was convinced that after these demonstrations of British disregard for their feelings it would be degrading for Indians to maintain their contact with British imperialism.[10] He therefore set out to formulate a programme of non-cooperation which Congress could offer to the nation in place of the reforms.

First, support for the institutions of British Indian government – offices, councils, courts, colleges and schools – should be withdrawn and Congressmen should devote themselves to the construction of national institutions in their place: 'a government of one's own within the dead shell of the foreign government'.[11] Resistance, non-violent and symbolic, might be offered to individual acts of British oppression, but the really important work was in national reconstruction.

For the nation as for the individual, Gandhi taught, salvation could be gained only by internal reformation. Society had to be rid of its evils, especially those of dissension and human exploitation. As a first step, he called for a reconciliation between religious communities and he took up the Khilafat issue as a means of cementing Hindu–Muslim unity. He also demanded that caste barriers be broken down and that the untouchables be accepted into the body of Hinduism. Congressmen of all castes should work with the Harijans (the children of God, as Gandhi called them) to help them rise from their degradation.

Similarly there had to be an end to economic oppression. Gandhi was adamant that self-government for India would be a travesty if the mass of the people were not freed from the exploitation of capitalists, land-holders and moneylenders. The nationalist movement had to be the people's movement, to benefit the mass of the people. 'I don't want

Swaraj at the cost of the depressed classes or of any other classes for that matter,' he wrote.[12] He therefore insisted that Congress demonstrate its concern for the welfare of the Indian poor by adopting a programme of economic rehabilitation. Congressmen should leave their urban professions and go into the villages to start cottage industries. The local manufacture of cotton cloth should be revived. The spinning wheel should become the symbol of India's new life and the wearing of *khadi* a gesture of the nation's rejection of imperialism.

Apart from having a rare ability to sway great masses of people, Gandhi was an astute politician, and throughout the first half of 1920 he was gathering around him an influential group of personal adherents on whose support he could rely when he put his programme of non-cooperation before Congress.[13] Despite this there remained powerful sections who were opposed to the adoption of the scheme and who were determined not to acquiesce in his domination of the nationalist movement. Foremost amongst these were the Bengali leaders.

An obvious reason for their opposition, and the one most often cited, was that they saw Gandhi as a rival. Chittaranjan Das certainly aspired to national leadership and his frequent appearances on public platforms outside Bengal in the preceding two years had already won him a national reputation.[14] Byomkes Chakravarti and Bepin Chandra Pal may have had similar ambitions.

Personal rivalry aside, there was reason for the Bengal nationalist leaders to be apprehensive, for Gandhi made it clear that there would be no room for dissenters in any political organisation which he commanded. '. . . so long as you choose to keep me as your leader,' he told a meeting of Muslims early in 1920, 'you must accept my conditions, you must accept dictatorship and the discipline of martial law.'[15] This was something new to Indian nationalism. Formerly the great Congress leaders – Naoroji, Mehta, Banerjea, Lajpat Rai, Gokhale, Tilak, Besant – had derived their power from one province and they had worked in alliance with leaders from other provinces on the understanding that there would be a minimum of mutual interference in regional activities. Gandhi relied far less on the support of any one area and his ambition was to subordinate regional differences to his national plan.

This the Bengal leaders were not in the least inclined to accept. Bengalis had enjoyed power in the nationalist movement for too long to be willing simply to abdicate on request. Nor were they willing to have an outsider dictate the form and content of their provincial politics. To Gandhi's insistent demands for a strong central authority under his control, they replied that personal dictatorship in the nationalist movement and a rigidly uniform policy would stunt national development. 'Blind reverence for Gandhiji's leadership,' wrote Bepin Chandra Pal, 'would kill people's freedom of thought and would paralyse by the deadweight of unreasoning reverence their individual conscience.'[16]

Personal ambition and a determination to maintain influence in the nationalist movement – these factors take us some distance towards an explanation of the opposition of the Bengal Congress leaders, but to go further we must understand the position which these men occupied in Bengal society, for in the last resort it was this that determined their attitude towards Gandhi's proposals. This social analysis will necessitate a short digression from our main theme, but throughout we shall highlight those elements which help to explain the dilemma facing the Bengal Congress in 1920.

III

The first and cardinal point is that almost all nationalist politicians in Bengal at that time, Extremist or Moderate, were bhadralok: 'respectable people'. The bhadralok were not a social class, economically or occupationally defined; they were a status group,[17] distinguished from other Bengali communities by their style of life and their sense of social propriety. Hence the significance of the term 'respectable people'.

The overwhelming majority of the bhadralok came from the three upper castes of Bengal Hindu society, Brahmin, Baidya and Kayastha, which in all numbered no more than 2,750,000 in a total provincial population of 46,500,000 (Hindus 20,250,000, Muslims 25,250,000).[18] From the proscriptions of these three castes, the bhadralok derived their basic social values, most significantly their aversion to manual labour and their belief in the inferiority of manual occupations. For many centuries there appears to have been an unusually wide gap between the high and low castes in Bengal, for there were few of the respectable intermediate castes which existed in other areas to act as a bridge. Unlike the high castes of some parts of India, those of Bengal did not till the soil. If they were engaged in agriculture they employed others to work their fields, for manual labour was considered degrading. The result was observed by an I.C.S. officer, J. C. Jack, in an economic survey of Faridpur district published in 1916:

Amongst the Hindus . . . landowners, clerks, professional men such as doctors, lawyers and priests, form a class apart. They are of the three higher castes in the

Hindu caste system and have for centuries lived in a different manner from the ordinary population. They have more wants and more ways of spending their money; they eat less but better food with greater variety; their houses are built on a different plan and are better furnished; their clothes although the same in cut display more variety in quality and colour.[19]

Reinforcing the bhadralok's distinctiveness and sense of superiority to the 'labouring classes' was their conviction that they had a vital role to play as guardians of a great cultural tradition. Theirs was the responsibility for the preservation of Hinduism in Bengal. They were the bearers of learning, the custodians of art, the interpreters of philosophy and doctrine. As a natural consequence they set great store by education. Here again they revealed their debt to high-caste values, but for them education was something far more than a mere traditional caste obligation. It was to education that the group had owned its success from the early nineteenth century onwards in gaining the lion's share of the new opportunities for professional, administrative and clerical employment which had accompanied the expansion of British rule in north India. Education, particularly English-language education, had been the making of the community under the British and it had become the hallmark of bhadralok status.

Not every individual who considered himself of the bhadralok could obtain an education. Not every bhadralok family could afford the education it desired for all its sons. But the ideal was accepted by all: an education, preferably in the English language, leading to a university college in Calcutta and 'white collar' employment. For the élite: the Presidency College, an English university or the Inns of Court in London, and success in the I.C.S. examination, at the bar of the Calcutta High Court or in one of the other learned professions of the capital. 'The school,' observed a Bengal Government report in 1928, 'is the one gate to the society of the bhadralok.'[20]

This points to another important characteristic of the group: the fact that it was not closed. For a low-caste Hindu or for a Muslim it was difficult to enter the charmed circle of the respectable, but it was not impossible and education was the way. 'We must remember that in Bengal the social order is a despotism of caste, tempered by matriculation,' remarked the 1914 Bengal District Administration Committee with some asperity.[21] Education, professional or clerical employment, the observance of bhadralok values and conformity to the proper cultural style – these were the means to acceptance as one of the respectable people.

Thus we can find among the bhadralok nationalist politicians of the second decade of this century a handful of men who were not Brahmin, Baidya or Kayastha: Muslim lawyers like Abdul Rasul from Chittagong, Abul Kasem from Burdwan and Fazlul Huq from Barisal; or Birendranath Sasmal, also a lawyer and a member of the agricultural Mahisya caste from Contai. Nor should it come as any more of a surprise to find in the Bengal Congress of that period men such as Bijoy Prasad Singh Roy, whose political and social style was typical of the bhadralok élite, in spite of the fact that he was a Kshatriya of Rajput origin and a great *zamindar* in Burdwan division. This points up another feature of Bengal society important to an understanding of the bhadralok: the fact that there was no clear-cut distinction between the landed and professional classes here as there was in many other parts of India. Many, perhaps most bhadralok families had some investment in landed rents to supplement, more or less adequately, the income of their members from professional or clerical employment. Landed property was valued for the status which its possession conferred and the bhadralok, as a group, thought of themselves as 'landed'.

Bijoy Prasad Singh Roy, we said, was typical of the bhadralok élite in his political and social style. Let us examine his career to see what this meant.[22] In the first place he had the 'right' education: Chakdighi village school; Hindu School, Calcutta; Presidency College; and the Calcutta University Law College; M.A., LL.B. Nor did his concern with education end with his graduation. He maintained a keen interest in college affairs and was ultimately a Fellow of Calcutta University. Involvement of this kind with educational administration, whether in a rural district, a mofussil town or in Calcutta, was characteristic of the bhadralok. Educational institutions were rungs in the community's ladder of preferment, and they were to be jealousy guarded and maintained with care. Moreover as one of the few avenues of constructive public activity open to them in their circumscribed colonial society, educational politics – particularly the politics of Calcutta University – had assumed an extraordinary significance for the bhadralok.

For a similar reason election to local self-governing bodies – local and district boards, and municipalities – was keenly sought, and thus we find Singh Roy serving for many years on the Calcutta Corporation and Improvement Trust, and later achieving the honour of Sheriff of the city. He had an equally distinguished career in the provincial legislature. Obviously direct participation of this kind in legislative politics was beyond the reach of all but a handful of the bhadralok, but even so parliamentary institutions were valued by many of the group as a potential instrument for the orderly achievement of self-government.

As a Calcutta High Court advocate Singh Roy was active in another area of bhadralok concern, the law. The community's keen attachment to legal institutions and the process of law was striking, and it is only partly explained by the career opportunities offered by the legal profession. Fundamentally the law was valued by the bhadralok – a socially privileged and consciously superior group – as the framework of social stability and order. We have just suggested that this concern for social order was a reason for the bhadralok's involvement with parliamentary institutions, and we should also recognise it as a factor underlying their ambition to furnish large numbers of recruits for the Indian and Bengal Civil Services, and their determination to control the institutions of education and local self-government.

In one other respect B.P. Singh Roy was representative of the bhadralok: in his nationalism. Nationalist politics in Bengal in the period which we are discussing, the end of the second decade of the twentieth century, were an exclusive bhadralok preserve, and (the other side of the coin) to be bhadralok and not to be a nationalist was to reject one of the common values of the group. Understandably there was wide and frequently acrimonious disagreement over methods of political action, and there was a variety of institutional affiliation, ranging from the Indian Association and the Moderate Party, through the Provincial Congress, to the revolutionary and terrorist *samitis*. But these were all bhadralok organisations[23] and the disagreements were disagreements between bhadralok.

No one man's career can illustrate all aspects of a society and we must take account of areas of bhadralok activity outside Singh Roy's experience. There were other important organisations, for instance the students associations which gave an institutional focus to the activities of bhadralok adolescents in their formative college years, when they were freed briefly from the narrow constraints of the joint family. There were the student messes in which those who went to Calcutta for an education found accommodation and security among bhadralok youths from their home districts.[24] There were the Peoples' and District Associations in the mofussil and the Ratepayers' Associations in the Calcutta suburbs, which, with the District Bar Associations, were the watchdogs of local bhadralok interests. There were the libraries, reading rooms and debating societies, found in every Bengal town supported by bhadralok money and managed by bhadralok committees, as centres for educated gathering and discussion. Equally as important as these formal institutions were the informal ties of tradition which bound the urban bhadralok to their ancestral villages, giving the group a communications network extending throughout Bengal; and the customary pattern of settlement in Calcutta which divided the bhadralok and other communities into separate *paras* (neighbourhoods).[25]

In all of these things there is indirect evidence of a distinct bhadralok identity. For a positive expression of that identity we can look to Bengali literature, for the literature like the politics of Bengal was the bhadralok's creation and cherished possession. Under the stimulus of European contact in Calcutta, the bhadralok in the nineteenth century had refashioned Bengali as a rich literary language, freely borrowing forms and techniques from English to enable them to grapple effectively with the intellectual issues introduced to their society by the European cultural intrusion.

Their achievement, now generally known as the Bengal Renaissance, is sufficiently celebrated as to need no elaboration, but we should consider its contribution to the formation of bhadralok identity. Primarily it gave the group a common syncretic culture which reinforced their distinctiveness from the lower strata of Bengal society and set them apart even from educated groups in other regions of India. Their inheritance was a passionate attachment to the Bengali language, an intense pride in their literature and an awakened consciousness of the history of Bengal. A sense of the past was accompanied by a growing sense of country, and the images of the Motherland and of Bengal the Nation filled their literature. The great literary figures were venerated, with the politicians, as heroes of nationalism. Of Rabindranath Tagore, most honoured of all, it could be said: 'He has sung Bengal into a nation.'[26]

But songs alone could not make a nation, as Vivekananda so eloquently emphasised. Courageous action was needed to prove Bengali manhood. 'What we want is muscles of iron and nerves of steel. We have wept long enough. No more weeping, but stand on your feet and be men.' After Vivekananda an emphasis upon the virtues of strength and vigour as the means of national regeneration was an article of the Hindu bhadralok creed. Bengal once strong in the classical age, it was said, had been emasculated by the quietest doctrines of Buddhism and the emotional popular cults of medieval Hinduism. The 'true Brahmanical virtues' of intellectual initiative and rational self-assertion had been neglected, and the degradation of the Muslim and British conquests was a natural consequence.[27] 'Let us think for a moment of the fatal and universal weakness which had beset our people when the English first came to this land,' Chittaranjan Das exhorted his fellow Bengal Congressmen in 1917. 'Our Religion of Power – the Gospel of "Sakti" – had become a mockery of its former self; it had lost its soul of beneficence in the repetition of empty formulas and the observance of meaningless mummeries . . . the Hindus of Bengal had lost strength and vigour alike in Religion, Science, and Life.'[28] To Das, as to his fellow Hindu bhadralok, it was self-evident that it was their ordained mission to restore the glory of Bengal through strength in action.

IV

We are now better equipped to look again at the clash in 1920 between Gandhi and the Bengal nationalist leaders. From our discussion of the Hindu bhadralok's ideal of political action, one area of disagreement will be readily apparent: Gandhi's philosophy of non-violence. Coming from a Gujerati trading caste, Gandhi had been strongly influenced by the quietest doctrines of Jainism and Vaisnavism, and it was one of the secrets of his mass appeal that he customarily used popular Vaisnava images in his speeches. By many of the bhadralok, modern Vaisnavism was despised as a lower-class survival of the obscurantist cults of medieval times.[29] The contrast between the 'beggarly and cringing' Vaisnava and the 'bold' Sakta, worshipper of the principle of strength in the goddess Kali, was familiar in their literature. Self-assertion, not self-abasement as Gandhi preached, was the doctrine of the bhadralok and their leaders refused to accept his philosophy of politics. Bepin Chandra Pal explained:

> I am not blind to the possibilities of good in the great hold that Mahatmaji has got on the populace; but there is the other side; and in the earlier stages of democracy these personal influences, when they are due to the inspirations of mediaeval religious sentiments, are simply fatal to its future. This does not remove the inherited slave-mentality which is the root of all our degradations and miseries.[30]

There was another more pragmatic reason why Gandhi's insistence on *satyagraha* was unwelcome to the Bengal leaders. It seemed, at least initially, to offer no prospect of a satisfactory engagement with the British. A resort to passive resistance was no doubt necessary on occasions for suppressed majority communities, but it was considered inappropriate for the bhadralok who were a dominant minority. Their politicians demanded a form of political action which enabled them to exert themselves against their adversaries, the British, without (and this qualification was important) endangering their hold on political life. These requirements were met by legislative politics and terrorism, both of which provided opportunities to hit at the British and yet involved relatively few people. It was in these activities that the bhadralok politicians were accustomed to engage. Thus Gandhi's insistence upon non-violence, as also his demand for a boycott of the legislative councils, threatened their political style.

His rationale for council boycott seemed absurd to most of the bhadralok leaders. He was arguing that Congressmen should withdraw from legislative councils and the other institutions of British Indian government because those institutions were alien and imposed. To many Bengal Congressmen such an argument was nonsense. In the past when they had boycotted the legislative councils it was not because the councils were foreign – because they were based on the English parliamentary model instead of an indigenous Indian model – but because they did not conform *closely enough* to the English model, their powers being so severely limited. The bhadralok wanted parliamentary self-government in Bengal, and, at least in part, terrorism was their protest against the British refusal to recognise the intensity of their desire or to admit their capacity for such a form of government.

This reveals the cultural gulf dividing Gandhi from the bhadralok. As Susanne Rudolph has demonstrated so convincingly, Gandhi was as concerned as any Bengali with questions of courage, and he was offering *satyagraha* to Indians as a way to prove their courage while maintaining their cultural integrity.[31] Yet for the bhadralok his exclusive emphasis on *ahimsa* and *satyagraha* offended dearly cherished values, and it was their cultural integrity which they felt to be threatened.

This threat was increased by Gandhi's espousal of the doctrine of 'creative crisis'. He proclaimed that he and his followers would harness the enthusiasm and energy generated by his campaign, to clear away the alien debris which overlay Indian society. Only in this way, he claimed, could national creativity be restored.[32] On the surface there was nothing novel for Bengal in this. Attacks on 'Anglicisation' and appeals for a return to the 'strength and simplicity of true Bengal life' had been heard frequently from political platforms throughout the province in the preceding fifteen years,[33] but formerly the orators were all bhadralok, often the most westernised élite politicians, men who valued the European elements in their culture too highly to consider acting on their own advice. Gandhi, on the other hand, had shown in his personal life that he meant what he said, and he was now insisting that all nationalists should follow his example. A return to simplicity of living to free the individual from the tyranny of material possessions; the renunciation of all non-essentials; a total commitment to the struggle against foreign domination – these were Gandhi's demands.

To the bhadralok leadership[34] this was philistinism. They were passionately proud of the richness of their culture and were unconvinced that they should strip their life bare in this way. Charles Freer Andrews, who had gained from his work with Rabindranath Tagore at Santiniketan a deep sympathy for bhadralok values, described their reaction. Writing to Tagore in January 1921 of the joys of painting, he remarked:

> Here are things which Mathatma Gandhi finds it difficult to understand, and he would suspend them all, while we get Swaraj – but not I, not I! I could *never* give up these! . . . No, there is some fundamental difference there: and perhaps it runs through the whole of Bengal as compared with Gujerat. Here, in Bengal, Mahatmaji is saying 'Let every student take up spinning and weaving, and drop everything else'. But the Bengali students say 'We will take up spinning and weaving, but we shall *not* drop everything else.' – There again, is the difference![35]

Tagore himself spoke from the heart of the bhadralok when he demanded rhetorically of Gandhi: 'The mind, surely, is not of less account than a length of cotton thread spun on the wheel!'[36] In a series of public addresses in Calcutta in August 1921 on his return from an extended trip abroad, he protested against Gandhi's anti-intellectualism and narrowness of view. Let us not obscure our vision of the wider world with the dust raised by political passion, he said. Let us seek universal truth, for 'India's awakening is a part of the awakening of the world.'[37] Earlier he had written: 'Our present struggle to alienate our heart and mind from the West is an attempt at spiritual suicide. . . . Let us be rid of all false pride and rejoice at any lamp being lit in any corner of the world, knowing that it is a part of the common illumination of our house.'[38] His attack brought Gandhi to Calcutta but discussions between the two men revealed (in the words of a contemporary) 'a difference of temperament so wide that it was extremely difficult to arrive at a common intellectual understanding'.[39]

These differences of culture and temperament certainly stood as barriers between Gandhi and the bhadralok nationalists, but there were other, less unimpeachable, reasons for their reluctance to follow his lead. This had been brought home to Andrews on a visit to Calcutta in September 1920 when he met a friend, Promothonath Chaudhuri, 'bitter beyond words and crying out against his countrymen for their folly in following any one who is an Ascetic, as though wisdom must necessarily come from fasting and starving and hunger-striking.'

But though my intellect went with Promotho Babu and I could never follow Mr Gandhi in his extravagances [Andrews recalled later] I could not help contrasting the other side: for there was Promotho Babu . . . and others in the Camac Street Club with every single luxury of a London Club-life around them, – playing bridge and taking their strong glasses of whisky and brandy. Say what one would to justify it they were parasites, living on immense fees taken from others. And if one had to choose, was not their judgement, – their *moral* judgement, – far more warped by luxury and luxurious living than Mr Gandhi's by starvation.[40]

There was more than politics and poetry to the good life which the bhadralok élite was defending.

V

The Bengal Congressmen's memory of the anti-partition agitation was another difficulty with which Gandhi had to contend in his effort to win Bengal for non-cooperation. 1905 was uppermost in bhadralok minds as they faced the decisions of 1920. 'I find our countrymen are furiously excited about Non-cooperation,' remarked Tagore in September. 'It will grow into something like our Swadeshi movement in Bengal.'[41] 'In Bengal we have passed through the stage of non-cooperation,' wrote Banerjea a month later. 'We practised it in the days of the *swadeshi* movement and the anti-partition agitation. We were non-cooperators before the rest of India thought of it.'[42] As this suggests there was a certain satisfaction in the thought that the rest of India was now following a path which Bengal had trodden fifteen years before, but there was also an element of pique at the temerity of an outsider like Gandhi in bringing forward as his own inventions and under labels of his own choosing, the old methods of boycott, *swadeshi* and national education.

Nor were the bhadralok leaders at all certain that they wished to retrace their steps. The campaigns of the partition period had been exhilarating but in retrospect the risks that had been taken seemed very grave. For a cause as dear to Hindu bhadralok hearts as the unity of Bengal those risks had been worth while, but were they similarly justified for 'a political chimera'[43] such as Gandhi's *swaraj*? Admittedly the anti-partition agitation had achieved its ultimate object and in Hindu bhadralok lore it was reckoned a great victory, but there were many secret doubts as to the efficacy of the political methods which had been used.[44] The effects of British retaliation had been serious. Public life in Bengal in the years following 1908 had suffered severely from the suppression of *samitis*, the imprisonment and deportation of political suspects, and the extended activities of the CID.[45] Bengal had pushed out its chin once and been punched hard. It was still suffering from the after-effects and it was naturally reluctant to invite another blow.

What carried even greater weight in the thinking of the Hindu bhadralok leaders was the social repercussions of the anti-partition agitation. In trying new methods of direct action in 1906 and 1907 in an effort to involve more people in their agitation against the British, the politicians had stirred up a hornets' nest of regional, communal and class dissension. To their acute embarrassment their bhadralok followers had responded with an enthusiasm which they could not control and their leadership had been discredited by this failure, which alone was sufficient to make them chary of ever repeating such an adventure. More disturbing still was the hostile reaction which they had evoked from communities, such as the Muslims, Namasudras and Marwaris, who previously had had no part in politics.[46] For thirty years the Bengal nationalists had maintained as their ideal the ultimate involvement of the 'masses' in the nationalist movement, but previously there had been no occasion for them to seek mass support, nor had they shown any particular concern at the lack of such an opportunity. As A.J.P. Taylor wrote of early nineteenth-century nationalism under the Hapsburg monarchy: 'The masses were evoked as a shadowy presence off-stage, reinforcements that were not expected to appear.'[47] The agitation of 1905–6, however, provided opportunities for political leadership to younger bhadralok, some of whom were determined to abandon the 'cautious' policies of their elders. They would involve the 'masses' in politics.[48] To their chagrin their appeals for support to non-bhadralok groups were hostilely rejected, and when a few Hindu bhadralok *zamindars* and lawyers attempted to use their economic and social power to coerce their inferiors, the result was communal violence.[49] This experience left a deep impression on Hindu bhadralok political thinking. Although the group's leaders did not totally discard the ideal of mass participation in nationalism, they were convinced that an incautious appeal for wider support might endanger the Hindu bhadralok's political, and even social, dominance. This reinforced their preference for the élitist and socially-secure forms of political action, such as legislative politics and terrorism, to which they were accustomed.

Seen against this background their reluctance to support the non-cooperation movement in 1920 can be readily understood. It was bad enough that Gandhi should insist upon their discarding 'safe' political methods in favour of direct action, but it was adding insult to injury for him to emphasise that it was the exclusive character of those old methods to which he objected. His aim was to take politics to the masses, and, by involving them in the nationalist movement, give them political education. He wanted to lead a people's movement. All of which was anathema to most of the Hindu bhadralok politicians, who had no taste for popular politics.

It must be recognised that apart from their aversion there were real difficulties in the way of their leading a mass movement. The great bulk of the peasantry, who comprised 75 per cent of Bengal's population, were Muslims, and even with the low-caste Hindus who made up the rest the Hindu bhadralok had little in common. As we have already observed, the manual labourer in Bengal was traditionally separated from his superiors by a wide social gap, and this had been maintained by the exclusive education system established under the British. The peasantry shared nothing of the bhadralok culture and their values were neither understood nor appreciated by the English-speaking urban professional men who were engaged in politics. In Bengal, as in most other parts of twentieth-century Asia and Africa, there was a great problem of communication between the small westernised intelligentsia of the cities, eager to build a nation free from European imperialism, and the rural populace, traditionalist and illiterate.

In an editorial published on the eve of the special Congress session in Calcutta in September 1920, the *Bengali* declared: 'We Bengalis are opposed to non-cooperation. For a period of 10 years, from 1906 to 1916, we played that game. And we are not prepared to take back what we rejected on deliberation then. Even Gandhi had admitted that to act up to this resolution would mean rebellion and revolution, and we are not ready to proceed to such a course.'[50] The *Bengali* was generally regarded as a voice of the Moderate party,[51] but on this occasion its concern at the effects of mass agitation was shared by a wide range of Bengal nationalists, Extremists as well as Moderates.[52] They were apprehensive that mass agitation would lead to violence, and that violence against the foreigner might quickly change to violence against the socially privileged. The Hindu bhadralok élite were afraid of the social consequences of a disturbance of the established political order.[53]

They were afraid because they had much to lose. This élite held much of Bengal's land and a significant share of its wealth. Their domination of all levels of the education system gave them almost exclusive access to the learned professions and government service. They controlled the press. They played a leading part in all forms of civic and village affairs. Politics was their business. They gave Bengal its literature, music and art. They were its cultural and social leaders. In city and countryside they were indeed the 'respectable people'. All of this they stood to lose from any social upheaval. 'Scratch a Hindu and you will find him a conservative,' remarked Surendranath Banerjea.[54] Certainly Banerjea's Hindus, the bhadralok élite, were conservative well might they be so.

It must be recognised that their fear was largely a fear of the unknown. They did not understand the 'masses' and they felt no confidence in their ability to lead or even control them should the existing order of political and social relationships be shaken. Their fear was blind but it was not unreasonable. A leap into the political unknown could well be a leap into revolution and anarchy. In a society like that of India of the early twentieth century, in which there was no system of communication extending vertically through the community; in which there were few universally accepted social values; in which there was no general knowledge of the functions of the state; in which there were great economic inequalities; and in which there were huge new urban centres, where traditional restraints had been weakened by the rapid influx of a heterogeneous migrant labour force, the line between order and disorder was thin. It was a perilous undertaking to rock the ship of state, even it it was officered by unwanted foreigners.

The events of the years immediately preceding 1920 had given the Hindu bhadralok politicians little reason for confidence. The war of 1914–18 had had a profoundly unsettling effect on Bengali society and this social unrest was aggravated in the immediate post-war years by economic difficulties. A succession of natural disasters in 1918 and 1919, including the great influenza epidemic, led to an extraordinarily sharp rise in the prices of foodstuffs and cotton goods,[55] and early in 1920 a severe slump brought to an end a five-year boom in Calcutta trade and industry.[56] Already there had been serious labour trouble in Bombay;[57]

there were disturbing rumours of peasant unrest in the United Provinces and Bihar;[58] and strikes among the migrant industrial workers of Howrah and Hooghly-side were becoming distressingly frequent.[59]

Events in Russia in 1917 had left the bhadralok élite extremely sensitive to any potential threat to property from labour. Indeed their reaction to the Russian revolution had laid bare their basic social conservatism. They had welcomed the success in March of Kerensky and his Provisional Government in deposing the Czar, as an exemplar for India's political emancipation,[60] but their delight had turned to dismay with the violent attack on the propertied classes which followed the Bolshevik revolution in November. They were afraid that a similar disaster might befall India.[61]

The Calcutta Muslim riots of September 1918 had shown how much inflammable social material was now available in Bengal for political incendiaries, and the concern of the bhadralok élite at this development had been manifest in the support accorded by the Hindu newspapers to the Government in its use of force to suppress the disorders.[62] This incident had also underlined the fact – a distressing fact for the Hindu bhadralok – that in Bengal it was Muslim rather than Hindu politicians who could best make use of a mass appeal. Although the Muslim leaders had to overcome the same problems of class distinction, and, to a lesser degree, differences of culture, sect and caste, they could speak directly to their co-religionists, in a way the Hindu bhadralok politicians could never do, in the name of Islam. There was a fraternity amongst Muslims such as was unknown to Hindus in Bengal. The best ground for an appeal was of course religious – Islam in danger – (again cool comfort to the Hindus) and in the post-war years the perfect issue was to hand in the Khilafat movement

Late in 1919 Khilafat committees had been established in various parts of Bengal 'to circulate news on the Moslem world',[63] and the official peace celebrations in December had provided their organisers with an opportunity to incite communal feeling against the British. 'So far as we are associated with the "Victory", it means defeat for Moslems,' declaimed the Bengali-language daily *Mohammadi* angrily. 'The bier of Moslem nationality is being carried out – are we to rejoice thereat?'[64] With the return to Calcutta in January 1920 of Abul Kalam Azad, a young Urdu-speaking Muslim journalist who had been interned for four years at Ranchi, the movement took a radical turn. Azad and his followers went among the Muslim workers in the mill

I

towns of West Bengal spreading propaganda about the British attitude to the Khilafat. When moderate appeals failed to stir up general anger, resort was had to provocative rumours. It was whispered that the Government had ordered prayers to be said on Sunday instead of Friday, and had proscribed the Koran.[65]

The dangerous possibilities of such an exploitation of religious fanaticism and ignorance were evident to the Hindu bhadralok leaders, and when Gandhi urged them to support the Khilafat movement in order to cement Hindu–Muslim unity, they angrily protested against his encouragement of such a campaign. Andrews reflected their mood when he wrote: 'The truth is that the "Khilafat" appeals to the very worst side of Islam – that religious arrogance, which is every whit as bad as racial arrogance.'[66] The Bengal Congressmen found it objectionable that Gandhi should insist upon coupling a communal issue of this kind with non-cooperation and accord to men like Azad a place of prominence in his movement. It strengthened their conviction that his campaign was fraught with danger.

VI

All that has been said about the attitudes of the bhadralok politicians towards the masses points a lesson of general application: that nationalist radicalism is not to be equated with social radicalism. It would seem a statement of the obvious to observe that the desire of colonial nationalists to rid their country of imperial domination is not, of necessity, accompanied by a desire to reconstruct the social order; yet the failure to grasp this point, or at best to state it explicitly, has been a frequent source of misunderstanding of the different forms which nationalism may take in colonial countries.

The confusion which prevails over the reasons for the Bengali reaction to Gandhi's non-cooperation proposals provides a striking illustration of this. Following the lead given by various participants,[67] commentators have applied the term 'Right Wing' to the Moderates and others who favoured council entry, and 'Left Wing' to the Extremists and terrorists.[68] By the logic of their metaphor they are then convinced that Gandhi's non-violent non-cooperation movement must have been of the 'Centre', and it is to their astonishment that they discover that while the Bengal nationalists favoured both council entry and terrorism (the 'Right' and the 'Left'), they were most reluctant to accept non-cooperation (the 'Centre').

It is evident that these writers have been led astray in their interpretation by their failure to distinguish between nationalist and social radicalism. The terms 'Right and Left Wing' which they employ have socio-economic connotations acquired from their European usage. If these terms are to have any meaning in this context (and their value is doubtful) both council entry and terrorism must be regarded as 'Right Wing', for they were esteemed by the bhadralok politicians as élite activities and non-cooperation as 'Left Wing', for it was regarded as socially hazardous.

Gandhi himself was aware of the importance of this distinction between nationalism and social radicalism. 'In fighting the Government the motives of co-workers can be mixed,' he explained. 'In fighting the devil of untouchability I have absolutely select company.'[69] Here in a nutshell is the explanation of the Bengal Congressmen's reaction which we have been seeking. Gandhi was not simply offering a fight against the Government. He was also calling for an attack on the devils in Indian society, and the socially conservative Hindu bhadralok politicians were convinced that these devils should be left well alone lest all hell be let loose.

VII

The trend of our argument has presented us with a logical problem: if, as we have asserted, the Bengal Congressmen were so implacably opposed to Gandhi and his programme of non-cooperation, why did they capitulate to him at Nagpur in December 1920? The answer basically is that he had undercut them by capturing the support of a section of their own community.

At the outset of our discussion of the bhadralok, we noted that they were a status group, not a class. We must now take account of the fact that there were class divisions within the status group, and that there was growing friction between the classes. In his definition of status group, Max Weber notes that social honour is usually determined by 'the average class-situation of the status-group members'. It appears that by the second decade of this century there was a large number of bhadralok who were discontented with their class-situation, believing it to be far below what was proper to their status. It is also apparent that this was the source of considerable tension within the group as a whole.

Between about 1880 and 1910 sections of the bhadralok appear to have been faced with serious economic difficulties. A marked rise in population in that period had been accompanied by increasingly frequent subinfeudation of landed rent holdings as a result of which the return from what had formerly been a major source of bhadralok income had been reduced to negligible proportions in many cases.[70] At the same time there was growing pressure on that limited area of 'white-collar' employment which the bhadralok considered respectable. Population growth was one reason for this and another was competition from Muslims and low-caste Hindus, who were now acquiring English-language education in small but significant numbers. Difficulties at home were compounded with difficulties 'up-country'. Throughout the cities and towns of north India, which up until the 1880s or 1890s had provided employment opportunities for enterprising Bengal bhadralok, new indigenous educated groups were appearing to contest the available jobs and to demand of the local Governments the exclusion of outsiders.[71] By 1900 office doors were shut to many younger bhadralok. So too were the doors to the best colleges, and the inferior institutions to which they were forced to turn were unsatisfactory substitutes. To all of these difficulties was added an unprecedented inflation in the basic cost of living in 1906 and 1907, accompanied by a shortage of credit, on which the bhadralok normally relied to finance their education and their prestigious religious ceremonies.[72]

Economic deprivation, frustrated ambition and injured pride made the lower-class bhadralok attentive listeners to the tales then current of the enormity of the drain of wealth from India to Britain. The same factors made them jealous of their fellow bhadralok who had obtained the education and jobs they desired. The vernacular press, which drew most of its readers from among the semi-educated, underemployed lower-class bhadralok, played upon this bitterness, ridiculing the élite for their English affectations of speech, dress and manners, accusing them of allying with the British bureacracy to their own advantage, and of selfishly excluding the mass of their fellow bhadralok from participation in politics.[73]

That there was real discontent over this last issue was demonstrated in 1905 and 1906 by young Extremists like Aurobindo Ghose and Bepin Chandra Pal, when they won the acclaim and support of the lower-class bhadralok by attacking the Moderates for their élitist politics and by calling for popular participation in the anti-partition agitation.[74] They brought the lower-class bhadralok onto the streets and fundamentally altered the character of the agitation but as we have seen they did not have the experience or techniques to control large numbers of followers, nor was it in their power to provide them with any permanent political role. With the withdrawal of the Extremists from the Congress and the collapse of the anti-partition agitation under British repression in 1908, the lower-class bhadralok were again condemned to the political wilderness.

It was eight years before there was another direct appeal to them and again it came from the Extremists. Attempting in 1916 and 1917 to reassert themselves in the Congress and to wrest control of the provincial political organisations from the Moderates, the Bengal Extremists raised the old cry of exclusivist politics. The way was prepared for them by the vernacular press which had maintained in the interim a constant attack on the Moderates on this ground. These papers had developed stereotyped lines of criticism, with a terminology which is highly misleading if taken out of context. When, for instance, they spoke of the 'babus' they referred to those objects of righteous scorn, the bhadralok élite. 'The people' or 'the mass' were their approving readers, the lower-class bhadralok. Their criticism was usually levelled at the 'babus' selfish disregard for 'the people', their 'Anglicisation' and divorce from 'true Bengali Hindu society', and their concern with British institutions, titles and honours. Two passages will serve as an illustration.

Dainik Chandrika, 30 December 1914
This is the Congress of the Babus. These irreligious, luxury-loving beggars are the creation of English education. The country and society have nothing to do with them. The mass do not know them, neither do they care for the mass. By virtue of their begging through the Congress they secure high posts, start subsidised papers and try to win fame and respect in the country.

Basumati, 17 April 1915
... whatever our Babus do, they do for the furtherance of their own self-interest and not for the benefit of the people at large. The Congress and conferences and what not keep these agitators perpetually before the public eye and bring them something for their pockets also. And that is all that our 'patriots' care for.

It is against this background that we can understand the applause with which Chitta Ranjan Das' maiden political speech – his presidential address to the Bengal Provincial Conference in April 1917 – was greeted by the old Extremist politicians and the vernacular press. Whether or not it was his intention (and there is reason to doubt that he meant his words to be interpreted so narrowly[75]) his speech was seen as an attack on 'babu' politics and as a direct appeal to the lower-class bhadralok against the Moderates.[76] If we compare his language with that current in the vernacular press, we can appreciate why this construction was put upon his words.

We have many dangers and difficulties in the path; but our chiefest danger is this that we have become largely and unnecessarily Anglicised in our education, culture and social practices. The mere mention of 'politics' conjures up before our eyes the vision of English political institutions; and we feel tempted to fall down before and worship the precise form which politics has assumed under the peculiar conditions of English history. . . . Only we neglect the one thing essential. We never look to our country, never think of Bengal or the Bengalees, of our past national history, or our present material condition. Hence our political agitation is unreal and unsubstantial – divorced from all intimate touch with the soul of our people. . . . We boast of being educated: but how many are we? What room do we occupy in the country? What is our relation to the vast masses of our countrymen? Do they think our thoughts or speak our speech? I am bound to confess that our countrymen have little faith in us. And what is the reason of this unfaith? Down in the depths of our soul, we, the educated people, have become Anglicised: we read in English, think in English and even our speech is translated from English. Our borrowed anglicism repels our unsophisticated countrymen: they prefer the genuine article to the shoddy imitation.[79]

This speech established for Das an immediate claim to inclusion in the first rank of Bengal politicians, and it was the keynote for a vigorous and successful Extremist effort to mobilise lower-class bhadralok support. In the battles of late 1917 and 1918 between the Moderates and Extremists for command of the local Congress machinery, the latter's ability on almost every occasion to produce a numerous and noisy backing to outvote and outshout their rivals was to prove the decisive factor.[78]

There was danger, however, in what the Extremists were doing. The nature of their appeal to the lower-class bhadralok, especially the terms they were using gave them a false appearance of social radicalism which might expose them to a charge of hypocrisy should there arise a demand for radical action. In fact the Extremist politicians were as much a part of 'Babudom' (as the influential Bengali daily *Nayak* described élite society[79]) as were the Moderates and should there be an attack on that society they were almost bound to turn in its defence – which is what happened when Gandhi appeared on the scene. Here was a man who spoke of 'the mass' and 'the people' without any mental reservations, who attacked Anglicisation root and branch, and who would sever all ties with British institutions. He offended the Hindu bhadralok politicians, Extremist as well as Moderate, and they turned against him, but in doing so they lost the support of their own lower-class who saw in this yet another example of 'babu' betrayal. *Nayak* spoke for them:

> The Babus openly advocate democracy to obtain cheap notoriety, while they secretly associate with Government, with a view to securing titles and high posts carrying fat salaries. When their object is accomplished they identify themselves with Government. This is the reason why one who is an Extremist today becomes a Moderate tomorrow. Mr Gandhi's non-cooperation movement strikes at the root of this turncoat policy, and this is why the Babus are opposed to it.[80]

With their excitement running high at their new share in politics, the lower-class bhadralok were in no mood to tolerate diffidence. If the 'babus' lacked the courage to lead them against the British, then they would find leaders who did not. At first they were doubtful that Gandhi was the man for the task, for the one thing that was clear among his otherwise perplexing political utterances was his unwavering opposition to any violent conflict with the British. However by the middle of 1920 as he clarified his ideas and they were given better publicity in Bengal, the lower-class bhadralok grasped the fact that he was offering a fundamental challenge to British authority and that his agitation would provide unprecedented opportunities for political involvement. Enthusiastically they declared for non-cooperation, and the cautions from the élite politicians about the dangers to Hindu bhadralok dominance of mass politics went unheeded. 'No one is listening,' wrote Andrews: 'all is clamour and noise and strife.'[81]

VIII

The Bengal Congressmen were now faced with a painful choice. Should they stand by their principles at the risk of committing political suicide and possibly being displaced by radical and irresponsible men? Or should they give way before Gandhi's popularity in the hope that ultimately they might be able to exercise some restraint on the agitation in Bengal? Fazlul Huq, presiding at the 1920 Provincial Conference in April, had given a pertinent word of advice: 'Leaders of the people must always have the courage to face the people and if they find that they can no longer lead, they must either give up their politics or be prepared to be led.'[82] As the year passed and Gandhi's following grew, many of the Bengal politicians decided that they would have to consent to be led. 'The whole country is with Mr Gandhi, but the politicians are holding back. Yet one by one they are obliged to declare themselves,' reported Andrews early in September.[83]

By that stage Gandhi, a master of political tactics, had manœuvred his opponents into a corner. In April and May he had arranged for the Central Khilafat Committee and the All-India Congress Committee to discuss non-cooperation, and it was announced that a special session of Congress would be held in September to decide for or against his scheme. In the meantime he went ahead with his own preparations and on 1 August began personal non-cooperation.[84] This forced the provincial Congress committees to reach some decision, and, with the knowledge that overt opposition to Gandhi would bring down upon them public wrath, they could do no more than search for some form of compromise. The Bengal committee decided for non-cooperation in principle but urged that the legislative councils should be boycotted from within.[85] All the leading Bengal Extremists were candidates for the first elections for the new legislatures to be held at the end of the year, but the uncertainty as to the policy which Congress would adopt was a handicap to them in their canvassing. Worse still their advocacy of council entry, even if the purpose were to obstruct from within, put them perilously close to the Moderates – and that was to court political disaster.

They went to the September Congress in this awkward, compromised situation, while Gandhi, well aware of his strength, went full of confidence. The main debate on non-cooperation took place in the Subjects Committee. For three days the Bengalis struggled vainly to swing the majority against Gandhi, who was obdurate in his insistence that Congress give immediate support to every item of his programme. When his resolution came before the full session on the 8th, Bepin Chandra Pal moved an amendment to accept the principle but delay the implementation of non-cooperation. His concern, he explained, was to avoid a failure on a national scale such as had occurred in Bengal during the *swadeshi* campaign of the partition period. In the voting on the following day, Pal's amendment was rejected and Gandhi's resolution carried by a large majority, against the votes of all but a handful of the Bengal delegates.[86]

What were Gandhi's opponents to do now? Should they withdraw from the Congress and go ahead with their preparations for the elections? Should they remain in the Congress in the hope that they could reverse the decision at the annual session in December? Or should they forget their qualms and accept non-cooperation? They were in a quandary, but they could not hesitate for long for they were under pressure from the Gandhians to declare themselves.[87] After a week of agonised debate, the main group in the Bengal Congress, under the leadership of C.R.Das and Byomkes Chakravarti, decided to adopt the second course: they would bow to the majority decision for the present but would work for its reversal at the end of the year. This meant, however, that they would be unable to contest the elections and on 15 September they issued a manifesto withdrawing their candidature.[88]

In the twelve weeks that remained before Congress met again at Nagpur there was much confused activity among Bengal Congressmen and Khilafatists. Abul Kalam Azad's party was busy discouraging Muslim voters from going to the polls,[89] while Das, Chakravarti and B.C.Pal travelled extensively in Eastern Bengal in an attempt to rally their dispersed supporters.[90] The popular excitement over Gandhi's activities which had been mounting steadily through the year had reached such a pitch that it had engulfed many who earlier had been sceptical. Andrews was one of them. 'It is good to be alive in these days,' he wrote delightedly on 1 November, 'even if one has not the heaven, which Wordsworth speaks of, of being young.' In this atmosphere there was no place for equivocation and the cry 'For or against?' became insistent. 'Are you a whole-hogger? If so you are a non-cooperator. Do you contend that some of the items in the programme are calculated to do more harm to the people than to the bureaucracy? Well, damn you, you are no non-cooperator but a renegade.'[91]

This mood augured ill for the success of the revisionist party at Nagpur, but it was determined not to let the issue go by default and it was as active as its opponents in organising supporters for the trip to the Central Provinces. The result was an extraordinary migration. '. . . whilst many of the prominent politicians were present, the Bengal contingent included hundreds of ex-detenus and the intelligentsia, which dominated earlier Congresses, seems to have been swamped in a mass of semi-educated persons swept up from all parts of India', reported the Government of India.[92]

Within the Bengal delegation there were a number of warring groups manoeuvring for ascendency, and feeling between them was so

embittered that the two meetings held on 26 and 27 December to
elect the province's representatives on the Subjects Committee, both
ended in ugly free-for-all fights. Order was restored only when Gandhi
intervened in person.[93]

Das had come to Nagpur determined to offer stout resistance to
non-cooperation but it was now clear that he could not even carry the
whole Bengal contingent with him if he opposed Gandhi. With a grand
gesture he turned defeat into victory. Having secured Gandhi's private
assurance that he would be left free to pursue his own political propaganda, he made the dramatic announcement that he would move the
main resolution in support of non-cooperation.[94]

With one stroke Das had dished his rivals. Provided he could carry
his own group with him – and his personal influence was sufficient to
enable him to do this – he now had a chance to unite the whole
contingent under his leadership. He had stolen his opponents' platform
and by securing Gandhi's endorsement had climbed a step above them.
They remained merely provincial politicians, while he had reasserted
himself as a national figure. Most important of all he could now return
to Bengal with a reunited battalion at his back and a job of work in
hand. Even had he been successful in persuading the Congress in favour
of council entry, he would have been unable to provide action for his
party, for the first elections were over and the Moderates ensconced in
the legislatures for a three-year term. With non-cooperation he had a
task for his eager followers, and a popular task at that.

IX

This story's epilogue was written by the Bengal Congressmen in 1921
in the distinctive (or, as Gandhi thought, deviant) character which they
gave the province's civil disobedience movement, and in 1922 in their
support for the Swaraj Party. But that epilogue must be told elsewhere
for we already have ample material on which to reflect.

The first general point to be made is one underlined by Das' action
at Nagpur: that in these twelve months there had been a profound
shift in the balance between national and provincial politics. Up until
this time nationalist politics in each province had been an almost
autonomous system. The power of nationalist leaders was regionally
based, and their authority, though not their influence, was regionally
restricted. They might advise or cajole their fellow nationalists in other
provinces, but they could not dictate their internal policy or interfere

in their internal organisation. A provincial leader with sound regional backing could comfortably disregard 'national' opinion. All this had been permanently changed in 1920. As Das acknowledged with his Nagpur decision, there were now two interdependent power structures, the national and the provincial, and to maintain his influence the nationalist politician would have to gain a secure position in both. The old-style Congress, a federation of provincial grandees, was being destroyed by Gandhi's consolidation of the powers of the All-India Congress executive and his intrusions into provincial politics.

How could Gandhi do what others had failed to do before him? Basically because his new appeals had won him the support of social groups which previously had had no share in nationalist politics. The dynamics underlying the emergence of these groups are still unclear for although it has long been conventional to comment on the significance of Indian social change in the second decade of the twentieth century, there has been as yet no serious analysis of it. Even so we can assert reasonably surely that Gandhi drew his most solid support from areas which formerly had played no major part in the nationalist movement, and, in the old nationalist regions, from social groups which had formerly no voice in nationalist policy.

For the old nationalist élites there were serious consequences. Their political power was simultaneously challenged at a number of levels, and, as a result, they felt threatened in their social dominance. They found that the organisational forms and techniques of leadership which had served them well in the past were no longer effective. At best they were uncomfortable with the new language and symbolism of mass politics which Gandhi had introduced to Indian nationalism. At worst they were totally inept.

In their attitude to Gandhi himself they were caught in a cleft stick. While on the one hand they could not deny his charism, on the other they resented deeply his imposition upon the nationalist movement of a doctrine of action which to them seemed the product of an alien culture. As though to rub salt in the wound, Gandhi described *satyagraha* as the traditional Indian mode of action, and offered it to his countrymen, particularly to the political élites, as an alternative to imported European methods – an alternative which would enable them to reassert their cultural integrity. To many of the élite this was an offensive assertion. In essence it appeared to differ little from the hated British jibe that they were not 'real Indians', and it showed a similar insensitivity to their intellectual and emotional commitment to the sophisticated syncretic cultures which they had developed and on which their identity was based. Here we are at the root of the conflict between Gandhi and the old political élites. Their visions of India, present and future, and Gandhi's vision differed fundamentally, and in defence of their visions of the future they resisted his ambition to use the extended powers of a reconstructed Congress to achieve his vision.

NOTES

1 1 Nov.[1920]. C.F.Andrews papers, Santiniketan (hereinafter AP).
2 I define group identity in this way: A group with identity has agreed values, understood internal relationships, accepted roles for various members at developing stages of life, a language and channels of communication, a shared interpretation of the past and hopes for the future, common heroes, common symbols and common myths. The members of such a group are aware of their membership, and the group is identifiable by other groups and individuals in the society.
3 *Amrita Bazar Patrika*, 2 July 1920. The source of all newspaper references in this chapter is the *Report on Native Papers in Bengal* (hereinafter *NP.*).
4 E.g. see B.C.Pal, *Nationality and Empire. A Running Study of Some Current Indian Problems*, Calcutta 1916, pp. 217–18.
5 *Amrita Bazar Patrika*, 1 Dec. 1919.
6 *Dainik Bharat Mitra*, 12 July 1918; *Dainik Basumati*, 13 July 1918; *Amrita Bazar Patrika*, 17 Aug. 1918.
7 Swami Vivekananda, *Complete Works*, Almora 1946–7, Vol. III, p. 224.
8 B.C.Pal, *Swadeshi and Swaraj; the Rise of New Patriotism*, Calcutta 1954, pp. 4 and 188. Aurobindo Ghose, *Speeches*, Calcutta, 2nd edn 1948, pp. 83–4, 88–9, 148 and 151–2. Rabindranath Tagore, *Towards Universal Man*, London 1961, pp. 49–66, and 101–28.
9 *NP*, Dec. 1919–Jan. 1920.
10 The development of Gandhi's thought in this period can be followed through his articles in *Young India, 1919–1922*, Madras 1922.
11 Andrews to Rathindranath Tagore, 6 Sept. [1920], AP.
12 Gandhi to Andrews, 23 Nov. 1920, quoted in B.Chaturvedi and M.Sykes, *Charles Freer Andrews. A Narrative*, London 1949, pp. 156–7.
13 J.Nehru, *Toward Freedom. The Autobiography*, New York 1941, pp. 51–3.
14 H.F.Owen, 'The Leadership of the Indian National Movement, 1914–20', unpublished doctoral thesis. Australian National University, 1965, particularly Chapter VI.
15 Nehru, *Toward Freedom*, p. 53.
16 Pal to Motilal Nehru, n.d., quoted in Atulchandra Gupta ed., *Studies in the Bengal Renaissance. In Commemoration of the Birth of Bipinchandra Pal*, Calcutta 1958, p. 577.
17 I am using Max Weber's definition of status group: 'What is a "status group"? "Classes" are groups of people who, from the standpoint of specific interests, have the same economic position. Ownership or non-ownership

of material goods or of definite skills constitute the "class-situation". "Status" is a quality of social honor or a lack of it, and is in the main conditioned as well as expressed through a specific style of life. Social honor can stick directly to a class-situation, and it is also, indeed most of the time, determined by the average class-situation of the status-group members. This, however, is not necessarily the case. Status membership, in turn, influences the class-situation in that the style of life required by status groups makes them prefer special kinds of property or gainful pursuits and reject others. A status group can be closed ("status by descent") or it can be open.

'It is incorrect to think of the "occupational status group" as an alternative. The "style of life", not the "occupation", is always decisive. This style may require a certain profession (for instance, military service), but the nature of the occupational service resulting from the claims of a style of life always remains decisive (for instance, military service as a knight rather than as a mercenary).' H.H.Gerth and C.Wright Mills eds, *From Max Weber: Essay in Sociology*, New York 1958, p. 405.

18   *Census of India, 1921*, Vol. I, Pt II, p. 3 ; Vol. 5, Pt I, pp. 350–6.

19   J.C.Jack, *The Economic Life of a Bengal District, A Study*, London 1916, p. 69.

20   *Indian Statutory Commission*, London 1930, Vol. VIII, p. 24.

21   *Bengal District Administration Committee, 1913–1914, Report*, Calcutta 1915, p. 176.

22   For biographical details see G.D.Binani and T.V.Rama Rao eds, *India at a Glance*, Bombay, revised edition 1954, p. 1726. Obituaries in *Amrita Bazar Patrika, Statesman*, Calcutta, and *The Times*, London 25 Nov. 1961.

23   This is based on an analysis of the lists of office-bearers of officially recognised associations, prepared annually by the Political Department, Government of Bengal. West Bengal Government Record Office, Calcutta (hereinafter WB Records), and *Sedition Committee, 1919, Report*, Calcutta 1918.

24   See N.C.Chaudhuri, *The Autobiography of an Unknown Indian*, London. 1951, pp. 301–4, M.K.Chakravarty *A Back Bencher's Autobiography* [Calcutta], n.d.

25   *Census of India, 1921*, Vol. VI, Pt I, pp. 36–7.

26   Ezra Pound, quoted in H.M.Hurwitz, 'Ezra Pound and Rabindranath Tagore'. *American Literature*, Vol. XXXVI No. 1, Mar. 1964, p. 54.

27   E.g., see J.C.Ghosh, *Bengali Literature*, London 1948, *passim*. N.C.Chaudhuri, 'Subhas Chandra Bose – His Legacy and Legend', *Pacific Affairs*, Vol. XXVI, 1953, pp. 354–5. S.C.Bose, *The Indian Struggle, 1920–1934*, Calcutta 1948, pp. 15 and 161–4. Rabindranath Tagore to Andrews, 5 Mar. 1921, R.N.Tagore, *Letters to a Friend*, London 1928, pp. 130–1.

28   'Bengal and the Bengalees', Presidential Address, Bengal Provincial Conference, Calcutta, April 1917. Rajen Sen, *Deshbandhu Chittaranjan Das, Life and Speeches*, Calcutta 1926, p. 11.

29 See the first two references given under note 27, above; B.C.Pal, *Bengal Vaishnavism*, Calcutta, 1962, Chapts V and VI.

30 Pal to Motilal Nehru, n.d., quoted in Gupta, *Studies in the Bengal Renaissance*, p. 577.

31 S.H.Rudolph, 'The New Courage. An Essay on Gandhi's Psychology', *World Politics*, Vol. XVI, No. 1, Oct. 1963, pp. 98–117.

32 E.g. see *Young India, 1919–22*, pp. 349–53, 373–83, 601, 608–13 and 668–75.

33 E.g. see C.R.Das, 'Bengal and the Bengalees', Sen, *Desbbandbu Chittaranjan Das*. Pal, *Swadeshi and Swaraj*, pp. 188 and 198–9. Motilal Ghose to G.K. Gokhale, 19 Oct. 1906. Gokhale Papers, Servants of India Society, Poona. Cf. *Nayak*, 3 Dec. 1912.

34 It is important that the reader should note the distinction which I draw between the attitudes of bhadralok leaders or politicians, and the bhadralok community as a whole; and, in the latter part of the paper, between bhadralok élite and lower-class bhadralok.

35 31 Jan. [1921], AP. Cf. Andrews to Tagore, 26 Jan. 1921, quoted in Chaturvedi and Sykes, *Charles Freer Andrews*, p. 176; and Tagore to Andrews, 5 Mar. 1921, Tagore, *Letters to a Friend*, pp. 131–3.

36 'The Call of Truth', speech at a public meeting in Calcutta, 29 Aug. 1921, Tagore, *Towards Universal Man*, p. 267.

37 Ibid., pp. 270–3.

38 Tagore to Andrews, 13 Mar. 1921, Tagore, *Letters to a Friend*, p. 136.

39 Quoted in Tagore, *Towards Universal Man*, p. 377.

40 Andrews to Tagore, 5 Oct. [1920], AP.

41 Tagore to Andrews, 18 Sept. 1920, Tagore, *Letters to a Friend*, p. 95.

42 *Bengalee*, 26 Oct. 1920.

43 An expression used in a manifesto opposing non-cooperation, which was published by five leading Bengali Extremists. *Servant*, 29 Sept. 1920.

44 E.g. see Tagore, *Towards Universal Man*, pp. 258–9. P.N.Bose, *Swaraj: Cultural and Political*, Calcutta 1929, pp. 157–9. Surendranath Ray speaking in Bengal Legislative Council, 26 July 1915, *Bengal Legislative Council Proceedings*, Vol. XLVII, pp. 437–8.

45 See S.N.Banerjea, *A Nation in Making: being the reminiscences of fifty years of public life*, London 1925, p. 247.

46 Dinshaw Wacha to Dadabhai Naoroji, 3 May 1907, Wacha letters, Bombay Presidency Association, Bombay. G.K.Gokhale to Sir William Wedderburn, 24 May 1907, Gokhale Papers; Government of India, Home Department Police Branch Proceedings, May 1906, A140–3 and B112–4. National Archives of India, New Delhi (hereinafter NAI); Government of Bengal, Political Department Proceedings, Nov. 1917, B65, File 8A-10(1), W.B. Records.

47 A.J.P Taylor, *The Hapsburg Monarchy, 1809–1918. A History of the Austrian Empire and Austria-Hungary*, London 1948, p. 30.

48   E.g. see Aurobindo Ghose, 'The Shell and the Seed, 17 Sept. 1906, and 'The New Faith', 1 Dec. 1907, *Bande Mataram* editorials, quoted in Haridas and Uma Mukherjee, *Bande Mataram and Indian Nationalism, 1906–8*, Calcutta 1957, pp. 19–20 and 54–7.

49   A.H.L.Fraser, Lieutenant-Governor of Bengal, to Sir Erle Richards, 20 Feb. 1907, Erle Richards Collection, MSS Eur. F122, No. 2 (e) (India Office Library, London). Government of India, Home Department Police Branch Proceedings, May 1906, A140–8 and B112–4, NAI.

50   11 Sept. 1920.

51   It was the Bengali-language counterpart of the *Bengalee*, Surendranath Banerjea's famous English-language daily.

52   E.g. compare the following extract from *Nayak*, 9 Sept. 1920: 'Should Gandhi's motion be carried, a revolution would break out in the country and there would be hostility between the rulers and the ruled. It is said that this will be a non-violent and bloodless war. Nevertheless, we must confess that this bloodless and non-violent revolution will surely terminate in bloodshed. Indeed, non-cooperation is another name for rebellion. So we are determined to protest against it at all costs. Let us tell Gandhi that the goal is yet far off!'

53   In his letters in this period C.F.Andrews frequently contrasted the eagerness of the peasantry to join in mass agitation, with the reluctance of the bhadra-lok. See Andrews to Rathindranath Tagore, 6 Sept. [1920]; Andrews to Rabindranath Tagore, 5 Oct.[1920], and 15 Oct.[1920]; Andrews to W. W. Pearson, 12 Nov. [1920], AP.

54   Banerjea, *A Nation in Making*, p. 397.

55   *Bengal Legislative Council Proceedings*, 3 Feb. 1920, Vol. LII, p. 104; and 10 Feb. 1921, Vol. I, Pt II, p. 195.

56   *Census of India, 1921*, Vol. V, Pt I, p. 34.

57   *Bangali*, 29 Jan. 1919.

58   NP, 1920, *passim*.

59   *Bengal Legislative Council Proceedings*, 23 Nov. 1921, Vol. V, pp. 182–3.

60   E.g. see *Modern Review*, April 1917; *Dainik Bharat Mitra*, 25 April 1917.

61   *NP*, 1918 *passim*.

62   *NP*, 21 Sept. 1918.

63   *Mohammadi*, 7 Nov. 1919.

64   Ibid., 5 Dec. 1919.

65   *Indian Statutory Commission*, Vol. VIII, pp. 98–9. Lawrence, Marquess of Zetland, *Essayez*, London 1956, p. 138.

66   Andrews to Rabindranath Tagore, 9 Aug. [1920], AP. Cf. B.C.Pal to Motilal Nehru, n.d., quoted in Gupta: *Studies in the Bengal Renaissance*, pp. 576–7.

67   E.g. Bose, *The Indian Struggle*, pp. 39–40, 46 and 55. *Reports on the Working of the Reformed Constitution*, 1927, Calcutta 1928, p. 173. Nripendra Chandra

Banerji, *At the Cross-Roads, 1885–1946. The Autobiography*, Calcutta 1950, p. 210.

68 E.g. see V.A.Smith *et al.*, *The Oxford History of India*, London, 3rd edn 1958, pp. 783 and 790. J.Coatman, *India. The Road to Self-Government*, London 1941, pp. 39, 82, 84, 97 and 101. R.C.Majumdar, H.C.Raychaudhuri and K.K.Datta, *An Advanced History of India*, London 1946, p. 955. R.C.Majumdar, *History of the Freedom Movement in India*, Calcutta 1963, Vol. II, p. 161.

69 Gandhi to Andrews, 23 Nov. [1920], quoted in Chaturvedi and Sykes: *Charles Freer Andrews*, p. 157.

70 *Census of India, 1921*, Vol. V, Pt I, p. 385. *Bengal District Administration Committee, 1913–1914. Report*, p. 13. Jack, *The Economic Life of a Bengal District*, pp. 89–95. B.B.Misra, *The Indian Middle Classes. Their Growth in Modern Times*, London 1961, pp. 276–7.

71 *Census of India, 1911*, Vol. V, Pt I, pp. 66 and 553–4. *Bengal District Administration Committee, 1913–1914*, Report, pp. 13–14, 19, and 176.

72 *Prices and Wages in India*, Calcutta, 24th issue 1907, p. 17; and ibid., 25th issue 1908, p. 12. (For this reference I am indebted to Gerald C.Barrier, University of Missouri.) *Census of India, 1911*, Vol. V, Pt I, pp. 64–6. Jack: *The Economic Life of a Bengal District*, pp. 98 and 103–4.

73 *NP*, 1903–8, *passim*.

74 Government of India, Home Department Public Branch Proceedings, July 1906, A124C. NAI. *NP*, 1906–7, *passim*. Also see references given under note 48, above.

75 Das alone among the prominent Hindu bhadralok politicians in the 1914 to 1920 period appears to have been deeply concerned with the absence of mass backing for the nationalist movement. At the Bengal Provincial Conference at Mymensingh in April 1919, for instance, he could find no support for a resolution to implement *satyagraha* in Bengal, and in disgust he threatened 'to leave the Conference and go to the masses.' (Government of India, Home Department Political Branch, Proceedings, May 1919, B494–7, NAI. For this reference I am indebted to Hugh Owen, University of Western Australia.) It is significant that he did not exile himself and was therefore available in the following year as a spokesman of the bhadralok's opposition to Gandhi. His attitude in 1919, however, does suggest an ambivalence towards non-cooperation and this no doubt eased the difficulty of his decision at Nagpur in December 1920 (see p. 252).

76 *NP*, April–May 1917.

77 C.R.Das, *About Bengal*, Calcutta 1917, pp. 4–5.

78 *NP*, Sept.–Dec. 1917 and July 1918. P.N.Dutt, *Memoirs of Motilal Ghose*, Calcutta 1935, pp. 262–3. Indian Association, Calcutta, Committee and General Meeting Proceedings, Jan. and July 1918.

79 8 Aug. 1916.

80   24 Dec. 1920.

81   Andrews to Rabindranath Tagore, 3 Aug. 1920, AP.

82   3 April 1920 at Midnapore. (Typescript collection of Fazlul Huq's speeches compiled by Azizul Huq, Dacca.)

83   Andrews to Rathindranath Tagore, 6 Sept. [1920], AP.

84   J. S. Sharma, *Indian National Congress. A descriptive bibliography of India's struggle for freedom*, Delhi 1959, p. 469–70.

85   *NP*, Aug. 1920.

86   *Servant*, 15 Sept. 1920. M. R. Jayakar, *The Story of My Life*, Bombay 1958–9, Vol. I, pp. 390–7.

87   E.g. see *Hindusthan*, 9 Sept. 1920.

88   *Servant*, 15 Sept. 1920.

89   Government of India, Reforms Office Proceedings, March 1921, B34–99. Bundle Jan.–March 1921 (5). NAI.

90   *Amrita Bazar Patrika*, 9 Nov. 1920.

91   Ibid., 24 Nov. 1920.

92   Government of India, Home Department Political Branch Proceedings, July 1921, Deposit 3 (Confidential) and K-W, NAI.

93   Banerji, *At the Cross-Roads*, p. 146. *Bengalee*, 30 Dec. 1920 and 1 Jan. 1921.

94   P. C. Ray, *Life and Times of C. R. Das*, London 1927, p. 159.

9

LANDLORDS AND PARTY POLITICS IN THE UNITED PROVINCES, 1934-7

★

P. D. Reeves

The elections held in February 1937 for the provincial legislature marked a turning point in the political development of the United Provinces. The main contestants were two landlord parties (the National Agriculturist Party of Agra and that of Oudh), the Indian National Congress and the Muslim League. Whereas the two latter were able to set the style of the campaign, with their use of mass ideology and party workers and funds on an unprecedented scale, the National Agriculturist Parties found difficulty in adjusting themselves to the new electoral conditions. Their sponsors, the landlords, were accustomed to the old political conventions of the United Provinces, formed in a period when the franchise had been restricted, when British administrators had cultivated informal relationships with local leaders, and when politics had been conducted on the assumption that the established social hierarchy and the landlord system were there to stay. The electoral contest involved, therefore, a conflict about the very nature of the political system of the province; the defeat of the National Agriculturist Parties would signify the eclipse of the landlords and the end of the structure of informal, consultative politics in which they had enjoyed so much power.

This chapter is concerned to show how and why such an outcome occurred. It will discuss why the landlords tried to form a political party and why they chose to challenge the Congress and the Muslim League in the election campaign; it will seek to account for their electoral defeat, and explore the reasons why this defeat undermined their position in the legislature and their ability to influence the government by informal means.

I

The idea that the landlords were the most powerful political group in the North-Western Provinces and Oudh (later called the United Provinces) began with the pacification of the provinces after the revolt of 1857. During the latter part of the nineteenth century, due to the untiring efforts and the growing influence of a group of administrators in Oudh, it came to be seen – and increasingly accepted – as the basic principle upon which rested the political system of the province.[1] By the beginning of the twentieth century the idea had been elaborated by these 'Oudh Men' into a doctrine of imperial government that was so clearly stated as to be identifiable as 'the Old Oudh School of States-manship'[2] or, more bluntly, as 'Oudh Policy, the aristocratic policy'.[3] In the 'Oudh' view, the landlords retained a position of social leader-ship in the rural areas that gave them control over their peasantry and, hence, a political dominance of that could be taken for granted: they were 'those whom the masses naturally and instinctively regard as their leaders'.[4] It followed that the landlords should be supported in order that their influence would be used to underpin British rule, and the 'Oudh Men' did all they could in their administration, particularly in agrarian matters, to bolster the landlords and preserve their local standing and influence. There were always opponents to this policy, both in Oudh and in the North-Western Provinces, but, as the 'Oudh Men' came to hold important positions in the administration after the amalgamation of the two sub-provinces in 1877,[5] their policy came to dominate provincial political thinking.[6] The influence of the 'Oudh Men' and their doctrine reached the peak of its influence in 1918 when Sir Harcourt Butler, 'Harcourt Butler of Oudh' as he was called,[7] the author of the pamphlet 'Oudh Policy' which had helped to sum up so much of the Oudh philosophy, was appointed lieutenant-governor of the United Provinces.

In the years between the revolt of 1857 and the First World War the landlords justified this belief in their 'natural leadership'. Even after 1920, when a legislative council with an elected non-official majority was established, the landlords managed to preserve their dominant position. In each of the four elections from 1920 to 1930 they obtained a majority of seats in the council. This was partly because of the favourable circumstances in which these elections were held. The electorate, enfranchised by moderately-high property qualifications, was relatively small and restricted: there were only 1,250,000 voters from a total population of nearly 50 millions.[8] About two-thirds of these voters were tenants,[9] which meant that the electors were those with whom the administrative machinery of the landlords' estates provided a ready contact. In this decade, too, the landlords faced little direct electoral opposition. The strongest of the nationalist groups, the Congress, did not contest the elections of 1920 or 1930 and in 1923 and 1926 it concerned itself mainly with defeating other parties (which posed a more immediate problem because they stood as alternative nationalist movements). In the Muslim constituencies, where the Congress had less influence, the landlords had an even freer hand, because the Muslim nationalist organisations were either closely tied to the Congress and its policies (as was the Khilafat movement in 1920), or in such disarray (as was the Muslim League throughout the period) that they did not contest the elections at all. But, favourable circumstances notwithstanding, the 1920s were important in maintaining the pre-eminence of the landlords in the governmental structure of the province.

In the 1930s, however, the provincial constitution underwent further changes, and some of the circumstances favourable to the landlords in the previous decade disappeared. Constitutional reforms enlarged the electorate fourfold and provided for autonomy in provincial matters to ministries to be formed from amongst the majority party in the lower house of the provincial legislature (the legislative assembly).[10] As a result of these changes, the landlords had to appeal to a much larger and more 'popular' electorate, and they had also to compete openly with the nationalist parties, for both the Congress and the Muslim League were drawn into the elections in the hope of securing control of the legislative assembly, from which, under the new constitution with its provisions for provincial autonomy, they would be able to exercise a greater measure of power within the province than had previously been possible. The danger to the landlords of the Congress entry into electoral politics was increased by the fact that sections of the Congress had begun to establish themselves as spokesmen for the tenants and had begun to adopt an increasingly hostile attitude towards the landlords. This alignment had begun in 1920[11] but it had been greatly strengthened by the effects of the economic depression of 1929-34. In those years, long-standing tenant grievances about rents, about security of tenure, and about exactions of illegal payments and forced labour were sharpened by the difficulties caused by the slump in prices for agricultural produce;[12] and as a result, tenants were drawn into political movements which promised support for their economic claims. The most important of those movements was the Congress 'civil disobedience movement' of the early 1930s which became for a time in the U.P., a no-rent campaign.[13] Thus, a combination of constitutional reform and growing militancy within the nationalist movement ushered in a new and dangerous era of political activity for the landlords.

The prevalence of 'Congress-cum-Bolshevik doctrines'[14] at this time of great constitutional advance, in fact, thoroughly alarmed both the landlords and their supporters. To the landlords, 'class war' seemed to loom over the countryside. 'Almost every day meetings are held in rural areas in which property rights are attacked', reported a landlord leader in 1931;[15] and in the years which followed he and his fellow landlords saw the object of these attacks written into the programmes and policies of the Congress.[16] Their supporters shared their alarm at the 'communism' of the Congress[17] but they saw more in these activities than simply an anti-landlord campaign. Congress policies, they were convinced, were the harbingers of revolution and chaos in the province. If the Congress came to power, the governor, Sir Malcolm Hailey, told a meeting of landlords in 1933,

> You will see the growth of bitter and aggravated relations between landlords and tenants, you will find an administration so chaotic that you may bid farewell to any hope of fostering those activities for your social and material progress to which you all look forward as a result of the greater political freedom you will then enjoy.[18]

And, as was to be expected in the U.P. with its background of landlord-based politics, men such as Hailey turned to the landlords as the men able through their political influence, to prevent such a catastrophe. From 1931 onwards efforts were made to convince the landlords that they should take steps to organise a political party, both to ensure their own continued predominance in provincial politics and to save the province from the disaster of Congress rule.

The earliest suggestion was for a 'Federal' or 'Centre' party linking the Indian princes, the landlords, the industrial and commercial interests and moderate politicians. A group of conservative leaders, prominent amongst whom were the Maharaja of Bikanir, one-time chancellor of the Chamber of Princes, T. B. Sapru, a veteran Liberal politician, and Raja Sir Rampal Singh, the dominant personality among the Oudh landlords, discussed the idea in 1931-2 and tried to establish the beginnings of an organisation.[19] Major D. R. Ranjit Singh, the energetic secretary of the largest landlord association in the province, the Agra Province Zamindars' Association (APZA),[20] took up the scheme and urged the members of his association to support it.[21] Sapru then interested Jwala Prasad Srivastava, an industrialist of Cawnpore who had become Education Minister in the U.P. in 1931, and with the help of the governor, Sir Malcolm Hailey, Srivastava acquired the management of the long-established Allahabad daily newspaper, the *Pioneer*, and made it a persistent advocate for the idea of a party to combine conservative and anti-Congress groups.[22]

This initial idea of a Centre Party did not last beyond mid-1932. Sapru's ardour cooled considerably as the party increasingly acquired what was to him an 'ultra-conservative' character and he dropped his association with it.[23] As time went by, the princes became less concerned with ideas of federation,[24] or of participation in British Indian politics, and they ceased to play any active part in the scheme. The basis for such a party, in fact, was reduced to the landlords in the U.P. and it became a major task for Hailey and his administration, for J.P. Srivastava and the *Pioneer*, and for Major Ranjit Singh of the APZA to convince the landlords that they should organise a party from among 'people who want to see a stable government and orderly progress'. Hailey regarded this as a most urgent duty and he used the entire administrative machinery to promote it.[25] His own occasional speeches to landlord associations, local-government bodies and meetings of moderates tirelessly propounded the idea, and where he did not go himself, the district officials[26] or the lecturers, the pamphlets and the 'demonstration vans' of the U.P. Publicity Department carried the message.[27]

The call penetrated to some of the more active members of the landlord associations. The Raja of Tirwa, for example, made an appeal for such an organisation in his presidential address to the first Agra province zamindars' conference in January 1932,[28] and later in the year he wrote privately to convince a sceptical fellow-landlord that their future depended on 'a strong party backed by people with plenty of stake in the country'.[29] In Oudh, individual landlords tried unsuccessfully[30] to have the British Indian Association of Oudh (BIA)[31] – the association of the taluqdars of Oudh – make adequate electoral arrangements. The only safeguard for the landlords, wrote one of these more perceptive taluqdars, Kunwar Guru Narain, was work 'on party lines'.[32]

At the time the landlords showed no inclination to take up any of these suggestions. Hailey complained in mid-1932 that it was still difficult to convince some landlords of the danger to their position.[33]

Similarly, in January 1933 the second Agra province Zamindars' conference resolved that the elections should be contested on 'party lines', but no action followed, and in July 1933 Major Ranjit Singh declared that he could not find 'any response whatever, not even a feeble response, to the great and important question of the Zamindars forming their own party and preparing the ground for the next election'.[34] The point was that many landlords believed that their position would be adequately secured by the provision of specially reserved seats in the legislature, and as long as constitutional reform discussions continued they were mainly concerned to present claims for landlord representation to the various committees of inquiry.[34] Others trusted that the efforts of individual landlords would be sufficient: an Oudh taluqdar suggested, for example, that the landlords should call their tenants together on their estates and get them 'to sign an agreement that they will not vote for any outsider without the consent of the landlords'.[36]

By 1933 it became clear that measures and hopes such as these would not be adequate. In the first place, the British government published in March 1933 a White Paper on Indian constitutional reforms which made it clear that the proportion of reserved landlord seats would not be maintained in any enlarged legislature.[37] 'We are now of less importance in the view of the British Government than even the depressed classes', wrote a dejected landlord in May 1933, giving voice to a widespread landlord feeling that they had been forsaken by their former champions.[38] And then, to add to their plight, Congress anti-landlordism became more vociferous. In October 1933 Jawaharlal Nehru published a critique of nationalist aims which held out the promise of a full-scale attack on the landlords.

> Nothing is more absurd [he wrote in a series of articles entitled 'Whither India?'] than to imagine that all the interests in the nation can be fitted in without injury to any. At every step some have to be sacrificed for others. . . . It is therefore essential that we keep this in mind and fashion our idea of freedom accordingly. We cannot escape having to answer the question, now or later, for the freedom of which class or classes in India are we especially striving? . . . To say that we shall not answer that question now is itself an answer and a taking of sides, for it means that we stand by the existing order, the *status quo* . . . India's immediate goal can therefore only be considered in terms of the ending of the exploitation of her people. Politically it must mean independence . . . ; economically and socially it must mean the ending of all special class privileges and vested interests . . .[39]

By late 1933 the landlords could no longer ignore these constitutional and political pressures, and they began to accept the proposition that in the new political era opening up before them they could no longer 'trust to the chance success which individuals, in one district or another, may win on the basis of some personal claim or territorial connection', and that they must instead have 'party organisation, supported by party funds and held compact by party discipline'.[40]

As they came to accept the need for a party, the landlords found that one of their leaders understood the implications of the new politics and was prepared to organise them. This was the Nawab of Chhatari, the leading landlord of Bulandshahr district who had entered the provincial legislature first in 1921, and had been between 1923 and 1933 successively minister, executive councillor and, on two occasions, acting-governor. Chhatari had never forgotten during those years that he was a landlord.[41] He had shown an interest in the proposals for a 'party of stability' from the beginning; as governor from April to November 1933 he had openly canvassed the idea himself;[42] and when he retired in November 1933 he made clear his intention to take the lead in the organisation of such a party from among the landlords. Elected president of the third Agra province Zamindars' conference in February 1934, he called for the maintenance of the landlords as 'a useful and influential class in the future policy of this country generally and particularly of these provinces' by means of an organised party in each district to supervise landlord participation in the elections.[43]

The zamindars' conference adopted Chhatari's suggestion and set up a committee to organise such a party, with Chhatari himself as chairman and Major Ranjit Singh as convenor.[44] Little progress was made up to mid-1934; but when the Congress began its preparations for the Indian legislative assembly elections to be held in late 1934, and a Socialist Party was formed within Congress with the avowed object of seeking 'the elimination of landlords without compensation and the distribution of land to peasants',[45] the landlord organisers hastened their own efforts. The zamindar committee elected in February met on 17 June 1934 and formed an 'advisory board'; and at the beginning of July Major Ranjit Singh published a provisional programme for a 'National Agriculturist Party' which was adopted by a meeting of the advisory board in Allahabad on 5 August 1934.[46] Shortly afterwards a similar party appeared in Oudh. On 25 February 1934 Kunwar Guru Narain called for the taluqdars to appoint a committee to ensure that each Oudh district had an association to help the landlords fight the elections, but this brought no action. On 12 August, however, following significantly upon the formation of the party in Allahabad, a taluqdar from Sitapur district, Maheshwar Dayal Seth, managed to get support for a conference later in the month to consider the question of a party. This conference met on 28 August and established a National Agriculturist Party for Oudh, under the aegis of the BIA.[47] By the end of August 1934, therefore, the two landlord-based NAPs were in existence.

These were the two landlord parties which contested the elections of 1937. They did so without success: they failed to win any substantial number of seats; the landlords were consequently unable to form a viable ministry to conduct the government of the province; and by the end of 1937 the NAPs had disappeared altogether.

Hitherto the NAPs have been dismissed as unimportant because of this electoral failure.[48] But it is precisely their failure that is significant, because it is this which marks the passing of the landlords and, with them, the decline of the landlord-based political system fostered by the 'Oudh Policy'. The reasons for the defeat of the NAPs in fact throws light upon the political transformation of the U.P. There were three major reasons for this defeat: the organisational problems which faced the organisers of the parties in the years from 1934 to 1936; the inadequacy of the methods which the organisers adopted for electioneering; and the changes which took place in the local position of the landlords in the late nineteenth and twentieth century and which falsified the assumptions on which the campaigning of the parties rested. The remainder of this essay will examine each of these in turn.

II

The establishment of the NAPs in August 1934 did not mean that the landlords were effectively organised for political purposes: indeed the parties never succeeded in completely mobilising the landlords as a political group. The two parties in fact represented not a coming together of the landlords as a whole but the expression of the political aspirations of a small group of landlords who acted as their organisers and leaders from the beginning. Chief among these men were the Nawab of Chhatari and the Raja of Tirwa in the Agra party and Rai Bahadur Maheshwar Dayal Seth and Kunwar Guru Narain in Oudh. These men saw the need for party organisation and understood something of what was required but they failed to enlist actively the majority of landlords in their enterprise because the modernising tendencies which they represented were not strong enough to cut across well-established landlord traditions of social and political 'style'. Regional jealousies among landlord organisations; an aristocratic disdain for mundane 'work'; personal vanities and rivalries; and a marked lack of commitment to anything but the preservation of their landed rights: all these traits had developed in the period of landlord predominance following the mutiny of 1857, and they continued to operate in the 1930s to hamstring efforts to obtain for the parties the allegiance of the general body of landlords. Some specific instances will illustrate how these traits operated and how they affected the NAPs.

Status was of overwhelming concern to the landlords, both amongst themselves as individuals and between the groups into which they tended to fall. There was for a start a long record of quarrelling between the different landlord associations in the U.P. over questions of precedence and rights. The Oudh taluqdars and the Agra zamindars conducted a bitter feud over the number of seats which the BIA and the APZA ought to hold in the provincial legislature;[49] and the APZA engaged in a fierce controversy with the older but smaller and less exclusive U.P. Zamindar Association as to which of them was the 'premier' association for Agra zamindars.[50] This concern for regional prestige affected the NAPs, too, and from the beginning, despite the efforts of their organisers, it proved impossible to unite the two parties. The very first meeting of the executive committee of the NAP of Agra on 6 August 1934 deputed Chhatari and Tirwa to negotiate with the taluqdars to secure 'co-ordination and co-operation between Agra and Oudh';[51] and at the beginning of September there were moves in Oudh by M.D. Seth and his brother, Bisheshwar Dayal, to effect an alliance.[52] But the older taluqdar leaders in Oudh were strongly opposed to any amalgamation.[53] In December 1934 it was reported that negotiations were under way for the formation of a united central board, but the statement made it clear that no 'formal merger' was contemplated: 'only matters which are common to the organisations such as the policy of the U.P. landlords in the provincial legislature will be regulated by the Central Board'.[54] Yet there was little progress with even this limited plan. A joint session of the executive committees of the two parties in late 1935 returned to first principles, and debated whether there should be 'amalgamation' or 'co-ordination'! In the end the meeting decided to work simply for co-ordination, and it set up an advisory committee with seven members from each party to bring about closer co-operation and draw up a joint electoral programme.[55] This committee, however, met only once, in July 1936, to discuss a draft election manifesto which was in fact never used.[56] For all practical purposes, therefore, the NAPs remained separate organisations, making it impossible for the landlords to present even a united provincial front.

Personal, no less than group, rivalries distracted the landlords. Nawab Muhummad Yusuf, a prominent member of the NAP of Agra went so far as to argue at the outset that the party should simply exist to help landlord candidates and adjudicate between rival nominees. 'The board', he wrote in July 1934, 'should have no other power otherwise there will be constant fight going on which would lead to serious disruption among the men belonging to our party.'[57] And indeed his own letter provided some evidence of this danger, for it was an attempt to gain the presidency of the nascent NAPA, an attempt which failed when the letter fell into the hands of the Nawab of Chhatari.[58] Again, there were instances of pique at what was felt to inadequate recognition of a member's status during committee elections at the inaugural meeting of the Agra party. Nawabzada Liaquat Ali Khan refused to be elected one of two joint secretaries (which, he felt, was too lowly a post) and he had to be made treasurer instead. And then Major Ranjit Singh, who had been one of the party's founders, dropped out of the party almost completely after he found that the only post he could be offered was that of 'honorary assistant secretary' because the 'higher' positions had been given to men of superior rank though of less ability.

In the NAP of Oudh there was a curiously inverted example of this concern for status. Raja Sir Rampal Singh refused to be a mere figure-head president of the party, and this brought him into collision with the organisers of the party and particularly with Maheshwar Dayal Seth. Rampal Singh had been the dominating figure among the taluqdars since 1921; he had been president of the BIA for a considerable part of that time, and he held that office in 1934 when the NAP was formed. It was a peculiarity of the taluqdari situation that the presidency of the BIA was a position of real power, and not a decorative post, and Rampal Singh assumed that the presidency of the NAP would be likewise. This, however, was not the case; the NAP was the creation of a particular group of taluqdars, of whom Maheshwar Dayal Seth was the leading representative, and these taluqdars were determined to retain control of its affairs. There was conflict from the beginning because almost immediately Rampal Singh, although he was in poor health, asserted his position. B. D. Seth, Maheshwar Dayal's brother, issued a statement claiming that there were 'definite prospects' of an alliance with the NAP of Agra but Rampal Singh contradicted him publicly and upbraided him for speaking without the authority of the president.[59] Over the next eighteen months, however, Rampal Singh let affairs slip more and more and more into the hands of M.D. Seth until, in November 1936, he asserted himself for the last time by resigning from the party and taking his personal following with him.[60]

Both the NAPs were, thus, dogged by disruptive personal conflicts. As one observer commented, 'The landlords of the U.P. as a class are perfect gentlemen but with rare exceptions they suffer badly from individualism and narcissim. Almost every landlord has notions about himself and few landlords are prepared to follow the lead of somebody else.'[61]

Moreover, while they were prepared to expend a great deal of energy on quarrelling, very few landlords were prepared to make the sustained effort needed to organise and maintain the parties. This work was left to one or two leaders: there was no general activity among the landlords on behalf of the parties. The organisers in Agra campaigned vigorously and some district branches were formed[62] but it was clear that everything depended on these few leaders. Things only happened when one of them was present; the party did not expand spontaneously. By 1936 they admitted as much themselves. 'The Zamindars have not endeavoured to make a success of it to the extent which they should have done', the Raja of Tirwa told the fourth Agra province Zamindars' conference in April 1936.[63] Twenty branches had been formed, he claimed, but they were invariably obstructed by the landlords' 'traditional indifference and lethargy'. With the Oudh party this was, if anything, more noticeable. There the organisation fell almost entirely upon Maheshwar Dayal Seth, the secretary. Except for participating in the central Indian legislative assembly elections in December 1934, there was almost no sign that the 'Lucknow NAP'[64] was active until M.D. Seth began a campaign to organise his own district (Sitapur) as a model for other districts;[65] and even this attempt ended farcically. Elaborate plans were drawn up for the organisation of branches even within the villages, and for a time great enthusiasm prevailed: meetings were held, and Maheshwar Dayal and the deputy-commissioner urged the landlords to unite. But then in March 1935 activity stopped almost as quickly as it had begun because Maheshwar Dayal decided to spend the summer in Europe, and went off leaving the affairs of the NAP in the hands of his private secretary![66] Nobody objected to this arrangement because nobody else was interested in undertaking the work of the party. Everything waited upon

Maheshwar Dayal. There was some further activity when he returned in September 1935, but still only at his direction. In June 1936 the *Leader* could claim that the NAP of Oudh was still 'little more than a collective name for its secretary and moving spirit Raja Maheshwar Dayal Seth'.[67] When firm arrangements were announced in April 1936 for the provincial elections to be held ten months later both NAPs had virtually to start from the beginning to organise themselves.

Poorly organised as they were in mid-1936, the NAPs were still furthered weakened before the elections took place in February 1937 because communal pressures greatly reduced the effectiveness of 'landlordism' as a political position. Raja Rampal Singh noted as early as July 1935 that many landlords 'kept two arrows to the string of their bows'. 'Their one foot', he continued, 'is in the Hindu Mahasabha, the Muslim League, the Muslim Conference or similar sectional institution and the other in the National Agriculturists' Party';[68] and as the demands of the religious communities for protection and religious expression grew stronger many landlords responded to these sectional interests to the detriment of the NAPs.

In the Agra party the pressure of these communal commitments brought about a bifurcation of the party into two communal 'wings' as a result of a struggle for control between the Muslim Nawab of Chhatari and the Hindu Sir Jwala Prasad Srivastava. Srivastava wanted the NAP of Agra to be a base for his personal political ambitions, but by 1935 he began to doubt the ability of the landlord leadership (Chhatari and Tirwa) to manage the party successfully.[69] He therefore began to take steps to consolidate his own position and to assume a controlling interest in the party.[70] He found his greatest asset in a communal issue, for in mid-1936 Chhatari, who had been active in Muslim communal organisations since late-1933, acquired unwelcome publicity when it was revealed that he and other Muslim landlords had hoped to use the NAP to advance Muslim interests.[71] This apparent duplicity lessened Chhatari's standing in the party as a whole and gave Srivastava an opportunity to press his claims for leadership and control. His first step was to attack Chhatari's organisation of the party. At a meeting of the executive board of the party on 21 June 1936, he presented 'a general review of the whole situation of the Party with a view to improve its position' in which he castigated the leadership of Chhatari and sought to bring the party machinery under his own direct supervision.[72] The clear lead which he offered on basic matters of party organisation convinced other members of the board and gave him an early advantage. When the board took up the question of the formation of an electoral board he was able to press this advantage home. The Muslims on the executive board insisted on the creation of a separate Muslim wing of the party,[73] despite the fact that this patently communal demand greatly embarrassed Chhatari. No final decision was reached at this meeting, and it was adjourned, but when it re-assembled on 23 June Srivastava completed his victory by turning the Muslim demand to his own advantage. The meeting elected a board of twenty-seven members divided into a Hindu wing of eighteen members under Srivastava and a Muslim wing of nine members under Nawab Muhummad Yusuf: Chhatari was to be simply the convenor of the board![74] Srivastava had won an initial victory in the tussle for control. Chhatari then attempted to reorganise his personal following but he failed to get the support that he needed either to regain his position in the NAP or to re-establish himself in Muslim circles.[75] At the same time, Srivastava, despite his initial success in the NAP, was also searching for a still stronger political base. Significantly, he too looked for communal support, but his attempt to form a Hindu party failed, and, simultaneously with Chhatari, he turned again to the NAP.[76] Here he still held the advantage, and in September he clinched his position by his election as chairman of the NAP parliamentary board. Chhatari was named as chairman of the general purposes sub-committee of the party, but in this position he was clearly ranked below Srivastava in the party hierarchy.[77] Srivastava played down his personal victory, but in doing so he underlined its real meaning. The 'only significance' of his election, he told T. B. Sapru, 'is that the Hindu landlords of the province are now prepared to stand up for what is their due'.[78]

In Oudh, communal pressures growing out of continuous activity in communal organisations by both Hindu and Muslim taluqdars, led to an exodus from the party. A group of Hindu taluqdars were active during 1935 in re-organising the Oudh Liberal League which came increasingly to espouse a concern for the protection of 'legitimate Hindu interests';[79] while important Muslim taluqdars held office in the All-Parties Muslim Conference and Unity Board in the early 1930s and then assisted in the revival and reorganisation of the Muslim League.[80] The organisers of the NAP of Oudh spoke out against this concern for communal organisation, but their protests were of no avail.[81] Important groups of taluqdars continued to participate both in these organisations and the NAP until, when election activity began in earnest, it became necessary for them to make a choice. At that time, in the latter part of 1936, the Oudh party was depleted as many taluqdars left it to join with the communal groups to which, in the final analysis, their stronger commitment apparently lay. The Muslims were the first to go. Following the controversy over the activities of the Muslim landlords in the NAP of Agra two important Muslim rajas, Mahmudabad and Salempur, resigned from the NAP in order to retain their places on the Muslim League Parliamentary Board and a third, the Raja of Jahangirabad, who was a vice-president of the NAP, announced that he would run as an independent.[82] Then later still, in response to fears aroused among Hindus by the revelation of Chhatari's plans for the NAP, a group of Hindu taluqdars who followed Raja Sir Rampal Singh began to leave and devote themselves to the quasi-communalist Liberal League.[83] Their departure, following upon that of the Muslims and added to the resignations of disappointed applicants for NAP nomination for the election, reduced the party by election time, as the Pioneer had feared it would, 'to a mere skeleton'.[84]

This, then, was the organisational record of the NAPs. The NAP newspaper, the *Pioneer*, asserted in December 1936, contrary to its own reports, that the two landlord parties had proved 'remarkably cohesive;' in February 1937 it added, in defiance of all indications to the contrary, that they were campaigning with 'vigour and discipline';[85] and throughout January 1937, by way of contrast, it sought to emphasise divisions of opinion within the Congress. But this was a campaign to boost morale, and it could not hide the fact that more than two years after their formation the NAPs were not effectively organised. Landlord style, which expressed itself in a preoccupation with status, an aristocratic lethargy and a marked lack of discipline, prevented the creation of a strong landlord political party to fight the elections of February 1937.

III

The lack of unity and of energy which marked the NAPs was the first major handicap with which the landlords entered the electoral contest. They were also hampered by the failure, even of their most active organisers, to see that the new situation with which they were faced demanded not merely organisation but new methods of electioneering in approaching the electorate and in seeking support for themselves at the polls.

The landlords still accepted in the 1930s the idea of their own 'natural leadership' in the rural areas. The Raja of Mallanpur in April 1933, for example, recommended that 'all the Taluqdars should hold a meeting of their tenants in the important places of their estates in the presence of a representative of the British Indian Association and ask the tenants what are their grivances [sic] and why they are so easily mislead [sic] by an outsider. The ancestral relations and the past and present favours of the landlords should be explained to them. They will say something which will be well-considered after which they should be asked to sign an agreement that they will not vote for any outsider person without the consent of the landlords.'[86] Again, after the 1934 elections to the Indian legislative assembly, Kunwar Guru Narain of Unao district spoke of his ability to 'deliver' votes at those polling stations where he had his 'estate and influence'.[87] The landlords' supporters, moreover, often re-assured them on this point. Hailey, for instance, insisted that 'with the influence they possess in the countryside, with all the traditions they have had in the past and the hold they still have on a very numerous tenantry' they could direct rural politics; while Hailey's successor, Sir Harry Haig, claimed that the landlords were still able to exercise 'that position of leadership which they have inherited'.[88]

It was from this premise of local landlord influence that the organisers of the NAPs started. They saw the parties as uniting and consolidating the position of the landlords as a political force, and in turn being guaranteed electoral success by the landlords' control over the rural electorate. Electoral organisation for the NAPs became, therefore, a matter of ensuring that the landlords' 'natural leadership' was brought into play. Schemes for electoral organisation in 1935 were clearly derived from this concept. In April 1935 Kunwar Guru Narain suggested that each taluqdar should be made individually responsible for the votes of his tenants;[89] and later, in September, M.D. Seth made this same principle of local responsibility the basis of his elaborate scheme for electoral machinery for the Oudh party.[90] Under a chief organiser, who was to be a landlord, there were to be hired organisers appointed for each tahsil. These tahsil organisers would prepare a list of 'persons who exercised influence' in the tahsil and then obtain from these persons a list of 'the tenants within the scope of their influence'. When their lists were completed, the chief organiser would tour the constituencies to meet the 'influential persons' and to 'make them responsible for the votes of their circle'. In this way the landlords would make sure of their control in each constituency. The party would carry on campaigns to publicise the landlord cause – leaflets and posters would be prepared by the chief organiser and distributed by the tahsil organisers, and there would be singing parties and dramatic performances – but the real basis of 'electioneering' and electoral success was to be the control exercised within the constituencies by the 'influential controllers of votes'.

During the campaigns for the elections these notions of electoral control did in fact govern the activities of the NAPs. The party organisers, and particularly M.D. Seth, travelled widely through the province to meet the 'leading men' and get their assurances that they would give 'their votes' to the NAP.[91] Almost invariably they returned with reports that they had received 'considerable' or even 'overwhelming' support. Candidates, moreover, canvassed influential men. Thus, Lady Kailash Srivastava, the wife of Sir Jwala Prasad, was assured by a prominent zamindar at an election meeting in Cawnpore district that 'all his tenants were ready to support and vote for her';[92] and it was reported that Kunwar Hirdey Narain of Unao had been successful 'in securing the support of big Zamindars and Taluqdars of Unao and retired civil and military officers' at the expense of the Congress.[93]

Such activity and reports encouraged the NAP leaders: they confidently predicted that their parties would win the elections and be able to form the new, autonomous ministry in the province.[94] In this they gravely miscalculated; they did not shirk the fight but the results were disastrous for them. Of the 564 candidates nominated for the 228 seats, 152 were from the NAPs as against 168 Congressmen and 36 Muslim Leaguers (who naturally contested only the Muslim constituencies). The NAPs won 21 seats, the Congress 133 and the Muslim League 27:[95] it was nothing less than a rout of the landlord forces.

As has already been suggested, the weak organisation of the landlord parties was one major cause of their defeat; but their electioneering methods were equally important. Electioneering by means of 'influential controllers of votes' had served the landlords well in the elections for the provincial council in the 1920s, but it was inadequate in the more exacting conditions created in the mid-1930s by a greatly expanded electorate and by the active participation in the contest of strongly organised rival parties. The inadequacy of the landlords' methods was given point, in fact, by the contrast that they presented to the methods of those other parties, and particularly the Congress. As the governor of the time, Sir Harry Haig, put it in an article several years later, the landlords were apathetic and disunited as compared with the Congress and their methods 'were often defective':

> The landlords thought they could depend on the traditional support of the tenants. . . . Electioneering to a great extent took the form in the large populous agricultural constituencies of obtaining the promise of the support of the

landlords instead of endeavouring to get into direct relations with the tenants. Very different were the Congress methods . . . they developed their activity not spasmodically, but continuously, through their resident workers in every village. Meetings and processions, slogans and flags, the exploitation of grievances, promises which held out the vision of a new heaven and a new earth, stirred the countryside into a ferment such as it had never before experienced.[96]

What was most significant was the contrast in attitudes towards the tenant-voter. The Congress was the more active and, on the whole, the more united party. The NAPs by contrast suffered from the lethargy and the squabbling of their members (for in campaigning, just as much as in party organisation, landlord style played its weakening role). But the Congress gained its clearest advantage from the efforts which it made to win the support of the tenants who formed the bulk of the electorate. Early in 1936 the Congress began a drive to increase its membership in the rural areas and there was some discussion of the best means by which kisans (peasants) and workers could be represented directly on Congress committees. The UPPCC eventually decided to give kisan sabhas and trade unions 25 per cent representation on delegations to Congress.[97] Then, through its election manifesto, it made an effort to identify itself with the aspirations of the tenants. There had already appeared in mid-1936 a Congress report on agrarian conditions in the U.P. which had attacked the landlords for their oppressiveness and had promised radical changes in land tenures, rents and revenue payments under a future Congress régime and the election manifesto took up this theme. It promised 'a reform of the system of land tenure and revenue and rent and an equitable adjustment of the burden on agricultural land, giving immediate relief to the smaller peasantry by a substantial reduction of agricultural rent and revenue now paid by them and exempting uneconomic holdings from payment of rent and revenue'.[98]

The NAPs, as Haig pointed out, gave little thought to making contact with the tenants. They talked at times of 'gaining the tenants' confidence' and of 'enlisting' their support;[99] but they did nothing practical. They quite foolishly underrated the tenant. The villager, wrote Maheshwar Dayal Seth, would be 'a willing tool in the hands of any self-seeking, intelligent man. His political life is blank. He is completely ignorant of his rights and privileges. Any man, with a little knowledge or power can lord it over him.'[100] He clearly believed that the NAP and its members had this knowledge and power, and consequently neither he nor his colleagues bothered to canvass the villagers directly.[101] In their electoral appeal, moreover, the NAPs made no attempt to voice the tenants' hopes or views. They simply offered to preserve the status quo – the existing agrarian system of landlord-tenant relationships[102] – or in short to preserve their own position.

Even when they had an opportunity to contact the voters and win them over, the members of the NAP refused to trouble themselves. A voter who supported the NAP claimed in a letter to the *Pioneer* that his attempts to organise support for the party in his own area had been spurned by the local NAP candidate.

> The NAP candidate visited me in his motor car at my home on 20 October last year [he wrote]. I advised him to organise a local Voters' Conference. He did not accept my proposal declaring it to be impracticable. However, I decided to call a local Voters' Conference at our central temple for 11 November. The NAP candidate thought it below his dignity to join it. The Congress candidate on the other hand snatched at the opportunity and joined in our deliberations on the appointed day. Our Voters' Conference decided to support him as our tribal candidate and consequently he won the election contest in our general rural constituency.[103]

This summarises the whole failure of the landlords' electoral campaign. Apathetic in their approach to electioneering, they continued to rely on a mode of political 'influence' and control which had been made less effective from the very beginning by the increased size of the electorate and which was countered by the forceful campaigning of the Congress as the campaign progressed.

What the landlords and their leaders in the NAPs failed to see was that the new political situation in the mid-1930s made it necessary for them to seek support by an appeal to the electors ('the new heaven and the new earth') and by a popular image broadcast by all possible means. Because they thought merely in terms of using their 'influence' and 'local control' they failed to use even the possibilities that were open to them. They did not realise that the electoral value of their position as landlords was that it provided them with a position for canvassing, rather than for actually controlling, the electorate. The point is well made in a recent study of the political influence of Irish landlords in the mid-nineteenth century which points out that the landlords' influence 'owed more to their powers of organisation than to their powers of intimidation: it was a matter of leadership, not of coercion'. These Irish landlords 'were the acknowledged leaders of practically every kind of local activity. . . . Many of them took a personal interest in their tenants, constantly inter-fering with advice, encouragement, criticism. . . . In these circumstances tenants would not find it extraordinary if their landlords took the lead at election time; if he arranged for them to be canvassed or brought to the poll. This would simply be an extension of his habit of leadership into the political field.'[104] Leadership working through organisation; leadership providing not a substitute but a basis for electioneering: it was this point which the U.P. landlords failed to perceive in 1936–7.

IV

Yet it is doubtful if a mere change of tactics would have helped them. Their general predicament was much too serious. Their social and political position, the entire basis in fact of their position in the rural areas, had been changing in such a way that only a complete re-orientation would have brought them political success in the countryside. Unlike the Irish landlords of the 1850s, the U.P. landlords were no longer 'the acknowledged leaders of practically every kind of local activity'. As a result of the changes wrought by British rural administration, they had begun to lose their position of 'natural leadership'. The fact was that in the period after the mutiny in which they and their supporters had been most active in affirming their pre-eminence, their standing had been gradually but surely declining.

This paradox rested on the misleading equation which the Oudh Men made of the position of the 'landed aristocracy' in the province before and after the assumption of British rule.[105] The whole basis of that position in fact had changed with the coming of the British power. Before the British gained control of the North-Western Provinces and Oudh many of the men who were later among the landlords had exercised a position of 'natural leadership'. But at that time they were not landlords but petty rulers, 'little kings'.[106] They were not owners of land, or proprietors of estates, but rulers of men, sometimes as heads of local lineages, sometimes as autocrats who had gained, and were able to maintain, their personal, local rule. These 'little kings' were put forward, or were accepted, as leaders in time of war; they were the representatives of their localities with the outside world; they were the final arbiters in times of dispute; and they were the executive heads of each locality. But under the land revenue settlement arrangements introduced by the British the basis of their position of rulership disappeared.[107] The British did not allow the landlords to perform the essentially 'royal' functions that they had discharged as 'little kings'. Instead, the British themselves provided the military and police forces; they broke down local forts; they assessed the revenue on the lands;

and they set up courts to arbitrate in disputes and punish offenders. Moreover, they did not give the landlords a new functional position of importance by which their local pre-eminence might be maintained.[108] The result was that the one-time rulers became simply landlords, owners of the lands of their erstwhile kingdoms with a right to collect rents from those who contracted to use it and with an obligation to pass on to the government a portion of those rents as the revenue from their lands. This landlord position could be an extremely powerful one for it gave the holder rights and privileges over the tenure and cultivation of lands, and over rents and the exaction of fees and services, which he could wield to enforce his will within his estate. In some cases it could be a more powerful position than that of the 'little king'; especially on estates where the will of the lineage had once imposed some restraint on the 'king's' power; or where (as in Oudh) the tenant was left very largely to the will of the landlord.[109] Nonetheless, it was a very different position from that of the petty ruler. For our present purposes it is most important to point to the differences in the links between the ruler and ruled in the pre-annexation 'little kingdom', and the landlord and tenant in the post-annexation estate. In the 'little kingdom' the ties were social and political in character: the subjects deferred to their king. On the estate, however, these ties became primarily economic and legal; the tenant accepted the superiority of the landlord from necessity. For his part, the landlord still exercised power not as a ruler of men but as a governor of tenants; not through social pressures derived from the deference of the people or the political pressures derived from the possession of the means of coercion or the kingly administrative, adjudicative and martial functions, but through economic pressures – rent enhancement, evictions and the exaction of dues (*abwab*). The landlords thus stood at the head of U.P. rural society. But they did not stand there 'naturally': they were maintained by the contractual agrarian system fashioned by the British administrators.

It is not suggested that these changes took effect immediately (or necessarily in all cases completely); but the new British settlements which established this 'landlord-aristocracy' represented the initial breach in the social and political ties which had linked the 'little king' and his subject. Landholders who resided in a village could exert through jajmani relationships, or their part in dispute-settlement processes, or their caste status, a position of authority within the village which was not merely agrarian. But these avenues of influence were less open, perhaps even non-existent, for the holder of a large estate (at least in the estate as a whole). On the landlord-estate, through the late nineteenth century and into the early twentieth century, social and customary links were increasingly replaced by agrarian and economic relationships.

As they became more important these agrarian links were themselves weakened. Many landlords lost contact with their tenants as they moved towards the urban centres in which they became key figures. In addition the landlord group changed in composition over the years as Rajput families in particular lost their estates to mercantile and banking groups. This was a fairly constant process which, if anything, gathered speed in the 1920s and 1930s.[110] Even if the other landlords had been able to exercise a 'traditional position' these newer landlords would have been hard put to do so. Moreover, not many of the old nor many of the new landlords made large-scale attempts to provide new links with their tenants by becoming improving landlords. In fact by the abuse of their new-found powers they made it difficult for their tenants not to feel hostile towards them. The good landlord became, in Indian parlance, one who left his tenants alone![111] These abuses in their turn led to legislation from the 1860s onwards to control rents, and evictions, and give the tenants more secure rights.[112] This tended to divorce the landlords from the control of the lands of their estates and so to make it more difficult for them to exercise pressure on his tenants. The increase in the exaction of premiums for entry on to a tenant-holding (*nazrana*) illustrates how these factors produced tenant resentment and government interference which estranged the landlords from their tenants even if they did not take away completely all his powers of coercion.[113] In 1886 the government tried to give greater security to Oudh tenants-at-will who were subject to considerable interference because of the Oudh landlords unrestrained use of their power to enhance rents. The government introduced a measure to fix rental enhancement of $6\frac{1}{4}$ per cent every seven years; the landlords, however, sidestepped this check to their powers by taking *nazrana*, a practice which grew, until *nazrana* became the focal point of tenant grievances against the landlords. In 1920-2 the popular slogan in tenant riots in Oudh was 'no *nazrana*, no ejectment'. The government then legislated to outlaw *nazrana* but without success. In the 1930s government officers still reported that premiums were being taken.[121] The corollary was, of course, that the landlords became steadily more unpopular and that there was mounting pressure for restrictions upon landlord powers.

In every respect, in fact, the landlords were in these years declining in power and prestige. Their earlier traditional position of rulership was steadily disappearing; and at the same time their new landlord position was being undermined. Moreover, they were not moving to restore the one or strengthen the other. Some of their supporters saw that they were losing their connection with the rural scene, and tried to give them the opportunity to bolster their failing position. When he was governor, Sir Malcolm Hailey, for instance, set his Publicity Department to work on government-financed 'rural uplift' in the hope that the improvement in village conditions would redound to the credit of the landlords. The landlords, he stressed, had to prove that they were 'an essential factor in rural life'.[114] Later, Jwala Prasad Srivastava used his ministerial position to organise another rural development scheme[115] as a way of helping the landlords find the means 'to forge afresh the links that once bound them to their peasantry, and re-establish themselves as the guardians of their interests'.[116] Sir Harry Haig, who succeeded Hailey as governor, commended the scheme to the landlords for this reason. They were being given an opportunity, he claimed, 'to prove convincingly that the order to which they belong is one that is capable of playing a valuable part in the rural organisation of the province. . . . The rural development movement lays particular emphasis on the emergence of rural leadership, through the agency which it proposes to carry out works of improvement. . . . The landlords have a great opportunity of exercising that position of leadership which they have inherited.'[117]

None of these schemes, however, succeeded in rousing the landlords. They ignored the chances presented to them by their supporters, and did not attempt to create new ones for themselves. Basically they were unconvinced of the need to do anything to win over their tenants: the politically-innocent villager, they assured themselves, would respond to the presence of his landlord and would acknowledge the influence of the landlord by his vote. They were content, therefore, to rely upon 'influence' and 'local control' and made no effort to establish an identity of interest with the tenants through their programmes: they offered not 'a new heaven and a new earth', but the status quo, which meant their own continued dominance. So it was that in 1937 they came to see 'before their very eyes . . . their own tenants voting against their wishes'.[118] An era had passed and the landlords could claim no longer that they were 'the chosen and natural leaders'[119] of the people.

NOTES

1 For the Mutiny and its effects on British policy see T.R.Metcalf, *The Aftermath of Revolt. India 1857–1870*, Princeton 1964; J.Raj, 'The introduction of the taluqdari system in Oudh, *Contributions to Indian Economic History*, I (1960), 46–79; and M.Maclagan, *Clemency Canning*, London 1962. For the development of the Oudh Policy, P.D.Reeves, 'The landlords' response to political change in the United Provinces of Agra and Oudh, India, 1921–1937' (unpublished Ph.D. thesis, Australian National University, 1963), esp. pp. 26–43.

2 *Express* (Lucknow), 4 Dec. 1902, in U.P., *Selections from the vernacular newspapers*, 1902, p. 726. The *Express* was the taluqdar newspaper.

3 S.H.Butler, *Oudh Policy, the policy of sympathy*, Allahabad 1906, p. 27.

4 Raja Udai Pratap Singh of Bhinga, *Democracy not suited to India*, Allahabad, 1888, p. 26.

5 For example, W.C.Benett became secretary to the Board of Revenue and J.R.Reid became a member of the Board and Sir John Woodburn became Chief Secretary.

6 Butler was jubilant, in 1906, at the ascendancy which the Oudh Policy had achieved: fears that it would be submerged had been unfounded, he claimed; 'Oudh Policy has not succumbed. For a while it was in captivity, it drooped but it escaped; and now, after many days, it has regained its former place and a wider ascendancy', *Oudh Policy*, p. 29, Cf. Sir John Hewett (Lt-Gov. 1907–12) in *Leader*, Allahabad, 27 Feb. 1921, p. 5, discussing influence of Benett and Butler on him: 'I can assure you that the feelings which animated these two most distinguished friends of Oudh were among the most dominant of those which guided my action while the province was in my charge...'.

7 Butler, speech to taluqdars, 15 Feb. 1915, Records of the British India Association of Oudh Lucknow (hereinafter BIA).

8 Great Britain, Parliamentary Papers (hereinafter PP), 1920, Vol. XXXV Cmd 812.

9 Government estimate of number of tenants, PP, 1919, Vol. XVI, Cmd 141, p. 651.

10 *The Government of India Act, 1935*, Delhi 1936, schedule VI.

11 See J.Nehru, *An Autobiography*, London 1936, Chs VIII, IX, X; M.K. Gandhi, *Young India 1919–1922*, 2nd edn, Madras 1924, p. 742; 'Kisans and non-co-operation', *Leader* (Allahabad), 18 June 1921, p. 3; *Report on*

the administration of the United Provinces (hereinafter *UP admin.*) *1920–21*, Allahabad 1922, p. xxi.

12   U.P., *Government resolution on the revenue administration for the revenue year 1929–30* (hereinafter, *Rev. admin*), pp. 2–3; *Rev. admin 1930–1*, p. 2; *Rev. admin 1931–2*, pp. 2–5; *Rev. admin 1932–3*, pp. 1–2. See also W.C. Neale, *Economic change in rural India. Land tenure and reform in Uttar Pradesh, 1800–1955*, New Haven and London 1962, p. 176 and indices af prices, rents and revenues for 1901/5–1930/4, p. 177.

13   See P.N.Chopra, *Rafi Ahmed Kidwai*, Agra 1960, pp. 31–3; S.Gopal, *The Viceroyalty of Lord Irwin, 1926–1931*, Oxford 1957, Chs. V, VI; Nehru, *Autobiography*, Ch. XXXII; *U.P. admin. 1930–31*, pp. iv.–vi. The landlords were too open to official retaliation to think of supporting a no-tax campaign: see action against Rajas of Kalankankar and Bhadri, the most prominent Congress-landlords in Oudh, *Leader*, 19 March 1931, p. 16 and 3 April 1931, p. 12; *Pioneer* (Allahabad), 19 March 1931, p. 1.

14   Letter, Raja Jehangirabad, *Pioneer*, 3 Sept. 1933, p. 2.

15   Raja Sir Rampal Singh to T.B.Sapru, 9 June 1931, Sapru Papers (2nd series), National Library of India, Calcutta (hereinafter, S.P. 2nd ser.). Cf. report of zamindar meeting Cawnpore, *Pioneer*, 1 Feb. 1932, p. 7; and letter, R.B.Chotay Lal of Moradabad, *Leader*, 2 March 1932.

16   The Congress Socialist Party was formed in 1934 with the elimination of the landlords without compensation and the distribution of land to the peasants as two of its major objectives: H.K.Singh, *A History of the Praja Socialist Party*, Lucknow 1959, p. 235. Congress resolved in 1936 to work for 'a thorough change in the land tenure and revenue systems': resolution, 12 April 1936, *Congress in evolution*, ed. D.Chakrabarty and C.Bhattacharyya, Calcutta, supplemented ed. 1940, supplement p. 6. In the early stages the Congress tried to re-assure the landlords: resolution of AICC working committee, *AICC Bulletin*, No. 9, 3 Jan. 1932, p. 2.

17   Sir M.Hailey, reply to address of Ballia Welfare League, 20 July 1932, *Leader*, 24 July 1932, p. 11.

18   *Pioneer*, 24 Jan. 1933, p. 9. For a compendium of his speeches on this theme at the time see *Current problems in the rural area. Vade-mecum for the rural propagandist* comp. S.S.Nehru, I.C.S., Naini Tal 1932. Nehru was the director of publicity. The second edition of these speeches entitled simply *Current problems*, Lucknow 1933, gives pride of place to 'the need for a stable party'.

19   See Sapru's correspondence with Bikanir and Bhopal in March–June 1931 and Jan.–Feb. 1932, S.P. (1st and 2nd ser.).

20   The Agra Province Zamindars' Association was founded in 1914. Its headquarters were in Allahabad and it admitted to membership zamindars who paid Rs 5,000 p.a. as land revenue. There was another association, with headquarters in the small western-U.P. town of Muzaffarnagar, with

some claims to being representative of the zamindars of Agra province. This was the U.P. Zamindars' Association which was founded in 1896. It was open to all zamindars, irrespective of the amount of revenue that they paid; in fact, it welcomed even tenants and those who were simply 'interested' in agricultural matters. See Reeves, 'The landlords' response to political change, pp. 54–65.

21 *Pioneer*, 24 July 1931, p. 12; *Leader*, 27 July 1931, p. 13. 'Political future of India's agriculturists', *Pioneer*, 27 Oct. 1932, pp. 2, 12; 'Landholders' party in U.P. *Landholders' Journal* (Calcutta) (hereinafter LJ) I (Aug. 1932), 132, Cf. statements in *Pioneer*, 28 Aug. 1932, p. 5; *Leader*, 7 Sep. 1932, p. 7 and letter in *Pioneer*, 21 Jan. 1933, p. 2.

22 See Sapru to Bhopal, 23 May 1931 and Sapru to Bikanir, 13 June 1931 in SP (1st ser.), VIII, 269–71; XXIV, 397. BIA, 'Memorandum on scheme to purchase The Pioneer (May 1932)', Statement of policy over Srivastava's signature, *Pioneer*, 8 June 1932, p. 1. Supplement, *Pioneer*, 18 Nov. 1932.

For an example of its advocacy of party idea see leading article 4 May 1932: 'The need of the moment is a party composed of all those stable elements – whose whole future depends on the maintenance of law and order and good government – to come out into the open and fight the Congress extremists'. See new column which began to appear, 'Pointers for politicians'.

23 Sapru to Srivastava, 29 July 1932 and Sapru to Clive Rattigan, 1 Aug. 1932, SP (2nd ser.).

24 V.P.Menon, *The Story of the Integration of the Indian States*, 1956, Ch. II, esp. pp. 31–3; R.Coupland, *The Indian Problem 1835–1935*, pp. 129–30.

25 Cf. above, page 284, note 18. Also, J.M.Clay, finance member U.P. government, address to district publicity officers, *Pioneer*, 4 Nov. 1932, p. 6: 'His Excellency has continually referred in public speeches to this question of a stable party. ... It is obviously a matter on which His Excellency has felt very strongly.'

26 Donaldson, collector of Allahabad, *Leader*, 3 July 1932, p. 10; Sucha Singh, assistant superintendent Dehra Dun, *Pioneer*, 28 Aug. 1932, p. 5.

27 *Pioneer*, 4 Nov. 1932, p. 6, Cf. 'Landlord and tenant', *Pioneer*, 4 July, 1932, p. 2.

28 *Leader*, 23 Jan. 1932, p. 12; *Pioneer*, 24 Jan. 1932, p. 5.

29 Tirwa to Nawab Syed Iqbal Bahadur of Shamsabad, 19 Oct. 1932, U.P. Zamindars' Association, Muzaffarnagar (hereinafter U.P.Z. Assn).

30 Letter from Dwarka Nath Seth forwarding resolution for meeting 20 Dec. 1932, BIA. Action was postponed according to a note on the letter. Letter, Seth O.N.Tandon, *Pioneer*, 13 Jan. 1933, p. 2. Register of executive committee, resolutions 12 Feb. 1933 (Seth O.N.Tandon) and 25 Nov. 1933, BIA.

31 The British Indian Association of Oudh was founded in 1861. Ordinary membership was confined to those who held taluqdari sanads and for them it was virtually obligatory, especially as the government collected the subscriptions for the association along with the land revenue. See Reeves, 'The landlords' response to political change', pp. 52–65.

32 Letter, *Pioneer*, 16 Mar. 1933, p. 2.

33 Reply to address, Benares District Board, *Leader*, 18 July 1932, p. 10; reply to address Bahraich Landholders' Assn, *Pioneer*, 24 Aug. 1932, p. 6.

34 *Leader*, 28 July 1933, p. 12; *Pioneer*, 29 July 1933, 6. There were reports of Ranjit Singh's activities in the districts during 1932 in *Leader*, 22 Jan. 1932, p. 7; 16 Oct. 1932, p. 3 and 29 Oct. 1932, p. 12.

35 Indian Statutory Commission, *Report, recommendations, memoranda and evidence*, 17 vols, London 1930, XVI, 386–9. Indian Central Committee, *Report*, Calcutta 1929, pp. 38, 49. Indian Franchise Committee, *Selections from memoranda submitted by individuals and oral evidence*, London 1932, pp. 791–801.

36 Raja Shri Prakash Singh of Mallanpur, 'Some of the means to organise suggested to the president of the B. I. Association, Lucknow, 7 April 1933', BIA.

37 *Proposals for Indian constitutional reform*, Delhi 1933, p. 79. The white paper was Cmd 4268 of 1932–3.

38 Raja Sir Rampal Singh to Sir H.Butler, 13 May 1933, BIA. Cf. letter, Major Ranjit Singh, *Pioneer*, 1 May 1933, p. 2, *Leader*, 30 April 1933, p. 7. Also *LJ*, I May 1933, pp. 836–7.

39 *Pioneer*, 9–12 Oct 1933; *Leader*, 12–14 Oct. 1933; the articles are reprinted in *India's freedom*, London, reprint 1962, pp. 20–34.

40 Hailey, reply to address of Ballia Welfare League, 20 July 1932, *Leader*, 24 July 1932, p. 11.

41 Nawab of Chhatari, *Speeches Delivered by H.E. Captain Nawab Sir Hafiz Muhammad Ahmad Said Khan [as] Governor of the United Provinces of Agra and Oudh*, Delhi, n.d., p. 96. This volume was printed by the Nawab of Baghpat, Chhatari's cousin.

42 See speeches to U.P.Z. Assn, Etah Reform League, Desh Hitkarni Sabha Allahabad and Agra Province Zamindars' Assn, Allahabad in *Speeches*, pp. 20–1, 40–1, 88, 100–1.

43 *Pioneer*, 5 Feb. 1934, p. 9; *Leader*, 5 Feb. 1934, p. 10.

44 *Pioneer*, 7 Feb. 1934, p. 6. See 'The Union and Progress Party', *Pioneer*, 20 April 1934, p. 8.

45 P.Sitaramayya, *The History of the Indian National Congress*, I, Bombay 1946, 571, 573. H.K.Singh, *A History of the Praja Socialist Party*, p. 235.

46 For meetings of committee see: *Pioneer*, 25 June 1934, p. 1; 9 July 1934, p. 5. For board: NAP, U.P., 'Proceedings of the meeting of the board

held on 5 Aug. 1934' in U.P.Z. Assn; *LJ*, II, 1934, 851–3; *Indian Annual Register* (Calcutta) (hereinafter, *I.A.R.*), II, 1934, 376–8; *Pioneer*, 8 Aug. 1934, p. 1; *Leader*, 8 Aug. 1934, p. 11.

47 Register of executive committee, 25 Feb. 1934; and 'proceedings of the conference of the agriculturists of Oudh', BIA. See reports in *Pioneer*, 15 Aug. 1934, p. 5 and 30 Aug. 1934, pp. 1 and 16; *Leader*, 19 Aug. 1934, p. 5 and 30 Aug. 1934, p. 5.

48 Cf. H.Tinker, *The Foundations of Local Self-government in India, Pakistan and Burma*, London 1954, p. 159: 'certain ephemeral organisations such as the "National Agriculturists' Party" . . . ' They receive a passing mention in R. Coupland, *Indian politics 1936–1942*, Oxford 1944.

49 Reeves, 'The landlords' response to political change', pp. 88–90, 296–7, 313.

50 Ibid., pp. 66–71.

51 'Proceedings of executive committee of the NAP held on 6th August 1934', U.P.Z. Assn.

52 *Pioneer*, 5 Sept. 1934, pp. 1, 16.

53 Letter, *Pioneer*, 15 Sept. 1934, p. 8. Cf. reports of their activities by APZA and BIA in *LJ*, III, 1934, 81–2. The APZA stressed how alike the parties were; the BIA emphasised how different they were!

54 *Pioneer*, 22 Dec. 1934, p. 3.

55 *LJ*, IV (1935), 231–3. *Pioneer*, 1 Dec. 1935, p. 6; *Leader*, 3 Dec. 1935, p. 6.

56 *Leader*, 29 July 1936, p. 3.

57 Yusuf to Anand Swarup, hon. secretary, 2 July 1934, U.P.Z. Assn.

58 Nawab of Baghpat to Swarup, 13 July 1934; Yusuf to Swarup, 25 July 1934, U.P.Z. Assn. (Note that Baghpat was Chhatari's cousin.)

59 Letter, *Pioneer*, 15 Sept. 1934, p. 8.

60 Letter of resignation, dated 11 Nov. 1936, *Pioneer*, 13 Nov. 1936, p. 8; *Leader*, 14 Nov. 1936, p. 11.

61 Rusticus, 'The political future of the landlords', *Pioneer*, 15 Feb. 1935, p. 8.

62 See *Pioneer*, 3 Oct. 1934, p. 6; 1 Dec. 1934, p. 7; 12 Aug. 1935, p. 6; 17 Aug. 1935, p. 3; *Leader*, 2 Dec. 1934, p. 14; 24 Aug. 1935, p. 13; 17 Aug. 1935, p. 13. Also, *LJ*, IV, 1936, 403–4.

63 Speech as chairman of reception committee, *Leader*, 13 April 1936, p. 13.

64 L.N. Sarin, 'Vested interests *vis-à-vis* the Congress. Is landlordism doomed?', *LJ*, III, 1935, 414.

65 *Pioneer*, 11 April 1935, pp. 8, 11. M.D. Seth, 'The NAP of Oudh – its aims and activities', *LJ*, III, 1935, 648–50.

66 Agha Syed Fateh Shah, hon. sec., 'The Sitapur District Association', *LJ*, III, 1935, 816–19. *Pioneer*, 31 Mar. 1935, p. 4.

67 *Leader*, 24 June 1936, p. 14.

68 *Leader*, 28 July 1935, pp. 9–10.

69 Cf. 'Notes', *Leader*, 8 July 1935, p. 8.

70   *Leader*, 2 Aug. 1935, p. 8 and *Pioneer*, 15 July 1935, p. 5. Cf. in *Leader*, 13 Sept. 1935, article 'The Liberals and the next elections' and cartoon 'The agriculturist party and the agriculturist onlooker'.

71   Reeves, 'The landlords' response to political change', pp. 341–9.

72   'Proceedings of the meeting of the executive board of the NAP (Agra Province) 21st June 1936', U.P.Z. Assn.

73   'Proceedings . . . 21st June 1936' and special correspondent, *Leader*, 14 June 1936, p. 14.

74   'Proceedings meeting executive board NAP (Agra Province), Naini Tal, 23rd June 1936'. Cf. *Pioneer*, 25 June 1936, p. 1; and *Leader*, 27 June 1936, p. 14.

75   *Leader*, 22 June 1936, p. 14; 2 July 1936, p. 9; 19 July 1936, p. 10; 3 Aug. 1936, p. 10; statement by Chhatari, *Pioneer*, 22 July, 1936 p. 9. Also, Khaliquzzaman, *Pathway to Pakistan*, Lahore 1961, p. 145.

76   *Pioneer*, 16 July 1936, 3. See letters between Sapru and Srivastava on 24 June, 19 July and 25 July 1936 in SP (2nd ser.).

77   *Leader*, 14 Sept. 1936, pp. 8, 10. Cf. K.N. Haksar to Sapru, 28 Sept. 1936: 'Tell me how JPS has outmanœuvred Chhatari?' SP (1st ser.), VIII.

78   Srivastava to Sapru, 23 Sept. 1936, SP (2nd ser.).

79   *Pioneer*, 4 April 1935, p. 4. Cf. address by the president of the Lucknow Division Liberal conference, Dec. 1936, who claimed that the Liberals were not communalist but that they had to advise Hindu voters to support only those candidates who were nationalists and who 'would not pose as disinterested spectators when Hindu interests are jeopardised'. Such advice, he claimed, was in harmony with a Hindu's duty 'towards Dharma, community, traditions and the country': *Leader*, 8 Dec. 1936, p. 8.

80   See, for example, details of activities of Raja of Salempur: *Leader*, 22 Feb. 1934, p. 8 and 14 Mar. 1934, p. 7; *I.A.R.* I, 1934, p. 320. Also Raja of Nanpara, *I.A.R.* II, 1935, pp. 313–15.

81   M.D. Seth at Kheri meeting, *Pioneer*, 24 Aug. 1935, p. 3; 'Landlords and the Hindu Party', *Pioneer*, 7 Aug. 1935, p. 8; letter from Guru Narain, *Leader*, 22 Sept. 1935, p. 7.

82   *Leader*, 16 Sept. 1936, p. 10. *Leader*, 27 Aug. 1936, p. 9.

83   For resignations see *Leader*, 11 Nov. 1936, p. 11; 25 Nov. 1936, p. 11; 23 Dec. 1936, p. 12. See report of Liberal League conference, *Leader*, 8 Dec. 1936, p. 8.

84   *Pioneer*, 3 Nov. 1936, p. 8; 24 Nov. 1936, p. 3.

85   *Pioneer*, 22 Dec. 1936, p. 8; 2 Feb. 1937, p. 5.

86   Raja Mallanpur, 'Some of the means to organise . . .', 7 April 1933, BIA.

87   *Pioneer*, 2 Dec. 1934, p. 8.

88   *Asiatic Review*, XXIX London, Oct. 1933, p. 613. *Leader*, 14 Aug. 1936, p. 4.

89 'Lessons of assembly elections', *Pioneer*, 26 April 1935, p. 8.

90 'The NAP of Oudh. V: Propaganda', *Pioneer*, 28 Aug. 1935, p. 7.

91 See *Pioneer*, 3 Dec. 1936, p. 4; 8 Jan. 1937, p. 16; 31 Jan. 1937, p. 5; 3 Feb. 1937, p. 3. Also, Chhatari, 12 Jan. 1937, p. 16.

92 *Pioneer*, 3 Dec. 1936, p. 17.

93 *Pioneer*, 1 Jan. 1937, p. 23.

94 M.D.Seth, 'The agriculturists' party and its rivals', *Pioneer*, 6 Jan. 1937; cf. *LJ*, V, 1936, 96. Also, G.Narain in *Pioneer*, 15 Jan. 1937, p. 11.

95 *Report of the first elections to the United Provinces legislature under the Government of India Act, 1935*, Allahabad 1937, p. 8. The report probably overstates the number of NAP candidates, but completely accurate party ascriptions are difficult to procure.

96 'The United Provinces and the new constitution', *Asiatic Review*, XXXVI, 1940, pp. 424–5.

97 See M.V.Ramana Rao, *Development of the Congress constitution*, New Delhi 1958, pp. 64–5. Also resolution of Faizpur Congress Dec. 1936, *Congress in Evolution*, supplement, pp. 13–14. For earlier discussions see *Pioneer*, 29 April 1936, p. 6; 13 May 1936, p. 6; 16 May 1936, p. 3. For sabha and union representation: *Pioneer*, 28 Aug. 1936, p. 5.

98 U.P.P.C.C., *Congress agrarian enquiry committee report*, Lucknow 1936. Election manifesto cited H.D.Malaviya, *Land Reforms in India*, 2nd edn, New Delhi 1955, pp. 65–6.

99 M.D.Seth, 'How to win the confidence of the tenantry', *Pioneer*, 26 Aug. 1935, p. 5; see also 'Constructive work by the taluqdars', p. 8; Chhatari, address to NAP (Agra), *LJ*, IV, 1936, 816.

100 'The villager's life', *LJ*, IV, 1935, 117.

101 Letter, 'One interested', *Pioneer*, 17 Oct. 1936, p. 8. See also 'post-mortem' letters in *Pioneer*: 'A heart-broken landlord', 16 Feb. 1937, p. 8; 'Disgusted', 20 Feb. 1737; p. 8; R.S.Rastogi, 24 Feb. 1937, p. 8; 'Saroj', 26 Feb. 1937, p. 8; N.H.Siddiqui, assistant sec., APZA, 9 March 1937, p. 23.

102 See the programmes of the two parties printed as an appendix to this chapter. It can be seen that they are couched in the most general terms – even those sections which are more specifically 'rural'. The organisers of the parties and their supporters on the whole saw this as sufficient; see, e.g., the Raja of Tirwa's statement in *Pioneer*, 20 Aug. 1934, p. 16: 'While it is true that there are many parties with more or less socio-economic aims and objects there has been so far none which had before it the ideal of establishing cordial relations between zamindars and tenants on the basis of a vigorous, well-chalked out and comprehensive economic programme'. Cf. 'A sound policy and programme', leading article, *Pioneer*, 22 Aug. 1934, p. 8; though the *Pioneer* did hope to see the programme amplified: 'A step forward', 31 Aug. 1934, p. 8.

103 'A loyal voter', *Pioneer*, 26 Feb. 1937, p. 8.

104   J.H.Whyte, *The Independent Irish Party 1850–9*, Oxford 1958, p. 79; also cf. pp. 76–8.

105   Most importantly in W.C.Benett's historical introduction to *The gazetteer of the province of Oudh*, Lucknow 1877, which was the historical and sociological manual of the Oudh Men. Benett's analysis is quoted, endorsed and expanded to bring it up-to-date, in Butler's *Oudh Policy*, 1906, esp. pp. 32–7. (Butler's pamphlet is in fact dedicated to Benett, 'The father of Oudh history, the champion of Oudh Policy'.)

106   I have taken this concept from the work of B.S.Cohn: 'Some notes on law and change in northern India', *Economic development and cultural change*, VIII, No. 1, Chicago Oct. 1959, 79–93; 'The initial British impact on India', *Journal of Asian Studies*, XIX, No. 4, Aug. 1960, 418–31; 'Political systems in 18th century India: the Banaras region', *Journal of the American Oriental Society*, LXXXII, No. 3, July–Sept. 1962, 312–20. Cf. Benett's introduction, *Gazetteer*, 1877, and W.Crooke, *The North-Western Provinces of India*, London 1897, p. 285. For a study of the taluqdars of Oudh before annexation see J.Raj, 'The revenue system of the Nawabs of Oudh', *Journal of the Social and Economic History of the Orient*, II, part 1, Leiden, Jan. 1959, 92–104. It is not suggested, of course, that all the villages of the province were incorporated in such 'little kingdoms'; but it is from these that the 'landlords' come, particularly in Oudh where British practice was able to change the system much less before it was 'frozen' in the 1860s.

107   S.C.Gupta, *Agrarian relations and early British rule in India*, London 1963, pp. 196–8, 299–303. Cohn, 'The initial British impact', pp. 429–30. This was also attempted in Oudh, but was reversed by the special conditions created by the events of 1857–8: see J.Raj, 'The introduction of the taluqdari system in Oudh'; and T.R.Metcalf, *The Aftermath of Revolt*, Ch. IV, 'The restoration of the aristocracy'.

108   Some were given a share of judicial or administrative power as *honorary* magistrates or deputy collectors/commissioners but there was not the power in these essentially subordinate posts to preserve their former 'royal' position. On the grant of these powers see Raj, 'Introduction of the taluqdari system', pp. 74–5; Metcalf, op. cit., pp. 154–6; and M. Maclagan, *Clemency Canning*, London 1962, pp. 289–99. The position which they needed to preserve their standing was that of a *ruling* prince; they came to see this themselves – for example, the memorial by a group of landlords in the Imperial Legislative Council in 1918 which propounded 'the paramount necessity [for 'constitutional reform'] of investing some of the leading zamindars of India with administrative powers within their territories', PP, 1919, XXXVII (Cmd 123), enclosure 10.

109   On the background to this – the Oudh Compromise of 1866 and subsequent legislation by which secure tenant rights were denied to any

but a handful of 'ex-proprietary' tenants – see Metcalf, op. cit., pp. 187–96; and Raj, 'Introduction of the taluqdari system', 66–9.

110 See, for instance, reports of transfers in the following settlement reports: Lucknow (1930), p. 2; Unao (1931), p. 4; Bara Banki (1931), p. 4; Partabgarh (1930), p. 3; Budaun (1929), p. 9; Hardoi (1932), p. 12. These reports are discussed in P.D. Reeves, 'Agrarian legislation and rural society in Uttar Pradesh, India. An historical study with especial reference to the period 1921–1958' (unpublished M.A. thesis, University of Tasmania, 1959), pp. 125–6. Cf. R.K. Mukherjee, ed. *Fields and farmers in Oudh*, Madras 1929, p. 190. Cohn, 'The initial British impact', shows this process in the early nineteenth century.

111 *Final settlement report of the Partabgarh district, Oudh* by J. Sanders, Allahabad 1896, p. 61. Sanders, it should be pointed out, was a most hostile critic of the taluqdars and Oudh Policy.

112 See Neale, *Economic change in rural India*, pp. 291–4, 'Digest of history of land tenure in Uttar Pradesh, 1775–1954'.

113 On early development cf. Neale, *Economic change in rural India*, pp. 97–102. For practice of nazrana in 1920s onwards see the following settlement reports: Rae Bareli (1929), p. 12; Unao (1931), p. 11; Bara Banki (1930), p. 11; Partabgarh (1930), pp. 15–16; Bahraich (1939), p. 17; Sultanpur (1940), p. 31; Bareilly (1942), p. 1; Aligarh (1940), p. 19; and *Rev. admin* 1930–1, p. 2. See Reeves, 'Agrarian legislation and rural society', pp. 76–7, 83, 86–7.

114 Reply to Benares Zamindars' Association, *Pioneer*, 15 Jan. 1934, pp. 1, 10. On 'rural uplift' movement see *Leader*, 18 July 1932, p. 11; *Pioneer*, 4 Nov. 1932, p. 6 and 26 Jan. 1933, p. 6.

115 *Leader*, 3 Oct. 1935, p. 11. Cf. 'Landlords and rural uplift', *Pioneer*, 17 Aug. 1936, p. 8.

116 'The future of the landlords', *Pioneer*, 11 Feb. 1935, p. 8.

117 *Leader*, 14 Aug. 1936, p. 4.

118 Rai Amar Nath Agarwal, secretary, APZA, *Leader*, 23 Mar. 1939, p. 12.

119 Raja of Bhinga, *Democracy not Suited to India*, 102.

APPENDIX

The 'aims and objects' of the National Agriculturists' Parties of Agra and Oudh

Agra

(a) To devise means for the peace prosperity and good government of the country.

(b) To adopt all constitutional means in order to obtain self-government in India.

(c) To create healthy public opinion.

(d) To protect and advance by all constitutional means the interests of the people generally and of the agricultural population particularly in these provinces.

(e) To help and advance the political, social, educational and economic uplift of the province.

(f) To create better and friendly relations between various classes and communities of the province.

(g) To encourage industries generally and cottage and agricultural industries particularly.

(h) To encourage the establishment of co-operative credit societies and land mortgage banks and to take steps to reduce the heavy burden of taxation.

(i) To help and improve medical and public health facilities generally and in the rural areas particularly.

(j) To regulate exchange policy in the interest of the country.

(k) To reduce expenditure and effect substantial economy in every branch of the government administration.

SOURCE: 'Proceedings of the meeting of the Board of the NAP, U.P., held on August 5th, 1934', p. 3. U.P.Z. Assn. Printed in *Landholders' Journal*, Vol. II, No. 12, Calcutta, July 1934, p. 852.

Oudh

1 To adopt measures for the peace, prosperity and good government of the country.

2 To oppose all subversive activities which tend to create class antagonism and cause political and social upheavals in the country.

3   To create healthy and responsible public opinion in the country and to inculcate the spirit of real service in the masses.

4   To adopt all means necessary to promote the agricultural and economic advancement of the rural areas.

5   To adopt means to secure unity among the various communities of India.

6   To promote the cause of Swadeshi, and to assist in the development of Indian manufactures and industries especially cottage industries.

7   To work for economy of administration and the reduction of the burden of taxation.

8   To maintain relations between landlord and tenants.

9   To adopt measures for the relief of agricultural indebtedness.

10   To encourage the establishment of co-operative credit societies and land mortgage banks.

11   To take effective steps for regulating the currency and exchange policy in the interest of the country.

SOURCE: 'Proceedings of the conference of the agriculturists of Oudh, August 28th, 1934', BIA. Printed in *Pioneer*, 30 Aug. 1934, p. 16.

The original draft of the 'Aims and Objects' for the Oudh party had included the following four sections which were deleted before the meeting; they are shown as originally numbered.

1   To adopt by constitutional means the attainment of complete Dominion Status for our motherland, The party will assist others by legitimate means to reach this goal.

9   To get all repressive laws repealed.

10   To maintain intact all that is best in the social structure of India.

11   To assist in the development of arts and languages.

The deletion of sections 1 and 9 left the Oudh party less 'political' than that of Agra, though the removal of section 10 made the programme a little less conservative than it might otherwise have appeared.

SIR TEJ BAHADUR SAPRU AND
THE FIRST ROUND-TABLE CONFERENCE

★

D. A. Low

There was once an American war of independence, and a Greek war of independence, and several Latin American wars of independence. More recently there have been wars of independence in Indo-China and in Algeria. There was once too an Italian revolution, and more recently an Indonesian one. But there was no Indian war of independence, and no Indian revolution either. For twenty years, moreover, after independence – and, conceivably, it could be for yet longer still – India has had a parliamentary régime, based very largely upon the Westminster model. This has not been the story in the overwhelming majority of the new nations. They seem to have become increasingly swift to take another course. To date India, however, has remained a parliamentary democracy in which free elections are as much taken for granted as they are in any other liberal democracy.

Why has all this been? An important part of the answer was stated by a member of the Indian constituent assembly in 1949.

We have to bear one fact in mind [he declared] – that although a revolution has been going on in our country for a long time, the immediate reason for the transfer of power was not a revolution, a revolution which would justify our upsetting everything that had existed before.[1]

Part of what existed before had been the quasi-parliamentary régime which the British had begun to institute, and since there was no traumatic break between the British period and the period of independence the traditions which this had generated were carried forward.

Why was there no traumatic break? Two of the answers that might be given would run like this. Mahatma Gandhi's campaigns of non-violent non-cooperation succeeded in forcing the British to leave India before a violent revolution became necessary. Or alternatively: it has always been the British way to transfer power in their empire by stages, and they were true to their tradition in India. There is a substratum of truth in each of these explanations. But both are myths, and they both ignore some quite vital considerations.

For a start the non-revolutionary transfer of power in India was in no sense a foregone conclusion. In the late 1920s and 1930s it would have been perfectly possible for the irresistable force of Indian nationalism to have met the immovable object of British imperialism and with violent results. It very nearly happened on three or four major occasions, and if nothing had occurred to resolve the crises which developed, it is difficult to believe that a violent upheaval would not have occurred sometime.

In retrospect it looks clear that the turning point came with the passage of the Government of India Act of 1935. The Oxford historian Robert Blake has called the 1935 Act 'one of the great liberal reform measures of modern times'.[2] Nothing could be further from the truth. The Act was stiff with illiberal 'safeguards'. But it was a great liberal victory. In the first place it paved the way for the establishment of full responsible government in all the provinces of India. As a result Congress took office for the first time and before long became so attached to a parliamentary system of government – for which many congressmen had in any event long had a private liking – that when at the end of the Second World War they came out of gaol after a final period of incarceration, they quickly took to it once again. Secondly, the Act proved to be a great liberal victory because its passage marked the defeat of the great Churchill-led, 'die-heard' attack against constitutional advance in India. It is true that up until the outbreak of the Second World War there was some doubt in British circles about the speed at which constitutional advance should be made. But the principles of responsible government in the provinces, and of 'responsibility at the centre', had been conceded by 1935, and were never seriously called in question again.

In 1945 *The Times'* leader writer on Indian affairs told an Indian correspondent: 'So far as India is concerned the situation can be described in a single sentence. The die-hards are extinct, public opinion is united in desiring India to obtain her independence just as soon as it can be arranged.'[3] is It clear, however, that even earlier – and for all the great conflict during the Second World War between the British and Congress – the crucial decisions had been taken.

I wonder what you thought of Winston's outburst yesterday evening? [Leopold Amery, the Secretary of State for India, wrote to his friend General

Smuts in November 1942] ... The idea that it might be possible to reconcile India to the Commonwealth by conceding Indian national aspirations under a workable constitution, just means nothing to him.... I need not tell you that on this issue the overwhelming bulk of the Conservative Party in this country have long since accepted my view and that Winston, if he did stump the country on this issue, would find practically no support.[4]

The great debate in Britain on the principle of India's early advance to independence was settled with the 1935 Act. It was certainly never revived.

Whilst it lasted it was a close run thing. On three or four occasions in 1929–30 the decision might have gone the other way. During the ensuing four years the 'die-hard' opposition to it in Britain became increasingly formidable. It forced the Government to adopt an increasingly illiberal attitude towards Indian reform, and at a crucial Conservative Party conference in December 1934 the 'die-hards' came within 23 votes – 543 to 520 – of upsetting the whole programme of reform. Had they succeeded, the consequences for India, and for British relations with India, would have been momentous.[5]

They did not succeed because there stood in their way a coalition of forces committed to India's constitutional reform which just succeeded in holding the line. This was spearheaded by a disparate collection of political leaders, drawn from all parties in Britain – all of whom would have been in an impossible position, and some of whom would fairly certainly have stood with the opposition, if there had not been a group of Indian leaders who showed themselves prepared to work with them on an agreed programme of constitutional change at the crucial moment. Most of these men were without connections with the Indian National Congress. In the face of much concerted Congress opposition they participated in the three Indian Round-Table Conferences of 1930–2. Without their work the reforms embodied in the Government of India Act of 1935 could never have become law, and without its passage it is difficult to imagine that a non-revolutionary transfer of power could have been effected.

On the Indian side the chief of them was Sir Tej Bahadur Sapru. The Aga Khan was Chairman of the British Indian delegation to the Round-Table Conferences, but it was Sapru's name that headed the list of those invited to the conference. Sapru was throughout much the most important and influential Indian figure. 'We agreed Sapru was the proper man to be leader'[6] wrote Srinivasa Sastri – himself a man with a claim to any leadership that was going – as the first Round-Table

Conference opened. 'Sapru was easily the most influential and able of us all',[7] he wrote once it was all over.

I

Tej Bahadur Sapru was born in 1875. He died in 1949. As a young man he had been a staunch Congressman. Jawaharlal Nehru has recorded how during the First World War he and his contemporaries had had great hopes that Sapru would give them a lead: 'He was emotional and could occasionally be carried by enthusiasm. Compared to him my father seemed cold-bloodedness itself.'[8] But it was not to be. Sapru was greatly incensed by the Government's arrest of Mrs Besant in June 1917 and promptly joined her Home Rule League; but within eighteen months he had left Congress for ever along with the rest of the minority that henceforward belonged to the breakaway National Liberal Federation.

Sapru's decision was completely characteristic. He was a staunch Indian nationalist. He wished, that is, to see India attain full self-government at the earliest possible opportunity. But he was, equally, a passionate devotee of 'the law' and of 'the rule of law', and he could never bring himself to support a programme like non-cooperation or civil disobedience which in his view threatened to destroy it: for this he felt would damage India at precisely the point in its changing political structure where it needed strengthening most.

This outlook derived from his own personal background. He was of the same profession, the same Bar, the same city, and the same community as the Nehrus. But he was truer to the traditions of their community – the Kashmiri Pandits – than they were: for the Kashmiri Pandits were pre-eminently a 'service' community, with close attachments to whatever government was in power. In Sapru's case this attachment was reinforced by the great influence upon him of his grandfather. Sapru himself was the only son of an only son, and as a young man he had been the light of his grandfather's eyes. The old man had lived through 1857 to become one of the first Indian Deputy Collectors. He instilled into his family a profound belief in the advantages which British rule had brought to India, from which Sapru, for all his periodic exasperation with the British, never prised himself loose. Such an outlook was buttressed in Sapru himself – or at least so his family assert – by his reaction to his father, a dissolute, ne'er do well, who battened first upon his father and then upon his son until his death in 1922. Sapru's uprightness, the integrity for which he was famous, was rooted in his revulsion to the human collapse that his father represented for him. It had its intellectual foundation in his distinctive brand of nineteenth-century liberalism. This had come to him from a true neophyte of the liberal holy-of-holies. As a student at Agra College, Agra, Sapru had been the favourite student of Principal Abrahams; and before coming to India Abrahams had been a close associate of John Stuart Mill himself. All these things were compounded by Sapru's great success first as a young lawyer in Allahabad – he was the first north Indian to procure an Allahabad LL.D. – and then in the U.P. and Imperial Legislative Councils between 1912 and 1922. He remained an Asquithian-type Liberal until his dying day.[9]

This meant that he would only have achieved personal fulfilment in politics if he could have been a member of an Indian cabinet supported by a political party of his own way of thinking. Half of him was fully engaged when, during 1920–2, he was Law Member of the Viceroy's Council under Lord Reading, and he proved to be much the most effective Indian member of it. But he had an acute sense of frustration with his lot, and took an early opportunity to resign. Thereafter – paradoxical as it may seem in view of his periodic involvement – he gave decreasing attention to the possibility of a political career, and abandoned any political ambitions. Once Gandhi, and then Jawaharlal Nehru, had come to dominate the Indian National Congress, there was no room for a man of Sapru's outlook within it. He accordingly returned to the Allahabad Bar. There he had a very large practice, and was widely renowned for the meticulousness with which he mastered a case, and the breath with which he argued it. There were several wealthier lawyers in India, and several who were more brilliant advocates. But from 1922 onwards, till he fell gravely ill in 1946, Sapru led the Allahabad Bar. Several Chief Justices owed their appointments to him, and in the whole of north India outside Calcutta he held the foremost place in his profession for a full quarter of a century. Given the central position of the law at this time in the Indian professional élite this meant that, whether he was an active politician or not, he was a man of outstanding public importance.

II

After 1922 it would have been easy for him, however, to have counted as little politically as most of the other breakaway Liberals, had he not suddenly been responsible for a remarkable political success. In 1923 he was appointed an Indian delegate to the Imperial Conference in London. At this the position of Indians in Kenya and South Africa was due to be discussed. Very recently a policy decision had been taken by the British Government which was extremely adverse to the Indians in Kenya. Sapru's closest associates urged him to boycott the conference in protest; but he declined, and almost single-handedly routed General Smuts, the South African delegate, who had wanted the conference to take the South African line on the position of Indians in the British Empire.[10]

For Sapru this proved to be a seminal achievement. Though now no more than an ex-member of the Viceroy's Council it put him right back in the Indian public eye. It persuaded him, moreover, of the virtue of resisting impassioned calls to boycott; and it encouraged him to believe that given the will as well as the arts of an informed, dedicated, and yet temperate advocate, there was nothing he could not effect in London, if he were given the opportunity.

Back in India he was much in demand for the chairmanship of public bodies; and back in India he began too to give his mind to the problem of India's constitutional future as no one else there ever quite decided to do. When in February–March 1922 Gandhi's first great non-cooperation campaign collapsed, Sapru had written to a friend:

> We have received a distinct setback . . . our task now will be of much greater difficulty than it has hitherto been. Hopelessly divided among ourselves, victimised by certain theories irrespective of their relation to realities [a clear reference to Gandhi] we have reached almost the brink of ruin.[11]

He was convinced that the only way to proceed was to get the British to move down the constitutional tracks which they had fashioned elsewhere, and which in a still fairly half-hearted way, they said they would proceed along in India.

> A constructive programme for further constitutional advance [Sapru told another correspondent in July 1922] must be settled carefully and thoughtfully long before there is hurry due to pressure.[12]

To this end, and whilst conducting his flourishing practice at the Bar, he turned himself into India's foremost constitutional lawyer. There was little of the British, the American, the Dominions', or the Swiss constitutions which he did not master. His growing expertise, moreover, very soon found outlets. He co-operated closely with Mrs Annie Besant's project for a draft Commonwealth of India Bill[13] which George Lansbury had read for a first time in the House of Commons in 1924. The next year he wrote a concise study of the existing Indian constitution,[14] and was then appointed a member of the Muddiman Commission which was set up to inquire into the operation of the Montagu-Chelmsford reforms.[15]

This was not, however, proving to be a very fruitful proceeding, and by 1926 he was coming to feel that, however expert one might be on constitution-making, 'the real question is one of policy, and it is obvious that on such a question English and Indian opinion has differed in the past, is differing today, and, I am afraid, will continue to differ in the future'.[16] The Commonwealth of India Bill had come to nothing. Sapru had felt impelled to append a sharp minority report to the Muddiman Commission. The intractable Lord Birkenhead continued to preside at the India Office, and the ruling interpretation of Montagu's declaration about responsible government in 1917 affirmed that it did not imply that India had been promised Dominion Status or full self-government.[17]

Steadily Sapru's exasperation with the British increased. It was exacerbated by a sharp distaste for Sir William Marris, the Governor of his own province, U.P. And in the end the final straw, for him as for so many other Indians, was the appointment by the British Government in 1927 of the all-white Statutory Commission under Sir John Simon to make recommendations about India's future constitutional progress. Sapru had just been to London and had tried to prevent any such decision being made. It was as intolerable to him as to any other self-respecting Indian that at this stage the British should still seek to decide India's future over India's head; and taking advantage of his position this year as President of the Indian Liberal Federation he was among the first to launch the vehement protests against the Simon commission which led to its widespread boycott.[18] Simon and the new Viceroy Irwin countered by establishing a consultative Indian committee called the Indian Central Committee; but to Sapru and most other Indian politicians this was adding insult to injury.

They smarted too under the taunt which Birkenhead hurled at them that Indians had shown no capacity to frame a constitution for themselves. To this the Congress leaders retorted by setting up a constitutional committee under Motilal Nehru as Chairman, and Jawaharlal Nehru as secretary to show precisely what they could do. Sapru was not only a leading member of this Committee. He was the most expert contributor to its deliberations, and did a great deal of the eventual drafting. In December 1928 the Nehru Report, as it was called, was accepted by an

All Parties National Convention in Calcutta as the reasoned basis for India to be a self-governing Dominion.[19]

All these events had generated a great deal of fervour. They were marred by sharp communal differences between the more intransigent Muslims and the more intransigent Hindus; and in the end they were overtaken by a deep rift between those who wished to secure Dominion Status for India and those who now wanted complete independence. The Madras Congress in 1927 had expressed a desire for complete independence. When an attempt was made to have this positively confirmed at the Congress meeting a year later, agreement was only reached on the basis that Congress would settle for Dominion Status for India if it were to be granted within a year: otherwise they would launch a full-scale civil disobedience movement. Up to this point Sapru had stood firmly with Motilal Nehru and Gandhi. There was no sign of any move by the British. Amid boycott and worsening disturbances, Simon soldiered on. The Viceroy, Irwin, protested to his visitors that the right to make decisions about India's future rested with the British Parliament, and that anything approaching a major concession was out of the question.[20] In these circumstances, with no sign of any kind of 'give' in the British position Sapru remained vehemently hostile to them.

Amongst some of the older Congressmen there was now, however, some increasing concern. The younger men, led by Jawaharlal Nehru, were now taking a sharply radical line both on constitutional and on social issues. Fearing the worst Vithalbhai Patel, Madan Mohan Malaviya and other older Congress leaders were accordingly soon beseeching the Viceroy to take some quite dramatic step before the upheaval they saw on the horizon, if the young men continued to make the running, took place.[21] There was an abortive attempt to get Sapru, as one of the leading participants in the Nehru committee, to see the Viceroy. Sapru seems to have made no move himself.[22] During the summer months of 1929, however, he was under increasing pressure from no less a person than Motilal Nehru himself – or at least so his surviving confidants vehemently assert – to see Irwin and press upon him the urgent necessity for a round table conference, so that Indian delegates might confront British delegates in a sustained effort to overcome the constitutional impasse. It was an idea that made a strong appeal to Sapru. He had very nearly brought about such a conference back in 1921. Eventually he was persuaded to accept an invitation to lunch with the Viceroy, and found himself sitting next to Simon.

III

His distaste for Simon and all his works was confirmed. But he was greatly struck by Irwin's personal integrity, and by his readiness to listen to suggestions. It suddenly seemed to Sapru that the British, or at any rate the Viceroy, were at last beginning to bend. For Sapru this immediately presented a profoundly important and altogether new opportunity.[23] Ever since 1921 the British had seemed to present an unwavering refusal to be guided by Indian advice, and Sapru had become increasingly disillusioned, along with most of his nationalist-minded countrymen. Suddenly he sensed a new situation. He had no love and less respect for a policy of simple defiance. As he saw it, it presaged little but violent, destructive conflict. If there was half a chance of taking another road – of peaceful, constitutional change – he was always amongst the foremost to exploit it. In private discussion with Irwin he pressed hard for a public assurance that India really would have Dominion Status and that a round table conference with Britain's leading political leaders would be called at which the details of India's constitutional future would be settled. Irwin for his part was now steeling himself to respond. He had underestimated the strength of Indian nationalism in his first two or three years as Viceroy. The situation, however, was now obviously very serious. Many of those who had been sharply separated from the main stream of Indian nationalism – and as a consequence had kept the existing constitutional régime in being – had in recent years become reassociated with it. Sapru, for example, had since 1927 stood firmly with Congress. And now another full-blooded non-cooperation campaign was promised unless Dominions Status was granted before the end of 1929. Irwin accordingly set his mind to detach 'moderate' opinion, both without Congress and if possible within Congress, from its attachment to any such course before a head-on collision between Britain and India occurred.[24] During 1928 he had tried to take a preliminary initiative along these lines but had been stopped by the Cabinet in London.[25] By mid-1929 the prospects were much more ominous.[26] There had already, however, been a change in the Secretary of State for India. There was now a change of Government in Britain when Labour came into office (on an overall minority) in June 1929.[27] Irwin, moreover, was due to go 'home' on leave. Nothing was quickly finalised, but the extent to which hopes had been raised is indicated by a letter from Sapru of 23 July 1929 in which he wished Irwin 'bon voyage' and 'every success in your high mission'.[28]

Irwin was now quite clear that unless some generous gesture were made fairly soon a direct clash with all the forces of Indian nationalism could not be avoided. He did not wish to see this occur because he wanted to keep India 'within the Empire'. It was clear that the Simon Report was not going to do the trick. If anything Simon himself had grown more rigid. In any event his Report was not due to be published until Congress' ultimatum had expired. When he reached London Irwin was dismayed by the lack of appreciation there of the seriousness of the situation in India, and appears to have gone about his negotiations with British political leaders in a somewhat circuitous way. He did not reveal what he had in mind before he left India, and when he got to London the first suggestion about a round table conference emerged out of the consideration of problems affecting the relationship between the Indian princely states – whose position had just been elaborately investigated by a committee under Sir Harcourt Butler – and the provinces of British India. The suggestion for a round table conference to deal with this question had Simon's full personal support, and it was accepted at the same time that some statement should be made that 'in due season' India would be 'a self-governing Dominion'. Before July was out the Cabinet had agreed to this procedure, though it wanted the agreement of both the Liberal and Conservative parties to it. By September some amendments had been made to the drafts as a result of representations by senior Government officials in India. They were clearly anxious to ensure that the concessions proferred did not prove empty (such as the establishment of the Indian Central Committee had proved to be), and they urged that the statement about Dominion Status should be quite explicit and the conference completely free. Simon now became somewhat concerned at the way things were developing. But the new draft was put to Reading for the Liberals – who so far had made no objection to the Dominion Status statement – and to Baldwin, for the Conservatives, who accepted it in principle. While Reading reaffirmed his support for the proposals about the conference, he now objected to the declaration about Dominion Status: and so did the Simon Commission when the draft was formally placed before them. Irwin was ready to make some verbal changes, but he resisted any attempt to emasculate his declaration, and was backed by the Cabinet. The seeds, however, were sown for the ensuing parliamentary controversy.[29] Irwin on his return to India saw Jinnah, Malaviya, Sapru and others. There was a last-minute suggestion from London that he should postpone his statement because of protests within the Conservative Party against it: but it had been too eagerly awaited in India, and too many people had been informed about its contents, for any delay to be feasible.[30] On 31 October 1929 Irwin accordingly announced that the British Government now considered 'that the natural issue of India's constitutional progress . . . is the attainment of Dominion Status', and that once the Simon Report had been published a conference would be held with a view to submitting 'proposals to Parliament which may command a wide measure of general assent'.[31]

IV

Sapru was among those who were delighted at the outcome. They would now be dealing not with the Government of India or the Simon Commission. 'It gives us,' he told Irwin, 'an excellent opportunity of putting our case before His Majesty's Government.'[32] An important meeting was held in Bombay on 1 November at which the declaration was welcomed by all but a few of the more radical members of Congress who were present. On the same day and on the next another meeting was held in Delhi at which a great many of the other most prominent political leaders were present including Gandhi, the two Nehrus, Mohammed Ali, Malaviya, S.C.Bose, and Sapru himself. There was a long discussion. Gandhi, Jawaharlal and several others wanted to insist upon a number of conditions before agreeing to attend the conference; but they were persuaded not to make them a *sine qua non*, while Sapru and others of a milder point of view, agreed to a statement that they understood 'that the Conference is to meet not to discuss when Dominion Status is to be established but to frame a Dominion constitution for India'.[33] These decisions were embodied in the so-called Delhi Declaration signed by all who were present except Bose.

Irwin was very well satisfied. So was Sapru. The leading Congressmen, he said, 'who had in the past refused to co-operate with the Government' had now said they were 'willing to tender their co-operation'.[34] But no one was out of the wood. In particular Indian opinion was inflamed by the storm which Irwin's statement had aroused in Conservative and Liberal circles in Britain. There were angry debates in both the Commons and the Lords, and it did not by any means look certain in their aftermath that any round table conference could hope to serve a useful purpose. 'The task of a peace-maker,' Vithalbhai Patel wrote to Sapru on 8 November, 'is always full of difficulties and he gets kicks from both sides.'[35] More precisely an important meeting of the

Congress Working Committee was due to be held on 26 November, and it was already beginning to look as if the Congress leaders would resile from the Delhi Declaration. At an earlier moment of crisis, in 1921, Sapru had negotiated with the Congress leaders, but only from a distance. He did not repeat the mistake this time. Whenever he could he entered into discussions with them directly.

From this point onwards we may follow the story in rather more detail.

Pandit Motilal Nehru came to me last night [Sapru wrote to Patel from his home in Allahabad on 11 November] and I went to him this morning. Last night's conversation left the impression on my mind that the Congress people were intending to go back on their acceptance at their meeting of the working committee on the 16th November. This morning I discussed the thing with him again at great length and pointed out to him the inadvisability of such a course and its repurcussions in the country. I said the enemies of the Indian progress would very much like that the chances of the conference coming about in London and being attended by the congressmen should be spoiled. . . . He said to me in reply that what they intended to say at the meeting of the 16th November was that they would go to the Round Table Conference only if their conditions were fulfilled. I begged of him to postpone such a decision . . .[36]

There was a gulf here yawning. So clear was Sapru, however, in his own mind that a round table conference imaginatively handled offered an unequalled chance of advance, that he had already decided on his own course of action. 'If Mr Gandhi and Pundit Moti Lal Nehru go back on the invitation to the Round Table Conference,' he affirmed, 'my support of it will continue to be unabated and unqualified.'[37] It was then arranged that in addition to the meeting of the Working Committee a meeting of the signatories to the Delhi Declaration should be held in Allahabad on 18 November. But as Sapru understood it Gandhi's difficulty was that

. . . he felt that the situation was such that the country expected that something should be done by the Government which would enable him to put the advanced section of his following consisting mostly of young men in a reasonable and hopeful frame of mind.[38]

So the problem was not easy. And there was a long discussion on the 18th. Malaviya backed Sapru warmly. In the end the Delhi Declaration was reaffirmed, and Sapru received a number of warm congratulations for his efforts.[39]

But he was far from being optimistic about their eventual outcome. It was quite clear that many congressmen were opposed to any participation in the conference whatsoever.[40] Patel, Sapru and others thought it would be worth while if the Viceroy could see Gandhi and Motilal. By the time this meeting was actually due to be held Jawaharlal had come out openly against the conference (and Irwin was informed that Gandhi had probably decided not to support it either).[41] Sapru, however, was not altogether downcast; he even began to feel that the omens were better than he feared. 23 December, the date eventually fixed for the meeting, was one of the Mahatmas's days of silence. The others spent the time in discussion, and according to Sapru 'were in complete agreement'. But his account of the day's proceedings then continues:

Mr Gandhi arrived at Patel's house at about 4 p.m. broke his silence at 4.15 p.m. and quietly went into the motor car with Pundit Moti Lal Nehru and drove to the Viceregal Lodge. We three, that is to say, Jinnah, Patel and I followed them in another car. When we went in Mr Gandhi first expressed his horror at the attempt to wreck the Viceregal train which had been made that very morning. After that throughout the conversation he was most truculent which took us all by surprise. Pundit Moti Lal Nehru was scarcely less stiff. Jinnah and I argued and reasoned with him, but it was all wasted on him. His point was that the Viceroy should guarantee that immediate Dominion Status would be granted. Our point was that the door of the Round Table Conference being open we could go in there and propose a scheme of full fledged Dominion Status and if doubts and difficulties were pointed out we would apply ourselves to a solution of those doubts and difficulties and that ultimately the question would resolve itself into one of providing safeguards and reservations for the period of transition. The Viceroy thought that we were right. Mr Gandhi however would not agree with us. He doubted British sincerity and then added, 'I am weak, I cannot go to London. There are enormous difficulties and differences among us and I cannot advise the Congress to take part in the Round Table Conference'. Pundit Moti Lal Nehru on his part denied the existence of any such difficulties. It was quite clear to Jinnah and myself that we had been badly let down and that these gentlemen had gone there determined to break off relations with the Viceroy. Both Jinnah and I were miserable, but the Viceroy maintained throughout a remarkable degree of patience, courtesy and reasonableness. We came back disgusted and did not talk after that.[42]

V

For Sapru it was the parting of the ways. The Lahore session of Congress, with Jawaharlal Nehru's first speech as President, and the 'independence' resolution followed. Congressmen turned their backs on the Round Table Conference; organised the holding of independence day on 26 January 1930; and set about making preparations for the civil disobedience movement under Gandhi's leadership to which so many of them had been looking forward for the past year.[43]

Sapru meanwhile took the train for Madras for the annual meeting of the National Liberal Federation. In recent weeks K.M.Munshi had urged him to take steps to rally those forces which were in favour of the Round Table Conference,[44] and to this Sapru now bent his energies. In Madras he secured the support of both the Liberals and the Justice Party. He won the support too of a considerable number of Muslim leaders. There were difficulties in securing the co-operation of the Hindu Mahasabha, and there was considerable Hindu–Muslim acerbity. Here the fact that Sapru was a Kashmiri Pundit with a deep love for Urdu and Persian stood him in excellent stead. He was a Brahmin but much of his culture was Muslim in origin. When coupled with his personal qualities – his renowned personal integrity – this made him a formidable mediator. During a long day of meetings in Delhi on 29 January 1929 he interviewed first the Muslim leaders and then the Hindu leaders. Both sides put their case strongly. Both, however, ended up by agreeing to attend an All-Parties Conference under Sapru's Chairmanship which was fixed for the end of February.[45]

When the Conference met, Sapru's mother was dying and he could not give his full attention to it. The Hindu–Muslim controversy took a new turn when Jinnah pressed his renowned Fourteen Points. Sapru, nevertheless, had quite succeeded in rallying those who were anxious to attend the Round Table Conference and advance the cause of Dominion Status for India. Some who were normally strong supporters of Congress – such as Mrs Naidu – attended, and an important meeting was held with some representative Princes.

But events now began to move very fast. Gandhi launched the civil disobedience movement with his 'salt march' to Dandi in March 1930. Thereafter for weeks on end thousands of men and women engaged in the most sustained defiance which the British had encountered in India since 1857. The government refused to arrest Gandhi immediately but did so on 5 May. Amidst the mounting excitement Sapru grew increasingly despondent. Civil disobedience was far more destructive of political order in India, he believed, than the non-cooperation movement he had helped to combat in 1921. This time 'the very framework of society' was being attacked. Moreover, his initially successful attempt

L

to rally the moderates was now running into difficulties, and he was worried about the delay in the publication of the Simon Report. Before very long he was appealing to the Viceroy to do something to quicken 'the execution of constructive policy. . . . The fact . . . is that those who want Dominion status plus a stable Government are disorganised and if I may say so demoralised.'[46] Irwin saw him on 7 May and reassured him. 'I do not lose any of my faith in the Conference policy,' Irwin told him, 'and I think we have all got to continue working quite steadily and un-shakeably to this end.'[47] With this Sapru agreed; but he now returned two or three times in his correspondence with Irwin to the theme that

> hasty action or indiscriminate use of force tends to alienate people more and more from the Government and to make the task of those who are anxious for a peaceful solution of the Indian problem and for the establishment of a stable constitution in this country increasingly difficult.[48]

For his part Irwin was very well aware that he was heavily dependent for the successful execution of his policy upon moderate support. By his Dominion Status declaration and his promise of a round table conference he had successfully wrenched moderate opinion away from its attach-ment to Congress. This meant that when Congress launched its civil disobedience movement, he was not faced by a completely united Indian opposition, as he looked like being a year before. It also meant that if he could keep the moderates satisfied, and thus keep open a way forward – the way of the Round Table Conference – he could treat the civil dis-obedience movement with impunity. All his conciliatoriness during 1930 was directed, therefore, not at Congress, but at keeping the moder-ates with him. 'I am constantly seeking,' he told Sapru 'means by which to ease the situation for persons like yourself, and indeed for the country generally.'[49]

It was not always easy. In June 1930 the Simon Report was published. Nowhere did it even mention Dominion Status[50]; and in seeking, as government action against the non-cooperation campaign mounted, to say something to assuage the moderates, the Viceroy ran headlong into the opposition of Liberal and Conservative leaders in Britain. In attempting to estimate the influence on British policy of moderate leaders like Sapru the following telegram which Irwin felt it necessary to send to Wedgwood Benn, the Secretary of State for India, on 28 June may be noted.

> The situation [Irwin telegraphed] is extremely difficult. We have had to take strong measures against civil disobedience which have had the effect of alienating

a great deal of non-Congress Hindu sympathy from the Government, and it is very likely as you know, in the very near future we may think it necessary to proclaim the Congress working committee and arrest Motilal. All this is popularly labelled repression and the natural tendency is to throw the people by reaction into greater sympathy with the Congress or, if not this, at least into attitude more critical of the Government. In such a temper it is, in our view, of great importance to give positive evidence that repression is not the sole policy of the Government but that desire to assist the constitutional development remains unimpaired.[51]

It succeeded in overbearing the Opposition leaders objections, and on 9 July in a speech to the Imperial Legislative Assembly, Irwin reiterated his Dominion Status statement and announced that the forthcoming Conference would be 'free to approach its task, greatly assisted indeed, but with liberty unimpaired by the Report of the Statutory Commission'. It was, he said, the Government's intention to treat the Conference 'not as a mere meeting for discussion and debate, but as a joint assembly of representatives of both countries on whose agreement precise proposals to Parliament may be founded'.[52] If one compares these words with Irwin's Dominion Status statement of the previous November, there is a marked advance in precision. The speech contained all the undertakings which Sapru believed to be essential if progress were to be made, and he was very well pleased.

The situation, however, was still extremely serious. When, therefore, there suddenly seemed to be an opportunity to make a move in another direction Sapru leapt towards it. On 20 June Motilal Nehru had given a seemingly conciliatory interview to George Slocombe of the *Daily Herald*.[53] With his Bombay associate Jayakar Sapru immediately took steps to try to see whether there was any possibility of a truce. The civil disobedience movement was at its height. There were obvious signs of disarray in the moderates own camp. And Sapru was beginning to look ahead.

Taking a long view of the situation [he wrote at this time] it would be most unfortunate if no attempt was made even at this stage to secure the presence of the Congress representatives at the Round Table Conference. We have to bear in mind the aftermath of the Conference and the people at large towards any constitution which may be enacted without their participation.[54]

He and Jayakar, therefore, approached Irwin who felt it would be 'morally wrong' not to see if a truce could be effected. Accordingly he gave Sapru and Jayakar every assistance within his power: the Nehrus were even moved from their gaol in U.P. to Gandhi's prison in Poona so that full discussions could be held. Irwin, however, was at this point 'quite determined that we should not abandon the main positions we have taken'[55] (the Liberal and Conservative stance in London had in any event left him with very little room for manœuvre). He never expected the negotiations to succeed. And his own primary concern was to see that 'if the Congress leaders are unreasonable [a breakdown would] have the effect of hitching Jayakar and Sapru pretty firmly to us'.[56] This was broadly what happened.[57] The Congress leaders wanted definite undertakings from the British that the Conference would only be concerned to draw up a Dominion Status constitution. This for the British, as everyone knew very well, was for the time being quite out of the question.

From Irwin's point of view, however, there can be little doubt that the Sapru–Jayakar negotiations served admirably to keep the moderates in line in the awkward three months between the peak of the repression of the civil disobedience movement and the opening of the Round Table Conference; and there can be little doubt too that Sapru and Jayakar were very much too sanguine in their belief that something might come of their negotiations. But from their point of view the effort served a purpose. It rallied the wavering moderate camp about them, and the eventual breakdown sealed their determination to see the Conference through. Their resolution was confirmed by what they had seen as they moved up and down the country in the course of their negotiations with the Congress leaders.

I have been compelled by personal experience to revise some of my opinion [Sapru wrote to Irwin just before leaving for England in September]. The Congress has undoubtedly acquired a great hold on popular imaginations. On roadside stations where until a few months ago I could hardly have suspected that people had any politics, I have seen with my own eyes demonstrations and heard with my own ears the usual Congress slogans. The popular feeling is one of intense excitement. It is fed from day to day by continuous and persistent propaganda on part of the Congressmen – by lectures delivered by their volunteers in running trains and similar other activities. Very few people understand what they say or what they do, but there is no doubt whatever in my mind that there is the most intense distrust of the Government and its professions. Indeed I have little doubt in my mind that the racial feeling has been fanned to a very dangerous extent. . . . It seems to me that the Congress is really fighting for its own supremacy in the country. As your Excellency knows very well I hold fairly advanced views on constitutional questions, but I am not for the break-up of the social system, much as I should like it to be improved in many ways, and yet men of my views must be content to be put down as old-fashioned Tories, if not worse.[58]

VI

There can be no doubt that Sapru – and Jayakar – felt as 1930 wore on that India was on the brink of a great upheaval. There can be no doubt too that the distance between Congress and the British was now very great indeed. The British were ready to call an unfettered Round Table Conference. But they would not give any undertaking that they would make any major concessions when it met. Congress had only to read the Simon Report; to note that it was being received in Britain as authoritative; and then read the speeches of many Conservative and Liberal leaders in the British Parliament (where in the Commons these two parties had a majority over the Labour Government) to be aware that they were not within even striking distance of their demand for independence. And this was not all. The distance between even a man like Sapru and the British was vast too. 'No section of articulate opinion including the Princes,' Irwin correctly reported to London on 28 June 'has failed to subscribe to general definitions of constitutional purpose as what they call "Dominion Status with safeguards".' On the British side this was still, for the immediate future, unthinkable. Irwin might make statements about Dominion Status, but only as 'the natural completion of India's constitutional growth'. The despatch which he and his government was now compiling on the Simon Report – for all its variations on the Simon proposals – still insisted that imperial control should continue at the centre; while the state of mind of British officials in Delhi may be gauged from a typical office memorandum written at this time by McWatters, the Financial Secretary of the Government of India. *Inter alia* he declared:

It may be laid down as axiomatic that any financial arrangements contemplated must be such as to ensure (1) the maintenance of credit and confidence in the financial stability of the country both in London and in India; (2) the provision of funds in London for payment of interest and repayment of capital of the sterling debt; (3) the provision of funds for the Defence forces; and (4) the payment of pensions, family pensions and provident fund charges for Civil and Army officers . . . the accepted goal of self-government for India must postulate ultimately the control of finance by an Indian Minister responsible to the Legislature . . . [but] the occasion for a transfer of responsibility is not one which can be . . . worked up to in any period which can now be defined.

All this, moreover, was endorsed by Sir George Schuster, the not illiberal Finance Member of Irwin's Council.

The point really is [he wrote] that, if the control of Finance and with it as a necessary consequence, the fulfilment of India's obligation to pay for the Army and meet her external debts, and the responsibility for the maintenance of stable conditions for trade, is handed over to an Indian ministry before India has done anything to correct the effects of the recently preached doctrines of repudiation and anti-British agitation, or in other words to gain the confidence of the world, then there may be a collapse of India's credit, external and internal, a flight of capital, complete devaluation of the existing currency, and general economic chaos...[59]

What was more, such an attitude was widely supported in London. It was not merely that even the more liberal-minded Conservative leaders were adamantly opposed to any idea of Dominion Status in the near future. The Liberal Party leaders were opposed to it as well. Lord Lothian said in September 1930 that they 'should make it clear to the Indians that they would not accept' a demand for 'responsible Self-Government at the Centre' – the one thing for which Sapru for one was after; while 'Lord Reading said that he held very definitely that the most serious thing we could possibly do at this juncture would be to weaken the Central Executive in India'.[60] As Sir Fazli Husein, the Muslim member of Irwin's Council, put it: 'Dominion Status ... does mean tremendously more than even the Labour Government may be ... permitted by the British electorate to go.'[61]

In going to England Sapru and his colleagues were thus pursuing – as they very well knew – a pretty forlorn hope. The truth was that there was nothing in common between any influential line of British thinking on constitutional change in India and any Indian thinking. There was direct opposition all along the line. And it was difficult to see what might be done to resolve it. Civil disobedience had settled nothing. It had not brought the Raj to its knees. The Government was still in control. And the truth was, as Gandhi quite correctly used to say, that the one thing which was necessary to bring about a different situation was a change of heart on the part of the British. Of this there was no sign. On the contrary their hearts were evidently hardening. The room for manoeuvre which was left even to Sapru and his associates was virtually non-existent, and the abyss yawned.

VII

The destiny of India, however, was at stake. So was Sapru's vision of the future; and he had the kind of rugged courage which made itself most felt just when the situation was at its most desperate. On this occasion he was strengthened by the clearness of vision which he brought to his task, and by the long preparation which he had given to it; and in an astonishingly short time a near miracle occurred. In doing more than any other man to bring it about Sapru reached the high point of his career.

It is worth recalling the assets he possessed as the Round Table Conference opened. In the first place he was no novice. Once before, at the Imperial Conference of 1923 he had tackled British politicians on their home ground – and with great success too. He knew that angry platform speeches would do more harm than good. Private meetings, personal lobbying, backed up by a consummate knowledge of the detail of the issues to be discussed, and, at the right moment, a firm, powerful and reasoned statement of the case – these, he knew, were the ways to over-bear them. He had the art at his finger tips. On that previous occasion he had defied those of his countrymen who had felt the Conference should be boycotted, and the results had justified the wisdom of his decision. He was not to be deterred by boycott cries now, and turned his back upon them imperiously. He never believed, moreover – as Jawaharlal Nehru did – that the British were quite intractable. He had a profound belief in the methods they had already employed elsewhere for the devolution of power within their empire. He believed that a peaceful transfer of power was possible. He had an acute sense of the streak of futility in Congress' blunt defiance, and he was not convinced that civil disobedience, however non-violent, did anything very much but choke up the jails. The great need to his mind was not to shame the British by a display of non-violence: it was to convert them to substantial constitutional change.

To this end he was never afraid to speak his mind. Sapru was no cringing sycophant. He was a staunch Indian nationalist, with a passionate concern for constitutional advancement. He differed from many of his countrymen about the best method to bring this about, primarily because he had his eye fixed upon the problem of the ultimate result as he saw it. He was second to none, however, in wanting India to be self-governing.

It was precisely this personal combination of an abiding faith in British constitutional procedures – if they could only be properly put into operation – and a deep concern for India's proper status which gave him his strength in London. It was reinforced by his unrivalled knowledge of all the relevant constitutional law and practice. As Law

Member of the Viceroy's Council in the early 1920s, he had gained a special knowledge of the Government machine from the inside. Among other things this had convinced him that provincial autonomy with a central government which was still solely responsible to the British Parliament was unworkable; 'that machinery will break down in the course of a week'.[62] For a decade, therefore, he had been clear in his mind that a central government bearing a very large measure of responsibility to a popular central legislature was an early necessity. No one in India had seen this issue quite so early or quite so clearly. Responsibility at the centre had become for him the dominant issue.

In defining and seeking it he was greatly assisted by all the experience he had gained through his own involvement in all the major constitutional exercises – apart from the Simon Commission – which had taken place in India during the 1920s – the Commonwealth of India Bill, the Muddiman Commission, and the Nehru Report. No one indeed had had a more extensive or more varied experience of drafting a constitution for India than he had. At the same time he had accumulated a vast knowledge of different constitutions in every part of the world. It was not just that he knew about the British, the Dominions, the American or the Swiss constitution. He knew about the German, the Japanese, the Czechoslovakian, among others, as well. When African constitutional conferences came to be held in London in the 1950s it became quite usual for academic constitutional experts to be called in to assist. At the Indian Round Table Conference this was quite unnecessary. There were several such experts among the Indian delegates, none of them more impressive than Sapru himself.

Yet this was not all. At the Conference one of the most difficult problems was the Hindu–Muslim controversy. As we have seen, Sapru, as a Kashmiri Pundit and a man of both cultures, was peculiarly at home here in the difficult role of mediator.

At the Conference few things, moreover, were more important than the part played by the Indian princes. Here again Sapru was in his element. He was legal confident to many of the more important princes – to the Nizam of Hyderabad, to the Maharajah of Kashmir, and the Maharajah of Patiala amongst others. He had a close understanding, therefore, of their constitutional position. At the same time he never believed that they could be roughly brushed aside. And, as it happened, his oldest boyhood friend, Colonel Haksar, was secretary to the Princes delegation. In every way, therefore, Sapru was as well positioned to tackle the Princes as he was the Muslims and the British.

On the British side no one was more important or more crucial to the outcome of the Conference than the former Viceroy, Lord Reading. As the chief Liberal spokesman on India, he held the delicate balance in British politics on Indian questions. Sapru was his former Law Member. As lawyers and Liberals the two men had a great deal in common. Sapru enjoyed direct access to Reading at any moment he wished, and, as a staunch believer in the doctrine of the ruling few, he made full use of it. In the Conference as a whole nothing was more important than the negotiations which these two men conducted both in private and in public to produce what Irwin was to call 'the Sapru-Reading line'. [63]

In half a dozen key ways, therefore, Sapru went to the first Round Table Conference with assets that were quite unrivalled. They were given cohesion, both by the dire straits into which Indo-British relations had now come, and, more positively, by the thought for Sapru himself that the conference represented the culmination of all his personal efforts over nearly a decade to bring about a conference of this kind. Congress was not there, and this was a great loss. But Sapru was determined that if it lay within his power this should not be crippling.

VIII

The crucial discussions on which everything hinged, began before the conference met – in the first place on the ship, the *Viceroy of India*, on which the main Indian delegates (some of them from British India, some from the Princely States) travelled to London. The idea of 'Federation' was advanced. The Princes had become much concerned about their position *vis-à-vis* the Government of India in the aftermath of the Butler Report (whose doctrine that 'paramountcy must remain paramount' was very distasteful to them); [64] and under pressure from Haksar – and his young associate the irrepressible K. M. Panikkar – they began to discuss the establishment of an Indian Federation in which the Princely States could participate fully (and thus escape some of the leading strings of the Political Department of the Government of India). [65] This had been mentioned as a possibility both by the Simon Report and by the Government of India in their despatch upon the Report. But no one hitherto had thought of it as an immediate possiblity. In their deepening reaction to the Butler Report, and in the atmosphere of tension engendered by the civil disobedience movement, the Princes – almost for the last time – warmed to the idea of a bold initiative.

The Federal idea soon took firm root when the Conference delegates arrived in England and found how adamant Liberal and Conservative politicians were against any idea of Dominion Status.[66] Sapru found Wedgwood Benn, the Secretary of State, 'determined to help us', but 'he warned me against Lord Reading and Lloyd George'.[67] The situation was somewhat complicated by a fresh outbreak of Hindu–Muslim contention.

The informal conversations proceeding between Hindus and Muslims [a Government telegram to Delhi reported on 13 November] are believed to lead to little result and differences are developing between Sapru who is most anxious to conciliate Muslims and thus secure united front for his demands, and Jayakar who is reluctant to surrender important points in Hindu position.[68]

But the Federation proposals went ahead very well nevertheless; and Sapru was right to the fore. The Princes set up a Committee to formalise proposals;[69] but

British Indian delegates [the Government of India was informed] such as Sapru are said to be interesting themselves considerably in these developments and hoping to get something out of them.[70]

Sapru was busy too seeing Baldwin, Lothian, Sir Herbert Samuel, and several other Conservative and Liberal leaders. He addressed a meeting of Labour Members of the House of Commons. He also saw Reading.

He was very nice to me personally [Sapru wrote on 14 November] and I believe I produced some influence on his mind, although I cannot say I have conquered his opposition altogether ... I am having an extremely busy time from 9 in the morning up to midnight.[71]

By the time the Conference opened, however, the Princes had undertaken to announce publicly their support for an early Federation, and the skies were beginning to brighten.

It now seems certain [the *Manchester Guardian* had written on 12 November] that the main interest will centre round the wholly unexpected revelation of the Princes' willingness to come out at once – on suitable terms – into an All-India Federation and to take part in an All-India Legislature with an Executive responsible to it ...[72]

At the first plenary session of the Conference Sapru was the first speaker.[73]

On the morning of the 17th [he told his son] I was quite bad and I was very nervous as to whether I should be able to speak at all as I had made no preparation for my speech whatsoever. Just at 9 o'clock while taking my coffee I thought of

the lines that I would take and at 10 o'clock I made my speech. I was extraordinarily well received in the Conference. Ramsay MacDonald, Henderson,
Wedgwood Benn and Lord Sankey and the Marquis of Lothian and Lord
Reading came up to me and warmly congratulated me. Ramsay MacDonald
said to me in the presence of Lord Reading, 'You have made a fruitful contribution, remember we will stand by you.'[74]

It was the speech of his lifetime. In ringing tones he demanded responsibility at the centre, and asked the Princes to support a Federation. The
Maharajah of Bikaner followed and on behalf of the Princes promised
to do so. Delegate after delegate rallied to their support, and as Delhi
was told shortly afterwards:

> Federal union for matters of common concern has certainly been transformed
> from a remote ideal into a practical problem and the whole question of Central
> Legislature may require to be re-examined.[75]

At joint meetings of the Liberal and Conservative delegations to the
Conference on 21 and 24 November, 'Lord Reading said that the idea
of an All-India Federation had . . . changed the whole position'; he also
affirmed that 'he did not wish to close the door to a discussion of responsible government at the centre, even if no Federal system were to emerge
from these discussions'.[76]

> The situation today [Sapru wrote on 19 November] is distinctly hopeful. . . .
> The English people are prepared in my mind to entertain the proposition of
> Federal Government with responsibility at the Centre. . . . A Federal Constitu-
> tion with responsibility at the Centre should at once give us the Status of a
> Dominion subject to safeguards as to the Army and the Foreign Policy.[77]

The corner had been turned.

There was no advance in the Hindu–Muslim negotiations. There were
indeed some bitter exchanges;[78] and before the Conference had finished
Sapru had resigned in disgust from the Indian Liberal Federation at its
anti-Muslim line. But for the rest everything proceeded admirably. Day
after day, more especially in the hastily arranged Federal Structure
Committee under the much admired chairmanship of the Lord Chancellor, Lord Sankey, the principal delegates, with Sapru always to the fore,
wrestled with the issues they had now successfully thrust forward. All
went well. 'The Prime Minister agreed with me,' Wedgwood Benn told
Irwin in January 1931, 'when I suggested that there had never been a
Conference where goodwill had lasted so well.'[79] The climax came after
Christmas. The prevailing atmosphere by this time was conveyed in a

revealing demi-official letter from an officer of the Reforms Department of the Government of India, who held a watching brief in London, to his chief, the Reforms Commissioner in Delhi:

> Even if the Conference [he wrote] were to break up now without deciding anything, its time would not have been wasted ... even the Conservatives ... can no longer stand where they did; while the Liberals in some directions may even snatch the lead from the Government ... you will have observed, the pace has quickened, and arrangements are already being regarded as practicable, which only a few months ago we would all have considered too advanced. The broad point which I am trying to convey to you is that there has grown up what may not unfairly be described as a very general acceptance of the notion of an entirely new relation between the two countries and all that implies. There is a much more widespread appreciation too of the dangers of delay. Unless the big thing is done quickly the more moderate elements in India drawn from the classes to which we would look to conduct an Indian administration will have been submerged. It would have taken endless Reports and Despatches to bring this home to English opinion ... it is becoming possible to see daylight in the Indian tangle.

And he went on:

> As regards individuals, Sapru spoke extraordinarily well on the subject of the responsibility of the central executive and his speech certainly made a deep impression on all who heard it. I would say that, as an individual effort, it ranks second in all the proceedings of the Conference, only to Lord Reading's contribution on the same subject.[80]

On the 15 January Sapru had lunch with the Prime Minister at the Athenaeum. Just as he had been the first Indian to make a speech at the first plenary session so he was the last Indian to speak at the final session. With the rest of the Conference he then heard Ramsay MacDonald announce that:

> With a Legislature constituted on a federal basis, His Majesty's Government will be prepared to recognise the principle of the responsibility of the Executive to the Legislature.[81]

It was music in Sapru's ears.

IX

He and his colleagues knew, however, that their task was only half done. They now set sail for India. Irwin assisted them by unconditionally releasing the Congress leaders from gaol, and the next step may be told in Sapru's own words written from his home in Allahabad on 11 February 1931.

I arrived here on Saturday the 7th instant and the same day I saw Pundit Jawahar Lal Nehru and Mr Gandhi. I met at Pundit Jawahar Lal's home Malaviyaji also. I had not much of a talk about the Round Table Conference, but I had a private talk with Malaviyaji and I found him to be in an extremely reasonable frame of mind. He was very appreciative of the work and he thoroughly approved of the idea of federation. The next day, that is to say on Sunday the 8th of February, I had a long conversation with Mr Gandhi and other Congress leaders including Malaviyaji, Pundit Jawahar Lal Nehru, Dr Ansari and Mr J.M. Sen Gupta. The conversation lasted from 1 o'clock in the afternoon to 7 o'clock in the evening. Mr Gandhi mostly listened to the conversation and did not express any definite views. . . . Yesterday, that is to say on the 8th February, we again resumed out conversation for several hours. Most of the preliminary conditions which he wants to be fulfilled are such that I can support him . . . We then discussed the constitutional issues at the Round Table Conference at great length. Pundit Jawahar Lal's main objection was that we got no control over the army, that we could not reduce the salaries of the services, that the Princes and the landlords were reactionary bodies, that the constitution as framed by the Round Table Conference would place the power in the hands of the vested interests and not bring any relief to the masses, that the financial safeguards were bad, and last that the army expenditure and the salaries of the public services would swallow such a large figure that nothing would be left to the Indian Government of the future to do anything for the masses. I contended everyone of these propositions. In short his attitude was very hostile. On the other hand Pundit Malaviya and Dr Ansari were obviously very anxious that a settlement should take place and they approved in substance the scheme outlined at the Round Table Conference. Today I have not gone to them as they are sitting in secret conclave and discussing the whole thing among themselves. Anyhow at 2 o'clock in the afternoon the information reached me that the position was slightly hopeful. At Mr Gandhi's request I have sent telegrams to Sastri and Jayakar to come and they are coming today.[82]

Sapru was also in touch with Irwin – 'I of course understand that you cannot come to Delhi till you have finished everything you can do in Allahabad.'[83] Jayakar and he saw the Viceroy on 15 February and arranged for Gandhi to meet him. The Gandhi–Irwin discussions followed. On 1 March they looked like breaking down over Gandhi's demand for an inquiry into 'police outrages'. Sapru and Jayakar intervened to support the Mahatma. 'I am afraid,' Irwin told Wedgwood Benn, 'partly by design and partly by accident, I rather lost my temper with them.'[84] They seem to have told Gandhi that Irwin would not give way; Gandhi acquiesced; and on 3 March the Gandhi–Irwin pact was settled. Gandhi called off the Civil Disobedience campaign and agreed to attend the next session of the Round Table Conference. Sapru had got him to do what he had twice before failed to get him to do.[85]

> While I recognise the wonderful work done by the Viceroy and Mr Gandhi [Sankey, the Lord Chancellor, wrote to him shortly afterwards] I know and feel personally that the real praise is due to you and to Mr Jayakar – I have seen the hands of the clock move, and I know that you and he have been the mainspring. . . . I am looking forward to joining with you again in our great task of bringing peace and happiness to India. I have no misgivings as to the ultimate result of our labours.[86]

Sankey's faith was not misplaced, but it was by no means all plain sailing. Gandhi very nearly did not attend the second Round Table Conference at the end of 1931. When it met a number of new complications, for example regarding the attitude of the Princes, had arisen. On his return to India Gandhi clashed with the new Viceroy, Lord Willingdon, and Civil Disobedience was renewed. Having now twice gone ahead successfully when all around him were crying 'boycott', Sapru was not to be deterred a third time. However in 1932 he resigned from any participation in further discussions with the British when the Government, inadvertently it would seem, appeared to be resiling from the Conference method. The Government, however, very quickly made amends. Sapru and a smaller number of Indian delegates attended the third Round Table Conference in 1932, as well as the meetings of the Joint Select Committee of both Houses which followed, at which he much enjoyed cross-examining some of the Conservative die-hards. He was by no means satisfied with the eventual result; but nothing supervened to put an end to the shifting of the logjam to which he had contributed more than any other man back in 1930.

X

The significance of the change which occurred can be measured in several ways. Two must suffice. Right at the end of 1932, after the second Round Table Conference had dispersed, Hoare, the new – Conservative – Secretary of State for India, had an exchange of telegrams with the Viceroy, Lord Willingdon. Willingdon was objecting to the cost of various missions which were being sent out from London – to do with finance, the franchise and so on. Hoare tartly replied, however, that he regarded it as the highest degree impolitic to have attempted to constitute these Committees without considerable leavening of Parliamentary membership.[87]

The political margin in Britain was so narrow that it was evidently necessary to resort to every expedient he could find to keep the coalition of liberal Conservatives, Liberals and Labour which was in favour of Indian reform in being. Without the positive response which Sapru and his associates had made at the first Round Table Conference it is difficult to think that it could have been constituted; and the consequences can be imagined. 'It is indeed curious [Sir Malcolm Hailey wrote to Lord Willingdon in 1933] that we should now find a small band of Conservative politicians who are pleading the Indian cause with all the fervour ... which was once displayed by Mr Montagu and who seem willing to run on the dangers which fell to his lot.'[88]

The change can be seen too in the *volte face* of a man like the Liberal party delegate, Lord Lothian. Before the Conference met he was foremost in insisting that the British parties must club together to resist any concession to men even of Sapru's outlook. After the Conference he was still concerned about British party unity: but for the rest his tune was now very different.

Everything ... to my mind [he wrote to Reading in July 1931] depends upon keeping the unity of the British delegation during the last stages of negotiations so as to ensure that whatever else may happen, a new constitution can be put on the Statute Book during the coming winter. The Parliament of Great Britain is the only body which can act in present circumstances and it is responsible for doing so. But if Great Britain does succeed in putting a reasonable solution of the Indian problem on the Statute Book, that is, one which reasonable opinion in India will privately agree is a fair solution there is, I think, good hope of a repetition of what happened in 1921. The choice before India will then be either to work it or **to** go into revolution. There will no doubt be a non-cooperation party as in 1921, but if enough Indians come forward to work the constitution as they did in 1921, the bulk of the non-cooperation will gradually come to heel as they did in India.[89]

So it transpired. The Act took very much longer than anyone anticipated to put on the Statute book, but the strategy succeeded. In all essentials it was Sapru's.

India would have been independent without Sapru, but the manner in which it became independent owed a great deal to men of his ilk; and one may reasonably doubt if India would have become independent without a violent revolution, or would then have sustained a parliamentary system of Government, but for his efforts and those of his colleagues in the tumultuous years 1929–31.

The enthisiasm which non-cooperation and civil disobedience served to generate did not by itself succeed in making the British move. It had, moreover, a way of running out into the sand. This had happened in 1922. It was happening again in 1931. It happened by 1934. The immediate effect on India's advance towards independence of the civil disobedience movement of 1930 was in fact limited. If anything, it only stiffened the British attitude towards independence for India. It was certainly never as successful in bringing the British to their knees as the earlier non-cooperation movement had been in December 1921. In a situation such as that of 1930 in which unrelieved opposition prevailed all along the line, the manœuvrings of Sapru and his like alone set things moving once again.

It must not be suggested that the civil disobedience movement served no purpose whatsoever. On the contrary, even within the limited sphere in which men like Sapru operated, it was of major importance. As nothing else ever did it made the British aware that enthusiasm for Indian nationalism had spread wide and deep and was not to be assuaged by anything less than a fundamental change in India's Government. For the British this meant that they had an enhanced and indeed now quite stark 'Indian problem' on their hands. In showing them a way by which they might deal with it within the terms of their own political traditions, Sapru and his colleagues were immensely strengthened by the ghoulish vision they could conjure up of the alternative. In a very real sense it was only Gandhi's civil disobedience movement which made Sapru's work possible.

But there is a very real sense too in which only he and men of his kind knew how to exploit the political force which civil disobedience had generated in a way which would make the British take a positive step forward. Gandhi himself seems to have recognised this. Immediately after his pact with Irwin he turned to Sapru, Jayakar and Sastri for a full explanation of the more complicated details of the settlement with the British which the first Round Table Conference had adumbrated.[90] And there can be little doubt that it was their unequalled ability to push ahead creatively with a full-scale settlement with the British when all the world around them was in storm which gave them their peculiar strength and their peculiar influence over events. It was also because they saw the way out of the impasse in terms which the British understood (and found that, despite a long series of fits and starts, it sufficed for the purpose) that no irretrievable damage was done to the traditions of British political practice which had begun to take root in India, so that they survived into the period of independence.

At the crucial moment the joker in the pack was Federation. It was never in fact established, and the Princes enthusiasm for it steadily evaporated as the '30s wore on. In its day, however, it served a vital purpose. It was the lever by which the British were moved to accept 'responsibility at the centre' – a decision from which so much else followed. It was frankly stated that it was only because the Princes would provide a 'stabilising force' at the centre that 'responsibility at the centre' could be allowed.[91] But on this issue Sapru for one was not concerned to quibble. Responsibility at the centre, even on terms, was, he believed, the first essential. Other changes could follow. He quickly discovered that there was no hope of securing this by asking for Dominion Status. It could be achieved, however, by asking for Federation. So this is what he pressed for.

During the last four years of his life he was for the most part bed-ridden. He died in 1949. He thought Partition a disaster. For him, as to some extent for Jawaharlal Nehru too, it meant a cleavage right down the middle of his own being. But for the rest Sapru died happy. He had seen India independent, with an established parliamentary régime, a system of cabinet government, all of it subject to the rule of law. He missed by a few weeks the London Declaration of 1949 whereby India retained its place within the Commonwealth when it became a republic, but the principle had been settled before he died. He could scarcely have asked for more.

It may be argued, of course, that if men of Sapru's cast of mind had continued to stand with Gandhi, not merely during 1927 and 1928 but during 1929 and 1930 the threat to the British position which was generated in India would have been very much greater. Of this indeed there need be little doubt – as the events of December 1921 would suggest.[92] Perhaps they should have been more resolute. But three things may be said about this. First, there is no evidence that the British would then have made a quicker exit. In 1929 they no longer suffered from the guilt complexes of Jallianwallah Bagh, as they had in 1921; and they were in no mood to treat unmitigated defiance with anything but hostility (tempered only by their readiness to introduce a modicum of change at a time of their own choosing). Secondly, Congress made no real move to meet men like Sapru halfway. If – as is clear – the moderates held the key to the situation on more than one occasion, the responsibility belonged to Congress if they treated them only with disdain. Sapru, of course, never had a popular political following. But a man who stands in the centre as he did, is not dependent for his influence upon a following; his strength derives from the fact that he is known to be independent, and in this respect it was very great indeed. It might have been exploited more. And then thirdly, it is necessary to insist that it was never spinelessness which determined the actions of a man like Sapru; but rather profound convictions. He was shocked to the core by the apparent refusal of the British at the time of Simon's appointment to allow Indians to participate fully in the making of their own constitution. But when in 1929–30 they seemed to be mending their ways he was amongst the first to seize the new opportunity. He had in these circumstances little patience with the alternative – which in any event he believed to be greatly destructive of much that was vital for India's future. Irwin (who became adept at putting the moderate point of view) expressed the sentiments of a man like Sapru exactly when he asked in July 1930:

> Is it not a very dangerous doctrine to preach to citizens of India that it is patriotic or laudable to refuse to obey laws or pay taxes? Human nature is often reluctant to do either; and if there is anything certain it is that, if society is once thoroughly inoculated with these noxious microbes the disease will perpetually recur, until one day it paralyses the Indian Government of the future which, by these methods, it is sought to bring into existence. It may not be too long before Indian ministers are responsible, for example, for the assessment and collection of land revenue or other taxes. They could have little cause to thank those who had allowed the impression to gain ground that the withholding of payments legally due was a proper method of voicing general political dissatisfaction with the established Ministry.[93]

It was because a man like Sapru held such beliefs so profoundly that he was ready to go into the political wilderness if his fellow countrymen would not heed him.

He had little patience with the cruder imperialists' jargon about the state of India prior to the British advent – or with its contemporary equivalent that lived on sidelong glances at the warlords' China. But he had little time either for Gandhi's lauding of *Ram Raj*; still less for the more apocalyptic doctrines of the Indian political left or the Indian political right. He wanted progress, but he also wanted order; and he had a profound concern, in an India that could not go back (for example to widespread traditional rulership), for the relationship between them. These indeed were the issues which dominated his thinking, and there can be little doubt that the eventual result – which eventually took a shape along lines of which he very much approved, and for which he had long been working – owed more to his efforts than has been generally recognised.

It is not difficult to see that his whole approach derived from the distinctive series of attributes which had come to make up his nature, and which had come to him from the surroundings in which he had been engendered – his family, his community, his education, and his profession, in all their various aspects. These had laid the foundations for the man that he was; and in the manner discussed here, had political consequences which were nothing less than immense. In the study of modern Indian history we are now much more aware than we used to be of the genesis of, the part played by, and the dramatic consequences which follow from the particular complex of attributes which mark a regional society, a religious community, a caste association, an élite, a widely-ranging socio-economic category, or a complex of people, large or small, who share certain common traditions. We may remind ourselves that these things are true for individuals as well.

NOTES

1 R.K.Chaudhuri, *Indian Constituent Assembly Debates*, X, No. 3, 38, quoted by Dietmar Rothermund, 'Constitutional Reforms versus National Agitation in India, 1900–1950', *Journal of Asian Studies*, XXI, No. 4, August 1962, p. 521.

2 Robert Blake, 'Baldwin and the Right', John Raymond (ed.). *The Baldwin Age*, London 1960, p. 65.

3 Rushbrook Williams to Sapru, 7 Aug. 1945, Sapru Papers (hereinafter SP), National Library of India, Belvedere, Calcutta. I am much indebted to Sri A.N. Sapru, I.C.S. for giving me access to his father's papers, and for much other help besides.

4 Amery to Smuts, 13 Nov. 1942, Smuts Papers, Vol. 67, No. 17. I am much indebted to Sir Keith Hancock for drawing my attention to this letter. It is quoted by permission of the Trustees of the Smuts Archive.

5 There is some useful information in S.C.Ghosh, 'Decision-making and power in the British Conservative Party: A case-study of the Indian problem 1929–34', *Political Studies*, XIII, June 1965, No. 2, pp. 198–212.

6 Sastri to V.S.Ramaswami Sastri, 30 Oct. 1930, T.N.Jagadishan, *Letters o Srinivasa Sastri*, London 1963, p. 199.

7 Sastri to Kunzru, 3 July 1931, ibid., p. 213.

8 Jawaharlal Nehru, *An Autobiography*, new edn. Bombay 1962, p. 34.

9 For all these details I am greatly indebted to Sri A.N. Sapru, I.C.S., and his elder brother Sri P. N. Sapru.

10 This episode is elaborately recounted both in the Smuts Papers and in the Sapru Papers. Sir Keith Hancock, the biographer of Smuts, and I will each be giving more extensive accounts elsewhere.

11 Sapru to Satyamurti, 1 June 1922, Satyamurti Papers. I am indebted to H.F.Owen for this reference, and the next.

12 Sapru to Annie Besant, 1 July 1922, Adyar Archives.

13 The Adyar Archives give details.

14 Sir Tej Bahadur Sapru, *The Indian Constitution*, Madras 1926.

15 *Report of the Reforms Enquiry Committee* (1924).

16 Sapru, loc. cit, p. vi.

17 Hailey in the Imperial Legislative Council, 8 Feb. 1924, *Debates* 1924, Vol. IV, Pt I, p. 365.

18 Presidential address, All-India Liberal Federation, 27 Dec. 1927, *Indian Annual Register*, 1927, Vol. II, pp. 425–9.

19 Rafi Ahmad Kidwai, *The Proceedings of the All-Parties National Convention*, Allahabad, n.d.

20 E.g. Irwin to Halifax, 1 April 1929, Halifax Papers (hereinafter HP) 29; Irwin to Peel, 4 April 1929, HP 5. Before he died the late Earl of Halifax generously gave me permission to see his papers.

21 E.g. Note by Irwin, 11 Jan. 1929; Irwin to Peel, 24 Jan., 28 Feb. 1929, HP 5.

22 Irwin to Peel, 4 April 1929, HP 5.

23 Irwin to Birkenhead, 13, 28 June 1928; Birkenhead to Irwin, 28 July 1928, HP 4.

24 Halifax in conversation with the author, May 1959, see Irwin to Halifax 5 June 1928, HP 27.

25 Irwin to Birkenhead, 13, 28 June 1928; Birkenhead to Irwin, 28 July 1928, HP 4.

26 Irwin to Benn, 13 June 1929, HP 5.

27 See Pole to Sapru, 6 June 1929, SP G112.

28 Sapru to Irwin, 23 July 1929, SP 15.

29 'Narrative of events leading up to the publication of the letters between Sir J. Simon and The Prime Minister, and of the Viceroy's Statement', 4 Nov. 1929, HP 5.

30 Benn to Irwin, tel., Irwin to Benn, tel., 29 Oct. 1929, HP 10.

31 *The Gazette of India*, 31 Oct. 1929.

32 Sapru to Irwin, 30 Oct. 1929, SP 18.

33 S. Gopal, *The Viceroyalty of Lord Irwin*, Oxford 1957, p. 51; Irwin to Benn, tel.; 2 Nov. 1929, HP 10.

34 Sapru to Irwin, 11 Nov. 1929, SP 19.

35 Patel to Sapru, 8 Nov. 1929, SP P11.

36 Sapru to Patel, 11 Nov. 1929, SP P12.

37 Sapru to Natesan, 11 Nov. 1929, SP N16: Sapru to Munshi, 15 Nov. 1929, SP M171.

38 Sapru to Irwin, 25 Nov. 1929, SP I13.

39 Patel to Sapru, 19 Nov. 1929, SP P15.

40 Shiva Rao to Sapru, 15 Nov. 1929, SP R73.

41 E.g. Sapru to Thakurdas, 24 Nov. 1929, SP T12.

42 Sapru to Graham Pole and Polak, 9 Jan. 1930, SP G121.

43 Gopal, *Irwin*, Ch. V.

44 E.g. Munshi to Sapru, 10, 20 Nov. 1929, SP M170, 172.

45 Sapru's undated statement, SP Misc. 7: Sapru to Ramaswami Aiyar, 14 Jan. 1930, SP A121.

46 Sapru to Irwin, 20 April 1930, SP I30.

47 Irwin to Sapru, 8 May 1930, SP I33.

48 Sapru to Irwin, 24, 31 May, 12 June 1930, SP I34, 36, 38.

49 Irwin to Sapru, 17 June 1930, SP I34: Irwin to Benn, 4 June 1930, HP 6.

50 See Irwin to Benn, 19 June 1930, HP 6.

51 Irwin to Benn, 28 June 1930, Reading Papers (hereinafter RP) 57. I am greatly indebted to the Dowager Marchioness of Reading for special permission to see some of her husband's papers.

52 Irwin's speech Imperial Legislative Assembly, 9 July 1930.

53 Slocombe to Sapru, 23 June 1930, SP S378.

54 Sapru to Irwin, 6 July 1930, SP I43.

55 Irwin to Halifax, 7 July 1930, HP 27.

56 Irwin to Benn, 18 July 1930, HP 6.

57 *Statement . . . by Sir Tej Bahadur Sapru and Mr M. R. Jayakar . . .* Cmd 3728, 1930.

58 Sapru to Irwin, 19 Sept. 1930, SP I60.

59 Note by Finance Secretary (with marginal comments), 27 July 1930, New Delhi, National Archives of India (hereinafter NAI) Reforms 67/VIII/30R.

60 Minutes of Liberal Delegation to Round Table Conference, 5 Nov. 1930, RP 56g.

61 Note, 18 Aug. 1930, on NAI Reforms 67/X/30R.

62 Sapru's speech at opening of R.T.C. see below.

63 Irwin to Hailey, 10 Jan. 1931, Hailey Papers, 34. I am much indebted to Lord Hailey for special permission to see his papers.

64 See Proceedings of the Informal Conference at the Viceregal Lodge, 14 July 1930, Chamber of Princes Archives, Patiala, V, 16.

65 The Princes at a meeting in Simla in July 1930 'decided in favour of co-operation in carrying out the design of ultimate federation of India', *The Times*, 15 July 1930.

66 Menon to Dunnett, 6 Nov. 1930, NAI Reforms 173/30I.

67 Sapru to P. N. Sapru, 23 Oct. 1930, SP Misc. 15.

68 Benn to Irwin, 13 Nov. 1930, NAL Reforms 147/30R.

69 *Manchester Guardian*, 17 Oct. 1930, also 6, 11 Nov.

70 Benn to Irwin, 7 Nov. 1930, NAI Reforms 147/30R.

71 Sapru to P. N. Sapru, 14 Nov. 1930, SP R66.

72 See also *Manchester Guardian* leader, 12 Nov. 1930.

73 *Indian Round Table Conference Proceedings, 12 November 1930–19 January 1931*, Cmd 3778, 1931.

74 Sapru to P. N. Sapru, 19 Nov. 1930, SP S17.

75 Haig to Dunnett, 19 Nov. 1920, NAI Reforms 147/30R.

76 Minutes, RP 57g.

77 Sapru to P. N. Sapru, 19 Nov. 1930, SP S17.

78 Hailey to Irwin, 15 Dec. 1930, Hailey Papers, 34.

79 Benn to Irwin, 13 Jan. 1931, HP 6.

80 Lewis to Dunnett, 6 Jan. 1930, NAI Reforms 173/30R.

81 See *Proceedings*, p. 506.

82 Sapru to Bikaner, 11 Feb. 1931, SP S174.

83 Irwin to Sapru, 12 Feb. 1931, SP I65.

84 Irwin to Benn, 2 March 1931, HP 6.
85 Gopal, *Irwin*, pp. 89 sqq.
86 Sankey to Sapru, 30 March 1931, two letters, SP S6/2 and 3.
87 Hoare to Willingdon tel. 20 Dec. 1931, NAI Reforms 182/31/Rd K.W.
88 Hailey to Willingdon, 26 April 1933, Hailey Papers.
89 Lothian to Reading, 17 July 1931, RP 56h.
90 Sapru to Bhopal, 10 March 1931, SP H162.
91 E.g. Minutes Liberal Delegation, R.T.C. 19 Nov. 1930, RP 56g.
92 I have discussed this in 'The Government of India and the first non-cooperation movement 1920–22', *Journal of Asian Studies*, XXV, No. 2, February 1966, pp. 241–59.
93 Irwin's speech, Imperial Legislative Assembly, 9 July 1930.

11

SYAMA PRASAD MOOKERJEE AND THE COMMUNALIST ALTERNATIVE

★

B. D. Graham

On 24 June 1953, Indian newspapers carried headlines announcing that Dr Syama Prasad Mookerjee had died while under detention in Srinagar. He had been arrested on 11 May as he attempted to cross a bridge over the river Ravi and enter the State of Jammu and Kashmir from the Punjab; his jeep had been halted by the Jammu police, who had served him with a government order forbidding him to enter the State on the grounds that he was 'about to act in a manner prejudicial to the Public Safety and peace . . .' This was the culmination of a noisy campaign during which Mookerjee, as a spokesman of extremist Hindu groups, had associated himself with the demand of Jammu's Dogra community that the State of Jammu and Kashmir should be brought fully under the Indian Constitution. When Mookerjee had made it clear that he had no intention of turning back, the police had at once produced an order of arrest, and after a long and uncomfortable ride to Srinagar, he had been placed under custody in a small cottage about eight miles from the city. He had begun to challenge the legality of his detention before the High Court of Jammu and Kashmir when he fell ill and died suddenly on 23 June.

The news produced a widespread reaction. Mookerjee's party, the Bharatiya Jana Sangh, was disturbed:

> Oh Heaven's weep! Bharat Bhushan Dr Shyama Prasad Mookerji is dead. Dead or murdered?

exclaimed its unofficial journal, the *Organiser*.[1] His native Calcutta, where his body was burnt on the Keortala Ghat, mourned him as one of its heroes. But for those liberal politicians and intellectuals who had seen in Mookerjee one of the outstanding men of their generation, the tragedy was of another order: as the Prime Minister told the Lok

Sabha, 'In any event his passing away would have been sad and a great blow to this House and the country, but in the peculiar circumstances in which this took place, naturally this added to our sorrow.'[2] How had Mookerjee, a former Vice-Chancellor of Calcutta University, an ex-Minister of the Union Cabinet, and a powerful opposition leader in the national parliament, allowed himself to become involved in the agitational politics which the Jana Sangh had made its *forte*? There were elements of tragedy, a uniquely Indian tragedy, about Mookerjee's last years. Despite his immoderate attacks on Pakistan and his admiration for the virtues of Hindu culture and tradition, Mookerjee was basically a rational man and a liberal. Why was it that he had rejected the ideals of secularism and moderate nationalism which animated such men as Jawarharlal Nehru, Maulana Azad, Govind Ballabh Pant and B. C. Roy? In posing this question we are also posing a question about Indian society in the decade after partition, for when Mookerjee definitely turned his face towards communalism and agitation, he became a hero for many thousands of his countrymen.

I

Mookerjee belonged to the Bengal bhadralok, a landed group which, early in the nineteenth century, had sensed the opportunities offered by Calcutta, the mode of Britain's commercial and political empire in India, and the importance of English education as a means of entry to the professions and the civil service. In Calcutta, they had begun to explore the relevance of Western ideas to their own experience and, as they became increasingly an urban class, their attitude towards the new culture became more ambivalent. Anxiety to avoid the rootlessness which alienation from their own traditions seemed to threaten caused them to strive for the highest standards of achievement in their new world. In literature, in law, and in the universities they succeeded; in politics they were frustrated, for while they admired and wanted to work British forms of government, particularly a fully representative parliament, many British administrators mistrusted or even despised them. The hardest blow to bhadralok pride came when Lord Curzon, Viceroy between 1898 and 1905, reduced the representative character of the Calcutta Corporation, increased official control over the city's University, and brought about the partition of Bengal, thereby diminishing the power of the Province's political leaders. From about 1905, bhadralok politics began to shift ominously towards extremism and violence and the annulment of partition in 1912 came too late to reverse the trend; the old style of liberal constitutionalism, personified by leaders such as Surendranath Banerjea, was still in evidence, but it was already giving way to a new style marked by strong anti-liberal, anti-European sentiments and by agitational and potentially violent methods. This was not a difference between generations so much as a difference between *tempéraments* or ways of feeling. In each bhadralok leader two men were at war – the liberal constitutionalist and the romantic revolutionary.[3]

In many ways, the story of Mookerjee's family is typical of the bhadralok pattern. His grandfather, Gangaprasad, came to Calcutta with his three brothers in the 1850s after the death of their father, and none of them appear to have retained any important economic links with their ancestral village, Jirat, in the Hooghly District. One of the first graduates of Calcutta University, Gangaprasad was awarded his B.A. in 1861 and his M.B. in 1866; he established himself as a general practitioner in the suburb of Bhowanipur and became a champion of Bengali traditions, publishing medical works in the vernacular and a Bengali version of the Ramayana. His son, Ashutosh (Syama Prasad's father), joined the famous Presidency College in 1880 and graduated M.A. in 1885. At first he thought of a career in higher mathematics but turned instead to law; here he did extremely well and in 1904 was appointed to the bench of the Calcutta High Court, a position which he held until just before his death in 1924. He dabbled in politics, was a member of the Bengal Legislative Council (1899–1904) and of the Imperial Legislative Council (1903–4) before joining the High Court, but his great interest was in the University, of which he was Vice-Chancellor between 1906 and 1914 and again between 1921 and 1923. He played an important part in building up the University's post-graduate work and encouraging its teaching of Indian vernacular languages. In one important respect, however, his career was untypical of the bhadralok. Most of his able contemporaries, such as Banerjea, lived for some time in England and were able to observe at first hand the workings of the British political system, thereby gaining a greater understanding of the values of constitutional liberalism. Ashutosh was unable to do so. His mother, a model of Brahman orthodoxy, made him decline Curzon's invitation to visit England and this gap in his experience seems to have affected his outlook fundamentally.[4]

Syama Prasad was born on 6 July 1901.[5] Like his father he was educated at Presidency College, from which he graduated B.A. with honours in 1921. His impressionable years were spent during the decade which saw the First World War, the growth of terrorist activities amongst bhadralok youth, the activities of the Home Rule Leagues, the disturbances caused by the prospect of the Montagu–Chelmsford reforms, and the increase in communal tension between Muslims and Hindus in Calcutta. His generation found its heroes in men such as Chittaranjan Das, who successfully challenged Banerjea's leadership of the Bengali Congress only to find himself, in his turn, faced with the problem of checking the Party's drift towards political extremism and Hindu communalism. When his father died in 1924, Syama Prasad appeared to be on the threshold of a successful legal career; having obtained his B.L. he enrolled as an advocate in the High Court, went to London to study at Lincoln's Inn, and was called to the English Bar in 1927. After his return to Calcutta he began to show some interest in politics; elected to the Bengal Legislative Council as a Congress member from the University constituency in 1929, he had to resign when the Congress began its Council boycott in the following year; however, he stood as an independent in the same constituency and was re-elected in 1931. Like his father, he took a special interest in the affairs of the University, and served as its Vice-Chancellor between 1934 and 1938.

By that time he was regarded as one of the leaders of the Bengali community and he reflected the frustration and insecurity which it felt in the face of continued British hostility and the rise of new social forces in the Province. The Muslim élite, headed by such men as Fazlul Huq, H. S. Suhrawardy and Sir Khwaja Nazimuddin and possessed of a strong mass following amongst the peasantry, was beginning to aggregate power rapidly; the *Namasudras*, low-caste Hindus, were responding to the sectional appeals of leaders such as Jogendra Nath Mandal; the bhadralok, their professional opportunities shrinking, their numbers increasing and their political power declining, were thinking increasingly in terms of authoritarian and violent forms of political action; and the Congress Party, weakened by a period of factional strife, was being slowly rebuilt by Subash Chandra Bose but remained a shadow of its former self. In such a situation, Mookerjee stood as an outspoken champion of Hindu rights. As early as 1930 he had opposed legislation designed to curb terrorist activities and had agitated against the Communal Award of 1932, which gave Muslims special electoral privileges. Elected to the Legislative Assembly in 1937, he began to gravitate steadily towards the Hindu Mahasabha, an avowedly communal and anti-Congress party, which he joined after encouragement from its president, Veer Savarkar, and from Dr Keshav Baliram Hedgewar, the leader of the Rashtriya Swayamsevak Sangh (RSS).[6] Mookerjee took a prominent part in the Annual Convention of the All-Indian Hindu Mahasabha in 1939, was its Acting President between 1940 and 1944, and became President of the Bengal Sabha in 1941.

The Hindu Mahasabha and the RSS were at that time the two most militant and firmly based political centres of Hindu communalism.[7] However, although both belonged to a tradition of revivalism and reformism which goes back to the Arya Samaj and to the writings of Dayanand Sarasvati and Vivekananda, their formal origins and early activities were widely separated. The Hindu Mahasabha of the '30s was composed of several different movements, each of which was strongly rooted in the politics of its province. In some cases the Hindu tradition-alists in Congress chose to limit their activities to argument and protest against the secular character of the national movement and its tolerance of Muslim claims, but in others they were taking a separate part in election campaigns. In the United Provinces election of 1926, for example, Madan Mohan Malaviya organised a Hindu traditionalist party in opposition to the *Swaraj* party led by Motilal Nehru.[8] In the early '30s, however, the Hindu Mahasabha as a whole became much more independent of Congress and much more willing to envisage separate electoral action. Under Veer Savarkar, who became its President on his release from prison in 1937 and remained so until 1942, the Mahasabha began to think of itself as a political party in its own right. The RSS, on the other hand, had never swerved from its course. Founded by Dr Hedgewar in 1925, it was organised on lines strongly reminiscent of the Italian blackshirts, with a military chain of command between clearly differentiated levels of leadership connecting rigidly disciplined units called *shakhas*. The members of each *shakha* attended daily training sessions devoted to drill in the use of *lathi* sticks, calisthenics and physical exercise, and were taught the virtues of unquestioning obedience to leadership and the principles of the Sangh's command and authoritarian ideology. For about a decade the organisation's membership was con-fined almost entirely to the Chitpavan Brahmans of Maharashtra, but the movement later spread through the towns of North India, until by 1938 there were some 400 RSS centres with a membership of 40,000 young Hindus.[9] After Hedgewar's death in 1940, Madav Sadashiv Golwalkar became the leader of the organisation. He, like Hedgewar, was not prepared to allow RSS members to play an open part in party politics; the true measure of their political importance was their potential capacity for agitational work and their unusual discipline.

In the Mahasabha and the RSS Hindu communalism had the means for political activity of either the constitutional or the agitational kind. The emergence of those organisations was in one sense a response by Hindu traditionalists to the rise of the Muslim League and its para-military extensions, particularly in Bengal, the United Provinces and the Punjab, and it betrayed their widespread fear that the Congress Party would make too many concessions to keep the Muslim community within a united nationalist movement. They extended their activities in the late '30s because they recognised that the acceptance of the Government of India Act of 1935 by the Congress Party had fundament-ally altered the character of Indian politics; by deciding to contest elections under the Act, the Congress had virtually signified its accept-ance of parliamentary institutions and a federal constitution for India. In terms of organisation, this meant that any political movement which hoped to increase its strength had to devote much more effort than previously towards electoral and parliamentary work while maintaining its capacity for agitation in the event of a future clash with the British. The Hindu Mahasabha represented the vehicle for electoral and parlia-mentary activities under the new constitution just as the RSS represented the potential for agitation. Mookerjee was himself aware of both per-spectives, and though he decided to join the Mahasabha because its ideals coincided more closely with his own, he also appears to have established contacts with the RSS.[10]

There are grounds for assuming that family influence also contributed to Mookerjee's decision to join the Mahasabha. In most bhadralok families, the mother, lacking the father's appreciation of Western culture, remained strongly attached to tradition, with the result that the children found the conflict of values actually personified in their home. In a fascinating passage of his autobiography, Banerjea describes how, although his father helped him in his plans to visit England, his mother considered the idea a terrible one and fainted with shock when she heard that he was actually about to go.[11] Syama Prasad's grandmother not only prevented his father from visiting England, but almost persuaded him not to accept his High Court post, the highest position open to an Indian, because she could not reconcile herself to her son's accepting service under the British.[12] His mother, the daughter of a respectable Krishnagar pandit, appears to have held equally strong views, and after the death of his wife in 1933, she was one of the most important influences on Syama Prasad's life. After his death in 1953 she declared: 'I had long dedicated my son for selfless service to the country and my son sacrificed his life for the cause of the motherland.'[13]

In the period 1940-7, Mookerjee was an important figure both in national and in Bengali politics. Within the Province he pitted the Mahasabha forces against Congress (he clashed with the Subash Bose machine in the Calcutta Corporation elections of 1940) and also against the Muslim League. Bengal was one of the Provinces which Congress had failed to capture in the 1937 elections and Fazlul Huq, the Muslim leader of the Krishak Proja Party, had been able to form a ministry. In August 1941, however, when he resigned from the Working Committee of the All-India Muslim League after a clash with Jinnah, his Muslim following in the Bengal Assembly broke up and a purely Muslim League group was formed under the leadership of Khwaja Nazimuddin. Huq resigned, arranged an alliance with other groups including the Mahasabha and in December 1941 formed a coalition ministry in which Mookerjee held the Finance portfolio. According to Madhok, Mookerjee's object was to prevent Huq's being thrown back into the arms of the League;[14] he resigned in November 1942 as a protest against the Provincial Governor's policy of repression which followed the Quit India campaign. In March 1943 Huq relinquished his post to make way for a Muslim League government headed by Nazimuddin and backed by J. N. Mandal's Scheduled Caste group. Mookerjee meanwhile continued to play a leading role in Bengali affairs; he organised relief during the terrible famine of 1943, founded an English daily newspaper, the *Nationalist*, in 1944, backed the Calcutta students who celebrated the National Army day in 1945, and formed the Hindustan National Guard during the communal rioting of 1946.

As one of the national leaders of the Mahasabha, he played an important part in the negotiations at the time of the Cripps Mission of 1942 and, after the war, in those which led to independence and partition. In 1942 he had backed the Congress line, but in 1946 he stood out against partition and against equal representation for Hindus and Muslims in the central government. When partition finally appeared inevitable, he became the spokesman for those who demanded that Bengal should not be regarded as a Muslim province, but that it should be divided into western (predominantly Hindu) and eastern (predominantly Muslim) portions.[15] Elected to the Interim Constituent Assembly from Bengal, he accepted a post in the first cabinet of independent India as Minister of Industries and Supplies, taking office on 15 August 1947. About this time, he advised the Working Committee of the Hindu Mahasabha to reorient its policies and confine its activities to social and cultural work as he saw no need for a separate political organisation confined to

Hindus as such after the attainment of independence. At first his suggestion went unheeded but the public reaction against communal organisations after the assassination of Gandhi persuaded the Mahasabha to give
way, and the Working Committee foreswore party politics on 15
February 1948. By November, however, it was once again beginning to
make political statements, criticising the Congress Party for having
accepted the idea of partition. Mookerjee resigned from its Working
Committee at the end of the month, and on 26 December, the organisation formally decided to resume political activity.[16]

By his resignation from the Mahasabha, Mookerjee at forty-seven
appeared to have reached a turning-point in his political career. As a
national politician he lacked both party and cause, and there seemed
little chance of his finding a place in the State politics of West Bengal,
where another son of the bhadralok, B. C. Roy, had just established himself as Congress Chief Minister, a position which he was to retain until
his death in 1962. With partition an accepted fact, and with the easing
of communal tensions in India, the old style of Mahasabha extremism
seemed hopelessly outmoded. Other than by joining the Congress
Party, Mookerjee appeared to have little political future. However,
certain events were soon to change the situation radically. In February
1950, there came news of communal rioting in Calcutta.

II

As always in such situations, there are several versions of how the
communal troubles began. Most Indian accounts state that the disturbances broke out in Kalshira village, in the Khulna District of East
Pakistan on 20 December 1949, when a small police party is alleged to
have mistreated women who refused to give information about Com-
munist suspects, whereupon they were attacked by villagers and one
policeman was killed. On the following day a larger party of police and
militia, aided by local Muslims, surrounded the area, destroyed houses
and assaulted a number of villagers, some of whom eventually escaped
across the border into West Bengal. Apart from the fact that the villagers
were Hindus, this had not been essentially a communal incident, but
once the refugees from Kalshira reached West Bengal, exaggerated
versions of their stories were repeated in Calcutta, where groups of
Hindus began attacking Muslims on 4 February. Within a week, rioting
had broken out in a number of parts of the city and in several surrounding districts such as Murshidabad. There were incidents in Dacca on the

10th, and later in Assam; then, at the end of the month, trouble broke out again in Calcutta and continued throughout March. Pakistani sources make light of the Kalshira incident and blame a Hindu Mahasabha conference, held in Calcutta between 24 and 26 December 1949, for intensifying the anti-Pakistan agitation which they allege had been going on for some time. They place the first riots as those resulting from the attack by Hindus on Muslims at Bongaon on 19 January and at places in the Murshidabad District on the 24th.[17]

The pattern of the conflict varied widely: in Calcutta, the attacks were directed mainly at the poor Muslims in the depressed quarters of the city, many of whom were employed in the jute mills; in Dacca, Pabna and other towns of East Pakistan, Muslim discontent vented itself against Hindu families engaged in business and in the professions; in the rural areas of East Pakistan, Hindu low-caste groups, such as the Namasudras and the Santhals, were harassed by the dominant Muslim peasantry. Before long the migration of refugees had reached huge proportions: according to figures which Nehru gave to the Indian Parliament in August, 857,579 Hindus had crossed into India and 378,778 Muslims had left for Pakistan between 7 February and 8 April 1950.[18]

Although India and Pakistan each blamed the other for the outbreak of the rioting, the real causes lay well back in the history of undivided Bengal. The memories and bitterness of more than two decades of atrocities and counter-atrocities, from the Calcutta riots of 1918 to the Noakhali disturbances of October 1946, were still very much alive in 1950. The partition of 1947 had not separated Muslims and Hindus in the east of the sub-continent as it had, amid incredible violence, in the west: East Pakistan, with a total population of 42 millions in 1951, contained 9 million Hindus, while West Bengal numbered 5 million Muslims amongst its population of 26 millions. But although partition had not been accompanied by widespread disturbances in Bengal, it had left the minorities with a feeling of insecurity which was aggravated by the inefficiency of the administrations on each side of the border. According to Nehru, 1,600,000 East Bengalis had migrated from East to West Bengal in the period after partition, and the flow had not been completely staunched before the fresh wave in 1950.[19]

Economic distress undoubtedly contributed to communal unrest. In September 1949, Pakistan had refused to follow India in devaluing her rupee to conform with the devaluation of the sterling pound, and difficulties over negotiating a new exchange rate had brought trade between the two countries to a standstill in December. India then took the drastic step of stopping coal supplies to Pakistan on the grounds that the latter was holding up deliveries of raw jute. East Bengal, which had produced 75 per cent of undivided India's jute was left with stocks of which it could not dispose, while in the West Bengal mills which had previously processed it, the factory workers found themselves out of employment.[20] The economic depression further aggravated the *malaise* of Calcutta, cut off by partition from its traditional hinterland. The anger of the mobs which burnt and pillaged Muslim quarters was at one with the frustration of the Hindu commercial groups who had seen their trade dwindle after the division of the Province. In fact, the riots in Calcutta were as much anti-partition as anti-Muslim. As the *Statesman* complained, outsiders

do not fully appreciate how full West Bengal is of discontent with present conditions. It is not only that people are deeply conscious of the plight of East Bengal Hindus. They are constantly aware also of past glories and present potentialities. They do not forget either that Calcutta was long the country's capital or that Bengalis took the lead in the freedom movement. Once they swayed the destinies of India; now they cannot even determine their own.[21]

Law and order were not enforced rigidly enough on either side, and it is probable that stronger governmental action, both on the part of B.C. Roy's Congress ministry and of Nurul Amin's East Bengal cabinet, could have done much to lessen the disorder. Extremist politicians in Calcutta and in Dacca were given unnecessary licence during the early stages of the rioting, and the press of both cities competed in making inflammatory statements – the *Amrita Bazar Patrika* went so far as to take a poll of readers' opinions as to whether India should go to war with Pakistan.[22]

Mookerjee, who was at this time still a member of the Indian Central Government, felt as a Bengali and a Hindu that firmer action should have been taken against Pakistan and it is probable that inside the Cabinet he backed Patel's proposal for a hard line with Pakistan and an exchange of populations.[23] N.V. Gadgil, one of the members of the Cabinet, has claimed that 'a police action on the Hyderabad style was thought of. But the idea was abandoned as, in the opinion of the generals, such a step would have led to riots.'[24] Throughout the disturbances, Nehru stood out for a negotiated settlement, arguing that war between the two countries would bring disaster to the whole sub-continent, and, on 17 March, after several visits to Calcutta and to West Bengal, he told the Indian Parliament very firmly that he would consider neither war nor an exchange of populations as a solution. Instead, he suggested that he and Liaquat Ali Khan, the Prime Minister of Pakistan, should make a joint statement assuring the minorities in both countries of protection and fair treatment,[25] and Liaquat Ali accepted his invitation to visit Delhi with this end in view.

The disagreements which undoubtedly occurred inside the Indian Cabinet at this stage were hinted at in the press, but they appear to have been much more serious than was then admitted. Although the two Prime Ministers did not begin their talks until 2 April, the general principle of an agreement had already been considered by the Indian ministers, and Mookerjee is reported to have expressed his lack of confidence in Pakistan's good faith and to have pressed for the insertion of a penal clause to provide for sanctions against whichever country failed to honour the agreement. Since such a demand would almost certainly have wrecked the ensuing negotiations, Nehru and the more moderate ministers rejected it strongly.[26] In consequence, Mookerjee tendered his resignation on 1 April, in circumstances which have only recently been described by Gadgil, who sympathised with his objections. According to Gadgil:

> Syama Prasad openly attacked Pandiji's [sic] policy [towards Pakistan]. For a long time Panditji was calm. Syama Prasad said: 'When Muslims in Kashmir were attacked you sent Indian armed forces and spent crores of rupees. What do you care for us Bengali Hindus? What do you care for the criminal assaults on our women?' Suddenly Panditji stood up and began to advance towards Syama Prasad. That tiger of Bengal also raised his hand and stepped forward. For a moment it looked as if the Cabinet meeting would become a battle-field. But I pacified Syama Prasad. When things came to such a pass Patel left the meeting. A couple of other ministers also left. I said to Panditji: 'Half the Cabinet has gone away. I think the meeting should be adjourned.' Panditji calmed down and the meeting was adjourned.
>
> I took Syama Prasad with me in the car. In the evening Sardar [Patel] rang me up and told me Syama Prasad had resigned. Later, at his suggestion, I met Syama Prasad, but he did not change his decision.[27]

On the following day Nehru and Liaquat Ali began their talks and on 8 April they signed the agreement which became known as the Delhi Pact, affirming the intention of their respective governments to protect their minorities, to assist those refugees who might wish to be repatriated, and to restore communal harmony in the two Bengals.[28]

Meanwhile both Nehru and Patel were trying to persuade Mookerjee to reconsider his resignation in the larger interests of the country, but without success, and on 19 April he attempted to justify his stand before Parliament. Appealing to the government to protect the Hindus of East Bengal, he alleged that it had dealt weakly with Pakistan and implied that it should consider war as a means of reunifying the sub-continent. Pakistan, being an Islamic state, would naturally oppress and harass its Hindu citizens, a fact which a limited agreement such as the Delhi Pact could not alter. There was, he maintained, a world of differ-ence between the way in which the two countries treated their minorities; Pakistan had not only fomented the recent riots in East Bengal but had exaggerated the extent of the disturbances on the Indian side of the border. The riots 'formed part of a deliberate and cold plan-ning to exterminate minorities from East Bengal; to ignore this is to forget hard realities'. Although he did not make an outright appeal for military action, there was no doubt in the minds of his hearers as to what he meant by his references to 'the only effective remedy' and 'alternative lines of action'; Pakistan should either treat her minorities properly or be prepared for war.[29] 'No permanent solution of the refugee problem is possible', he said later, 'unless India is reunited or Pakistan declares herself a modern democratic State'.[30]

His resignation accepted, Mookerjee returned to Calcutta by train, addressing at each stop the crowds who had gathered to meet him. At Burdwan he told them, 'Bengal shall never die, none can kill Bengal. Rather Bengal will save India.' When his train pulled into Howrah Station on 21 April there were about 40,000 people awaiting him with shouts of 'Mookerjee ki jai' and he was garlanded by the representatives of thirty organisations, including the Hindu Mahasabha and the Hindu-stan National Guards.[31] At public meetings in Calcutta, he renewed his attack on the Delhi Pact and proposed that, if Pakistan continued to deny her Hindu minority its rights, India should demand an exchange of population and property between East Bengal on the one hand, and West Bengal, Assam and Tripura on the other.[32] If the migration of Hindus from East Bengal continued, he claimed, this would impose an intolerable burden on West Bengal's economy; nor would the scattering of refugees throughout India be an acceptable solution. 'We shudder to anticipate a complete disintegration of the Bengali race and not merely the sufferings of millions of East Bengal Hindus. We do not deserve this fate, as Bengal has contributed her best towards the cultural, economic and political uplift of India.'[33] He was rapidly becoming identified as the spokesman for Bengal; full coverage was given to his statements by such Calcutta papers as the *Amrita Bazar Patrika, Juganter*, the *Hindusthan Standard* and the *Ananda Bazar Patrika*, and at public meetings which he addressed the platform was usually crowded with leading representatives of the city's establishment. Hindu Calcutta had seldom given such enthusiastic backing to a political leader, and even those people who realised that Mookerjee's stand was impractical admitted that his views were shared by an appreciable number of Bengalis and that his resignation from the Cabinet had raised him in their estimation.

From his base at Calcutta, Mookerjee moved rapidly to establish new areas of support. He took up the cause of the thousands of refugees who were crammed into rehabilitation centres and camps in and around the city and in Assam, calling for adequate compensation for them and denouncing the Delhi Pact.[34] The refugees were important not only in terms of numbers (in August there were in the Indian Union some 2,521,681 displaced persons who had come since 1 January from East Pakistan)[35] but their relief camps, of which there were 28 in West Bengal, 25 in Assam and 41 in Tripura,[36] affected the surrounding regions with their communalist sentiments. Politically, they constituted one of the most unstable and explosive elements in eastern India. Mookerjee found a national forum for his ideas at the large conference of refugee organisations which was held in Delhi at the end of July. Leader of the Bengal delegation, he reached the capital on the evening of the 26th, to be met at Old Delhi Station by a reception committee which included such figures as Dr Choitram Gidwani, President of the All-India Refugees Association, and V. G. Deshpande, General Secretary of the All-India Hindu Mahasabha. Heavily garlanded, he moved to his car through crowds of young men who held banners proclaiming, 'We Do Not Want Nehru's Anti-Hindu and Cowardly Government', 'Nehru has failed to protect Hindus and Rehabilitate Refugees' and 'Nehru-Liaqat Pact Murdabad'. Mookerjee told reporters that it was not possible for Hindus to live in East Pakistan any more than in West Pakistan – 'only after we have realised this fact, we can expect to find a proper solution of the problem.'[37]

The main political figures at the conference were Mookerjee himself, Purushottamdas Tandon, President of the Uttar Pradesh Congress Committee and a confidant of Patel, and Dr N. B. Khare, the President of the Hindu Mahasabha. They represented the three main regions of Hindu communalism – Bengal, Uttar Pradesh and Maharashtra – and each had political motives for attending. Within a few months Tandon, encouraged by Patel, was to make his successful bid for the Presidency of the Indian National Congress; Khare was preparing to lead the Mahasabha in its first major election; and Mookerjee, who was now a power to be reckoned with in Bengal, was establishing a new range of political contacts.[38]

After the conference, Mookerjee remained in Delhi for the brief emergency session of Parliament which had been called to discuss the outbreak of war in Korea. Nehru took the opportunity to review also the Bengal situation and the working of the Delhi Pact. It had been 'meant to stop a certain drift towards catastrophe', and he maintained that it had in fact reassured the minorities.[39] Figures which he gave showed that many refugees were now returning to their homes; between 9 April and 25 July, 541,251 Hindus had left India for Pakistan as compared with the 1,284,623 who had come into the country, and the outflow of Muslims (449,968) had not been much larger than the inflow (304,255).[40] Mookerjee, who spoke soon after Nehru, questioned these figures and produced some of his own to show that the exodus of Hindus from East Pakistan was continuing unabated. Citing several instances in which Hindus had been brutally treated, he returned again to his thesis that the Delhi Pact could not deter Pakistan from her plan to create an Islamic State. He then outlined three courses of action which India might follow: she could declare that Pakistan's failure to protect her Hindu citizens had destroyed the basis of partition and that India would now assume the responsibility for protecting them; she could demand one-third of the territory of East Pakistan for the resettlement of her refugees; or she could oblige Pakistan to agree to an exchange of populations in the eastern part of the sub-continent. Speaking of the first proposal, he said, 'I know the danger of it. I know what it means. It means war. This is a method which was contemplated by Mahatma Gandhi himself in extreme circumstances.'[41]

When Nehru spoke again at the end of the debate, it was against this part of Mookerjee's speech that he directed most criticism. Now that their differences were public, Nehru had come out strongly against Mookerjee's views and showed unmistakeable concern at the drift of his arguments. As he had told a South Indian audience,

I respect him for his ability and I have no doubt that he loves this country and wants to serve it. But that is not enough for me. There are people who love their country and wish to serve it, but go in the wrong direction. It becomes my duty to oppose them with all my strength and so far as I am concerned, on this issue of communalism, I give no quarter to anybody. I shall be prepared to fight to the utmost, anybody, anywhere and everywhere, wherever it raises its head.[42]

Summing up after the debate, he told Parliament that talk of reunification through war only made things more difficult for the minorities, who would be the first to suffer if war actually came, and would never be able to live with any feeling of security while such propaganda was going on. Suggestions that there should be an exchange of populations were also

completely devoid of sanity, reason, logic or any sensible approach to this problem. I say it is an approach which has nothing to do with the problem. This approach can only be due to one of two things. It is either an approach of despair where through anger and passion we look out for a way out and catch hold of anything that somebody says, without realising its consequences. Or it is a definite political approach which has nothing to do with this problem. It is raised for political reasons, just to embarrass the Government, just to create difficulties in the way of this Government, just to come in the way of rehabilitation, in the way of normality coming back to the minds of the minority in East Bengal and elsewhere, so that the trouble may continue. I cannot find any explanation except these two, . . .[43]

Mookerjee remained unconvinced. 'The present policy of appeasement of Pakistan must cease', he told a meeting on his return to Calcutta. 'Whether we start with a definite plan of economic sanctions or we intensify military action is a matter of procedure and strategy, . . .'.[44] His love of Bengal, his pride in Bengali achievements, his revulsion at the barbarity of the riots all help to explain his attitude, but another factor, the fear of disorder, was present as well. As an upper-caste Hindu, Mookerjee saw communal riots as bringing not only the prospect of cruelty and dispossession, but also the prospect that the widening circle of disorder would ultimately destroy the structure and moral basis of Hindu society itself. He strongly preferred state action, even at the risk of war, to social action in communal crises. In a significant passage during his April speech in Parliament, he had said that during the riots of January and February

we allowed weeks to go by and we could not decide what was the right course of action. The whole nation was in agony and expected promptness and firmness, but we followed a policy of drift and indecision. The result was that in some areas of West Bengal and other parts of India, people became restive and exasperated and took the law into their own hands. Let me say without hesitation that private retaliation on innocent people in India for brutalities committed in Pakistan offers us no remedy whatsoever. It creates a vicious circle which may be worse than the disease; it brutalises the race and lets loose forces which may become difficult to control at a later stage. We must function as a civilised State and all citizens, who are loyal to the State, must have equal rights and protection, irrespective of their religion and faith. The only effective remedy in a moment of such national crisis can and must be taken by the Government of the country and if the Government moves quickly, consistent with the legitimate wishes of the people and with a full sense of national honour and prestige, there is not the least doubt that the people will stand behind the Government.[45]

Another factor which influenced Mookerjee's stand was his idea of the nature and function of the State, an idea which stood in direct contrast to that held by Nehru. The Prime Minister saw the State as standing for certain principles of international and social relations even when those principles were unpopular amongst the masses – hence his distinction between 'democratic' and 'majority' rule.[46] He firmly maintained that India could not interfere in the internal affairs of another polity, in this case Pakistan, even when the question at issue was the future of Pakistan's Hindu minorities. While he agreed that India was greatly concerned about the Hindus in East Bengal, he told Parliament that 'protection in Pakistan can only be given obviously by Pakistan. We cannot give protection in Pakistan.' Again, 'Now it is patent that the kind of protection that [the Hindu minority] can get in their territory can only come to them in the existing state of affairs through the Government that controls that territory. There is no other way. . . . so long as there is a Government dealing with a situation, you have to deal through that Government.'[47] For Mookerjee, on the other hand, the mere fact that they were Hindus was sufficient justification for India's taking action on their behalf. By leaving part of 'the Hindu nation' in an alien State, he argued, partition had created an unnatural and unstable political situation, a fact which became clear whenever Pakistan mistreated its Hindu minority. On such occasions, their Hindu 'brothers' in India would become restless and, in the absence of strong leadership, disorderly. Nehru's essential failure had been his refusal to face the fact that the Indian State must stand for strong action against the national enemy, Islamic Pakistan, if it were to survive and be healthy.

Mookerjee was an honest and honourable politician, and it would do him less than justice to allege that he left the Union Cabinet in April 1950 with the deliberate intention of forming a new, nationalist, communalist party. He resigned because he could not support a policy and a theory of Indo-Pakistani relations which conflicted fundamentally with his own ideas and temperament, and in doing so he acted out what many Congressmen would have liked to have done themselves.[48] This is why his subsequent career must be set firmly against the background of the Bengal riots of February–March 1950; his action in that situation marked him as a man of integrity and a man of political courage. It was inevitable, however, that he should also calculate his chances carefully, and it is clear that he based his actions on the assumption that the Indian national movement was, in 1950, on the verge of one of its great transformations, those revolutions of feeling, of organisation and of ideology which had occurred in 1920–2, 1929–34 and 1942–5. As before each of these earlier crises, there was in 1950 an air of uncertainty, of popular restlessness, of emotionalism and romantic idealism – but with one important difference; the potential enemy was now not the British, against whom all communities could be mobilised, but Pakistan. Hindu communalism, always latent in the national movement since the days of Tilak and Malaviya, seemed to have found its opportunity. Mookerjee was to shape his political strategies in this expectation.

III

In October 1951 Mookerjee became the leader of a newly formed party, the All-India Bharatiya Jana Sangh, which was intended to provide a Hindu traditionalist alternative to the Congress in the impending general elections. Although there is evidence that Mookerjee was considering the formation of such a party in 1950, it is by no means certain that this was his only or even his most important plan at that time; he was dealing with the fluid and uncertain political situation which preceded the 1951 elections, not with a stable and fixed party system in which circumstances dictated clear strategies. Until after the election, the great question was that of the future of the Congress Party, whose morale was weak, whose provincial ministries were unstable, and whose leadership was divided.

One real possibility in the summer of 1950 was that the forces behind Sardar Patel and those behind Nehru might come into open conflict. Within the cabinet, the two leaders observed a kind of division of labour, Nehru concentrating on foreign affairs and the Kashmir problem and Patel devoting himself mainly to home affairs, but within the Congress Party they had become symbols almost despite themselves. While Nehru had great popularity amongst the masses and a loyal following amongst the young intellectuals of his party, Patel enjoyed the confidence of the Hindu traditionalists and of Indian business interests – the former angered by Nehru's conciliatory policy towards Pakistan and by his effort to push through Parliament the Hindu Code

Bill, and the latter alarmed at the outlook of the Planning Commission appointed in March 1950. Nehru found his authority and his doctrine of secular nationalism challenged sharply and he had to fight hard to hold his ground. The first phase of the struggle began on 2 September 1950, when the AICC office announced that Purushottamdas Tandon, President of the Uttar Pradesh Congress Committee and a well-known traditionalist, had defeated Acharya Kripalani in the contest for the Congress presidency, an outcome which was interpreted as a victory for Patel, who had backed Tandon, and a setback for Nehru, although he had not endorsed Kripalani's candidature.[49] Noting that 'Communal and reactionary forces have openly expressed their joy at the result', the Prime Minister reaffirmed his faith in secularism and demanded that at the forthcoming session at Nasik, the Indian National Congress 'should declare its policy in this matter in the clearest and most unambiguous terms.'[50] At the Nasik Congress (20 and 21 September), Nehru insisted on the adoption of resolutions which confirmed his policies, especially those relating to communalism and Indo-Pakistani relations.[51] Tandon retaliated by excluding several of Nehru's most prominent followers, such as Rafi Ahmad Kidwai (Minister of Communications), from his Working Committee,[52] and by publicly expressing his views about the need for a firmer policy towards Pakistan over the question of the East Bengal Hindus.[53]

During the Nasik session, Kripalani had formed the Congress Democratic Front to press from within for the reform of the Congress organisation, and after the Congress had ended he and Kidwai set about rallying the pro-Nehru forces against the Tandon establishment. Tandon's response was to insist that the Front be dissolved, but he for his part would not make any concessions, refusing to reconstitute the Working Committee or to admit the Front's representatives to the Central Election Committee. When all efforts to restore unity had failed, Nehru decided that the only course was to have the Front disband itself, and this was done on 3 May 1951. However, in June most of the dissidents met at Patna and founded an independent party known as the Kisan Mazdoor Praja Party (KMPP). Kidwai, who was closely associated with this venture, in July sent in his resignation as a member of the Union Cabinet, but was persuaded by Nehru to remain for the public interest. Tandon objected on the grounds that non-Congressmen should not be ministers and on 2 August Kidwai finally left the Cabinet. Nehru, who disagreed with Tandon's idea that 'the Prime Minister and his Cabinet are responsible to the Congress',[54] decided to force the issue;

on 6 August he resigned from the Working Committee and the Central Election Committee. His position within the party had been steadily improving, particularly as Patel's death in December 1950 had deprived the traditionalists of one of their most able leaders, and when the Congress Parliamentary Party met on 21 August he received a vote of confidence. The contest was his when, on 8 September at a meeting of the AICC, he became Congress President as well as Prime Minister, having virtually obliged Tandon to resign from the former post.[55]

Although in one of its aspects this struggle represented a clash of personalities, it was above all a bitter war between the two forces within Congress – the secular nationalists and the Hindu traditionalists – to control the Party's election policies. Certainly this was the light in which both the *Organiser*, the pro-RSS weekly journal, and the Mahasabha's *Hindu Outlook* viewed the situation.[56] Nehru's victory was by no means certain even as late as August 1951, and until the outcome of the struggle was clear, the Hindu traditionalists hesitated to form a strong party to challenge the Congress.

This is surely the explanation for Mookerjee's delay; his close touch with Patel and his contacts with Tandon would have made his entry into the Congress Party almost a certainty had that party changed its direction. Although, as we shall see, Mookerjee had been exploring the possibility of founding a new party in 1950, the fact remains that he made no public move to do so until April 1951, a delay which is even more significant when it is remembered that, until November 1950, it was widely expected that the first general election under the new Constitution would be held in mid-1951. The RSS, which collaborated with Mookerjee in founding the Jana Sangh, may also have had ideas of working with the Congress Party had the Tandon forces been able to maintain their ascendancy. Its unofficial journal, the *Organiser*, was frankly sympathetic towards Tandon, and Curran, who had been closely studying the RSS leadership in 1949 and 1950, noted that the group with which it seemed likely to form some kind of connection was the Congress.[57] Perhaps it was the hope that the Tandon forces would win the struggle that caused the founders of the Jana Sangh to delay the formation of the party's main provincial units until about six months before the election campaign and of the All-India party until after the campaign had actually begun.

The RSS had been working under considerable difficulties. The man who assassinated Gandhi on 30 January 1948 had once been an RSS member but had severed his connections with the organisation before the war: the Government of India none the less banned the RSS in February 1948 and the restrictions imposed were only removed on 12 July 1949, following Golwalkar's assurance that his organisation would abstain from politics and devote itself to 'cultural' work. As Myron Weiner has pointed out, its political ambitions were far from quelled and one of its main objectives was to guard against being banned on another occasion by a Parliament which was unsympathetic to its policies and to its ideas of Hindu nationalism. Two courses were open to it: one was to infiltrate the Congress Party, and the other was to set about forming a new, Hindu-oriented party. The first course presented difficulties: in October 1949 the Congress Working Committee actually decided the RSS members should be allowed to join the party, but this decision was reversed in the following month.[58] With regard to the second course, Vasantra Rao Oak told Myron Weiner that he and a number of other RSS leaders had discussed the formation of a new party with Mookerjee in 1949, and had, in the following year, urged him to leave the Union Cabinet, promising that if he did so the RSS would help in founding a new party; Golwalkar, according to Oak, neither welcomed nor discouraged the idea.[59] According to Golwalkar, however, Oak did not meet Mookerjee until after the latter's resignation from the cabinet; Oak had then introduced Golwalkar to Mookerjee and the two men had had several discussions about the new party idea. Golwalkar claims that, having pointed out to Mookerjee that the RSS should remain outside politics and pursue 'cultural' work, he nevertheless agreed that RSS workers might assist Mookerjee in organising his movement.[60]

Care has to be exercised in drawing conclusions from this evidence. For one thing, it is clear that Mookerjee was accessible, not only to Oak, but to other RSS cadres such as Balraj Madhok, who had been in touch with Mookerjee as early as 1948 over the ban on the Jammu Praja Parishad;[61] while there can be no doubt that Oak and others had discussed the new party proposal with him, this probably was not the main reason for their contacts. It is in fact highly likely that in 1950 both Mookerjee and the RSS were much more attracted by the idea that there might be a place for them in a reformed Congress Party dominated by Patel and Tandon. Certainly, the external evidence advanced in the previous section strongly suggests that Mookerjee resigned in April 1950 not with the intention of forming a new party but rather to oppose publicly what he considered to be a weak policy towards Pakistan.

At the same time, of course, both the RSS leaders and Mookerjee had to take account of the possibility that the Nehru forces might win their struggle with the traditionalists and to frame an alternative strategy. As early as mid-1950, there is evidence of tentative moves towards founding a new party. One course was to take over and transform an existing party, the Hindu Mahasabha, which had resumed political activities and which in December 1949 had chosen as its leader the unpredictable but energetic Dr N.B.Khare, a Chitpavan Brahman in the Tilak mould. Despite the undoubted differences of temperament and age which separated the RSS leaders from those of the Hindu Mahasabha,[62] and Mookerjee's lack of standing with the latter because of his failure to protect them in 1948, it would be wrong to under-estimate the restlessness which some of the Mahasabha's more dynamic leaders, such as V.G.Deshpande, the Organising Secretary, and Ashutosh Lahiri, felt because of the narrow role their organisation had adopted under Savarkar's direction. A section of the Mahasabha's leadership was anxious in 1950 to throw its membership open to all Indians, not just to Hindus, and to broaden its appeal by toning down its emphasis on *Hindu Rashtra* (Hindu nationalism). It would be interesting to know more of a Delhi meeting which Dr Khare claims to have had with Mookerjee, in the presence of Deshpande and Lahiri, at the house of the Managing Director of the Punjab National Bank on either 31 July or 1 August 1950. Khare says that Mookerjee asked him:

> to wind up the Hindoo Mahasabha and join his new party which he was going to establish under his own leadership with the help of Mr M.S. Golwalkar of the Rashtriya Swayam Sewak Sangh. I was very much surprised at the suggestion of Dr Mukherjee and I said to him, 'Your new party is just in the air yet. Its programme also is not yet chalked out. How can I wind up an organised old party and join your new party under these conditions? It will be highly improper to do so....'

Addressing Mookerjee directly, Khare went even further. '*I emphatically tell you in the language of Churchill that I have not become the President of the Hindoo Mahasabha to liquidate the organisation.*'[63] Not only does this incident establish that Mookerjee was already in contact with Golwalkar about the new party idea as early as July 1950, but it strongly suggests that the absorption or transformation of the Hindu Mahasabha was being seriously considered as one of the possible steps towards that end.

This may add significance to the efforts which were made late in 1950 to convert the Mahasabha into a less exclusive and more effective party. Its Working Committee recommended, after a meeting at Moradabad on 2 October, that non-Hindus should be associated in future with the

Mahasabha's parliamentary groups (obviously as a token gesture),[64] and this, along with a more revolutionary proposal that the Mahasabha should bring all 'democratic and nationalist elements' into a new National Democratic Party, was referred to a general conference at Poona in December. Both encountered opposition from the firmly entrenched oligarchies of the Uttar Pradesh, Punjab, West Bengal and Maharashtrian Sabhas, who wanted the organisation to retain its explicitly Hindu and traditional character. Their weight was sufficient to guarantee the proposals' rejection by the Poona conference and by the subsequent provincial conferences to which they were referred,[65] but a special general session held at Jaipur on 28 April 1951 was able to resurrect the Moradabad resolution about widening the parliamentary groups, and it authorised the Working Committee to select non-Hindu candidates for the coming election.[66] There the matter rested. The Poona conference had given a fairly clear indication that the Mahasabha was incapable of reforming itself, and it is probably significant that January 1951 saw the first concrete steps taken by Mookerjee and his RSS supporters to go ahead with their own plans.

Madhok has given a full account[67] of a meeting held in Delhi on 16 January at which the formation of a new party in the States of Punjab, PEPSU, Himachal Pradesh and Delhi was discussed. Mookerjee wanted consideration to be given to the establishment of an all-India party as well, and a sub-committee was appointed to go into proposals for a manifesto and platform. Provisionally, the name Bharatiya Jana Sangh (Indian People's Party) was adopted. According to Madhok, Mookerjee took the view that the Jana Sangh should uphold the values of *Hindu Rashtra* as he understood it, defining Hinduism as nationality rather than simply community or religion. In terms of this concept, first discussed systematically by Veer Savarkar in *Hindutva* (1924), Indian nationality was a product of several factors such as country, race, culture, language and religion;[68] some Indians had lost their true identity and, by turning to Islam or western culture, had denied their inheritance; the remedy was to convince them of their error and to persuade them that the release of the creative spirit in Indian society could be brought about only when all Indians became aware that Hinduism was the true nationalism and that the secular nationalism of Nehru and his Congress followers was alien to Indian experience. Mookerjee, however, realised that there were people who were not prepared to accept the word 'Hindu' as a synonym for 'Indian'; consequently 'Bharatiya' was chosen on the grounds that it would be acceptable to all Indians. During the discussion of the Hindu Code Bill in Parliament Mookerjee's own belief in the value for India of its Hindu identity came out clearly:

> ... we should never tolerate any criticism from any quarter, especially from a foreign quarter when they say that Hindu civilisation or Hindu culture has been of a static nature or of a stagnant nature or of a decadent nature. There is something in our culture and civilisation which is of a dynamic character and which has lived from generation to generation. Even when India was a subject nation people were born in this country, men of our soil, who stood up for great ideals which gave a new lease of life under new and modern conditions to the eternal tenets of Hindu civilisation.[69]

The work of building up the regional units began in the summer. A Bengal Jana Sangh was formed on 28 April under Mookerjee's leadership;[70] a branch covering the Punjab–PEPSU–Himachal Pradesh–Delhi area was established at Jullundur on 23 May;[71] a conference at Lucknow on 2 September set up the Uttar Pradesh party;[72] and later on organisations were founded in Bihar, Madhya Bharat, Orissa and Rajasthan – but not, it should be noted, in Maharashtra, where the local RSS cadres were not enthusiastic about the venture,[73] or in the southern parts of the country. Finally, the All-India Bharatiya Jana Sangh was formed at a convention in Delhi on 21 October 1951; Mookerjee was appointed President, a Working Committee chosen, and a platform and constitution adopted.[74]

For all its Sanskrit terminology, the Jana Sangh's constitution envisaged a structure very much like that of the Indian National Congress. Membership was open to any 'national of Bharat' of sixteen or more years who subscribed to the party's objectives and was willing to pay a nominal fee of four annas; from local committees at the base, tiers of institutions mounted upwards, through Constituency, District, State and All-India Committees, with the appropriate executive bodies at each level; like their counterparts in the Congress, the State and All-India Presidents were entitled to nominate their respective Working Committees; but most other executive posts were elective.[75] Here was the framework for a mass party, functioning to some extent as a democratic body. In fact, however, the Jana Sangh did not become a mass party; by 1954 its membership was still only 143,000 and by 1959 it had risen to 210,000.[76] By comparison, Congress members in 1951 were said to number 34 million[77] and the formal adult membership of the RSS was estimated at 631,500 of which Uttar Pradesh accounted for 200,000, Madhya Pradesh for 126,000, Punjab for 125,000, and Bombay 60,000.[78]

The latter comparison is the more significant, especially beside the fact that, whereas in 1950 there were 5,000 established centres of the RSS in India,[79] in 1954 there were only about 2,000 local committees of the Jana Sangh.[80]

There was little more to the early Jana Sangh than the armature of well disciplined RSS cadres in northern India and Mookerjee's personal following, poorly organised, in West Bengal and Assam; of the two, the RSS component was the more important. It was the young workers of the RSS who built the party up in 1951 and who carried it through the 1951–2 elections. Their price was organisational control; rather than adapt themselves to the democratic requirements of the formal constitution, they aimed deliberately at taking over the focal executive positions of secretary, organiser and treasurer in the State and All-India Working Committees, and from these they set out to control the day-to-day functioning of the party. A measure of their success was provided in November 1954, when Mauli Chandra Sharma, one of the organisation's founders and at that time its national president, resigned his office and charged the RSS with exercising undue influence within the party. Within a few days, Guru Dutt, another founding member and President of the Delhi State Jana Sangh, resigned on the same grounds. From the statements of these two men, it would appear that the RSS had tried to influence the choice of election candidates and party officers to the extent of antagonising the 'liberal' party members, many of whom belonged to the RSS but felt that the Jana Sangh should be run on democratic lines. The implications of RSS control had been discussed at the Jana Sangh's All-India Committee in August 1954 but the matter had been referred to a subsequent meeting which the General Secretary, Din Dayal Upadhyaya (a former RSS man), had refused to convene. Sharma had submitted his resignation as President in the belief that this would oblige Upadhyaya to call the All-India Committee together, but Upadhyaya (who is said to have consulted Golwalkar) referred the matter instead to the Working Committee, dominated by an RSS majority, which accepted the resignation and appointed an interim president. Sharma claimed that trouble with the RSS was not a new thing.

The late Dr Mookerjee was often seriously perturbed by the demands of RSS leaders for a decisive role in matters like the appointment of office-bearers, nomination of candidates for elections and matters of policy. We however hoped that the rank and file of the RSS would be drawn out into the arena of democratic public life through their association with the Jana Sangh.

A vigorous and calculated drive was launched to turn the Jana Sangh into a convenient handle of the RSS. Orders were issued from their headquarters through their emissaries and the Jana Sangh was expected to carry them out. Many workers and groups all over the country resented this and the Delhi State Jana Sangh as a body refused to comply.[81]

When another group of 'liberals' left the Jana Sangh in July 1961, they told similar stories. They claimed that the initial decision to found the party had been taken by the RSS Working Commitee shortly after the lifting of the official ban on 12 July 1949, that Golwalkar had delegated RSS organisers to hold key posts in the newly formed party, that the RSS always took an active interest in the choice of Jana Sangh office-bearers, and that Golwalkar and his lieutenants were consulted before the selection of top leadership and the making of policy decisions.[82]

While these revelations must be treated with caution as coming from party dissidents, they strongly suggest that the relationship between the Jana Sangh and the RSS, although perhaps not a formal one, was much closer than that which had existed earlier between the Hindu Mahasabha and the RSS; in short, that the Jana Sangh was, to a very real extent, a projection of the RSS into constitutional politics. Most of Mookerjee's key organisers had come from the RSS and their experience in the hard work of establishing and sustaining local committees made them indispensable: Din Dayal Upadhyaya, who was chosen as the party's General Secretary, was an RSS cadre who had worked amongst the villagers of Uttar Pradesh and had impressed Mookerjee with his ability as Secretary of the Uttar Pradesh Jana Sangh; Atul Behari Vajpayee, one of the party's All-India Secretaries, had joined the RSS during his student days and had later worked as editor on several nationalist Hindu journals, including the Delhi *Vir Arjun*; Professor Mahavir, a member of the Central Executive and Professor of History at New Delhi's Camp College, had been an RSS worker for almost twenty years; Balraj Madhok, founder of the Punjab Jana Sangh, had been during the war a full-time RSS organiser in Jammu and Kashmir; and Bapu Saheb Sohni had been appointed RSS organiser in Berar in 1936 and later became one of the most influential members of the Jana Sangh's All-India Working Committee.[83] The early Jana Sangh had two aspects, one the tough, authoritarian aspect of the RSS men and the other the moderate, flexible Hindu traditionalism of Mookerjee's generation; in a photograph of the group sitting on the platform at the founding convention, the mild faces of Mookerjee and other middle-aged leaders contrast with the tense, controlled expressions of their young lieutenants.[84]

As a political figure in Bengal, Mookerjee was already securely established but he knew that he lacked sufficient backing to become the leader of a national party; consequently, he turned for support to the RSS. This was a dangerous move, for he must have realised that if the Jana Sangh did badly in its first election and failed to establish sizeable parliamentary groups, he would be under pressure to forsake moderate and constitutional strategies for the techniques of agitation, *satyagraha* and mass action, a prospect for which he had little taste: 'Our aim,' he told a press conference, 'is to form a healthy constitutional Opposition both inside and outside the Legislatures . . .'[85] Despite his irrationality over questions concerning Pakistan, Mookerjee was essentially a man of order. 'What does India ultimately stand for?', he had asked Parliament in March 1951. 'We have made up our mind about this. We have embodied it in our Constitution. We believe in democracy. We believe in the rule of law. We believe in the supremacy and the sovereignty of the people.'[86]

He drove himself hard during the election campaign, touring the Punjab and Madhya Pradesh in November 1951, West Bengal, eastern Uttar Pradesh, Rajasthan and Bihar in December and Delhi State in January. Despite his periodic outbursts about Pakistan, his speeches were moderate as compared with those of the Hindu Mahasabha and Ram Rajya Parishad leaders. Instead of a repeated and wearying emphasis on *Hindu Rashtra*, Mookerjee addressed himself to a wide range of issues, speaking very much as the leader of a constitutional opposition. The fragments of table talk which Madhok has recorded confirm this impression: 'I will set this man right,' he said of Nehru, 'if I can take even ten members with me into the Parliament.'[87]

He maintained that India was losing direction under Congress rule, which had fostered corruption, inefficiency and undemocratic practices. 'The country today is passing through a great crisis and one-party rule is tending towards malevolent dictatorship.'[88] Nehru, he said, had fostered communalism by consenting to partition and by granting special privileges to the Muslim minority within the Indian State; moreover his support of the Hindu Code Bill showed that he was willing to undermine the basis of true nationality in his country. Jana Sangh, on the other hand, was offering the chance of a new unity.

We have thrown open our Party to all citizens of Bharat irrespective of caste, creed, or community. While we recognise that in matters of custom, habits, religion and language, Bharat presents a unique diversity, the people must be united by a bond of fellowship and understanding inspired by deep devotion and loyalty to the spirit of a common mother-land.[89]

He promised that Muslims and other non-Hindus would receive fair treatment so long as they behaved as true sons and daughters of the motherland.[90] Nehru, who made a special point of attacking the Hindu communalists during his own campaign, said that in their communalism he saw 'germs of fascism.'[91] To such charges Mookerjee replied that Nehru and the Congress were the people guilty of surrendering to communalism, for partition was in a large measure due to their placation of the Muslim League; but at the same time he took pains to point out that, although some of its members were RSS men, the Jana Sangh was separate from the RSS.[92]

In the economic sphere, Mookerjee claimed that the Jana Sangh would work to increase the production of food and other essential commodities, that it favoured zamindari abolition, and that it would sanction the State's acquiring some land for the landless. 'While it is in favour of nationalisation of key industries, it will fully encourage private enterprise subject to two conditions, namely, prevention of undue profiteering and of formation of groups or cartels wielding large-scale economic power.'[93] On relations with Pakistan, however, Mookerjee's intolerence came to the fore. Describing partition as a 'tragedy' which the Congress could have avoided had it not been 'impatient for power', he declared that the Jana Sangh 'believes that the future welfare of the people of India and Pakistan demands a reunited India. . . .'[94] He strongly implied that military action was legitimate in order to ensure fair treatment for the Hindu minority of East Bengal and to secure the removal of Pakistani troops from Azad Kashmir;[95] India should withdraw the Kashmir dispute from the United Nations and refuse to hold a plebiscite.[96]

In the elections, which were held over a period of several months during the winter of 1951–2, the Jana Sangh failed to reach even the modest limits it had set itself. It contested 93 of the 489 Lok Sabha constituencies but won only three seats, two in West Bengal and one in Rajasthan; altogether it polled 3,246,288 votes, or 3·1 per cent of the total. Mookerjee was returned for Calcutta South-East with 44·96 per cent of the valid votes but the party's performance was generally disappointing; taking the Lok Sabha votes, it polled best in the small States of Delhi (25·9 per cent), Ajmer (16·2 per cent), Vindhya Pradesh

(12·7 per cent), and Himachal Pradesh (10·7 per cent) and scored reasonably well in Madhya Bharat (9·7 per cent) and in the large States of Uttar
Pradesh (7·0 per cent), Punjab (6·0 per cent) and West Bengal (5·9 per
cent).[97] Most of its support had come from the large towns of the north
and from pockets of refugee concentration (which explains, for example,
why the Delhi vote was so high) but it had failed to gain much of a rural
following. Even so, as Weiner has pointed out,[98] it did better, and enjoyed a wider regional support, than either the Hindu Mahasabha or
Ram Rajya Parishad.

Apparently not discouraged, Mookerjee did his best to form a number
of the non-Congressmen in the Lok Sabha into a united Opposition
party, the National Democratic Group.[99] A preliminary conference held
on 29 March 1952 found about 40 members who indicated their willingness to co-operate; but some later changed their minds, and by June the
Group numbered 34, drawn from such parties as the Hindu Mahasabha,
the Commonweal Party, the Tamil Nad Toilers' Party, the Akali Dal
and Ganatantra Parishad and some Independents.[100] Naturally such a
medley lacked coherence and a common cause and by 1953 Mookerjee's
over-riding concern with Pakistan had driven some of the South Indian
members away.[101]

When Mookerjee had resigned from the Union Cabinet in April 1950
he had appeared to be well placed for a strong political drive, comparable
to that by which Gandhi had brought himself to the head of the national
movement in the period 1918–20 or that by which Subash Chandra Bose
had achieved fleeting success in the period 1938–9. If the dangerous
undertow of anti-Muslim feeling built up during the Bengal riots of
1950 had become much stronger, Nehru might well have lost his battle
for the secular and non-communal ideals of the old Congress, and in a
rising current of Hindu extremism Mookerjee, along with Congress
traditionalists such as Tandon, might have taken Indian nationalism in a
new direction. When instead, Nehru won the day, Mookerjee was left
with the task of carrying through the role he had set himself in 1950.
Having been disappointed in his hope that the Jana Sangh would win
sufficient seats in the Lok Sabha to enable it to follow a constitutional
rather than an agitational course, and having seen the National Democratic Group, after some early promise, come to nothing, it was almost
inevitable that Mookerjee should find himself compelled increasingly
by the young men of the RSS to resort to *satyagraha, hartal,* demonstrations and protest marches, as if the Congress were the British all over
again and Jana Sangh the spearhead of the new nationalism. Mookerjee

the leader of the constitutional opposition gave way steadily to Mooker-jee the leader of the communal agitation for the integration of Kashmir into the Indian Union.

IV

By 1952 Sheikh Abdullah's policy of maintaining Kashmir's special position within the Indian Union had come under strong fire from the Hindu community of Jammu, represented by the Praja Parishad Party, and the Buddhist leaders of Ladakh. The situation became critical when the main Indian communalist parties, the Jana Sangh, the Hindu Mahasabha and the Ram Rajya Parishad decided to come out strongly in support of the Praja Parishad's demand that the State be fully integrated with India.

In Jammu and Kashmir, deep-seated communal differences lay just below the surface of party politics. While Abdullah's own party, the National Conference, was identified with the predominantly Muslim population of the Vale of Kashmir, the Praja Parishad reflected the interests of the Hindu minority, concentrated in Jammu, and the frustration of the proud Dogra community, who had formed the Hindu ruling group under the previous dynasty.[102] The Dogra Maharajahs who had ruled the area since 1846 had been a byword for oppression, and it is not surprising that the Muslim Conference, founded in 1932, should have been both communal and agrarian-radical in character. In 1938 it became the National Conference and in the following year threw open its membership to all communities; subsequently it adopted a radical economic and political programme[103] and identified itself with the broader movement of the Indian National Congress. Abdullah began a 'Quit Kashmir' agitation in 1946 but was imprisoned by the Maharajah, who nevertheless found his power weakening as the events of 1947 led steadily towards independence and partition. He first tried to negotiate standstill agreements with both India and Pakistan, but in October 1947 he was obliged to appeal to Delhi for military aid to curb a revolt of frontier tribesmen (said to have received support from Pakistan) and, on the 26th signed an Instrument of Accession to India. This agreement was not recognised by Pakistan, which retained control of a portion of Kashmir after a cease-fire had been arranged.

Under the Instrument of Accession, Jammu and Kashmir acknowledged the authority of the Government of India over Foreign Affairs, Defence, and Communications, but remained sovereign in other fields of policy. On 5 March 1948 the Maharajah issued a proclamation making Abdullah Prime Minister of the State, and subsequently surrendered more and more power to the National Conference leader. The protraction of the international dispute over Kashmir, and the respect which the Indian Government accorded the Abdullah régime, meant that the State came to enjoy a status quite different from that of the other Princely States which had also acceded to India. Whereas these had either accepted integration into existing Provinces, or had been represented on the India Constituent Assembly and were thus bound by the subsequent Constitution, Kashmir remained separate and did not send representatives to the Constituent Assembly until June 1949. The Indian Constitution, which came into force on 26 January 1950, recognised in Article 370 that the provisions applying to the other Princely States (contained in Article 238) should not affect Kashmir and that the power of the Parliament of India should be limited to the fields specified in the Instrument of Accession (Foreign Affairs, Defence, and Communications). However, it also provided that this power could be extended to other matters by Orders of the President of India, acting with the concurrence of the Kashmir Government and subject to the eventual approval of the Kashmir Constituent Assembly. In accordance with this provision, the President made the Constitution (Application to Jammu and Kashmir) Order, 1950, specifying those parts of the Constitution which would not apply to Kashmir and those which would, while leaving no doubt that the executive and legislative powers of the Kashmir Government in the internal affairs of its territory remained virtually unimpaired.[104]

Under Abdullah's influence, the General Council of the National Conference on 27 October 1950 adopted a resolution calling for the election of a constituent assembly to decide the 'future shape and affiliation of the State of Jammu and Kashmir'.[105] Despite protests from Pakistan that this proposal ran counter to India's undertaking to the United Nations Security Council to hold a plebiscite, elections to the Constituent Assembly were held between August and October 1951, an overwhelming majority of the seats being won by the National Conference. In November the Assembly adopted the *Jammu and Kashmir Constitution Amendment Act*, which provided a temporary constitution declaring the sovereignty of the State Government in all fields except the three given to India under Article 370 of the Indian Constitution.

Displaced from power and feeling their landed rights to be in danger, the Dogras joined forces with the Praja Parishad, formed in 1947 as a respectable substitute for the illegal RSS. The Parishad had been resisting trends towards a separate Kashmiri state almost from the time of accession, and as early as 20 May 1949 its Working Committee had called for 'full and unconditional accession' of the State to India.[106] Its tough, wiry leader, Prem Nath Dogra, had been imprisoned during most of 1948 for his opposition to the Abdullah régime and in 1951 he committed his community to a life and death struggle against the government's policies. (This was the year in which the State's *Big Landed Estates Abolition Act* was passed, confiscating and redistributing to the tillers the holdings of the large landlords, most of whom were Dogras.) Claiming that the electoral officers had unfairly refused to accept many Praja Parishad nominations for the Constituent Assembly elections, Prem Nath Dogra came to Delhi towards the end of 1951 to ask Mookerjee's advice about boycotting the polls; through Madhok, Mookerjee recommended that the Parishad should go ahead and fight the election. 'His view was that legislatures were the only effective forums for giving vent to diverse view points on Governmental policies. Therefore, it would be worth while fighting the elections if thereby the Praja Parishad could send into the Assembly even one single spokesman.'[107] However, the Parishad decided to maintain the boycott. On 8 February 1952, police broke up a procession in support of students who had protested against the raising of the National Conference flag at a function at the Gandhi Memorial College in Jammu[108] and on 12 February, Mookerjee referred to the matter in Parliament, calling for the integration of Kashmir in India.[109] When, in March, the subject came up again in Parliament, Sheikh Abdullah defended the right of the people of Jammu and Kashmir to decide whether their State should retain its existing autonomy or cede more powers to the Centre.[110] By now the Jana Sangh was becoming thoroughly embroiled in the Kashmir situation, and Mookerjee found himself being committed step by step to the agitational course which the Praja Parishad had chosen. On 26 June he pleaded with the Union Government to persuade the Kashmir Government to accept full integration under the Indian Constitution rather than permit it to become 'a republic within a republic'; Mookerjee disliked the fact that Kashmir was not subject to the central controls of the Auditor-General or to the jurisdiction of the Supreme Court of India; he complained further that repressive security laws still prevailed in Kashmir, and that Urdu was being promoted at the expense of Hindi. He suggested that Abdullah should be invited to Delhi to discuss the position anew: 'Prime Minister must firmly assert that we do not want this kind of Kashmiri nationalism; we do not want this "sovereign Kashmir" idea. If you start doing it in Kashmir, others also will demand it.' If, however, the National Conference insisted on preserving the State's internal autonomy, then both the Hindus of Jammu and the Buddhists of Ladakh should be given the opportunity of declaring for full accession of their areas to the Indian Union.[111]

In reality, the Central Government had very little ground for manœuvre; if it insisted on full accession, it ran the risk of inflaming Muslim feeling both in the Vale of Kashmir and in Pakistan-held Azad Kashmir, a turn of events which would have damaged India's case in the Kashmir dispute and strengthened the possibility that, if a plebiscite were held under United Nations' auspices, the vote would go against union with India. Added to this, there was more than a suspicion that Abdullah hoped to make Kashmir a semi-independent state, with something approaching the status of Nepal, and the Indian Government was reluctant at this stage to do anything which might antagonise him and drive him further away. This was the background to an agreement concluded between Nehru and Sheikh Abdullah in July 1952, which reaffirmed Kashmir's special status within the Union, acknowledged India's sovereignty in matters of defence, foreign policy and communications, and granted that the power of the Indian President to proclaim a general emergency (under Article 352) should apply to Kashmir except when the threat arose from an internal disturbance (or its likelihood), in which case the concurrence of the Kashmir Government was required. The Agreement also accepted the decision of the Kashmir Constituent Assembly to replace the hereditary Dogra dynasty by a constitutional Head of State (Sadar-i-Riyasat), elected by the State Legislature and recognised by the Indian President.[112] This arrangement was confirmed by a Presidential Declaration on 15 November 1952.

Besides finding the internal situation a delicate one, the Government of India was annoyed at the bad publicity which the Parishad agitation was giving India during the discussion of the Kashmir dispute before the United Nations. Mookerjee claimed that for two years Prem Nath Dogra and other Parishad leaders had been begging Nehru for an interview and that, by refusing to see them, the Prime Minister was forcing the protest upon them; this Nehru denied, saying that he had refused to meet the Dogra leader only once, after the latter had misrepresented what had occurred at an interview granted him in February 1952, and that since then the question of Nehru's seeing him had never arisen.[113] In any event, as the months slipped by, Mookerjee found increasing difficulty in persuading his own more militant supporters and the Parishad against embarking on their threatened agitation; when he visited Jammu in August 1952 he conferred with both Abdullah and Prem Nath Dogra, advising the latter to be patient and pointing out that *satyagraha* was an extreme step to be used only as the last resort.[114] However, after a meeting with Prem Nath Dogra at Jullundur on 8 November, he finally gave way and agreed that, if the Parishad decided to begin its agitation, the Jana Sangh would rally support in the rest of India (from the Jana Sangh point of view it was essential to the cause of national solidarity that all territories of the Union should be subject to the same constitutional provisions and that Pakistan's interest in the affair should be unambiguously denied). Soon afterwards, some incidents relating to the State flag, one of which resulted in the arrest of Prem Nath, sparked off a *satyagraha* movement which was to last for more than seven months.[115] In keeping with Mookerjee's earlier commitment, the Jana Sangh's national conference, held at Kanpur on 29–31 December, supported the Parishad's demand for the integration of Kashmir with India and Mookerjee was empowered to form an 'Agitation Committee' for the purpose of widening the *satyagraha* if the Government still refused to meet the challenge. Some of the more militant delegates even hoped to serve the government with an ultimatum but Mookerjee pleaded for caution, and was authorised to write to Sheikh Abdullah and Nehru in a final effort to find a solution.[116]

On 9 January 1953 he sent a letter to Nehru suggesting that they two and Abdullah should confer about the problem. This was the first of a remarkable exchange of letters between the Jana Sangh leader and his two opponents, ending with his last declamatory appeal to Abdullah on 23 February.[117] The letters do not mark the course of an ordered negotiation, gradually narrowing down to areas of agreement, but an elaborate striking of attitudes; however, it is possible to discern in Mookerjee's writing a tension between his desire to make the case for integration and his concern to have the bargaining transferred from the streets of Jammu to conference tables in Delhi. His basic request, expressed most clearly in his letter to Nehru of 12 February, was that the Prime Minister and Sheikh Abdullah should agree to discuss the matters in dispute upon which the Parishad's agitation would be called off. By this time, however, the *satyagraha* was being extended to the rest of India. On 8 February representatives of the Jana Sangh, Hindu Mahasabha and Ram Rajya Parishad had met in Delhi to co-ordinate their plans[118] and on 5 March, set aside as 'Jammu and Kashmir Day', public meetings and processions were held in Delhi and other major cities. Slogans about integrating Kashmir were shouted out in the streets. Mookerjee and some companions were arrested on the 6th for defying a ban on public meetings and processions but were released five days later, after filing a *habeas corpus* writ with the Supreme Court; although Mookerjee was still involved in court proceedings, he paid a bond of Rs 100 to remain at large.[119]

While young agitators poured into Delhi from Bengal, Bihar, Uttar Pradesh, the Punjab and Madhya Pradesh to carry on the *satyagraha*, the response on the part of the public was disappointing, and Mookerjee and his lieutenants found themselves increasingly restricted by the ban on public meetings. It was at this point that Mookerjee decided to visit Jammu and issued a statement explaining his purpose in doing so – to study the situation for himself and to explore the possibility of obtaining a peaceful settlement.[120] In fact, it is extremely doubtful whether he expected to be allowed to enter Jammu while the situation there was so disturbed.[121] Almost certainly, he believed that the Indian authorities would refuse to let him into the State without the permit usually required, and, as his statement explained, he had not applied for one, for

Mr Nehru has repeatedly declared that the accession of the State of Jammu and Kashmir to India has been one hundred per cent complete. Yet it is strange to find that one cannot enter the State without a previous permit from the Government of India. ... I do not think Government of India is entitled to prevent entry to any part of the Indian Union which according to Mr Nehru himself includes Jammu and Kashmir. Of course if any one violates the law, he will have to face the consequences.[122]

In other words, Mookerjee would seize the opportunity, in the proceedings which he believed would follow his attempt to enter Jammu, to appeal to the Supreme Court about the alleged unconstitutionality of the permit system, and to broaden his attack on the Central Government's refusal to question Kashmir's special status under Section 370. He set out from Old Delhi Station on 8 May, and we know that he expected to be back in Delhi by 13th to meet Adlai Stevenson.[123] However, events worked out differently from what he had planned. When he reached the border on 11 May, he was arrested not by Indian but by Kashmiri police, who issued him with an order barring his entry under Section 4 of the *Jammu and Kashmir Public Security Act* and then, after he and his companions had signified their intention to continue their journey, arrested and later interned him under Section 3 of the same statute.[124] As we have seen, his death was to follow before a month had passed, and on 7 July the *satyagraha* was called off.[125]

V

Mookerjee must have been well aware of the dangers in the course the *satyagraha* was taking; having failed to arouse much popular enthusiasm in support of the Praja Parishad, it had moved from protest to open defiance. His realisation that extreme elements were likely to come to the fore and to lead the Jana Sangh 'down the slope of hate with gladness', allied to the fact that he was always more at home in legal battles than in this type of agitation, would explain why he was anxious to transfer the centre of interest to an appeal in the Supreme Court.

Mookerjee was neither an agitator nor a fanatic; he was a liberal constitutionalist pursued by the furies of communalism and tradition-alism. With the bhadralok leaders of an earlier generation, he wanted to reconcile Hindu traditions with parliamentary institutions. Whereas on the one hand he hoped to give Indians a broader and more intense awareness of their Hindu identity, of the essentially religious and romantic character of their nationalism, on the other he realised the value of a parliamentary system as a means of ensuring a stable political order. Unlike Nehru, who was working to establish India as a secular state, Mookerjee was a communalist to the extent that he could not conceive of an Indian polity which was not characteristically Hindu; he was convinced that the parliamentary order would be stable only if it expressed the will of the people, not only ensuring respect for govern-ment but strengthening the social order against alien traditions, whether those of Islam or those of the West.

When Mookerjee resigned from the Central Cabinet in April 1950, he believed that Nehru's concept of the secular State and his policy of conciliating Pakistan were about to be rejected by the Indian people, and he saw himself as one of the leaders of the new, essentially Hindu, nationalism which would reshape the State in its image. Combined with Tandon's drive to gain control of the Congress organisation, his assertion of traditionalist and communal values had an immediate impact on Indian politics; for the first time, important national leaders were challenging the secularism of a section of the Congress Party, the authenticity of its nationalism, the soundness of its international policies. The challenge failed, but for almost a year the issue was in doubt.

Partly because he identified himself so strongly with the general traditionalist campaign against Nehru's policies, Mookerjee delayed too long in his move to found a constitutional opposition to the Congress Party. Hastily drawn together in the last half of 1951, the Jana Sangh was unable to focus its resources to the best advantage in the general election and Mookerjee found himself without enough members in the Lok Sabha to do anything more than create the wraith-like National Democratic Group. Had he formed the Jana Sangh in the heat of 1950, when the Bengal riots had aroused considerable anti-Muslim feeling throughout northern India, he might have drawn away traditionalist strength from Tandon and would have been much better placed to challenge the Congress in elections and parliament.

In the 1952 Lok Sabha, Mookerjee was once more the effective, intelligent critic of government measures, but he lacked the mass following essential to him if he were to provide a serious electoral challenge to the Congress Party. At this point he faced two possible courses of action; he could either act out his role as leader of the constitutional opposition and build up the Jana Sangh's organisation for the 1957 elections or he could go out once more to the people and try to recapture the spirit of 1950. Everything, his temperament, his hostility towards Pakistan, his need for popular support, impelled him to pursue the second course, and he allowed himself to be committed to the campaign for integrating Kashmir in the Indian Union. Kashmir, however, was not East Bengal – there was no mass migration, no sudden political crisis to stir communal feelings to life; and as Mookerjee waited in vain for the return of popular enthusiasm he was forced step by step to sanction the strategy which led to the agitation of March and April 1953 and to his last journey.

The agitation which ended in his death could almost certainly have been avoided had he acted with greater caution and, in his dealings with the Praja Parishad, with greater firmness. Had he lived he may well have built the Jana Sangh into a much larger and more responsible party than it is today, for he came closer than any other Indian leader to embodying in a coherent form the powerful current of Hindu traditionalism which still flows strongly in the national movement. However, his addiction to militant action may well have proved to be greater than his respect for legitimate procedures; he was attracted to the techniques of agitation even while he appreciated their threat to order, and in this he epitomised the historical dilemma of his social class, the Bengal bhadralok.

Even today Indians have different ways of regarding his death. For the men of Jana Sangh, he is a martyr who died in the cause of true nationalism, but by liberals he is regarded as an intelligent parliamentarian and a responsible social leader who was blinded by communalist prejudice. There is more common ground between these attitudes than may at first appear; indeed, partly because Mookerjee was an enigma, he appealed powerfully to the darker strain in the political life of his countrymen.

NOTES

1 *Organiser*, 29 June 1953.
2 *P.D. (L.S.)*, Part 2, VI, 3 Aug. 1953, c.2.
3 This paragraph is based on Chapter I of J.H.Broomfield, 'Politics and the Bengal Legislative Council, 1912–1926', unpublished Ph.D. thesis, Australian National University, 1963.
4 See Lalitmohan Chatterjee and Syamaprasad Mookerjee 'Asutosh Mookerjee', *Representative Indians*, Calcutta 1936, pp. 97–145.
5 The fullest biography of Mookerjee is Balraj Madhok, *Dr Syama Prasad Mookerjee, A Biography*, New Delhi, n.d. [1954], also published in a Hindi edition (Delhi 1954). See also R.C.Banerjee, 'Dr Syama Prasad Mookerji', *Organiser*, 24 Dec. 1951.
6 Madhok, *Mookerjee*, pp. 5–8; Banerjee, op. cit.
7 On Hindu Mahasabha and Hindu Communalism generally, see Donald E.Smith, *India as a Secular State*, Princeton, 1963, XV; Myron Weiner, *Party Politics in India, the Development of a Multi-Party System*, Princeton 1957, VIII and IX; Richard D.Lambert, 'Hindu Communal Groups in Indian Politics', in Richard L.Park and Irene Tinker, eds, *Leadership and Political Institutions in India*, Princeton 1959, pp. 211–24; and several special articles in the *Times of India* (Delhi), Sunday magazine, 24 Dec. 1950. The basic source for the history of the RSS is still J.A.Curran, *Militant Hinduism in Indian Politics. A Study of the R.S.S.*, New York 1951. See also D.V. Kelkar, 'The R.S.S.', *The Economic Weekly* (Bombay), 4 Feb. 1950, pp. 132–4 and 137–8.
8 See P.D.Reeves, 'The Landlords' Response to Political Change in the United Provinces of Agra and Oudh, India, 1921–1937,' unpublished Ph.D. thesis, Australian National University, 1963, pp. 211–25.
9 Curran, p. 14.
10 See, for example, an account of his meeting with Dr Hedgewar in 1940, 'Dr. Mookerji and Dr. Hedgewar, when the two Doctors met . . . ', *Organiser*, 15 Aug. 1954.
11 Sir Surendranath Banerjea, *A Nation in Making*, Calcutta 1963 (reprint), p. 9.
12 Chatterjee and Mookerjee, *Representative Indians*, pp. 106–7 and 138–9.
13 Madhok, *Mookerjee*, pp. 3–4.
14 Ibid., p. 11.
15 V.P.Menon, *The Transfer of Power in India*, Calcutta 1957, pp. 143–4 and 245; Madhok, pp. 13–20; Syama Prasad Mookerjee, *Awake Hindusthan*,

Calcutta, n.d. [1944], gives Mookerjee's speeches 1940–4 as leader of the
Hindu Mahasabha.

16   Lambert, p. 220. See also Mookerjee's obituary notice, *Statesman* (Calcutta),
25 June 1953, p. 4.

17   See the following statements by Nehru (*Indian P.D.*, Part 2, I, 23 Feb. 1950,
pp. 749–55), Dr Ishtiaq Husain Qureshi (*Pakistan Constituent Assembly
Debates*, I, 17 Mar. 1950, pp. 105–10), and Liaquat Ali Khan (ibid., 28 Mar.
1950, pp. 443–8). One of the most important documents on this subject is a
letter published by Mr J. N. Mandal following his resignation from the
Pakistan Cabinet (see *Times of India*, 9 Oct. 1950). It should be read in
conjunction with Liaquat Ali's reply *Statesman* (Delhi, 15 Oct. 1950) and
Mandal's rejoinder (ibid., 31 Oct. 1950). Lambert (p. 221) deals with the
Hindu Mahasabha Conference of December 1949.

18   *P.D.*, Part 1, IV, 1 Aug. 1950, cc. 33–4; also *Statesman*, 2 Aug. 1950. Unless
otherwise specified, the *Statesman* references in this paper come from the
New Delhi edition.

19   Ibid., Part 2, III, 17 Mar. 1950, p. 1701.

20   *The Times* (London), 2 Jan. 1950; ibid., 'The Two Bengals, Challenge to
Indian and Pakistani Statesmen', 15 April 1950.

21   *Statesman*, 24 June 1950.

22   *Amrita Bazar Patrika* (Calcutta), I, 16 March 1950. For representative quotes
from the East Bengal press see *Pakistan Constituent Assembly Debates*, I,
16 March 1950, pp. 58–64 (speech by Bhupendra Kumar Datta).

23   Michael Brecher, *Nehru. A Political Biography*, London 1959, p. 428;
Madhok, *Mookerjee*, pp. 41–2.

24   Article in the Maratha weekly, *Lok Satta*, 7 July 1964, cited in *Organiser*,
27 July 1964.

25   *P.D.*, Pt 2, III, 17 March 1950, pp. 1700–8, esp. pp. 1705–6.

26   Ibid., IV, 19 April 1950, p. 3017; *Pioneer* (Lucknow), 6–20 April 1950.
See also Mookerjee's recollection, *P.D.*, Pt 2, XIV, 10 Aug. 1951, c. 365.

27   *Lok Satta*, 7 July 1964, cited in *Organiser*, 27 July 1964. Gadgil does not give
the date for this incident, but the sources cited above show 1 April as the
day on which Mookerjee first submitted his resignation. (Note: 'Panditji'
is the familiar term of address for Jawarharlal Nehru.) Gadgil also claims,
in the same article, that the original draft of the Delhi agreement contained
two clauses 'which gave reserved seats, reserved jobs and special representation to Muslims. In exchange, a similar arrangement was to be made in
Pakistan.' When these were considered by a cabinet meeting, Gadgil
writes that he objected to them, that N. Gopalaswami Ayyangar offered
to redraft them, but that he (Gadgil) insisted on their outright rejection.
He alleges that Nehru then became angry, pointing out that he had already
reached agreement with Liaquat Ali but finally admitting that he had told
the latter that the proposal would have to have cabinet approval. The

meeting was adjourned at the suggestion of Sardar Patel, who visited Gadgil on the evening of the same day and found him still in favour of rejecting the disputed clauses. Patel then turned down Ayyangar's proposed redraft and wrote to Nehru asking him to delete the section involved. This was done and the subject was not raised again when cabinet met on the following day. Gadgil does not give the date of the above incident but it most probably occurred on 3 April, the first day after the Nehru–Liaquat Ali talks had begun.

28 For the text of the agreement see *Pakistan Constituent Assembly Debates*, I, 10 April 1950, pp. 746–50. Under the terms of the Pact, Minority Ministers were appointed to the Governments of both Dominions, Mr C.C.Biswas in the case of India and Dr A.M.Malik in the case of Pakistan. Minority representatives were also included in the Governments of East Pakistan and West Bengal and Minority Commissions were established in these two States and in Assam. Commissions of inquiry were formed to investigate the occurrences of February–March 1950 and to recommend steps for preventing a similar outbreak in future. See Nehru's statement, *P.D.*, Pt 1, IV, 1 Aug. 1950, cc. 7–13. A supplementary agreement was signed on 16 August 1950 (*Statesman*, 17 Aug. 1950).

29 *P.D.*, Pt 2, IV, 19 April 1950, pp. 3017–22.

30 *Times of India*, 12 June 1950.

31 *Pioneer*, 22, 23 and 28 April 1950.

32 Mookerjee is said to have advocated the population-exchange scheme while still a member of cabinet (see *Economic Weekly*, 22 April 1950, p. 390), but the scheme, had it been applied to the sub-continent as a whole, would actually have involved cession of territory by India.

33 *Pioneer*, 22 May 1950.

34 See his speeches at the East Bengal Refugees' Rehabilitation Convention, Calcutta, on 11 June, *Times of India*, 12 June 1950; at Shillong on 18 June, *Statesman*, 19 June 1950; at Gauhati on 19 June, ibid., 21 June 1950; at Karimganj on 25 June, ibid., 26 June 1950, and a statement which he and other Calcutta leaders issued on 20 July, ibid., 22 July 1950.

35 *P.D.*, Pt 1, IV, 1 Aug. 1950, c. 56.

36 See ibid., Appendices, Third Session 1950, Appendix III, Annexure No. 19, pp. 319–20. See also Appendix V, Annexure No. 20, p. 446.

37 *Times of India*, 27 July 1950.

38 For the fullest account of the conference proceedings, see ibid., 29–31 July 1950.

39 *P.D.*, Pt 2, V, 7 Aug. 1950, cc. 398–417.

40 Ibid., Pt 1, IV, 1 Aug. 1950, cc. 33–4; *Statesman*, 2 Aug. 1950.

41 Ibid., Pt 2, V, 7 Aug. 1950, cc. 425–61.

42 *Statesman*, 4 June 1950.

43 *P.D.*, Pt 2, V, 9 Aug. 1950, c. 617. Whole speech cc. 597–622.

44   *Times of India*, 4 Sept. 1950.

45   *P.D.*, Pt 2, IV, 19 April 1950, p. 3020. Cf. Kripalani's presidential speech to a meeting of the AICC on 14 and 15 June 1947, when he described his reaction to the communal rioting at Noakhali in October 1946. 'The fear is not for the lives lost or of the widows' wail or the orphans' cry or of the many houses burnt. The fear is that if we go on like this, retaliating and heaping indignities upon each other, we shall progressively reduce ourselves to a state of cannibalism and worse. In every fresh communal fight the most brutal and degraded acts of the previous fight become the norm. So we keep on degrading each other, and all in the name of religion. I am a Hindu and am proud of the fact. But this is because Hinduism for me has stood for toleration, for truth and for non-violence, or at any rate for the clean violence of the brave. If it no more stands for these ideals and if in order to defend it people have to indulge in crimes worse than cannibalism then I must hang down my head in shame.' *Congress Bulletin* (issued by the Office of the All India Congress Committee), No. 4, 10 July 1947, p. 9.

46   The following extract from Nehru's speech at the Nasik Congress Session (September 1950) serves to illustrate this distinction. 'What has happened to the minds of Congressmen, ... Do they want today to bow before what a mob says, and compromise their principles? I have not learnt to bow before anybody. I do not agree that democracy means that Congressmen should do what the large majority of people ask to be done.'

'The majority has a right to dictate its terms. If the majority today wants to tread a path which is opposed to the one it has been following all these years, and if this involves compromise of democratic principles, it can do so. If Congressmen have also started thinking in those terms, it is open to them to have a Government of their choice. But, strictly speaking, this compromise will be opposed to the principles of democracy, and will be fought by democratic people, whatever the majority says.' *Statesman*, 22 Sept. 1950.

47   *P.D.*, Pt 2, III, 17 March 1950, cc. 1707–8, 1742.

48   On the tensions within the Parliamentary Congress Party caused by the East Bengal situation, see *Economic Weekly*, 25 March 1950, pp. 305–6 (Delhi Letter).

49   The college for the election was composed of duly elected delegates to the AICC, who voted at their respective Pradesh Congress Committee headquarters on 29 August 1950, the sealed ballot boxes being sent to the AICC Office, Delhi, for counting (*Congress Bulletin*, No. 5, July–Aug. 1950, pp. 192–3, 197–201). The result (given in ibid., p. 210) was as follows:

Purushottamdas Tandon	1,306
Acharya Kripalani	1,092
Shankerao Deo	202
Invalid	18
	2,618

It should be noted that of the 3,100 enrolled delegates, fully 570 were from Uttar Pradesh; most of these would have been committed to Tandon (*Statesman*, 29 Aug. 1950). In an interview with the writer (Lucknow, 29 Jan. 1964), Kripalani said that Patel called several Chief Ministers to Delhi and solicited the votes of their delegates for Tandon.

50 *Statesman*, 13 Sept. 1950.

51 *Congress Bulletin*, No. 6, Sept.–Oct. 1950, pp. 224–37. For the resolution on communalism, see pp. 228–9. Weiner (p. 71) implies incorrectly that the presidential election was held at the Nasik Session itself.

52 Announced on 16 October (see *Congress Bulletin*, No. 6, Sept.–Oct. 1950, p. 238). Nehru had at first refused to join the Committee but eventually agreed to do so.

53 See for example *Statesman*, 2 Oct. 1950.

54 *Times of India*, 23 July 1951.

55 The fullest account of this complicated struggle is given by Brecher (pp. 429–37). On the Congress Democratic Front and the KMPP, see Weiner, pp. 65–84. Several exchanges of letters arising out of the negotiations were released to the press, namely, those between Kripalani and Tandon (*The Hindu* (Madras), 14 May 1951 and *Times of India*, 18 May 1951); Nehru and Kidwai (*Statesman*, 3 Aug. 1951); Nehru and Tandon (ibid., 11 Sept. 1951).

56 See comment in the following issues of the *Organiser*: 11 Sept. 1950; 2 July, 27 Aug., and 3, 10, 17 Sept. 1951.

57 Curran, pp. 64 and 67–8.

58 Ibid., pp. 65–8.

59 Weiner, pp. 185–6.

60 'A Tribute to Dr Shyamaprasad, How Jana Sangh was born', *Organiser*, 25 June 1956.

61 Interview with Balraj Madhok, New Delhi, 20 Dec. 1963.

62 On this question, see Weiner, pp. 197–8, and Curran, pp. 63–4.

63 Dr N.B.Khare, *My Political Memoirs or Autobiography*, Nagpur [1959], pp. 427–8. It should be noted that the Punjab National Bank Limited, founded at Lahore in 1894, had retained its early connection with Arya Samaj and was the main bank serving Hindu refugees from the western Punjab (see *National Herald*, Lucknow, 13 April 1965, Supplement on the Bank's history and business).

64 *Statesman*, 3 Oct 1950; *Times of India*, 27 Dec. 1950.

65 Ibid., 25–27 Dec. 1950; 26 Feb. 1951 (conference of Maharashtrian Sabha); 27 Feb. 1951 (conference of U.P. Sabha). See also *Statesman*, 31 Dec. 1950.

66 *Hindu*, 29 April 1951. See also statement by V.G.Deshpande (*Times of India*, 24 May 1951) that, although non-Hindus who accepted the Hindu Mahasabha manifesto could be put up as election candidates, membership of the organisation had not been thrown open to non-Hindus.

67 Madhok, *Mookerjee*, pp. 55–7. See also *Times of India*, 15 March 1951.

N

For a report on trends in the RSS at this time see the *Hindu*, 8 Jan. 1951, cited by Weiner, p. 190.

68 On this question, see Smith, *India as a Secular State*, pp. 458–9, and Balraj Madhok, *Hindu Rashtra. A Study in Indian Nationalism*, Calcutta 1955.

69 *P.D.*, Pt 2, XV, 17 Sept. 1951, c. 2715.

70 *Times of India*, 29 April 1951. See also *Organiser*, 7 May 1951, although this source gives an incorrect date for the conference.

71 *Times of India*, 29 May 1951; Madhok, *Mookerjee*, pp. 57–8.

72 *Organiser*, 10 Sept. 1951.

73 Weiner, pp. 191–2.

74 *Organiser*, 29 Oct. 1951. See also *Times of India*, 11 Sept. 1951, for the preparations.

75 For the constitution as finally approved by the Working Committee on 14 and 15 June 1952, see *Organiser*, 23 June 1952.

76 Ibid., 8 Feb. 1954; 12 Jan. 1959.

77 *Statesman*, 26 Feb. 1951.

78 Curran, p. 44.

79 Ibid., p. 43.

80 *Organiser*, 8 Feb. 1954.

81 *Statesman*, 4 Nov. 1954. See also ibid., 2, 5 and 8 Nov. 1954, and *Times of India*, 5, 6, 14 Nov. 1954.

82 *Link* (Delhi), 6 Aug. 1961, p. 13.

83 See the biographies of Jana Sangh leaders given in *Organiser*, Aug. 1956 (special number), pp. 26–32.

84 *Times of India*, 22 Oct. 1951, p. 3.

85 Ibid., 1 Dec. 1951.

86 *P.D.*, Pt 2, IX, 28 March 1951, c. 5279.

87 Madhok, *Mookerjee*, pp. 84–5.

88 *Times of India*, 4 Oct. 1951. Agency reports of Mookerjee's speeches during the campaign are scrappy and unreliable. The best sources for his views at this time are: his speech at the founding convention of 21 Oct. 1951 (*Why Bharatiya Jana Sangh – The Presidential Address of Dr Syama Prasad Mookerjee at the Opening Convention of Akhil Bharatiya Jana Sangh*, Delhi 1951); and an article he wrote for the *Statesman* (Delhi), 21 Dec. 1951. See also the reports of his press conferences in *Times of India*, 23 Oct., 1 and 9 Dec. 1951. Cf. *Manifesto of All India Bharatiya Jana Sangh* (Delhi 1951), which he drafted in collaboration with Madhok, Professor Mahavir and Mauli Chandra Sharma (Madhok, *Mookerjee*, p. 63).

89 *Organiser*, 29 Oct. 1951.

90 *Times of India*, 15 Dec. 1951.

91 *Statesman*, 3 Oct. 1951.

92 *Times of India*, 4 Oct. 1951.

93 *Statesman*, 21 Dec. 1951.

94 Ibid.

95 *Times of India*, 15 Oct. 1951.

96 *P.D.*, Pt 2, IX, 28 March 1951, cc. 5274–8; Pt 2, XIV, 10 Aug. 1951, cc. 352–9.

97 Election Commission, *Report on the First General Elections in India 1951–52*, Vol. II, Delhi 1955, pp. 7, 11, 90–1.

98 Weiner, pp. 195–6.

99 Lanka Sundaram (Madras) said that Mookerjee wrote inviting him to join such a group in January 1952. See A. B. Lal (ed.), *The Indian Parliament*, Allahabad 1956, p. 63.

100 *Organiser*, 5 May, 30 June 1952; Madhok, *Mookerjee*, pp. 96–9.

101 See Selig Harrison, *India. The Most Dangerous Decades*, Oxford 1960, pp. 291–2.

102 On the Kashmir issue, see Michael Brecher, *The Struggle for Kashmir*, Toronto 1955; Josef Korbel, *Danger in Kashmir*, Princeton 1954; and 'Kashmir', *Seminar*, No. 58, June 1964. For a Jana Sangh viewpoint, see Balraj Madhok, *Kashmir. Centre of New Alignments*, New Delhi, n.d. [1963]; Madhok, *Kashmir Divided*, Lucknow, n.d. [1950]. I am indebted to Mr Matin Zuberi, who both permitted me to read his paper, 'The Kashmir Problem', and made helpful suggestions about this section.

103 See *New Kashmir. With an introduction by Sheikh Md. Abdullah, Constitution and Outline Economic Plan for the State of Jammu and Kashmir, including Ladakh and the Frontier regions and the Poonah and Chinani 'ilaqas'*, Kashmir Bureau of Information, New Delhi, n.d. [c. 1944].

104 On the interpretation of these provisions, see Alan Gledhill, *The Republic of India. The Development of its Laws and Constitution*, 2nd edn, London 1964, pp. 154–6; Durga Das Basu, *Commentary on the Constitution of India*, 4th edn, Vol. 5, Calcutta 1964, pp. 243–5.

105 *United Nations, Security Council, Official Records, Sixth Year, 1951, Special Supplement No. 2*, Document S/2375), Report of the United Nations Representative [Frank P. Graham] for India and Pakistan to the Security Council, 15 Oct. 1951, p. 24.

106 Madhok, *Kashmir Divided*, Appendix III, pp. 197–8.

107 Madhok, *Mookerjee*, pp. 130–1.

108 *Times of India*, 14 Feb. 1952. See also the accounts of Maulana Masuodi (*P.D.*, Pt 2, II, 3 March 1952, cc. 1807–19); Professor S. L. Saxena (ibid., 4 March 1952, cc. 1936–42); and Sheikh Abdullah (ibid., 5 March 1952, cc. 2018–26).

109 Ibid., Pt 2, I, 12 Feb. 1952, cc. 300–3.

110 Ibid., Pt 2, II, 5 March 1952, cc. 2018–26.

111 Ibid., (*L.S.*), Pt 2, Vol. II, 26 June 1952, cc. 2570–86.

112 Ibid., Pt 2, III, 24 July 1952, cc. 4501–21 (speech by Nehru).

113 Ibid., Pt 2, I, 17 Feb. 1953, cc. 326–7; 18 Feb. 1953, cc. 471–2.

114 Madhok, *Mookerjee*, pp. 145–55.

115 Ibid., pp. 156–8.

116 Ibid., pp. 201–8; *Organiser*, 5 Jan. 1953.

117 Madhok, Mookerjee, pp. 209–234. See also the following pamphlets: *Kashmir Problem & Jammu-Satyagrah*, Bharatiya Jana Sangh, Lucknow [1953]; Balraj Madhok, *Kashmir Problem. A Story of Bungling*, New Delhi [1952]; *Why Jammu Satyagraha? Dr Mookerjee's Last Letter to Sheikh Abdullah & Report of Repression in Kashmir*, Allahabad [1953].

118 Weiner, p. 200. Weiner suggests (pp. 215–18) that since Mookerjee had sources of political power outside the Jana Sangh he had no firm attachment to it, and that he was interested primarily in forming as broad an Opposition front as possible, by linking together such parties as the Hindu Mahasabha, Ram Rajya Parishad, Ganatantra Parishad and the Akali Dal (see also pp. 247–9). This interpretation ignores, however, the fact that although Mookerjee undoubtedly hoped to attract the older parties to Jana Sangh, he wished to do so very much on his own terms. As a practical politician, he was well aware of their ineffectiveness as mass parties and knew that his only hope of building up a sound electoral base in the Hindi-speaking States was by working through the well-disciplined cadres to which Jana Sangh had access through its connection with the RSS. Moreover, Mookerjee's experience as Minister of Industries and Supplies had convinced him of India's need for much more progressive economic policies than those to which the older communal parties subscribed.

119 Madhok, *Mookerjee*, p. 242; *P.D.(L.S.)*, Pt 2, II, 9 March 1953, cc. 1571–3.

120 Madhok, *Mookerjee*, pp. 251–6.

121 See his reported conversation with Meghnad Saha, *P.D.(L.S.)*, Pt 2, VIII, 18 Sept. 1953, c. 4253; and Madhok, op. cit., pp. 252–3.

122 Madhok, op. cit., pp. 252–3.

123 Madhok, op. cit., p. 250.

124 For statements and documents relating to the arrest and internment, see Umaprasad Mookerjee (ed.), *Syamaprasad Mookerjee. His Death in Detention. A Case for Enquiry*, Calcutta 1953. See also the text of a telegram from the Chief Secretary of the Government of Jammu and Kashmir to the Deputy-Speaker of the Lok Sabha, *P.D. (L.S.)*, Pt 2, V, 12 May 1953, cc. 6423–5.

125 *Statesman*, 8 July 1953. When addressing a public meeting at Jammu on 9 April 1964, shortly after his release from prison, Sheikh Abdullah said that there should have been an inquiry into Mookerjee's death. He claimed that, at the time, he was not aware of Mookerjee's illness and that, after his death, he had requested B.C.Roy, the Chief Minister of West Bengal and a medical doctor, to conduct an inquiry, only to meet with refusal (*National Herald*, Lucknow, 11 April 1964).

GLOSSARY

abhanga A religious poem, verse or hymn; notably composed by *bhakti* (q.v.) saints.

abwab Exaction of cesses or additional dues from tenant by landlord.

adawlut Court of justice; justice, equity: a term inherited from the Muslim rulers by the British.

advaita 'Non-dualism', the classical monistic Vedanta (q.v.) philosophy and probably the predominant school in Hindu thought.

ahimsa 'Not killing', i.e. non-violence.

Akali Dal A militant Sikh political party which has demanded a separate Panjabi-speaking (i.e. Sikh) state within India.

alankar 'Belles Lettres'.

Amil Literally 'revenue collector'; the outstanding caste of the Hindu minority of Sind; originally administrators in the service of the Muslim rulers of Sind, they have traditions of scholarship.

Arain A low market-gardening and cultivator caste in the Panjab.

Arora Hindu trading caste in the Panjab.

Arya Samaj Hindu sect founded by Dayanand in the Panjab, whence it spread into the United Provinces in particular; opposes caste restrictions, aggressively proselytising, especially *vis-à-vis* Muslims.

ashraf 'Honourable', Muslims of highest status, who traced their descent to homelands outside India.

Azad Kashmir 'Liberated Kashmir', the Pakistani designation of the portion of Kashmir held by Pakistan.

Babu Originally a title of respect attached to a name in Bengal. Used by the Bengali-language press as a pejorative designation for the anglicised, bhadralok élite.

Baidya (Vaidya) A physician; the medical caste – one of the three upper castes in Bengal.

Bania A Hindu trader, shopkeeper or money-changer; the name of certain trading castes; the trading castes generally.

baproti Patrimony.

Baqr-Id A festival observed by Muslims on the 10th of the month Zil-hijja – the feast of the ox, in commemoration of the offering of Ismail by Abraham (according to Muslim tradition).

beegah (*bigha*) A measure of land. In northern India it was usually 3025 square yards. The Maratha *bigha* was 400 square *kathis* ('rods'): as the rod varied so did the *bigha*; under the Adil Shahi dynasty it was 4383 square yards.

bhadralok 'The respectable people', the three upper castes of Hindus in Bengal, Brahmin (q.v.), Baidya (q.v.), and Kayastha (q.v.).

bhakti Devotion: the reforming *bhakti* cults in Hinduism stress devotion and love, as opposed to knowledge or duty, as the means of realising God.

Bhatia Trading caste from Gujarat, important in Bombay, claiming Kshatriya status.

bhayachara *Bhai*, 'brother'; *achara*, 'custom': land-tenure system in the United Provinces under which the revenue assessment of the village was distributed among its members by the brotherhood.

bhumidar A landowner; proprietor; head-man; chief.

Biloch Muslim tribe of the North-West Frontier and the Panjab.

birader bhaus Legal brother: an outsider permitted to buy land from, and to enter, a *jatha* (q.v.).

Bohra (*Borah*) 'A trader'; a caste or group originating in Gujarat, converted to Shia Islam; generally associated with banking or commerce, but in Gujarat numbers are agriculturists.

Brahma Samaj (Bengali: *Brahmo Samaj*) 'The Divine Society', a monotheistic sect founded by Raja Rammohan Roy. It found its support among the westernised intelligentsia of Bengal.

Brahmin The highest, or priestly, *varna* (q.v.) among the Hindus.

burud Classification of cultivable soil type according to fertility.

bustee Any inhabited place; more specifically a squalid shanty area.

carcoon (*karkun*) A clerk; in Maharashtra any agent or subordinate in revenue collection.

chawl Tenement; the open space between blocks of such buildings in Bombay.

Chitpavan (*Brahmin*) Caste of Maharashtrian Brahmins, traditionally dominant in Maharashtra since the rise of the Peshwa from among them.

chowar A Maratha measurement of land, theoretically 120 *bighas*, but supposedly taking soil quality into account.

chowrie Village place of assembly.

dakshina Presents made annually by the Peshwa to Brahmin scholars at Poona and continued as an allowance applied partly to them and partly to the maintenance of the Poona College by the British Government.

deshmukh Chief; hereditary officer in pre-British times exercising chief police and revenue authority over a district; under the British a district revenue officer expected to assist in revenue settlements.

dharamsala (*dharmsala*) A building for any legal or pious purpose, a resting-place for travellers and pilgrims.

Dharamshastra (*Dharmashastra*) The collective texts of the Hindus on their laws and institutions. The Hindu code.

dharma Moral duty, law; more broadly, religion.

Dogra The predominant Hindu caste in Jammu, from whom came the former Rajas of Kashmir.

Durga 'The Inaccessible', the Mother Goddess, popular especially in Bengal and Assam; the consort and *sakti* (or active principle) of Siva. Also known in her grim aspect as 'Kali' or 'Candi'.

Durga Puja The worship of Durga, celebrated for 10 days in the month of Aswin (September–October) with particular pomp in Bengal.

durwan Watchman, guard.

dyarchy 'Rule by two', term applied to the form of government introduced in the Indian provinces by the Government of India Act (1919), responsibility being shared between British officials and elected Indian representatives.

gaduda Huge stone.

Ganatantra Parishad A conservative party in Orissa organised by the dispossessed rajas.

Ganpati Alternative name of Ganesh, the propitious god for all undertakings, round whose worship Tliak built a nationalistic festival.

ghadr 'A mutiny'; specifically a revolutionary anti-British movement among Sikhs in the World War I period, fostered by overseas Sikh communities.

ghar baus House brother: one belonging by blood ties to a landowning *jatha* (q.v.).

ghutkool (*gatkul*) Gat, 'gone', *kul*, 'family'. Property, the proprietors of which are extinct; lands thus considered as belonging collectively to the village.

Gondal Agricultural and pastoral tribe in south-western Panjab.

Gujar A great agricultural (and pastoral) caste in north and north-western India; some have converted to Islam.

harijan 'Children of God.' Gandhi's name for the untouchables.

hartal Closing of all shops in a market as passive resistance to exaction;

hence suspension of work and business as a mark of indignation.

Hindu Mahasabha, All-India   The oldest Hindu communalist party, founded 1915, especially active from mid-1920s.

Hindu Rashtra   'Country of Hinduism', Hindu nationalism.

ilaqa   Dependency, district, jurisdiction.

istawa   The practice of letting land at a reduced rate, increasing progressivley until it reaches the full sum imposable, to encourage cultivation.

jagir   An assignment of the land revenue of a territory to a chief or noble for specific service.

jajmani   A prescriptive or hereditary right to receive, provide or exchange services as between members of higher and lower castes, with or without the payment of fees.

Jammu (and Kashmir) Praja Parishad   A Hindu communalist party founded by B. Madhok and Prem Nath Dogra, affiliated with the Jana Sangh in 1952.

Jana Sangh, All-India Bharatiya   A leading Hindu communalist party founded in 1951.

Jat   A numerous and proud race of agriculturists in the north and north-west of the sub-continent. May be Hindu or (by conversion) Muslim or Sikh.

jatha (jat, jati)   Family group; clan; tribe.

jerayet   Inferior (or unirrigated) category of cultivable land.

jyotish   Astronomy, astrology.

Kakezai   Pathan tribal name assumed by Muslim Kalals.

Kalal   A distiller; caste in the Panjab whose hereditary occupation was distillation and sale of spirituous liquors. In British times they turned to trade and agriculture. May be Hindu, Muslim or Sikh.

kamal   'Entire, perfect', the augmented (Maratha) assessment of land revenue (i.e. tax); introduced in the 1760s under Peshwa Madhav Rao.

kanungo   Literally 'a speaker', 'an expounder of the laws'; village or district revenue officer or accountant.

Karnatak   The Kannada-speaking area of Bombay Presidency of British India, now absorbed in Mysore State. (Sometimes has a more extended meaning, and when spelt 'Carnatic' is usually applied to south-east India.)

Kayastha   Hindu caste, traditionally writers or accountants, associated with learning and with administration under Muslim rulers in northern India.

kesari 'Lion' (Marathi); clothed in yellow, indicating desperate valour. Name of Tilak's Marathi-language newspaper.

khadi Cloth hand-woven from hand-spun thread.

Khalifa 'Successor', the religious and temporal head of Islam (as acknowledged by Sunni Muslims)'

Khatri Panjabi Hindu trading caste which, however, is regarded as of the Kshatriya (q.v.) *varna.*

Khilafat 'Sovereignty', the office of Khalifa.

' ... *ki jai*' 'Victory to ...' or 'Hail ...'

kisan A peasant; cultivator.

Kisan Mazdoor Praja Party (*K.M.P.P.*) Peasants' and Workers' People's Party, founded by J. B. Kripalani in 1951 calling for a return to Gandhian principles on socialist lines.

Kisan Sabha 'Peasant association.'

Kshatriya Generalised term for castes of the second (warrior, kingly and noble) status, or *varna.*

kshetrapala 'Lord or protector of the field (or region)'; tutelary deity who sanctioned the allocation of property in land to the founding families of a village.

kunbi Chief cultivating caste-cluster (often grouped with the Marathas) in central and western India, whence 'cultivator' in general.

Labana Cultivator caste in the Panjab (Hindu and Sikh), whose hereditary occupation was the carrying trade.

lathi A stick, fighting staff, bludgeon.

Lohar Blacksmith caste; in the Panjab a few were hereditary land-owners (Sikh and Hindu).

Lokhitwadi 'Advocate of the People's Welfare', title given to G. H. Deshmukh.

Lok Sabha 'The House of the People', the lower house of the central legislature of the Indian Republic.

Mahajana Sabha, Madras The leading Moderate political association in Madras, founded in the 1880s.

Mahatma 'Great Soul', title given to Gandhi, and also to others, e.g. Jyotirao Fule, Swami Shraddhananda.

Mahisya An agricultural caste in Bengal.

mali A gardener; a market-gardening caste.

Marwari A native of Marwar (Rajasthan); settled widely in other parts of India, usually following business of banker, broker, merchant: mostly of Jain religion.

Maulana Title of a learned Muslim, teacher.

maya   Illusion.

mayukh   Jurisprudence.

merras (*miras*)   Inheritance; village land belonging to the *meerasdar* (q.v.).

meerasdar   Freehold owner of land by hereditary right (in British times, subject to payment of land tax).

misl   'Similitude', a company or group of Sikh confederate clans.

mofussil (*mufassal*)   The rural localities of a district (or region) as distinguished from the chief station (or capital).

Mogul (*Mughal*)   The designation of one of the great Tartar tribes, the Mongols, or of a member of it.

Moharrum (*Muharram*)   The first month of the Muslim year; also the ten days' mourning at the beginning of that month commemorating the deaths of Hasan and Husain, especially venerated by Shias.

mukkadam   The headman of a village; more particularly, in Maharashtra, the senior member of a *patel* (q.v.) family.

mullah   A Muslim lawyer or learned man. Also the village Muslim schoolmaster who has charge of the village mosque.

Namasudra   Low-caste or outcaste Hindu agriculturists in Bengal.

nayaya (*nyaya*)   Logic.

nazrana   'A present', premium paid by tenant to landlord for entry onto a tenant-holding.

Pachada   Muslim agricultural and pastoral tribe in the Panjab.

panchayat   Panch, 'five'; a council of five (or more) persons from a caste, village or other body assembled to decide on matters affecting that body.

pandit   A learned Brahmin; may be applied to a caste of Brahmins, e.g. the Kashmiris.

Pan-Islamism   Movement for the rehabilitation of international Islamic brotherhood aimed at arresting the decline in Islam in the nineteenth century. Introduced to India about 1880; revived in the early twentieth century.

para   Neighbourhood.

Parsi   Race, originally from Persia, settled chiefly in Gujarat and Bombay city, who observe Zoroastrian religion; distinguished as merchants, industrialists.

patel   In western and central India, the (sur)name of the family chosen to represent the village in the collection and payment of land-tax.

Pathan   Afghan; one of the four groups comprising the *ashraf* (q.v.).

Pathare Prabhu   Writer caste of western India (cf. Kayastha, q.v.), claiming Kshatriya (q.v.) status which was denied by the Brahmins.

patwari   A village accountant, who kept accounts of all lands, produce and revenue assessment in the village.

PEPSU   Patiala and East Panjab States Union, a strongly Sikh state formed after Independence and merged in the Panjab in 1956.

Peshwa   'Second Minister', the Brahmin minister of the Maratha rajas who became *de facto* ruler of Maharashtra from *c*. 1714.

prakrit   'Not refined', the common language (or people).

Prakriti   Primeval substance; used in Sankhya texts to denote the material universe in general.

Prarthana Samaj   'The Prayer Society', the western Indian equivalent to the Brahmo Samaj (q.v.), which undertook social reform.

puranik   Religious man learned in the Puranas.

Purusha   'A man', the Primeval Man, from whom the universe is sprung.

raja   Ruler, king, prince; a title also borne by landlords.

Rajput   'Son of a king'; the formerly dominant Hindu landholding caste in northern India, generally accorded Kshatriya (q.v.) status; numbers converted to Islam, or (in central Panjab) to Sikhism.

Ram Lila   'The Sport of Rama', dramatic presentation of the adventures of Rama (an avatar of Vishnu), performed in the month of Aswin.

Ram Raj   'The Rule of Rama (i.e. God)'; the golden age of Hinduism.

Ram Rajya Parishad   'The Party for a return to Ram Raj', an ultra-conservative party founded by a religious leader in 1948; somewhat successful in Madhya Pradesh.

Ramayana   The story of Rama; one of the great Hindu epics.

Rao Bahadur   (Combination of Hindu and Mughal terms for noble), a title given to Indians by the British.

Rao Saheb   A title given to Indians by the British.

Rashtriya Swayamsevak Sangh (*R.S.S.*)   'Society of Servants of the Country', Hindu communalist organisation founded in 1925.

rivaj   Customary rates of land tax in Maharashtra which pre-dated the Peshwa's settlement.

rudrabhumi   Cremation ground.

ryot   A peasant.

ryotwari   'Of the *ryot*', a land-revenue settlement in which the peasant enters into a direct contractual relationship with the state.

sabha   An assembly, association.

sakta   Relating to *sakti* (q.v.); an individual or sect, especially in Bengal, who worships the goddess Durga or Kali, either publicly or privately. Such worship was associated with certain Bengali anti-British, terrorist associations after 1905.

sakti   Power, especially of a goddess; the goddess herself.

samiti   An association, society.

sanad   A document conveying to an individual emoluments, titles, offices, or government rights to revenue from land.

Sankara (charya)   A famous South Indian Saivite Brahmin who propounded the *advaita* (q.v.) philosophy.

Santhal   Low-caste or tribal Hindu group in north-east India.

saraswati   A learned brahmin (priest or religious man).

Sarvajanik Sabha   'People's Association', representative association founded in a number of towns in Maharashtra in the nineteenth century; the most outstanding was at Poona.

satyagraha   'Truth-force' or soul-force. A term coined by Gandhi to cover forms of non-violent coercion, e.g. civil disobedience.

Sayyid (Said)   'A chief', designation assumed by Muslims claiming descent from Husain, grandson of the Prophet.

Servants of India Society   Society founded by G. K. Gokhale in 1905, members of which pledged themselves to poverty and to the social and political service of India. It provided administrative personnel for the Moderate Congress sessions.

Shaikh   'An elder'; designation of Muslims claiming descent from Muhammad, Abubakr and Omar.

shakha (sakha)   Literally 'a branch', division of any social organisation; unit within the R.S.S. (q.v.).

shastra   A scripture; collectively, religion and law.

shastri   A man of learning, an expounder of Hindu law.

Shiah (commonly Shia)   The second in point of numbers of the two great divisions of Muslims, who believe Ali, son-in-law of Muhammad, to have been his lawful successor, and reject the first three *khalifas* (q.v.) as usurpers: cf. Sunni.

Shivaji   Maharashtrian hero and king (r. 1674–80) who, by military and organisational ability and assassination of a Muslim general, launched the Marathas on the road to power.

Sial   Agricultural and pastoral tribe in the Panjab.

Sircar (Sarkar)   The government; generally applied to the British government of India and to any of its officers.

sirdar (sardar)   Chief, title of honour.

sirdar 'A holder of *sir* [originally a personal land-holding]', tenants of the state with no rights to mortgage or sell their land.

smriti The body of recorded Hindu law.

Sonar Goldsmith caste; traditionally supposed to have sprung from a Brahmin father and Sudra mother, but in Maharashtra some Sonars claim to be 'minor Brahmins' and wear the sacred thread.

sthul Estate in a village, originally held by one *jatha* (q.v.).

Sudra The fourth or lowest *varna* (q.v.) of caste Hindus, embracing broadly agriculturists and artisans.

Sunni 'A follower of the *Sunna* [traditions of Muhammad]', the larger of the two great divisions of Muslims, who recognise the first four *khalifas* (q.v.): cf. Shiah.

sutra Precept, aphorism; a rule briefly expressed; a form commonly used in the oldest Sanskrit compositions.

suttee (*sati*) A virtuous wife, especially one who consummated a life of duty by burning herself on her husband's funeral pyre.

swadeshi Belonging to, or made in, one's own country.

swaraj 'Self-rule', self-government; had been used of the Marathi-speaking areas ruled by the house of Shivaji (q.v.).

tahsil A revenue subdivision of a district.

taluka 'Dependence, estate', area of administration next in size below a district.

taluqdar 'Holder of a *taluqa*, *taluka*', contractor for revenue (in Oudh chiefly), granted proprietary rights by the British; cf. *zamindar* (q.v.).

taluqdari Refers to the post-Mutiny system in Oudh whereby the *taluqdars* were re-established as the land-tax collectors, and were given proprietorship in the land.

tankha The oldest revenue assessment in the Deccan, fixed in money.

Tarkhan Carpenter caste in the Panjab.

teeka Small plot, subdivision of estate in Maharashtra.

Theosophical Society Founded in 1870s by Mme Blavatsky and Colonel Olcott to expound the thesis that all religions are paths to truth and to investigate occult phenomena. Strongly influenced by religions of Indian origin, its Brahmanical Hindu elements were emphasised by Mrs Besant.

ulema Plural of *alim*, those specially trained in the knowledge of Muhammadan religion and law, who are regarded by Muslims as the authorities on these matters.

upree 'Stranger', a cultivator considered as not belonging originally to the village and hence holding land on inferior or less secure tenure than the *meerasdar* (q.v.).

Vaisnava   A worshipper of Vishnu.

Vaisnavism   The worship of Vishnu.

Vaisya (Vaishya)   Generalised term for the castes of the third (trading) *varna* (in which Manu also included agriculturists). Bania (q.v.) is used similarly.

vakil   A pleader, or lawyer.

varna   A class, the generalised fourfold status-rankings into which Hindu *jatis* or castes are grouped.

varnashramadharma   The Hindu system of duties according to *varna* (q.v.) and stage in life.

Veda   One of the four original Hindu scriptures: *Rig Veda* (hymns), *Sama Veda* (arrangements of the *Rig*), *Yajur Veda* (sacrificial formulae) and *Arthava Veda* (magical spells).

Vedanta   'The End of the Vedas', the most important of the six systems of Hindu philosophy, fundamentally monistic and based on the Upanishads.

vyakaran   Grammar.

vydic   Indigenous medicine.

watan   'Native country, home', a hereditary land-holding in western or central India.

zamindar   'A possessor of land', formerly a revenue farmer; in Bengal, Bihar, eastern United Provinces and parts of Madras they were accorded proprietary rights by the British; in Panjab and western United Provinces any cultivator, but especially one who held village lands in common with others.

INDEX